NBER
*Macroeconomics
Annual 1999*

Editors
Ben S. Bernanke and
Julio J. Rotemberg

THE MIT PRESS
Cambridge, Massachusetts
London, England

Send orders and business information to:
The MIT Press
Five Cambridge Center
Cambridge, MA 02142

In the United Kingdom, continental Europe, and the Middle East and Africa, send orders and business correspondence to:
The MIT Press, Ltd.
Fitzroy House, 11 Chenies Street
London WC1E 7ET England

ISSN: 0889–3365
ISBN: hardcover 0–262–02476–4
    paperback 0–262–52271-3

Contents

Editorial, NBER Macroeconomics Annual 1999

This volume of the *NBER Macroeconomics Annual* focuses primarily on explantions of current notable macroeconomic phenomena. Some of the papers also discuss policy responses. In particular, the paper by Jonathan Parker tries to understand the increase in the consumption-to-GDP ratio in the United States, the paper by John Heaton and Deborah Lucas tries to explain the rise in U.S. asset prices, the paper by Fernando Alvarez and Marcelo Veracierto seeks to rationalize unemployment in European countries, and the paper by Takeo Hoshi and Anil Kashyap explores the causes and implications of the Japanese banking crisis. The other papers in the volume deal with international financial and economic crises: Roberto Chang and Andrés Velasco propose a theory of liquidity crises in emerging markets and derive its policy implications, while Michael Mussa and Miguel Savastano discuss the IMF approach to dealing with stabilization and balance-of-payments crises.

The recent increases in both consumption and asset prices in the United States are related, because the latter is often used to rationalize the former. There is little doubt that a stock-market crash would dampen consumer spending. However, there is also an undeniable tension between explanations of the two phenomena. For example, one potential explanation for the rise in consumption is that people have become more impatient. On the other hand, an increase in impatience would normally require that asset prices fall, so that people would be willing to hold on to their assets. Thus, a potential explanation for the increase in asset prices is that people have become *more* patient. One common feature of the papers by Parker and by Heaton and Lucas is that they both dismiss monocausal explanations of the rises in consumption and asset prices, respectively, attributing these phenomena instead to a combination of factors.

Parker is able to cast doubt on a number of the single-cause explanations that have been offered for the rise in the ratio of consumption to income. These include the changes in the age composition of the population, changes in government tax, transfer and spending policies, changes in access to credit, and, mostly notably, the aforementioned increase in asset prices. Parker in fact offers both timing and cross-section regression evidence that the increase in asset prices has relatively little to do with the consumption boom. By contrast, the possibility that increased impatience accounts for the increase in consumption cannot be ruled out, particularly as we have recently seen increases in real interest rates on fixed-income securities that exceed even the increase in the rate of growth of consumption.

Heaton and Lucas take aim at the claim that the stock-market boom in the United States can be explained by increases in stock-market participation. They point out that, even though many more individuals hold some stocks, the bulk of shares in publicly traded companies are still held by a very small fraction of the population. They also cast doubt on other single-cause explanations of asset price increases, including the suggestions that they reflect expected higher earnings growth or increased patience. However, by combining the various explanations, and in particular by giving a large role to increases in average diversification brought about by the explosive growth in mutual funds (which they model in a novel way), the authors can account quantitatively for the increase in U.S. stock prices. In his discussion, John Campbell argues that for the story to work diversification would need to have increased for the richest wealthholders as well, and he wonders whether this occurred in practice. This is now left as an important question for future research.

The volume includes two papers on crises in financial markets. The first, by Hoshi and Kashyap, is a study of the origins and likely future evolution of the problems of the Japanese banking system. Hoshi and Kashyap argue that, as in the case of many other banking crises, the origins of this problem can be traced to financial deregulation. In the Japanese case, this led the banks' best customers to borrow elsewhere. The authors show that much of the cross-sectional distribution of bank returns in Japan can be explained by the degree to which banks relied on large corporate customers who defected to the capital markets when deregulation permitted. A key question at this point is whether Japanese banks' fortunes can be expected to improve over time without much in the way of government help. This would be possible, for instance, if future bank profits could be expected to cover some of the losses that have yet to be recognized formally.

Hoshi and Kashyap argue forcefully against the optimistic view, on the basis of two pieces of evidence. First, a rereading of the accounting evidence suggests to them that the magnitude of Japanese bank losses is very large. Second, they expect the Japanese banking system to shrink over time, rather than grow. The main basis for this conclusion is that they expect financial-market deregulation to lead Japanese borrowers to become as dependent on banks as U.S. borrowers are. Since many firms in Japan still rely on bank financing to a larger extent than similarly placed U.S. firms, the implication is that bank lending in Japan will begin to shrink substantially. Thus there is little chance that the bad-loan problem of Japanese banks will cure itself without substantial outside help. As the discussants emphasized, the future of Japanese banks would be much brighter if they could expect to increase their fee income to the extent that U.S. banks have done. Hoshi and Kashyap suggest that this is one respect where, unfortunately, the institutions in the two countries do not appear to be converging, as Japanese banks still derive very little of their income from fees.

The second paper on financial-market crises is by Chang and Velasco, who focus on recent financial problems in emerging markets. The aim of their paper is to discuss the properties of these crises as well as the policy implications derived by considering a very specific interpretation of these crises. In particular, motivated by the observation that many of these crises occurred in situations where countries' reserves were low relative to their short-term loans from abroad, Chang and Velasco consider a theoretical setting in which the crises are essentially the results of bank runs. Foreigners lend funds to banks in emerging markets, which in turn use the funds to finance illiquid investments. If domestic residents run on the banks, then the investments must be liquidated, the returns are low, and foreigners cannot all be repaid.

Chang and Velasco use a model that has much in common with the celebrated Diamond–Dybvig model of bank runs. However, their setting differs in that, unlike a central bank in a closed economy, the government of a small open economy cannot act as a lender of last resort if the exchange rate is fixed, or if all transactions are carried out in foreign currency. It is for this reason that regulatory interventions can be much more appealing in the open-economy context. For example, an emerging-market government may wish to encourage domestic banks to borrow long-term even though individual banks prefer to borrow short-term. The reason is a type of externality, arising because individual banks ignore the effects of their increased short-term borrowing on the likelihood of a run on the entire banking system. Similarly, Chang and Velasco show that financial-market liberalization may make emerging economies more vulnerable to runs. The exchange-rate regime also has implications for the financial fragility studied in this paper: In particular, the existence of flexible exchange rates, together with the requirement that domestic residents make their deposits in domestic currency, makes it possible for emerging-market governments to act as lenders of last resort after all. Under these conditions the government can respond to an impending run by printing the requisite domestic currency, then allowing the currency to depreciate. In the Chang–Velasco model this strategy avoids runs altogether.

Several commentators noted that these issues of financial fragility were not central in Mussa and Savastano's discussion of the IMF approach to economic stabilization. Rather, their paper suggests that the IMF views the countries that seek its support as requiring changes in "fundamentals," so that their current-account financing problems do not recur. The required changes in fundamentals involve fiscal and monetary contractions as well as reforms of institutions. The liberalization that lies at the heart of many of the proposed institutional reforms is seen as necessary to increase sustainable growth. The paper spends relatively little time defending these specific institutional reforms against their critics, however. Rather, the paper deals explicitly with several other criticisms of IMF programs. It argues, for example, that IMF programs are not all identical; for example, the magnitudes of fiscal and monetary adjustments that are proposed differ by country. The paper emphasizes that, in addition, IMF programs react flexibly to evolving circumstances. Initial IMF targets are not rigidly maintained over time but rather are allowed to change as new information accumulates. Mexico's successful adjustment to the 1994 crisis, for example, involved the violation of several interim program targets.

The authors see the need for fiscal contraction as relatively noncontroversial, because it improves the current account by reducing imports. That these contractions can also reduce the feasible repayment to foreign creditors by reducing asset values is recognized indirectly, by acknowledging that the required fiscal adjustments are sometimes modest. Still, the extent to which the IMF takes this problem into account is quite controversial. The lack of a precise formula by which fiscal adjustments are set, while probably a strength given the myriad considerations that make each country a special case, naturally complicates the judgment of whether the IMF staff is giving these considerations their proper weight.

Mussa and Savastano recognize that the domestic credit creation targets are more controversial. One reason for this is that one cannot forecast future credit creation (or money growth) without a model for money demand, and estimated money demand curves have large residuals. They thus take pains to argue that these targets are not rigidly adhered to as circumstances change. Since there has been a shift (in both academic discourse and central bank practice) back towards thinking of monetary policy in terms of interest rates, the IMF might be able to silence this criticism at low cost by describing its suggestions for monetary policy in these terms. It might then be easier to communicate that the IMF cannot accept blame simultaneously for raising interest rates and for allowing currencies to devalue, given that it sees interest-rate increases as the only short-term method for preventing depreciation.

Alvarez and Veracierto return to a topic that has long occupied the *Macro Annual*, namely the increase in European unemployment. The authors try to deduce the importance of European labor-market policies by studying these within a simple calibrated model of search, in which unemployed individuals are indifferent between searching and staying out of the labor force altogether. They focus, in particular, on minimum wages, increases in wages brought about by unions, firing taxes, and unemployment insurance. Even setting the minimum wage so that it covers 90% of the average wage has very little effect on unemployment in the model. Minimum wages might well have larger effects if the model were extended so that workers would not all earn the same wage in the absence of the search frictions. While unions also raise wages, they raise wages for everyone, and the result is that they have much larger effects on unemployment. One attractive feature of the authors' model with unions is that it can easily match both the size of the union wage premium and the fraction of the U.S. workforce that is employed by unions.

As in many previous studies, firing taxes are found to have relatively modest effects on unemployment, because they discourage both hiring and firing. By contrast, unemployment insurance acts as a firing subsidy in this model. It thus leads to a substantial increase in the number of temporary withdrawals from work that are rewarded by the government. While this means that UI has a large effect on unemployment, Alvarez and Veracierto show that the effects implied by their model are similar in magnitude to those estimated by Nickell (1997) using a cross section of countries. The fact that such strong policy conclusions follow from such a stripped-down model led many commentators to worry about the robustness of the results. It was generally agreed, however, that the advantage of the broad modeling framework of the paper is that it can be modified to study many aspects of the labor market while providing a range of testable implications.

We close with some acknowledgments. We owe a tremendous debt of thanks to the NBER's conference department, who as usual did a superb job with the logistics. Refet Gurkaynak did a fine job as assistant editor of this volume. We also wish to thank Martin Feldstein, the National Bureau of Economic Research, and the National Science Foundation for their continued support of the *Macro Annual* conference, now in its fourteenth year.

This is the last volume for which Julio Rotemberg will serve as coeditor. Julio would like to express his thanks to the authors, discussants, and conference participants who over the years have made his job so interesting.

Ben S. Bernanke and Julio J. Rotemberg

Abstracts

Liquidity Crises in Emerging Markets: Theory and Policy
ROBERTO CHANG AND ANDRÉS VELASCO

International illiquidity—defined as a situation in which a country's consolidated financial system has potential short-term obligations in foreign currency that exceed the amount of foreign currency to which it has access on short notice—was a common element in recent financial and exchange-rate crises in Mexico, East Asia, Russia, Eduador, and Brazil. Illiquidity can render economies vulnerable to self-fulfilling panics. If creditors lose confidence and stop rolling over existing loans—whether to the private sector as in Asia or to the government as in Mexico or Brazil—the collapse of the currency or the financial system or both is the likely outcome. We build a model of crashes driven by illiquidity and show how and in what circumstances self-fulfilling collapses can occur. Vulnerability depends on a host of factors, such as the maturity and currency denomination of debts, the health of the banking sector, the fiscal stance, and the exchange-rate regime. We also use the model to analyze options for crisis prevention and crisis management. Certain kinds of capital controls, stringent bank regulation, and flexible exchange rates are among the policies that can reduce illiquidity and limit financial fragility.

The IMF Approach to Economic Stabilization
MICHAEL MUSSA AND MIGUEL SAVASTANO

This paper explains the IMF approach to economic stabilization, with emphasis on its quantitative aspects. It argues that a Fund-supported program is a process, comprising six broadly defined phases, that evolves along a multiplicity of potential pathways delimited by the Fund's policies governing assistance to members and by the member's resolve to implement the measures needed to restore external payments viability. The paper discusses the three-pronged approach to stabilization that is at the core of all IMF programs, stresses the iterative character of the Fund's "financial programming" framework, and explains the rationale for setting quantitative performance criteria for fiscal and monetary policy in all Fund arrangements. A main theme of the paper is that IMF programs contain a great deal of flexibility to respond both to differences in circumstances and to changes in conditions in individual cases.

The Japanese Banking Crisis: Where Did It Come From and How Will It End?

TAKEO HOSHI AND ANIL KASHYAP

We argue that the deregulation leading up to the Big Bang has played a major role in the current banking problems. This deregulation allowed large corporations to switch quickly from depending on banks to relying on capital-market financing. We present evidence showing that large Japanese borrowers, particularly manufacturing firms, have already become almost as independent of banks as comparable U.S. firms. The deregulation was much less favorable for savers, and consequently they mostly continued turning their money over to the banks. However, banks were also constrained. They were not given authorization to move out of traditional activities into new lines of business. These developments together meant that the banks retained assets and had to search for new borrowers. Their new lending primarily flowed to small businesses and became much more tied to property than in the past. These loans have not fared well during the 1990s. We discuss the size of the current bad-loan problem and conclude that it is quite large (on the order of 7% of GDP). Looking ahead, we argue that the Big Bang will correct the aforementioned regulatory imbalances. This will mean that banks will have to fight to retain deposits. More importantly, we expect even more firms to migrate to capital-market financing. Using the U.S. borrowing patterns as a guide, we present estimates showing that this impending shift implies a *massive* contraction in the size of the Japanese banking sector.

Stock Prices and Fundamentals

JOHN HEATON AND DEBORAH LUCAS

We consider a variety of fundamentals-based explanations for the recent stock price run-up, including changes in preferences, dividend growth rates, and the extent of risk sharing. In a calibrated OLG model we focus on two aspects of risk sharing—the market participation rate and the degree of diversification. We conclude that the relatively small changes in participation that have occurred over this decade are unlikely to be a major part of the explanation. Increased portfolio diversification, however, is likely to have had a larger effect. There is empirical evidence that households have significantly diversified their portfolios, selling individual stocks and buying mutual funds. An important difference between poorly diversified portfolios and investment in a market index is the reduced likelihood of catastrophic outcomes. When this is reflected in model parameters, the expected equity premium falls by more than 4%. More generally, we construct scenarios that are loosely consistent with the data in which the required return on stocks falls by 2%. Using a calibrated Gordon growth model, we find that this change in expected returns goes at least halfway towards justifying the current high level of the price–dividend ratio in the U.S. stock market.

Labor-Market Policies in an Equilibrium Search Model
FERNANDO ALVAREZ AND MARCELO VERACIERTO

We explore to what extent differences in employment and unemployment across economies can be generated by differences in labor-market policies. We use a version of the Lucas–Prescott equilibrium search model with undirected search and endogenous labor-force participation. Minimum wages, degree of unionization, firing taxes, and unemployment benefits are introduced and their effects analyzed. When the model is calibrated to U.S. observations, it reproduces several of the elasticities of employment and unemployment with respect to changes in policies reported in the empirical literature. We find that: (1) minimum wages have small effects; (2) firing taxes have similar effects to those found in frictionless general equilibrium models; (3) unions have large and negative effects on employment, unemployment, and welfare; and (4) unemployment benefits substantially increase unemployment and reduce welfare.

Spendthrift in America? On Two Decades of Decline in the U.S. Saving Rate
JONATHAN A. PARKER

During the past two decades, the personal saving rate in the United States has fallen from 8% to below zero, and the share of GDP that households consume rose by 6 percentage points. This increase in the share of consumption was concurrent with a reduction in the growth rate of real consumption spending per person, high real rates of return, and an increasing ratio of aggregate wealth to income. Despite this last fact, wealth changes can explain little of the boom in consumption spending: The largest increases in national wealth postdate the consumption boom, and households with differing wealth levels nevertheless had similar increases in consumption. The changing age distribution of the U.S. population does not explain the consumption boom, either: While it may be that younger, wealthier cohorts are driving this boom, the preponderance of evidence suggests rather that the rising consumption-to-income ratio is due to a common time effect. The main findings of the paper are consistent with either an increase in discount rates or a general belief in better economic times in the future. Alternatively, the low rates of saving could be due to a combination of factors, such as the increase in intergenerational transfers from the Social Security system, which has raised the consumption of the elderly, and increased access to credit and an expanded menu of financial instruments raising the consumption of the young.

Roberto Chang and Andrés Velasco
FEDERAL RESERVE BANK OF ATLANTA; AND NYU AND NBER

Liquidity Crises in Emerging Markets: Theory and Policy

1. Introduction

The recent literature offers no shortage of villains to blame for the financial crashes in Mexico, East Asia, Russia, and Brazil: corruption and cronyism, lack of transparency and imperfect democracy, misguided investment subsidies and loan guarantees, external deficits that are too large (or sometimes too small), fixed exchange rates that are maintained for too long (or abandoned too readily), poor financial regulation, excessive borrowing abroad—the list goes on and on.

It is tempting to argue that several or even all of these factors mattered for recent meltdowns. But such a kitchen-sink approach would help little in understanding why, when, and where these crises happened. Which one of the many weaknesses exhibited by the afflicted countries is *necessary* for a crisis to occur? Can any of them conceivably be *sufficient* to trigger a collapse? There is also the pesky need to formulate policy. Central bankers and finance ministers can at best tackle a few issues at a time. Where should they focus their efforts to have the best chance of avoiding financial vulnerability?

At the risk of oversimplifying, in this paper we focus on a single factor behind financial and currency distress: *international illiquidity,* defined as a situation in which a country's consolidated financial system has potential short-term obligations in foreign currency that exceed the amount of

We thank Philippe Aghion, Abhijit Banerjee, Ben Bernanke, Dean Corbae, Laura Hastings, Julio Rotemberg, Nouriel Roubini, Aaron Tornell, Chris Waller, and seminar participants at Harvard, Yale, the University of Kentucky, and the University of Pittsburgh for useful comments. The opinions expressed here are ours only and not necessarily those of the Federal Reserve Bank of Atlanta or the Federal Reserve System. Velasco acknowledges the support given by the C. V. Starr Center for Applied Economics at NYU.

foreign currency it can have access to on short notice.[1] Illiquidity is certainly not *necessary* for currency crashes to occur. The EMS troubles of the early 1990s, for instance, had more to do with governments' desire to fight unemployment than with any difficulties in servicing short-term obligations.[2] But illiquidity comes close to being *sufficient* to trigger a crisis. The options left after creditors lose confidence and stop rolling over and demand immediate payment on existing loans—whether to the private sector as in Asia or to the government as in Mexico and Brazil—are painfully few. The collapse of the currency, of the financial system, or perhaps both is the likely outcome.[3]

We restrict our focus even further by stressing the role of domestic banks in causing and transmitting situations of illiquidity. In doing so we miss some of the action: the world now knows that in Indonesia it was corporates that did much of the borrowing and that faced severe illiquidity when foreign lending stopped. Yet a focus on banks is justified for two reasons. The first is the high observed correlation between exchange-rate collapses and banking crises. In the Southern Cone of the Americas in the early 1980s, Scandinavia in the early 1990s, Mexico in 1995, and Asia more recently, the currency crashed along with the financial system. Formal econometric work, such as that reported by Kaminsky and Reinhart (1996), shows that a bank crisis helps predict a currency crisis.[4] The second is that banks play a much larger role in emerging than in mature economies; this justifies focusing on banks to the neglect of other financing mechanisms such as equity.

Emphasizing illiquidity is natural for emerging markets because of their limited access to world capital markets. When fractional-reserve banks in mature economies face a liquidity problem, they are likely to get emergency funds from the world capital markets as long as they are solvent. This is seldom the case in emerging economies: a private bank in Bangkok or Mexico City will get many international loan offers when things go well, and none when it is being run on by depositors. The combination of fractional reserve (and hence potentially illiquid) banks

---

1. This is close to what Dornbusch (1998) calls "balance sheet vulnerability." See also Feldstein (1999) for a set of policy recommendations that focus on increasing liquidity.
2. This point has been forcefully argued by Obstfeld (1994).
3. We say "close to sufficient" because, as Obstfeld and Rogoff (1995) have stressed, any central bank that has enough resources to buy back the monetary base is capable, in a technical sense, of maintaining an exchange-rate peg. But, as Obstfeld and Rogoff themselves recognize, in situations of financial distress the de facto claims on central-bank reserves may be as large as M2 or larger. In those cases, as we study in detail below, maintaining the peg becomes a more treacherous task.
4. Also, Sachs, Tornell, and Velasco (1996b) find that the previous speed of bank credit growth helped explain which countries were affected by the tequila effect.

and external credit rationing is potentially devastating, and is the focus of our analysis below.

International illiquidity is what the very diverse recent crises in emerging markets have in common. Recently, troubled countries in Asia[5] had high and sharply rising ratios of hard-currency short-term liabilities, especially external debt, to liquid assets. They were therefore extremely vulnerable to what Calvo (1998) terms the *sudden stop syndrome:* a massive reversal of capital inflows, which occurred in the second half of 1997.[6] Bankruptcies, payments moratoria, and collapses in asset prices (including the exchange rate, the price of domestic money) proliferated. The financial panic fed on itself, causing foreign creditors to call in loans and depositors to withdraw funds from banks—all of which magnified the illiquidity of domestic financial institutions and forced yet another round of costly asset liquidation and price deflation.

Our intention is not to provide yet another answer to the question of "who lost Asia." Nor do we want to compete with the many good and detailed accounts of what happened.[7] Rather, we tackle three sets of questions:

Analytics: What is the right theoretical framework for illiquidity-driven crises? We have well-established "first generation" models of how loose money causes currency crashes, and "second generation" models of why governments may choose to devalue in response to mounting unemployment. By contrast, models of crashes caused by illiquidity and balance sheet vulnerability are still in their infancy.[8]

Crisis prevention: Can illiquidity-driven crises be avoided, and how? The easy yet useless answer is to require financial systems to be always liquid. Full liquidity is costly and may dispense with all benefits of financial intermediation: banks are in the business of transforming maturities, and there is no way to do this without a mismatched balance sheet. Hence, countries attempting to prevent crises face some unpleasant trade-offs, involving not only domestic financial regulation but also monetary, fiscal, and exchange-rate policy.

5. Although our review is restricted to the Asian crisis, international illiquidity is also found in other crash episodes. For instance, in Chang and Velasco (1998c) we have argued, in this respect, that the recent Asian crisis resembles the experience of Chile in 1982 and Mexico in 1994.
6. Radelet and Sachs (1998) estimate a capital outflow of US$ 34 billion from the Asean-5 countries in the second half of 1997, equivalent to a negative shock of 3.6% of GDP.
7. See, especially, Corsetti, Pesenti, and Roubini (1998a, b) and World Bank (1998).
8. We have made some preliminary progress in Chang and Velasco (1998a, b, 1999). Other papers in the same research line include Calvo (1995, 1998), Detragiache (1996), Goldfajn and Valdés (1997), Jeanne (1998), Aghion, Bacchetta, and Banerjee (1999), and Krugman (1999).

Crisis management: How should one respond to a crisis caused by international illiquidity? In the aftermath of Asia there have been furious debates over the wisdom of increasing interest rates or letting the exchange rate go in the face of an attack. But the "correct" answers should hinge on the nature of the crisis. Current-account-driven crises require a real depreciation and a contraction of demand; illiquidity-driven crises may call for different answers.

We study a model of a bank situated in a small open economy with limited access to international capital. This simple setup attempts to capture the main features of what Krugman (1998) has tentatively termed "third generation" crisis models, and enables us to discuss, in a unified way, a number of issues raised by the recent sequence of crises in emerging markets. In particular, we discuss the role of capital inflows and the maturity of external debt, the way in which real exchange-rate depreciation can transmit and magnify the effects of bank illiquidity, options for financial regulation, the role of debt and deficits, and the implications of adopting different exchange-rate regimes.

Clearly this is not the only potentially useful way to study crises. Several analysts of recent crashes—most visibly Corsetti, Pesenti, and Roubini (1988a, b)—have stressed the role of bad shocks and bad policy, presumably leading to insolvency. That emphasis leads to very different policy implications than does a model like ours, which stresses illiquidity and multiple equilibria. We can offer the usual disclaimer: both approaches are necessary and may turn out to be complementary. But it is important to realize that in our approach the line between illiquidity and insolvency is a fine one. Being illiquid can cause some investment projects to be left unfinished and others to be liquidated early. If this is sufficiently costly, illiquidity can breed insolvency. In practice, the bankruptcies and weak balance sheets recently observed in crisis countries may well be consequences rather than causes of the crisis.

2. International Illiquidity in Recent Crises

Financial fragility is associated with the concept of *international illiquidity,* defined as a situation in which a financial system's potential short-term liabilities in hard currency exceed the amount of hard currency it can have access to on short notice. International illiquidity was crucial in triggering recent crises. To make this case, we shall analyze data from the so-called Asean-5 countries (Korea, Indonesia, Malaysia, Thailand, and the Philippines) and also from comparable Latin American countries.[9] We need to answer at least two questions: how illiquid were the Asean-5 countries at the time the crisis erupted? And were the Asian countries systematically different from otherwise similar ones in terms of international illiquidity? Answering these questions requires making the concept of "international illiquidity" operational, which in turn requires identifying the institutions that constitute each country's "financial system," as well as their relevant "short-term assets and liabilities in hard currency." The appropriate definitions depend on government policy.

Our definition of a financial system will naturally include domestic banks and other domestic financial entities that perform banklike operations (such as Thailand's finance companies). In addition, because the countries under discussion had governments committed to act as lenders of last resort of private financial institutions, their central banks will be included as well. This is sensible because, in the presence of such a commitment, a crisis affecting private financial institutions will force a central bank to honor it, and this may pull the government itself into the crisis. Indeed, we shall argue later that a balance-of-payments crisis is best understood as a situation in which a central bank runs out of international liquidity in an attempt to fight a financial crisis.

Accordingly, an ideal definition of the liquid international assets of the financial system would include not only the short-term external assets of private financial institutions, but also the amount of foreign currency available to the central bank for last resort lending in the event of a crisis. (Notice that the latter should, in principle, exclude the amount of reserves that has already been committed, implicitly or explicitly, to other uses in a crisis, such as the repayment of *tesobonos* in Mexico in 1994.) The definition would also include the amount of international loans that the financial system can have access to in the short run as well as the liquidation value of fixed assets. While a measure of short-term international liquid assets embodying these desiderata can perhaps be constructed, because of data constraints we use the stock of international reserves of the monetary authorities as a proxy for the ideal measure.

Similarly, an ideal definition of the short-term international liabilities of the financial system would include its short-term foreign debt as well as demandable deposits denominated in foreign currency; the only difference, from the perspective of international illiquidity, is that the former are obligations to foreigners while the latter are obligations to domestic residents. In addition, if there is a fixed exchange rate, demandable deposits in domestic currency should also be included, since fixed rates imply that such deposits are effectively obligations in foreign currency.

9. The discussion below is essentially taken from Chang and Velasco (1998c).

The relevant data on deposits in the consolidated financial system are available from the International Financial Statistics (IFS), but the situation for international debt is less satisfactory. As discussed by Corsetti, Pesenti, and Roubini (1998a), the most useful source of evidence on short-term external debt is published by the Bank of International Settlements (BIS). But the BIS data are restricted to the indebtedness of a country's residents against foreign banks. More importantly for our purposes, available BIS tables are not broken down sufficiently to identify the short-term external debt of the financial system. However, they do contain data on the short-term external debt (against BIS reporting banks) of a country as a whole, as well as on the amount of external debt (including debt of longer maturity) contracted by domestic banks. These aspects of the data force us to treat domestic deposits and external debt separately.

Keeping data limitations in mind, we now turn to the available evidence. The data on the Asean-5 countries does suggest that the international liquidity position of their financial systems deteriorated before the crisis. This is can be seen most clearly from the BIS data on foreign bank lending. Table 1 shows the behavior of the ratio of short-term loans from international banks to reserves; obviously, an increase in the ratio implies a higher likelihood of international illiquidity. The upper panel of the table shows that among the Asean-5 the ratio increased between mid-1994 and mid-1997 in every case except for Indonesia, where the ratio was stable. (In Korea, Malaysia, and Thailand the ratio had also increased between 1990 and 1994. It had fallen in Indonesia, but not by much. It had fallen sharply in the Philippines, but this was probably an anomaly following the Philippine Brady debt restructuring of 1991.)

It is also remarkable that the ratios of short-term debt to reserves at the end of 1996 were substantially above one in Korea, Indonesia, and Thailand. This suggests a financially fragile situation, in the sense that international reserves would not have been sufficient to repay the short-term debt had foreign banks decided not to roll it over. While the ratio was below one in Malaysia and the Philippines (the two countries among the Asean-5 least affected by the crisis), it doubled between mid-1994 and mid-1997.

As shown by the lower panel of Table 1, the corresponding data for Latin American countries look rather different. The ratio of short-term debt to reserves was stable and below one in Brazil, Chile, Colombia, and Peru; in Argentina and Mexico it was approximately 1.2 in mid-1997, thus exceeding one but not by much, and had been falling. The Latin countries appear to have been in a much less vulnerable position.

The BIS tables suggest, in addition, that the proportion of foreign bank

Table 1   SHORT-TERM FOREIGN DEBT/INTERNATIONAL RESERVES

			Ratio		
Date[a]	*Indonesia*	*Korea*	*Malaysia*	*Philippines*	*Thailand*
1990	2.21	1.06	0.22	3.18	0.59
1994	1.73	1.61	0.25	0.41	0.99
1997	1.70	2.06	0.61	0.85	1.45
			Ratio		
Date[a]	*Argentina*	*Brazil*	*Chile*	*Mexico*	*Peru*
1990	2.09	2.63	0.89	2.24	3.87
1994	1.33	0.70	0.51	1.72	0.38
1997	1.21	0.79	0.45	1.19	0.50

Source: BIS, IMF.
[a]June.

lending intermediated by the domestic banking sector was stable in each Asian case except Thailand. In the case of Thailand, the decline in the share of the domestic banking sector in foreign borrowing is attributable, by and large, to the increased importance of finance companies. Finance companies seem to have emerged in response to regulatory distortions, but performed banklike functions. In fact, they are included in the IFS as part of the group "Other Banking Institutions"; the IFS notes that although finance companies were "not licensed to accept deposits from the public," they "issued promissory notes at terms comparable to the time deposits at commercial banks." The importance of Thailand's finance companies in the financial systems was also underscored by the fact that the Bank of Thailand was committed to support them as a lender of last resort.

The evidence thus strongly indicates that the short-term external liabilities of the relevant Asian financial systems were growing faster than their liquid international assets. In our interpretation, this trend weakened the international liquidity position of the Asean-5 countries to the point where a loss of confidence from foreign creditors could force the financial system into a crisis. The same was not true in Latin America.

The behavior of domestic deposits vis-à-vis international reserves shows a similar picture. The upper panel of Table 2 shows the evolution of the ratio of M2 to foreign reserves for the Asean-5 economies before their crises. The high level of the M2-to-reserves ratio seems consistent with the hypothesis of international illiquidity. At the end of 1996, the ratio was 6.5 or above in Korea and Indonesia and 4.5 in the Philippines.

Table 2   M2 AS A MULTIPLE OF FOREIGN RESERVES

Date	Indonesia	Korea	Malaysia	Philippines	Thailand
			Ratio		
1993	6.09	6.91	2.09	4.90	4.05
1994	6.55	6.45	2.47	4.86	3.84
1995	7.09	6.11	3.33	5.86	3.69
1996	6.50	6.51	3.34	4.50	3.90
	Argentina	*Brazil*	*Ratio* *Chile*	*Mexico*	*Peru*
1993	3.30	1.85	1.73	4.44	1.91
1994	3.73	2.30	1.52	12.63	1.27
1995	3.64	2.22	1.75	4.37	1.31
1996	3.41	2.75	1.91	4.65	1.24

Source: IMF.

As the lower panel in Table 2 reveals, the same ratio was only 3.4 in Argentina, 2.7 in Brazil, and less than 2 in Chile and Peru. It was higher in Mexico (4.65), but there it had been falling; it is notable (and maybe more than a coincidence) that it had been over 7 there in June 1994, just before Mexico's own crisis!

The M2-to-reserves ratio was stable in each of the Asean-5 countries, except in Thailand, where it was falling. The behavior of the Thai ratio most likely reflects, as we discussed above, that the relevant measure of the liabilities of Thailand's financial system vis-à-vis domestic residents should include the promissory notes of the finance companies, which are not included in M2.

In short, the ratio of M2 to reserves in the Asean-5 countries had been high in each case but Thailand. By contrast, in comparable Latin countries the ratio was relatively high only in Mexico, where it had been falling drastically. This evidence, which proxies the short-term asset and liability positions of each financial system vis-à-vis domestic depositors, also favors the view that the Asean-5 but not the Latin countries had a problem of international illiquidity when the crisis started.

We conclude from this quick review of the data that international illiquidity was in fact a distinguishing characteristic of the Asean-5 economies prior to their 1997–1998 crises. Latin countries did not suffer from that condition—and did not go into crisis.[10]

10. In contrast, the performance of several key real variables was not that different across regions. East Asian countries often had large current account deficits in the 1980s and early 1990s, but the crash did not happen until 1997. In the mid 1990s a number of Latin

Two caveats are in order. First, it bears repeating that, because the Asean-5 countries had effectively fixed exchange rates, our accounting includes domestic currency deposits as obligations in international currency. The magnitudes of deposits relative to international reserves implies that the latter would not have been sufficient to honor the outstanding stock of deposits at the fixed exchange rate. Given this condition, a run by domestic depositors was bound to result in either the bankruptcy of the financial system or the abandonment of the fixed exchange rate. The M2-to-reserves ratio, however, overstates international illiquidity in countries with flexible exchange rates, such as Mexico and Peru, to the extent that M2 includes deposits in domestic currency. This is because, in case of a crisis, a central bank can always print enough domestic currency to honor those deposits; see Section 8 below.

The second caveat is that, because comparable data are not currently available, we have not included short-term domestic public debt in our liquidity measures. In the Asian crisis, this is not likely to be an important omission. Around the time of the collapse there does not seem to have been much short-term public debt in the strongly affected countries of Indonesia, Korea, and Thailand (see Table 3 of Ito, 1998). However, public debt may have played a role in other episodes. We know that the Mexican government's inability to roll over its large stock of short-term debt (in particular, the infamous *tesobonos*) was to prove key in triggering the financial crisis in December 1994. More dramatically, Brazil's debt situation seems to be crucial for understanding its current predicament.[11] This raises the question of whether our international-illiquidity view of crises can be reconciled with the presence of fiscal and/or domestic debt problems. We delay our answer until Section 7.

3. A Basic Framework

Focus on a small open economy with three periods indexed by $t = 0$ (the *planning period*), 1 (the *short run*), and 2 (the *long run*). There is a single, perishable consumption good in each period. The consumption good is

---

countries, including Brazil, Chile, and Colombia, had external deficits over 5% of GDP. Mexico, Malaysia, Thailand and Brazil surely suffered from real exchange rate misalignment, but so did Argentina, Colombia, Chile and Peru, and no crisis has yet hit these South American countries. For a detailed discussion, see Chang and Velasco (1998c).

11. Except for Brazil, public debt has not been a major problem recently for comparable Latin American countries either. Mexico managed substantially to extend the maturity of its public debt after the 1994 collapse. At the end of September 1994, its short-term domestic federal debt was equivalent to U.S. $26.1 billion; by the end of June 1997 this figure was down to less than U.S. $8.5 billion. Argentina, Chile, and Peru have not issued domestic short-term debt in any substantial magnitude.

freely traded in the world market; we take its world price to be the numeraire, or, equivalently, we assume that the price of consumption is fixed at one unit of an international currency (the *dollar*).

The economy is populated by a continuum, whose measure is normalized to one, of ex ante identical individuals, whom we refer to as *depositors* for reasons that will become clear shortly. Each depositor is endowed with an amount $a \geq 0$ of the single good only at $t = 0$. Depositors maximize expected period-2 consumption.

They have access to a world capital market where interest rates are zero. Each depositor can lend as much as she wants in the world market; more precisely, in each period she can purchase any nonnegative quantity of a world *liquid* asset that yields a zero interest rate and can be costlessly liquidated at any time. In contrast, each depositor can borrow at most an amount $f > 0$ and then only from a continuum of identical foreign *creditors*, whose measure is also unity. Each foreign creditor is risk-neutral, can freely borrow or lend in the world market, and maximizes expected second-period consumption. Hence creditors will lend to domestic agents if and only if they are offered an expected net return of zero.

Domestic depositors can also invest in a *long-term* asset with the following characteristics. Each unit of the consumption good invested in this asset at $t = 0$ yields R units of consumption at $t = 2$. However, with probability λ, the investment is hit by a bad shock, in the sense that it needs a further infusion of resources in period 1 if any yield can be collected in period 2. The required infusion is of size $i < a + f$, and is independent of the size of the initial investment in the long-term asset. In other words, when a long-term investment of size k is hit by a shock, period-2 output is Rk if and only if an additional i is invested in period 1.

Assume that $R(1 - \lambda) > 1$, that is, the long-term asset's expected yield is higher than the world interest rate even though it can go to waste when hit by a shock. Assume also that the long-term asset k can be liquidated at $t = 1$ for rk units of output in that period, where $r \in [0, 1)$.[12] These assumptions ensure that the long-term asset is very profitable in the long run but illiquid in the short run.

Information about types is private: whether an agent is unlucky, in the sense that her long-term asset is hit by a shock, is only observed by that agent. Finally, shocks to long-term investment are i.i.d. across consumers and there is no aggregate uncertainty, so λ is also the fraction of the domestic population that turns out to be unlucky.

---

12. Notice that the investment has a positive liquidation value regardless of whether it was hit by the shock. Assuming that only healthy investment has positive liquidation value would change nothing substantial, but would complicate the algebra slightly.

Clearly, in the absence of shocks to illiquid investments, each domestic resident would borrow up to her credit limit f and invest all of her resources in the illiquid asset. On the other hand, if she knew in advance that she was unlucky, she would hold enough liquidity to finance the resource infusion i in period 1.[13]

As the appendix shows in some detail, this uncertainty makes the trade-off between holding and not holding sufficient liquidity very unattractive for the individual agent. She can do better by joining a bank, as we now see.

3.1 A BANK

What banks do is allow agents to take advantage of the law of large numbers to predict more accurately their needs for costly liquidity. The bank pools the resources of the economy (including the endowment a and the maximum credit level f belonging to each depositor) in order to maximize the welfare of its representative member. In doing so, it needs to respect resource constraints and informational constraints.[14]

Formally, the bank's problem is to maximize expected consumption subject to the following constraints. First, it must distribute the period-0 resources $w \equiv a + f$ to the long-term asset and the liquid asset, and hence it must respect the budget constraint

$$k + b \le w, \tag{1}$$

where b and k denote, respectively, investment in the liquid and illiquid assets. In period 1, the bank may or may not spend i to shore up each of the λ investments hit by a shock. In period 2 the bank collects the result of its investments, repays the external debt f, and pays c to each depositor.[15] Finally, these choices must satisfy the incentive compatibility constraint

$$i \le c. \tag{2}$$

An explanation of this last inequality is in order. To simplify exposition, we assume that unlucky agents cannot lie about their types. In contrast, a lucky agent can claim to have been hit by a bad shock, obtain i from the

---

13. Hence shocks to long-term investment play here a role analogous to preference shocks in models in the tradition of Diamond and Dybvig (1983).
14. In this subsection we characterize the best that the bank can do for its members; the next subsection deals with whether and how this solution can be decentralized.
15. This is without loss of generality, although in principle the bank may pay different amounts to lucky and unlucky agents. With risk neutrality, this would not make any difference. As long as there is even a small degree of risk aversion, however, it becomes strictly optimal to pay the same to both types.

bank, and *abscond* with the payment. In that case, she cannot be caught, but is entitled to no period-2 consumption.[16] To prevent absconding, c cannot be smaller than i.

To characterize the solution (whose values are denoted by hats), ignore the incentive constraints for the moment. It can be shown that the bank will hold enough liquidity to shore up bad investments,[17] that is,

$$\hat{b} = \lambda i, \tag{3}$$

which implies that consumption in period 2 is

$$\hat{c} = R\hat{k} + (\hat{b} - \lambda i) - f = R(w - \lambda i) - f. \tag{4}$$

[It is easy to show that the equality in (3) must hold.] Note that $\hat{c}$ is not only the total consumption in period 2 but also the expected utility of depositors.

One still has to check that the incentive constraint $\hat{c} \geq i$ is satisfied, or

$$i \leq \frac{Rw - f}{1 + R\lambda}, \tag{5}$$

which we assume from here on.

One can now check that $\hat{c}$ is greater than optimal consumption under individual autarky (the latter is derived in the Appendix). The bank improves matters over autarky; the reason is that the bank faces no uncertainty, and hence may plan to hold less liquidity than an individual in isolation.[18]

The optimal bank allocation differs from the autarky solution along several other dimensions. In particular, since the current account deficit in period 0 is given by $k - a$ and the amount k devoted to illiquid investments is larger under a bank, it follows that financial intermediation enlarges that deficit. It also changes the net foreign asset position of the economy as a whole. In period 1, the net foreign asset position is given by $b - f$; since financial intermediation reduces the amount b held

---

16. Lucky agents cannot, however, withdraw i in period 1 and c in period 2. The implicit assumption is that types become public information at the beginning of period 2.

17. If it were optimal for the bank to plan not to shore up bad investments, it would be optimal to set $b = 0$. Total consumption in period 2 (and also ex ante utility) would then be given by $[(1 - \lambda)R + \lambda r]w - f$. But assumption (32) in the Appendix (necessary so that agents in autarky choose to be liquid) implies that this is less than $\hat{c}$ as given by (4).

18. Compare (3) and (33) in the Appendix.

abroad, the net foreign asset position is smaller with a bank than in autarky.[19]

3.2 DEMAND DEPOSITS AND ILLIQUIDITY

The previous subsection identified the best allocation that the coalition of depositors can achieve in principle. In practice, the bank may rely on alternative systems to attempt implementing the social optimum. Following much of the literature, the rest of the paper is concerned with the study of one such system, which we call *demand deposits*. Our focus on demand deposits makes sense not only because they are often observed in reality, but also because, as we shall see, they are able to implement the social optimum.

Given the optimal allocation $(\hat{c},\hat{k},\hat{b})$, a demand-deposit system is a contract that works as follows. Each depositor agrees to surrender her endowment and her borrowing capacity to the bank at time 0. In period 1 she may withdraw i from the bank on demand, so that she can shore up her illiquid investment if necessary. (This resembles actual demand deposits in that depositors may withdraw i at their discretion). In period 2, depositors have the right to withdraw $\hat{c}$, provided they have not absconded.

To finance its operations, the bank borrows f in period 0, invests $\hat{k}$ in the long-term asset, and invests $\hat{b}$ in the world liquid asset. We shall assume, for the time being, that foreign debt contracted in period 0 is due for repayment in period 2 at a contractual interest rate of zero; the significance of this assumption will be discussed at the beginning of the next subsection. The bank agrees to use $\hat{b} = \lambda i$ to finance period-1 withdrawals, and $R\hat{k} = R(w - \lambda i)$ to repay the external debt and service withdrawals in period 2.

We impose two additional assumptions on this system. First, in period 1 the bank must serve depositors on a first-come, first-served basis.[20] In period 1 depositors visit the bank in random order. Upon arrival at the bank, and assuming the bank is open, each depositor may withdraw i on demand. To service withdrawals, the bank liquidates its world asset $\hat{b}$ until exhausted, and then it proceeds to liquidate long-term investments. If all assets are liquidated while there are agents still in line attempting to withdraw, the bank goes bankrupt and closes. Second, if the bank did not close in period 1, in period 2 output (if any) is collected, depositors and foreign creditors are paid, and any surplus is distributed

---

19. These assertions follow from the Appendix.
20. Wallace (1996) derives this *sequential service constraint* from more primitive assumptions on the environment.

to depositors. We shall assume that, in period 2, the bank serves first those depositors that did not withdraw i in period 1.[21]

In the demand deposit system just described, depositors face a strategic decision of how and when to withdraw. In other words, depositors are engaged in an anonymous game, whose equilibria naturally characterize the outcomes of the system. We are now ready to describe those outcomes.

A first result is that the demand deposit system has an *honest* equilibrium, in which all depositors withdraw according to their true types, the bank honors all of its commitments to foreign creditors, and the socially optimal allocation is obtained. The intuition is simple. By construction, the demand deposit system is feasible if depositors act honestly. Then the incentive compatibility constraints ensure that lying about shocks and absconding cannot be profitable for lucky depositors.

The previous result implies that the demand deposit system can decentralize the preferred allocation. But this is not the only possibility. The problem is that, because holding liquidity is costly, the bank may choose to become illiquid in the short run (i.e. in period 1) in the sense that

$$\hat{b} + r\hat{k} < i. \tag{6}$$

This *international illiquidity* condition says that the *potential* short-term obligations of the bank may exceed its liquidation value. International illiquidity is crucial, since it is necessary and sufficient for a *bank-run* equilibrium to exist.

To see that international illiquidity is a sufficient condition for the existence of a bank-run equilibrium, observe that a bank run occurs when all depositors withdraw i and lucky ones abscond. Given (6), this behavior will force the bank to liquidate all assets and close. As a consequence, depositors will not be paid anything in period 2, which in turn implies that it is individually optimal for each of them to run on the bank. Conversely, if (6) fails, then the bank will not exhaust its resources even if all depositors collect i in period 1. This, together with the assumption about seniority of claims, implies that lucky depositors that wait until period 2 will be able to collect at least the promised $\hat{c}$ from the bank. But then it cannot be individually optimal for them to participate in a run.[22]

---

21. For instance, suppose that in period 1 each depositor can either stand in line at the bank or walk to the next day's line and wait there.

22. A formal proof is as follows. Let λ^r be the fraction of depositors reporting bad luck; in a run, $\lambda^r > \lambda$. The bank will be forced to liquidate $l = (\lambda^r - \lambda)i/r$ units of $\hat{k}$ in period 1. The bank will be able to repay $\hat{c}$ to the $1 - \lambda^r$ depositors that wait if $R(\hat{k} - l) \geq (1 - \lambda^r)\hat{c}$, or if $R\hat{k} \geq R(\lambda^r - \lambda)i/r + (1 - \lambda^r)\hat{c}$. But this must be the case if (6) fails.

Since (6) is equivalent to

$$r \leq \frac{[1 - \lambda(1 - r)]i}{w},$$

a bank run will be possible if and only if liquidation of the long-term asset is sufficiently costly.

In short, a demand-deposit system may emerge in this economy as a collective attempt to implement the social optimum. The system may succeed in this purpose if every depositor believes that all others will behave honestly. However, the system may also fail: self-fulfilling bank runs are possible because the social optimum may imply international illiquidity.

As we argued at the outset, in this model illiquidity and insolvency are closely related. We have stressed that a certain illiquidity condition must be satisfied for run to occur. But in that case the runs are self-fulfilling precisely because they lead to insolvency. Bank creditors who do not run (or who cannot run, like external creditors) get nothing in period 2 because all bank assets have been liquidated. And it is precisely the costly nature of this liquidation that turns an illiquid bank into an insolvent one.

3.3 THE PROBABILITY OF CRISES

In the preceding subsection we ignored the fact that, if a bank run occurs, the external debt contracted in period 0 is defaulted on. This is consistent with our earlier assumption of zero interest rates on foreign borrowing only if foreign creditors believe, at $t = 0$, that a crisis will occur with zero probability. The analysis of the previous section may need to be modified if creditors are rational and crises occur with positive probability when they are possible. More generally, while we stated that runs may take place, we did not discuss the probability of such runs, nor the effects that such a probability may have on the bank's problem.[23]

How to deal with this issue is controversial; our strategy follows Cooper and Ross (1998). We postulate the existence of a publicly observed random variable that takes the value 1 with probability $p \in [0,1]$ or 0 with probability $1 - p$. The nature of that random variable is arbitrary but immaterial, as long as depositors and creditors may condition their

---

23. In this subsection we keep the assumption that all foreign debt contracted in period 0 is due in period 2. This is only to simplify the exposition, but in fact the distinction between short-term and long-term debt has been crucial in recent crises. We deal with that issue in the next section.

behavior on its realization; however, we assume that payments promised at $t = 0$ cannot be made contingent on it. We also assume that p is sufficiently small so that $R(1 - \lambda)(1 - p) > 1$. Otherwise, the long-term asset is insufficiently productive (in an expected-value sense), and it is optimal to invest everything in the liquid world asset.

The bank's problem is now to choose an allocation (c, k, b) to maximize the expected utility of its representative depositor, taking into account the following observations. First, the allocation must be feasible if there is no crisis. Second, the allocation will determine whether or not a crisis can occur. The results of the previous section imply that a given allocation may result in a crisis if and only if

$$i > b + rk, \tag{7}$$

in which case we assume that a bank run occurs with probability p.

Second, if a bank run occurs, not every depositor will collect what she is owed by the bank. Our assumptions imply that in a run each depositor will be served (and thus be able to withdraw i) with probability $(b + rk)/i$.[24]

Finally, if a bank run occurs, foreign loans contracted in period 0 will be defaulted on. This implies that foreign creditors will demand an interest rate greater than zero on these loans in order to compensate for the probability of default. Denoting the interest rate on two-period loans to the bank by r_l, it is readily seen that

$$r_l = \begin{cases} p/(1 - p) & \text{if (7) holds,} \\ 0 & \text{if not.} \end{cases} \tag{8}$$

In this simple model, the solution of the resulting problem is straightforward if p is small enough. If an allocation satisfies $b = \hat{b} = \lambda i$ (so that bad investments can be shored up) and (7) (so that a run is possible), period-2 total consumption conditional on no run taking place is

$$R(w - \lambda i) - (1 + r_l)f = \hat{c} - \frac{pf}{1 - p}, \tag{9}$$

and hence the expected utility of such an allocation is

$$c^* = (1 - p)\left(\hat{c} - \frac{pf}{1 - p}\right) + p\left(\frac{b + rk}{i}\right)i \tag{10}$$

$$= (1 - p)\hat{c} + p(\hat{b} + r\hat{k} - f). \tag{11}$$

---

24. This follows because only a fraction $(b + rk)/i$ of all depositors will be served. Hence the probability that a particular depositor will be served equals the probability that a uniform $[0, 1]$ random variable is less than or equal to $(b + rk)/i$.

Note that c^* converges to $\hat{c}$ as p goes to zero, as should be expected.

On the other hand, runs will not occur if the inequality in (7) is reversed. This requires holding liquid assets at least as large as

$$b^{**} = \frac{i - rw}{1 - r}. \tag{12}$$

Since $b^{**} > \lambda i$ for r small enough, the expected utility of such a runproof allocation is

$$c^{**} = Rw - (R - 1)b^{**} - \lambda i - f.$$

Therefore, the bank will choose the socially optimal levels $(\hat{b}, \hat{k})$, and promise a last-period payment of $\hat{c} - pf/(1 - p)$ to depositors, leaving itself vulnerable to a run, if $c^* > c^{**}$. This requires the probability of a crisis to be less than

$$p^* = \frac{\{i[1 - (1 - r)\lambda] - rw\}(R - 1)}{(1 - r)\,[(R - r)\,(w - \lambda i) - \lambda i]}. \tag{13}$$

A run will occur with probability p if and only if $p < p^*$.

It follows that the analysis of the previous subsection remains essentially valid if p is small enough. In this simple model, in fact, the bank's investment decisions will be exactly the same as with $p = 0$; hence, for the analysis of many questions it is legitimate to proceed as if p were in fact zero. On the other hand, allowing p to be positive will turn out to be informative in the analysis of some issues, such as the determination of asset prices and the structure of interest rates. We will exploit these degrees of freedom in the exposition that follows. It is to be understood that results obtained with $p = 0$ will carry over to the case in which p is small but strictly positive.

3.4 WHY THIS MODEL?

We now have a simple framework with some desirable attributes:

Holding liquidity is costly, and international illiquidity emerges endogenously as the optimal response of agents to their environment. The consequence is that *bad* equilibria caused by self-fulfilling pessimistic expectations are possible.

Financial institutions may choose to leave themselves illiquid and therefore vulnerable to crises even if such crises happen with positive probability. This does not imply that illiquidity and crises are always an inevitable outcome of an optimal plan: as we show below, distortions can affect allocations and hence vulnerability to crises.

Domestic banks have two types of creditors: domestic depositors and foreign lenders. The interaction between them can give rise to a rich set of outcomes, with the size and maturity of loans from abroad mattering a great deal. This is particularly important in light of the recent Asian experience, in which capital inflows were large before the crisis and a run by foreign creditors triggered much (but not all) the trouble faced by domestic banks.

Crises have real effects, in contrast with first- and second-generation models. Costly liquidation (or, more generally, projects that are left unfinished or not undertaken because of lack of funding) can cause illiquid banks to suffer real losses and become de facto insolvent.

Government's policy can matter here in two ways. First, policy can conceivably help agents relax some of the constraints placed by the environment—for instance, by using the government's power to tax and borrow, making resources available to the bank when they are needed most. Second, policy can attempt to offset distortions that lead to too much borrowing or too little liquidity, if any exist.

Next we put this model to work for the analysis of several issues related to emerging markets crises.

4. Debt Maturity and Capital Flows

Most accounts of the Asian crisis stress the role of short-term debt.[25] Countries affected were peculiar in that their foreign debts were mostly of short maturity, and crises occurred when foreign creditors panicked and refused to roll over their short-term loans.[26] Furman and Stiglitz (1998) write: "The ability of this variable, by itself, to predict the crises of 1997, is remarkable."

Banks and governments in emerging markets often explain that they prefer to borrow short-term "because it is cheaper." This sounds sensible enough. But the term structure of interest rates is determined by the riskiness of different debt maturities, and these should in turn reflect the possibility of a crisis associated with illiquid portfolios. Consequently, the role of short-term debt in generating a crisis can only be analyzed in

25. Among them Corsetti, Pesenti, and Roubini (1998a), Radelet and Sachs (1998), and Furman and Stiglitz (1998).
26. For arguments of this sort in the context of the Asian crisis, see Radelet and Sachs (1998) and Chang and Velasco (1998c).

a model of the *simultaneous* determination of debt maturity and the term structure of interest rates. In this section we propose one such model and derive its policy implications.[27]

4.1 THE TERM STRUCTURE OF INTEREST RATES

Consider the model of the previous section, now allowing the bank to take both short- and long-term debt. Let d_l be the amount the bank borrows for two periods starting in period 0, and d_s the amount it borrows in period 0 to be repaid with interest in period 1; of course, under appropriate conditions this loan can be rolled over in period 1. The two amounts must satisfy the credit ceiling

$$d_l + d_s \leq f. \tag{14}$$

We know from (8) what the contractual return is on two-period loans. What about r_s, the contractual return one-period loans? If the loan is renewed in period 1, the net interest rate must be zero. But starting in period 0 for loans repayable in period 1, two cases are possible. If the bank chooses an allocation in which a run is not possible, there is zero probability of default and r_s must be zero. But if the allocation is such that a run may happen, lenders may not receive full payment, and this will be reflected in the interest premium they charge. The seniority of claims in the event of a run will determine the size of this premium. For the sake of brevity, we study here only the simplest case in which all short-term claims are equally senior in period 1: in the event of a run, domestic depositors and foreign creditors all "get in line" at the bank, with their place in line being determined randomly.

Given any allocation, total liquid resources available to the bank in the event of a run equal $b + rk$. A straightforward extension of the analysis of the previous section implies that a run is possible if and only if

$$i + (1 + r_s)d_s > b + rk, \tag{15}$$

which is the appropriate international illiquidity condition.[28]

If a run is possible, it will happen with probability p, and in that case each short-term creditor will collect the promised repayment only with probability

27. This section largely follows Chang and Velasco (1999), except for the analysis of externalities, which is new. Obstfeld (1994) has also discussed the role of debt maturity in generating self-fulfilling crises, although he did not endogenize the choice of maturity.
28. For the "only if" part, we modify the seniority assumption of Section 3.2 in a natural way: if the bank is alive in period 2, it honors first the claims of those depositors and foreign short-term creditors that did not collect in period 1.

$$q = \frac{b + rk}{(1 + r_s)d_s + i}.$$ (16)

Since creditors are risk-neutral and have a zero opportunity cost of funds, r_S will be determined by the condition that the expected net return on a short loan is zero. That is,

$$(1 + r_s)(1 - p + pq) = 1.$$ (17)

This implies that if a crisis is possible, $r_s < p/(1 - p) = r_l$. Hence a *term structure* of interest rates emerges endogenously, and in this term structure short-term debt is less expensive (in the contractual sense) than long-term debt. The intuition is that in the event of a crisis, the default on long-term debt is complete, while under our assumptions short-term debt will be at least partly honored.

4.2 ENDOGENOUS MATURITY STRUCTURE

The bank's problem is now to choose its investment portfolio and the optimal maturity structure of its foreign debt in order to maximize the welfare of its representative depositor. The analysis of this problem reduces to that of two simpler subproblems. First, suppose that the bank had to solve the above problem respecting the additional constraint that no crises can be possible. Then the constraint $i + d_s \leq b + rk$ would have to be respected. Since it is easy to see that the implicit cost of that constraint is minimized by setting $d_s = 0$, the value of such subproblem would just be given by c^{**}, as derived in Section 3.3. Note that the subproblem, and hence c^{**}, do not depend on p.

Alternatively, suppose that the bank had to choose an allocation consistent with crises. In that case, it can be shown that it is optimal to set again $b = \hat{b} = \lambda i$, and $\hat{k} = w - \lambda i$. If no crises occurs, therefore, total period-2 consumption will be given by $R\hat{k} - (1 + r_s)d_s - (1 + r_l)(f - d_s)$. Hence the value of this subproblem is

$$\bar{c} = \max_{d_S} \ (1 - p) \left[R\hat{k} - (1 + r_s)d_s - (1 + r_l)(f - d_s) \right] + pqi$$ (18)

subject to (16) and (17).

Clearly the overall bank's problem can now be solved by solving the above two subproblems and comparing their values. This implies that the value of the bank's problem is given by the maximum of $\bar{c}$ and c^{**}. But $\bar{c}$ must be at least as large as c^* as derived in Section 3.3; hence it must also be larger than c^{**} for p small enough. In other words, for p

small the best allocation will be such that a crisis is possible, and we shall focus on that case.

What is the optimal level of short-term debt when the bank chooses to make itself vulnerable? In this simple model with linear preferences and technology, the answer is simple (in fact, too simple): $\bar{c}$ turns out to be the same for all d_s in $[0, f]$, and hence the optimal debt structure is indeterminate.[29] The intuition is that, while short-term debt is contractually less expensive than long-term debt, the cost difference only compensates foreign creditors for the partial defaults associated with the two kinds of debt. As a consequence, the choice between short-term debt and long-term debt is immaterial for final consumption, which coupled with risk neutrality explains the result.

However, if the model is amended so that domestic residents are even mildly risk-averse, optimal debt maturity is pinned down: we show in the Appendix that the bank will find it *strictly* optimal to set $d_s = 0$. The intuition is that, while the choice between short- and long-term debt does not affect expected consumption, it changes the allocation of risk. Taking short-term debt increases expected consumption conditional on a crisis not happening, at the expense of reducing the probability that domestic depositors will be served when a crisis happens. This is cannot be optimal if depositors are risk-averse.

It follows that, in this model, short-term borrowing is indeed suboptimal. How can one reconcile this result with the observed bias towards short-term borrowing emphasized in the recent literature? One possibility is that the bias reflects some distortion not captured by our assumptions. We discuss this next.

4.3 MARKET FAILURE

There may be many reasons why debt choices by individual borrowers might be distorted, so that private and social incentives do not coincide. One of them is that individual borrowers fail to take into account the fall in country risk ratings that may result from their own higher borrowing. A related reason is that, because of informational limitations, foreign lenders cannot distinguish across borrowers from the same country, and treat them all as equally risky. Indeed, the policy of *sovereign ceilings* followed by rating agencies, in which no single company can have a rating higher than the government of its country, suggests that this may well be so.[30]

To illustrate, consider a simple case in which the short maturity of

---

29. The determination of $\bar{c}$ and of the optimal debt maturity is analyzed in the Appendix.
30. See Furman and Stiglitz (1998) for additional reasons as well as an extended discussion.

foreign debt is due to the fact that banks fail to internalize the social effects of reducing their liquidity. Suppose that there are not one but many banks, each of which solves the same problem as in the previous subsection but with one crucial difference: each bank takes the interest rate r_s [instead of the arbitrage condition (17)] as given in its optimization problem. Of course, (17) must hold in equilibrium.[31]

In the Appendix we show that, under our benchmark assumption of risk neutrality, equilibrium requires that $d_s = f$—that is, all debt is to be *short*-term. The intuition is, obviously, that if banks are indifferent as to debt maturity structure when they correctly evaluated the cost of short-term borrowing, they must strictly prefer short-term to long-term debt when that cost is underestimated.

This result is extreme due to risk neutrality, but the point is general: the prevalence of short-term borrowing may be reflecting an externality of the kind just discussed. If that is in fact the case, government intervention to discourage short-term borrowing is justified.[32] Our analysis implies, however, that while optimal intervention would reduce short-term borrowing, it would *not* eliminate the possibility of crises: if policy were successful in eliminating the effect of the externality discussed here, it might be still optimal for banks to choose an internationally illiquid allocation and be subject to crises.

4.4 POLICY IMPLICATIONS: CRISIS PREVENTION

Given that short-term debt is a potential cause of liquidity problems, if there is too much of it because of the kind of market failure just discussed, there may be a case for policies that lengthen the maturity of that debt. A natural candidate is a tax on short-term capital inflows, such as that used by Chile and Colombia. Soto and Valdés-Prieto (1996), Larrain, Laban, and Chumacero (1997), Cárdenas and Barrera (1997), and Montiel and Reinhart (1997) estimate that a shift in composition toward longer foreign-debt maturities is precisely what the taxes seem to have accomplished in both countries. But such a conclusion is subject to two important caveats.

In our model, as in the real world, short-term debt serves some useful functions. Here, it serves to share some of the risk of runs between domestic and foreign creditors, and hence lower the contractual cost of borrowing. The same would be true in a world with stochastic shocks to

---

31. More precisely, an equilibrium of this model is given by an allocation and a short interest rate such that (i) the allocation is optimal for each bank when it takes interest rates as given, and (ii) the allocation and the short-term interest rate satisfy the arbitrage condition (17).

32. In this model, however, the externality causes no distortion and there is no welfare loss. This is clearly a consequence of our strong assumptions; in general, the externality will decrease welfare.

exogenous variables. Alternatively, short-term debt may serve as a commitment device, as in the models of Jeanne (1998) and Rodrik and Velasco (1999). Policies that effectively prohibit short-term debt, regardless of circumstance, need not enhance social welfare.

The other very important caveat is that foreigners are not the only short-term creditors. Hence, abolishing short-term debt is neither necessary nor sufficient for ruling out crises. As Krugman (1998) has stressed, that still leaves all holders of domestic claims on the commercial and central banks ready to run. Policies other than limits on short-term inflows are necessary to deal with this problem. We examine some of those policies below.

4.5 POLICY IMPLICATIONS: CRISIS MANAGEMENT

Short-term debt makes a *coordination failure* among lenders possible. A main task of crisis management is to attempt to coordinate their behavior on the good outcome. Of course, that is easier said than done. In this model, the key is to avoid the real costs (liquidation and others) imposed by early repayment. Hence, a simple suspension of payments that preserves the present value of the creditors' claims makes everyone better off. This kind of logic leads Kenen (1998) to wonder whether in recent policy debates "there has been too much talk of the need for permanent debt workouts as distinct from short-term suspensions of debt service payments."

In practice lenders are wary of such responses. From New York or London it is hard to distinguish the payments moratoria that are justified by liquidity considerations from those that are veiled attempts at default. When in doubt, bankers are likely to suspect the latter. There is also the logistical problem of coordinating the actions of many bondholders (the norm for most capital flows today) rather than a few banks.

But the fact that the task is hard should not keep policymakers from trying. Payments reprogrammings that are accompanied by serious macroeconomic policies and signals of orthodoxy (such as fiscal retrenchment) may prove more palatable. In Korea, for instance, American, European, and Japanese banks jointly agreed in December 1997 to an orderly rollover of existing short-term loans. Major creditor countries helped by anticipating the disbursement of a fraction of the bailout package the IMP had just approved. Those two measures effectively ended the financial panic that had gripped Korea for several months.[33]

In our model, a good part of the problem comes from the bank's inabil-

---

33. This description follows Corseti, Pesenti, and Roubini (1998b). They also note that the rescheduling of loans was a much more daunting task in Indonesia, where there were large numbers both on the lenders' and on the borrowers' side.

ity to sell rather than liquidate its illiquid assets in the event of a squeeze. That assumption is realistic insofar as, in a crisis situation, there are few domestic agents with the cash in hand to buy the real capital. But foreigners are in a different position. Everyone would be better off if through foreign direct investment liquidation could be avoided—even if the price is that of a fire sale, below the present value of capital's real yield in the future.[34] Hence, foreign direct investment should be encouraged for these purposes. Debt–equity swaps involving foreign creditors played a role in the resolution of the 1980s debt crisis, and could be useful again in the current context.

Multilateral lenders can also help. They can lend "into arrears" when appropriate to strengthen confidence in the borrower's prospects. They can also encourage the adoption of clauses in international bond covenants that facilitate negotiations between debtors and creditors even when debt service is suspended. As Kenen (1999) points out, such proposals were endorsed by the G-10 back in 1995, but have yet to be implemented in full.

5. Bank Regulation

In this section we study how changes in regulation or in the availability of deposit insurance can affect the banks' vulnerability to runs.

5.1. FINANCIAL LIBERALIZATION

Both casual observation of recent crises and formal econometric work suggest the existence of important links between financial liberalization and crises. The econometric work of Kaminsky and Reinhart (1996) and Demirguc-Kent and Detragiache (1998) has shown that financial liberalization precedes financial crises. Similar stylized facts have emerged from case studies of many notorious crisis episodes, including Chile in 1982, Sweden and Finland in 1992, Mexico in 1994, and Asia in 1997.[35]

Lowering reserve requirements on commercial banks is a common liberalization move. Mexico, for instance, lowered required reserves on peso sight deposits all the way to zero in the first half of the 1990s. The rationale is usually that such reductions enhance the efficiency of financial intermediation. Our analysis implies that the conjecture is correct,

34. Because the world rate of interest is zero and one unit of healthy capital yields R units of the tradeable good in period 2, the "fundamental" price is R. But any price smaller than R and bigger than r makes the bank and its creditors better off, while giving the foreign investor an abnormally high rate of return.
35. See Velasco (1987, 1992), Dornbusch, Goldfajn, and Valdes (1995), Sachs, Tornell, and Velasco (1996b), and Radelet and Sachs (1998).

but also that there is a side effect: lower reserve requirements increase banks' vulnerability to runs.

To fix ideas, assume that $f = 0$, and consider a polar policy of *narrow banking*, in which intermediaries are required to keep liquid assets in an amount equal to potential liquid liabilities: $b \geq i$. Clearly, no self-fulfilling runs can take place. But, at the same time, there is a loss in welfare relative to the no-run equilibrium. In fact, in this very simple model, narrow banking is equivalent to autarky; requiring it does away with all the benefits of financial intermediation (this is not necessarily true in more complex models—see Chang and Velasco, 1998b). This captures in a nutshell a result that turns up several times throughout this paper: making yourself liquid is easy, but it is also potentially expensive. Not any policy to enhance liquidity will do.

Another popular liberalization policy is to lower barriers to entry into the banking sector (whether by domestic or by foreign banks), presumably enhancing competition and efficiency. But the problem is that the additional competition may also encourage greater risktaking by banks. Typically the argument is phrased in terms of "franchise values," which presumably fall with competition, so that banks have less to lose and therefore behave less prudently. Garber (1996), for instance, writes: ". . . the sudden admission of foreign banking competition into a system with low capital can further reduce the franchise value of domestic banks and lead to a crisis within a few years as domestic banks compete to retain market share."

Models like the one in this paper can deliver similar results. While we have treated the bank as a coalition of individual agents bent on maximizing their joint welfare, an alternative interpretation of our model is that the bank is a perfect competitor in a banking market into which there are no barriers to entry. Free entry would ensure that equilibrium profits were zero, and in order to attract customers and not be undercut by competitors banks would have to offer depositors contracts that promised as high a level of expected utility as possible.

To assess the effects of liberalization, one may analyze how a less competitive banking system would behave in this context. We study that question in Chang and Velasco (1998b), using a related model that draws directly on Diamond and Dybvig (1983). There we find that a monopoly bank is less prone to runs than competitive banks; the greater fragility of competitive banking arises from the larger rate of return it offers to short-term depositors. Relative to competitive banks, the monopoly will reduce payments to depositors. This hurts depositors, but in general it also implies that the potential short-term obligations of the bank are smaller. This means that the monopoly bank will be *less* illiquid. The implication is that enhanced competition in the financial sector may improve depositors' welfare if no runs take place, but at the same time it may make crises more likely.

5.2 DEPOSIT INSURANCE

It is a plausible conjecture that self-fulfilling crises would disappear if governments of emerging economies established adequate deposit insurance institutions. Presumably, if domestic deposits were guaranteed by the government, depositors would have no incentive to run on commercial banks. In addition, this would seem to entail no cost, since the insurance funds would not be needed in equilibrium. In this subsection we examine this conjecture. Deposit insurance funds may indeed eliminate crises, provided that they are of sufficient size. But deposit insurance is not costless and may result, at best, in the implementation of a suboptimal allocation.

Here and in the rest of the paper we assume, for simplicity, that $p = 0$. Consider the simple setup of Section 3.1, except that the government requires the bank to pay a lump sum z in period 0 in order to finance an insurance fund of the same size. The government agrees to keep z in liquid form, and to take over the servicing of deposit withdrawals in period 1 in case the commercial bank runs out of resources in that period; otherwise, z is returned to the bank in period 2.[36]

The bank's planning problem is the same as in Section 3.1, except that the resources it can invest in period 0 are given by $w - z$ instead of w, and that it will anticipate a lump-sum transfer z in period 2. Hence, if z is not too large, the solution is very similar to that in Section 3.1: the bank will hold just enough liquidity, λi, to keep alive the unlucky long-term assets, and invest the rest, now $k' = w - z - \lambda i$, in illiquid assets. Expected and total consumption in period 2 will now be

$$c^+ = Rk' - f + z = \hat{c} - (R - 1)z. \tag{19}$$

The last expression implies that building the insurance fund is costly and necessarily results in a suboptimal allocation. The intuition is that the insurance fund must be kept in liquid form, whose opportunity cost is $R - 1$ per unit.

Assume now that the bank implements its desired allocation via a demand deposit system. If

$$b + rk' + z = \lambda i + r(w - z - \lambda i) + z \geq i, \tag{20}$$

36. Readers familiar with Chang and Velasco (1998a) will recognize that this definition of deposit insurance is similar to the "war chest" policy of central banks.

it should be intuitively obvious there cannot be an equilibrium run on the bank. Indeed, in a run a lucky depositor would receive i by withdrawing i in period 1 and absconding, while she would receive c^+ in period 2 by not withdrawing i in period 1. But then it cannot be optimal for her to participate in the run. Hence an insurance fund large enough would eliminate the possibility of runs, but cannot be optimal.

It is also of interest to analyze what would happen if (20) failed, that is, if the insurance fund were insufficient. In that case, a run would clearly be possible, in the sense that it would be an equilibrium for all depositors to attempt to withdraw i from the bank. The interesting observation about such a crisis is that it would be expressed as a failure of *deposit insurance,* since it would be the insurance fund that would not be capable of honoring its commitments.

A related point is that, in order for deposit insurance to eliminate crises, the insurance fund must be sufficient to cover the risk of a *generalized* banking panic, not only bank-specific risk. To see this, suppose that depositors are equally allocated not to one but two banks called A and B, and that there are two symmetric states of nature. In one state, the fraction of illiquid assets hit by a bad shock is $\psi > \lambda$ in bank A and λ in bank B, and vice versa in the other state. Hence there is no aggregate uncertainty, although there is bank-specific risk. Suppose now that there is an insurance fund of size $z = (\psi - \lambda)i$ to be used to help a bank if it has to service more than λ depositors in period 1. Then, clearly, there is an honest equilibrium in which all depositors withdraw according to their true type and the insurance fund is used to help fund unlucky long-term investments. But if (20) fails, a bank run is clearly an equilibrium. This may be the reason why deposit insurance institutions that perform well in "normal" times seem underfunded in times of crisis.

The main conclusion: for a country to "self-insure" its banking system is possible, but costly. Can it be done better by purchasing such insurance abroad? After all, if lenders can diversify away the risk of country-specific bank runs, such insurance need not be expensive. This is presumably the logic of the Argentine policy of contracting a line of credit (for which a premium is paid annually) to be used in case of bank troubles.

The idea is appealing, but not without potential difficulties. First, if there is regional or global contagion, the risk of bank runs may not be easily diversifiable for lenders. Second, the obvious potential for moral hazard makes such contracts hard to write and enforce. Third is the issue of size: press accounts put the Argentine line of credit at U.S. $6 billion, which is a small fraction of M2. Whether larger amounts may be provided by the market at a reasonable premium is unclear.

5.3 POLICY IMPLICATIONS

Furman and Stiglitz (1998) write that "the evidence that financial liberalization increases the vulnerability of countries to crises is overwhelming." The examples we have just examined suggest precisely the same. It would seem, then, that the case for strengthening supervision and carrying out liberalization very carefully is also very strong. And indeed, one finds such advice being freely dispensed in the post mortems on the recent crises.

But one should not trust financial regulation alone as the panacea of crisis prevention. As we have seen, mandating institutions to remain liquid is not cheap. There is also the issue of design and enforceability of financial regulation. Regulators have been overwhelmed, and financial crises have occurred, in countries as advanced as Japan, Sweden, and the United States. Why should emerging markets do any better?

And macroeconomic conditions, if sufficiently severe, can overwhelm even the best-managed financial system. Developed country banks might not have survived the massive depreciations and external credit squeezes that financial institutions in Thailand, Korea, or Brazil have had to face. This suggests that most financial crises are also macroeconomic. To that issue we now turn.

6. The Real Exchange Rate

So far in the analysis, all real consequences of financial distress have come from the early and costly liquidation of investment. Interpreted in a literal sense, such liquidation an also account for only a small part of the output losses that we observe in Mexico or Thailand. A broader interpretation, which included projects left unfinished or not undertaken for lack of finance, would take us farther. But, as Krugman (1999) has argued, ". . . the main channels though which financial panic has turned good assets into bad involve not so much physical liquidation or unfinished projects as macroeconomic crisis: companies that looked solvent before the crisis have gone under because collapsing investment has produced a severe recession, or because capital flight has led to currency depreciation that makes their dollar debts balloon. . . ."

Accordingly, we are led to explore how our framework can be extended to allow for such endogenous liquidation effects, and thereby provide a more realistic account of crises. The key, as conjectured by Krugman (1999) and earlier by Calvo (1998), is the behavior of the real exchange rate. Indeed, real depreciation may be crucial in making bank runs possible and multiplying their deleterious real effects.

Take the same model as before, recalling that we are imposing $p = 0$, but adding a nontraded good. This good is produced by many competitive firms with a simple technology: a dollar invested in period 0 yields $A > 1$ of the nontradable in period 1. This output is then stored and consumed in period 2, along with tradables consumption.

Firms in the nontradable sector must borrow the dollars needed to invest in period 0 from the commercial bank. Clearly, for the bank to be indifferent between lending to the nontradable-good firms and investing in tradable goods, the rate of interest paid by the nontradable producers must be the same as the marginal return earned by tradable production: R.

It follows that the profits, denominated in dollars, earned by the representative nontradables producer are $Ah/e - Rh$, where h is the amount invested by the typical nontradables firm, and e is the price of tradables in terms of nontradables—that is, the *real exchange rate*. The zero-profit condition ensures that this relative price is given in equilibrium by

$$\bar{e} = \frac{A}{R}, \tag{21}$$

where overbars denote equilibrium values.

The composition of output is determined on the demand side. Assume that consumers have Cobb–Douglas preferences and allocate a fixed portion θ of total consumption expenditure in period 2 to nontraded goods, and a portion $1 - \theta$ to traded goods. Since the resources allocated by the bank to domestic investment are $w - b$, the amount going to production of tradables is $w - b - h$. It follows that output and consumption of tradables is $R(w - b - h)$, while output and consumption of nontradables is Ah. Consumer optimality conditions then dictate that

$$\theta R(w - b - h) = (1 - \theta)\frac{A}{e}h. \tag{22}$$

But, in equilibrium, the real exchange rate is expected to be $\bar{e} = A/R$. Inserting this value into (22) and solving the resulting equation implies that total investment in the nontradables sector is $\bar{h} = \theta(w - b)$ and, correspondingly, in the tradables sector is $\bar{k} = w - b - \bar{h} = (1 - \theta)(w - b)$.

It only remains to check whether it is optimal for the bank to hold enough liquidity to shore up distressed investments in tradables. If so, the dollar value of total expected consumption is $R(w - \lambda i) - f$; if not, it is $[(1 - \lambda)R + \lambda r](1 - \theta)w + R\theta w - f$. The first option dominates provided that

$$w(1 - \theta)(R - r) > Ri,\tag{23}$$

which we assume.[37] As a consequence, $\bar{b} = \lambda i$.

We conclude that investment in tradables is $\bar{k} = (1 - \theta)(w - \lambda i)$, and investment in nontradables is $\bar{h} = \theta(w - \lambda i)$. The dollar value of total output accruing to the bank in period 2 from the two sectors, given the real exchange rate in (21), is therefore simply $R(w - \lambda i)$.

Consider now how this allocation can be decentralized by means of a demand deposit system, in which agents' depositors surrender their endowments for the right to $R(w - \lambda i)$ dollars in period 2 plus i dollars in period 1 if unlucky. Using arguments identical to those in earlier sections, one can show that, if the incentive compatibility constraint (5) is satisfied, there is an honest equilibrium to the game among depositors, in which everyone reports truthfully.

It is also possible to have self-fulfilling bank runs, as in earlier sections. However, there is a mechanism here that was not present before. The key observation is that the dollar resources at the bank's disposal in period 1 are its liquid-asset holdings λi, plus the liquidation value of tradables investment $r\bar{k}$, *plus* the dollar market value of the repayment of the loan made to nontradables production. But this last quantity varies with the real exchange rate. Indeed, we saw above that a relative price $\bar{e}$ guarantees zero profits for the borrower, which then transfers the whole value of his revenue—equal to $A\bar{h}/\bar{e} = R\theta(w - \lambda i)$—to the bank. At a more depreciated real exchange rate (a higher e), on the other hand, the nontradables firm is broke, and cannot repay the whole amount owed to the bank. Indeed, for $e > \bar{e}$ the bank will get only $(A/e)\bar{h}$ dollars, which is less than it is contractually entitled to.

Now, if there is a bank run the total supply of tradeables in the economy is only $\lambda i + r(1 - \theta)(w - \lambda i)$ which, by (23), is smaller than the $R(1 - \theta)(w - \lambda i)$ units that would have been supplied with no run. Hence, the real exchange rate is now given by a condition similar to (22) but evaluated at the new output and consumption levels[38]

$$e^r = \left(\frac{A}{R}\right)\frac{(1 - \theta)\,R(w - \lambda i)}{\lambda i + r\,(1 - \theta)\,(w - \lambda i)} > \frac{A}{R}\tag{24}$$

37. In the model with only one good the equivalent condition was $w(R - r) > Ri$, which was guaranteed by our assumptions. Here an amended version of that condition would read $(1 - \theta)\lambda(R - r)w \geq [R - (1 - \lambda)]i$. That would guarantee that in this two-good model agents in autarky held positive liquidity, and so did the bank [condition (23) would always hold].

38. Notice that no consumption takes place until period 2. But all output to be consumed in period 2 reaches the public already in period 1. Hence, one can assume that all trades take place in period 1, satisfying the consumption optimality conditions that must prevail in period 2. During trade the real exchange rate e is determined.

It follows that in a run the bank can at most have access to $A\bar{h}/e^r + r\bar{k} + \lambda i$ dollars to meet withdrawals in period 1. The illiquidity condition that is necessary and sufficient for a run to be an equilibrium is therefore

$$i > \frac{A}{e^r}\bar{h} + r\bar{k} + \bar{b}, \tag{25}$$

which, using (24) and the definitions of $\bar{h}$, $\bar{k}$, and $\bar{b}$, can be written as

$$r \leq \frac{(1 - \lambda - \theta)i}{(w - \lambda i)(1 - \theta)}. \tag{26}$$

As in the case of the model with one good, a sufficiently small r is necessary to make self-fulfilling runs possible.

The crucial part of the argument is that the liquidation value of the bank is now *endogenous*. It depends on the real exchange rate, through the value of the loans to the nontradables sector; in turn, the real exchange rate is determined by whether a crisis happens. This can be seen most clearly if $A\bar{h}/e^r + r\bar{k} + \bar{b} < i < R\bar{h} + r\bar{k} + \bar{b}$. In this case, a crisis can happen if and only if a real depreciation is expected in period 1.

One might have thought that the presence of nontraded goods would give the government greater latitude in dealing with crises. After all, it is traded goods that are "scarce" in period 1 when the economy is internationally illiquid. But as long as the withdrawal of size i that agents can make is denominated in tradables, that conjecture is incorrect.[39] For instance, giving the government the right to borrow from the nontradables sector in period 1 does not help. The proceeds of the loan still would have to be converted into tradable goods, because it is such goods that are needed to stop an incipient bank run. And since only $\bar{b}$ such goods are available, liquidation would still have to take place.

The main point of this section is that introducing a second good gives macroeconomic phenomena a role both in producing financial crises and magnifying their effects. In this setup, the coefficient θ is the share of the traded sector in the economy. Since this is also the sector in which capital is illiquid, θ is also the proxy for the extent to which liquidation is the source of the real costs of a financial crisis. The coefficient θ does not to be particularly large for (26) to be satisfied and crises to be possible.[40] This implies that a good chunk of the fall in bank income in a crisis may

---

39. We analyze below the case in which this liability is denominated in terms of nontradables.
40. For instance, (26) shows that if $r = 0$, it is sufficient that $\theta > 1 - \lambda$.

come from the real depreciation and the resulting bankruptcy of nontradables producers, and not from the physical liquidation of assets.

From a modeling point of view, real effects here result from the interaction of a financial-sector inefficiency with the behavior of the real exchange rate. In that sense, this model is similar to those by Calvo (1988) and Krugman (1999). The only difference is in the assumed financial problem: Calvo assumes bankruptcy costs and Krugman collateral constraints, while we assume costly liquidation in the tradables sector.

6.1 POLICY IMPLICATIONS: CRISIS PREVENTION

Forcing domestic banks that borrow in dollars to lend in the same currency is a popular way to minimize risk. Our analysis suggests that that policy is largely useless. In the preceding subsection, all bank borrowing and lending was in terms of tradable goods (loosely, in terms of foreign currency), but that did not insulate the bank. The reason is that the real devaluation risk is simply passed on to firms in the nontradables sector, who default partially on their loans when the relative price of their output falls unexpectedly.

What would work in this context is to have both loans to the nontradables sector and at least some bank liabilities denominated in terms of the nontradable good. To see this more formally, imagine that the contract now requires the bank to pay unlucky depositors the tradables equivalent of $\bar{e}i$ units of nontradables. That is to say, the portion of the contract covering period-1 payments now denominates these withdrawals in nontradables but continues to make them payable in tradables. Clearly, this does not affect the properties of the honest equilibrium: a measure λ of depositors still withdraw $\bar{e}i/\bar{e} = i$ units of tradables, which allows them to restore damaged investments. But, as one can readily show, the illiquidity condition for a run equilibrium to be possible changes to

$$i\frac{\bar{e}}{e^r} > \frac{A}{e^r}\bar{h} + r\bar{k} + \bar{b}. \tag{27}$$

Since $\bar{e}/e^r < 1$, the preceding condition is more stringent than the one for the case in which allowable withdrawals are denominated in tradables, (25). Hence, changing the denomination of bank liabilities makes the bank less vulnerable to a run.

The intuition is simple: in the event of a run the relative price of nontradables falls, which reduces the number of units of tradables the bank must hand over to those who visit in period 1. Notice that this logic could be extended to foreign debt contracts, which we have neglected to consider here. If foreign loans were denominated in terms of nontradables, their service cost would also fall in the event of a run-induced real depreciation, further alleviating the liquidity position of the bank.

How to achieve this in practice? One possibility is to restrict the domestic bank to borrow only from local lenders. This is plausible if national savings are high and the domestic capital market deep (Chile is often lauded on these grounds, partly because of its privatized pension system). But capital-poor emerging economies will still typically want to run current account deficits and import capital from abroad; if banks are not allowed to do this, someone else (like Indonesian corporates) probably will. An alternative is to encourage foreign lenders to lend in domestic currency, and hence share with local borrowers some of the exchange risk. Loans in nominal pesos are unlikely, but loans indexed to the domestic price level have more of a ring of plausibility. Again, Chile has made some progress along these lines, encouraging a nascent market for indexed foreign loans.

6.2 POLICY IMPLICATIONS: CRISIS MANAGEMENT

In this model the real exchange rate depreciates because output and consumption of tradables falls relative to that of nontradables, so the relative price of the former must rise. The best way to deal with this, of course, would be to get real resources to the hands of the bank before it liquidates its investment, thereby preventing the fall in tradables' output. An equivalence policy would be to extend emergency nonbank credit to firms in the tradables sector, so that they could repay their loans to local banks without having to cut down trees or padlock factories.

In practice neither policy is likely to be very useful. Getting the money to the right place quickly enough is difficult. Informational asymmetries (why would foreign banks lend to firms that are being refused local credit?) and the potential for moral hazard make matters even more complicated.

Straight balance-of-payments support might be easier and just as effective. The problem here is that local output of tradables falls and so does their consumption. But tradables can also be imported, propping up consumption levels and hence avoiding real depreciation. Foreign lenders and multilaterals may frown at the thought of emergency loans to finance consumption, but in that context that is exactly what is needed. And a penny of support may do a pound of good: high levels of tradables consumption prevent bankruptcies in the nontradables sector and prevent a harmful multiplier effect from kicking in.

7. Government Debts and Deficits

In the so-called first-generation models of crises (Krugman, 1979), balance-of-payments crises were ultimately caused by ongoing fiscal deficits. However, fiscal accounts were essentially in balance before the Mexican 1994 and the Asian 1997–1998 crashes, and hence first-generation models have fallen a bit out of fashion. This does not mean that fiscal debts and deficits are irrelevant to recent crises, but instead that the relevant channel is not what the earlier literature stressed. The channel from deficits to crises runs not through the monetization of government financing gaps; the problem has more to do with the effects that government debt—especially if short-term—has on the overall liquidity position of the country's financial system. Calvo (1995) was the first to recognize this.

The role of the infamous *tesobonos* in the Mexican 1994 crisis—upon which Calvo's observations were based—is now well known; a more recent example is Brazil. Bevilacqua et al. (1998) report that by year-end 1996, the Brazilian government had approximately U.S. $150 billion in outstanding domestic securities, with an average maturity of 180 days. While data on the precise maturity structure are not available, this number alone is cause for concern: on average, U.S. $75 billion had to be rolled over by the Brazilian government every semester. By contrast, international reserves were only slightly above U.S. $58 billion at the end of 1996. This potentially explosive situation suggests why Brazil was the Latin economy hardest hit by the reverberations of the Asian meltdown in the second half of 1997. In November of that year a speculative attack against the real forced the authorities to increase interest rates to 42% (at a time when domestic inflation was running at less than 5% per annum) and to announce cuts amounting to 2% of GDP from the government budget. The cuts were never implemented, and the astronomical real interest rates created a sharp monetarist arithmetic problem. A second and more dramatic package was launched in late 1998, this time with IMF blessing, but the currency collapsed anyway in January 1999. At the time of writing, real interest rates remain high, and debt dynamics are still explosive or close to it. Domestic debt has risen to over 54% of GDP. With massive rollovers necessary every month, Brazil remains vulnerable.

Suppose that the government has to raise some funds in period 0. Specifically, suppose that it needs to finance some expenditure that costs g dollars, and it has decided to hold x dollars in liquid form—say, for deposit insurance purposes—that will be transferred to the commercial bank if there is no need to fight a run.

One way to finance the required amount $T = g + x$ is to tax domestic residents in period 0. From the viewpoint of the commercial bank, its planning problem is the same as in Section 3.1, except that the resources that it can invest in period 0 are given not by w but by $w - T$, and that the bank will receive a transfer x in period 2. It is not hard to show that the expected utility for consumers of this option is

$$c_a = R(w - T - \lambda i) - f + x = \hat{c} - (R - 1)x - Rg.$$

Relative to the social optimum $\hat{c}$, this option implies a cost of holding liquidity, $(R - 1)x$; in addition there is the cost of paying for government expenditure, Rg.

Suppose now that there is an alternative: the government can borrow T in international markets. In order to repay its debt, suppose that the government can levy a tax, whose rate is τ, on the return to long-term investment in period 2. The commercial bank's problem is the same as in Section 3.1, except that the perceived return to long-term investment is $R(1 - \tau)$ instead of R, and that it will receive a transfer x in period 2. Hence expected consumption will be

$$c_b = R(1 - \tau)(w - \lambda i) - f + x. \tag{28}$$

Now, for the government to be able to repay its debt, it must be that

$$\tau R \hat{k} = \tau R(w - \lambda i) = T. \tag{29}$$

Combining the two previous expressions, we obtain

$$c_b = R(w - \lambda i) - T - f + x = \hat{c} - g, \tag{30}$$

implying that $c_b > c_a$. Hence it is efficient for the government to borrow in order to finance its needs in period 0.

We have, therefore, a situation in which it is good for the government to be in deficit. However, a crucial point is that, while fiscal deficits may not be bad per se, they may create problems because of their financing. To see this, suppose that the government borrows a fraction σ of the T dollars needed in period 0 as a short-term loan. The reader can check that, if all foreign creditors roll over their loans in period 1 and all depositors withdraw honestly, there is no panic and consumption is given by (30). However, suppose that foreign creditors refuse to roll over their loans to the government, and that domestic depositors also panic. Then, if

$$i + \sigma T > x + \hat{b}b + r\hat{k}, \tag{31}$$

expectations of a crisis must be self-fulfilling: all assets of the economy will be liquidated, and the commercial banking system will become bankrupt.[41]

Why would foreign creditors stop lending to the government? Because the crisis implies that all of $\hat{k}$ will be liquidated in the period 1, and hence there will be no fiscal revenue in period 2. In other words, the expectation of a fiscal crisis would trigger the refusal of foreign lending, which itself creates the fiscal crisis.

This all assumes that the crisis happens with zero probability. If it happened with positive probability, then risk-neutral foreign lenders would ask to be compensated for the loss in the event of a run. Contractual interest rates on loans to the government would exceed world rates—again, we would have a term structure of interest rates, and high rates all around. None of which, of course, bodes well for stability. High rates increase the servicing cost of debt, and can easily lead to a monetarist arithmetic problem (in fact, this is plausible interpretation of Brazil's recent travails). But if the government tries to lower servicing costs by resorting to short-term debt (increasing σ), vulnerability is increased.[42]

One other aspect deserves attention. Condition (31) may be satisfied even if the insurance fund x seems sufficient to cover systemic risk, that is, (31) and $i \leq x + \hat{b} + r\hat{k}$ may hold simultaneously. In this case, a crisis cannot be possible unless foreign creditors refuse to roll over their short-term loans.

7.1 POLICY IMPLICATIONS: CRISIS PREVENTION

The strongest implication of the preceding analysis is that the fisc's short-term debt position should be taken into account when trying to measure the degree of potential illiquidity of a country. Measures like M2 over reserves or short-term private debt over reserves typically fail to do this. By late 1994 Mexico had U.S. $29 billion in liquid *tesobonos*, and only U.S. $6 billion in cash reserves (plus another $6 billion in credit lines from NAFTA partners). Hence, net of government short-term dollar commitments, Mexico had negative reserves.[43]

41. We are making an implicit assumption that in period 1 the government's and the commercial bank's balance sheet can be effectively consolidated. Such would be the case if, for instance, the government were able to tax the bank in period 1 in order to finance the difference between T and x.
42. Of course, the problem would disappear if σ were zero, that is, if all government debt were long-term. But the government, just like the bank whose problem was discussed in Section 3 above, may find it optimal to borrow short-term.
43. Notice that, if the exchange rate is fixed, such netting out should include all short-term public debt, not just dollar debt. This point, which was mentioned in Section 2, is implied by the analysis of the next section.

7.2 POLICY IMPLICATIONS: CRISIS MANAGEMENT

A very controversial point in recent discussions is the degree to which IMF disbursements should have been conditional on sharp fiscal retrenchment by the troubled countries. Many critics have accused the fund of worsening the crisis by insisting on fiscal austerity as a precondition for lending. Our model lends some support to this criticism. Suppose that T is a loan not from private creditors but from an international institution, such as the IMF. Suppose also that, in keeping with current practice, disbursement of T in period 1 is conditional on prospective fiscal discipline. In an honest equilibrium, fiscal revenue in period 2 is large, and justifies the release of the T dollars in period 1. But in a run equilibrium, tax revenue in period 2 is destroyed and T is not released. Ex post, it will look as if the international agency's decision to withhold T had been justified. But clearly the crisis would have not occurred if the agency had committed T unconditionally. Of course, there are many other reasons for conditionality. And fiscal adjustment may indeed be needed, especially if debt has built up and the costs of bank bailouts are mounting. But in advocating such conditionality one should be mindful of the potentially self-defeating mechanism highlighted here.

Also, the discussion in Section 3 of how to deal with coordination failure by lenders remains applicable. In the event of a crisis lenders are panicking, and everyone would be better off if their actions could be coordinated. Negotiated debt rollovers and similar strategies are clearly of use here as well.

8. The Exchange-Rate Regime

Our analysis so far has abstracted from monetary considerations. Yet they are clearly crucial for policy purposes. Only after extending the model to introduce domestic currency can one discuss the proper role of central banks in providing credit, regulating the money supply, or managing exchange rates.

In this section we modify the basic model of Section 3 to allow for the existence of domestic and foreign money.[44] As suggested in that section, assume that there is an international currency ("dollars"), and that the dollar price of a unit of consumption in the world market is fixed at one. With this trivial extension, the analysis of previous sections can be interpreted as applicable to an economy that is completely "dollarized."[45]

---

44. This section is based on Chang and Velasco (1998a).
45. While this observation is trivial from a theoretical perspective, it has nontrivial consequences in practice, in particular for the ongoing debate on replacing Latin American currencies with the U.S. dollar.

In order to allow for other possibilities, assume that there is a domestic currency, referred to as "pesos." Pesos are costlessly issued by a domestic central bank. A demand for pesos can be introduced in several ways, but for the sake of simplicity assume here that there is a legal restriction that forces domestic banks to pay its depositors in pesos.

Since the bank's sources of funds are in dollars, there must be some arrangement by which the central bank provides pesos to the commercial bank. Since depositors receive peso payments from the commercial bank but need dollars to buy consumption in the world market, there must be some system by which the central bank sells dollars to depositors. These arrangements are what we call a *regime*. Difference assumptions about the central bank's credit policy, or about its exchange-rate policy, give rise to the study of different regimes.

8.1 A CURRENCY BOARD

The simplest regime is a currency board. In a currency board, the central bank stands ready to sell or buy pesos for dollars at a fixed exchange rate, which we shall fix at one. (It is useful to think of the central bank as a vending machine, which gives one peso for each dollar deposited in it, and vice versa.)

Given a currency board (or in fact any of the other regimes we shall study), the bank's planning problem is the same as in Section 3.1. The interesting question is: how successful is a demand deposit system in implementing the social optimum in the different regimes? In order to answer it, we need to alter the assumptions of Section 3.2 to accommodate the use of different currencies. It is simplest to modify the sequential service constraint in the following way. As in Section 3.2, at the beginning of period 1 depositors visit the commercial bank in random order. Each depositor may, upon her arrival at the bank, withdraw i pesos on demand, assuming the bank has not gone bankrupt. The main assumption is that, after visiting the bank, depositors join a second line, this time at the central bank, to exchange whatever pesos they may hold for dollars at the fixed exchange rate. The commercial bank, in turn, services withdrawals by liquidating its assets and selling the resulting revenue (which is in dollars) for pesos at the Central Bank.

Given the timing of events, the central bank cannot run out of dollars to honor its exchange-rate commitment; in other words, with a currency board there cannot be a *balance-of-payments* crisis. However, there may still be a *banking* crisis: as before, the commercial bank goes bankrupt in period 1 if, after liquidating all of its assets, there are still depositors in line attempting to withdraw i.

If the bank did not close in period 1, in period 2 the bank liquidates all of its investments and repays foreign creditors and depositors; the latter are paid in pesos that the bank obtains from selling dollars to the central bank. Depositors then visit the central bank to exchange their pesos for dollars which can be used to buy consumption.

This completes the description of a currency-board regime. Aside from the fact that the commercial bank pays deposits in pesos that depositors exchange back for dollars, the model is essentially the same as in Section 3.2. As a consequence, a currency-board regime implies the same outcomes as in that subsection. There is one honest equilibrium in which the social optimum is obtained. But also, there a run equilibrium in which all agents attempt to withdraw i pesos and the commercial bank goes bankrupt in period 1 if and only if the illiquidity condition (6) holds.

In short, the analysis of a completely dollarized economy in previous sections applies to a currency board. More important, the currency board is no panacea: while balance-of-payments crises are not possible, bank crises may still occur. This is, in modern language, a conclusion that economists have known at least since Bagehot: systems that tie the central bank's hands and prevent it from printing money also prevent it from coming to the rescue of banks in times of trouble. Under a currency board or the gold standard, the domestic banking system has no domestic lender of last resort. The price of low inflation may be endemic financial instability.

Not everyone feels this is a problem. Dornbusch (1998) has recently written: "The counter argument that currency boards or full dollarization sacrifice the lender of last resort function are deeply misguided. . . . Lender of last resort can readily be rented, along with bank supervision, by requiring financial institutions to carry off-shore guarantees." But how exactly does one rent such a lender? We argued in the discussion on deposit insurance that credit lines Argentine style are a step in the right direction, but they are unlikely to be large enough to cover the bulk of the liquid liabilities of a country's financial system. A currently fashionable alternative is to encourage foreign ownership of domestic banks, hoping that equity holders abroad will serve as lenders of last resort. Again, this is probably a good idea, but is a completely untested one. Will Citibank U.S. ride to the rescue every time that Latin or Asian bank in which it has a 10% equity stake gets into trouble? Perhaps. But hanging a whole financial system's health on that conjecture seems risky indeed.

8.2 FIXED RATES WITH A LENDER OF LAST RESORT

The rules of a currency board prevent the central bank from assisting the commercial bank in the event of a run. This may suggest that crises may be avoided if the central bank lends enough pesos to the commercial bank to prevent its failure. There is much evidence that monetary authorities have done precisely this in times of recent trouble. The problem is that, by doing so, they have also precipitated the end of many a fixed exchange rate. Díaz-Alejandro (1985) and Velasco (1987) argue that it was precisely a money-financed bank bailout that caused the end of the Chilean *tablita* (and then the fix) of the late 1970s and early 1980s. Sachs, Tornell, and Velasco (1996a) claim that it was the fragility of the banking system that prevented Mexican authorities from raising interest rates in 1994 to defend the peg. In Asia the problem recurs. Corsetti, Pesenti, and Roubini (1998b) write: "Well before the onset of the crisis, several governments were engaged in an extensive policy of bailing out financial institutions. Such a policy was by itself a source of monetary creation. . . . As it turned out, it eventually induced a continuous spiral of currency depreciations. . . ."

To examine this issue, assume that the central bank grants a credit line to the commercial bank to be used in case of an attack—that is, if more than λ depositors attempt to withdraw i. In such case, the central bank agrees to lend, at a zero interest rate, as many pesos as needed for the commercial bank to service further withdrawals. In exchange, the central bank obtains temporary control over the remaining assets of the commercial bank, including the right to liquidate them as necessary to honor its exchange-rate commitment. The latter assumption implies that the central bank is committed to defending the fixed exchange rate for as long as it is feasible.

Consider what may happen in period 1. Depositors arrive at the commercial bank in random order and may withdraw i. The bank services withdrawals first by liquidating $\hat{b}$, and then by borrowing pesos from the central bank. Hence the commercial bank cannot go bankrupt. After all depositors have visited the commercial bank, the central bank starts buying pesos back, first with the dollars bought from the commercial bank, and then with dollars obtained from the liquidation of the bank's long-term assets. If the central bank completely runs out of assets while there are depositors attempting to exchange pesos for dollars, it closes its window, and we say that there is a *balance-of-payments crisis*.

Somewhat surprisingly, this regime has essentially the same outcomes as a currency board. There is an honest equilibrium that results in the social optimum and in which the emergency credit line turns out to be unnecessary. But also there is a balance-of-payments crisis equilibrium if and only if the same illiquidity condition (6) holds. In a balance-of-payments crisis, all depositors attempt to withdraw i pesos and exchange it for dollars at the central bank, and the central bank liquidates all of its assets and has to close its window. To see that this can be an equilibrium, suppose that all depositors withdraw i pesos and attempt to exchange them for dollars at the central bank. To honor its exchange-rate commitment, the central bank will have $\hat{b}$ dollars obtained from the commercial bank; in addition, it can raise $r\hat{k}$ more dollars from exercising its right to liquidate the long-term asset. So the central bank will not be able to honor its commitment if i exceeds the resulting sum, $\hat{b} + r\hat{k}$; but this is precisely the international illiquidity condition (6).

The intuition is that, with fixed exchange rates, the ability of the central bank to act as a lender of last resort is limited by the extent of its own international liquidity. While the central bank can print pesos freely, it cannot print dollars. With fixed rates each peso is a potential dollar liabilities liability, and a balance-of-payments crisis occurs when depositors realize that the central bank's potential dollar exceed its liquidation value.

It is remarkable that, under fixed exchange rates, the possibility of a crisis depends only on the underlying international illiquidity of the economy. It does not depend on whether the central bank acts as a lender of last resort, which only determines how the crisis becomes manifest: as a bank failure or as a currency collapse.

8.3 FLEXIBLE EXCHANGE RATES

If the combination of fixed rates and potentially unstable rates seems to be dangerous, what about a regime in which the central bank acts as a lender of last resort but allows exchange rates to be flexible? The easiest way to model this situation is to retain the assumptions of the previous subsection, except that there is no line at the central bank. Instead, the exchange rate is determined, after depositors have visited the commercial bank, by an auction in which the central bank offers some amounts of reserves and depositors offer their holdings of pesos.

To be concrete, suppose that in period 1 the central bank fixes its supply of dollars at the auction at $\hat{b} = \lambda i$, the amount of dollars previously bought from the commercial bank. Then, if λ^r is the fraction of depositors withdrawing i in period 1, equality of supply and demand in the auction amounts to

$$\lambda^r i = E\lambda i,$$

where E is the exchange rate (pesos per dollar). It follows that $E = \lambda^r/\lambda$: naturally, pesos lose value if more depositors withdraw i in period 1.

What are the outcomes of this regime? It should be intuitively obvious that honesty is still an equilibrium. Indeed, if only unlucky agents withdraw i, then E must be one, and our previous arguments imply that it is individually rational for lucky depositors not to withdraw early. Hence, flexible rates may implement the socially optimal allocation.

But now a run *cannot* occur. To see this, notice that for a run to occur, λ^r must exceed λ; hence E must be greater than 1. By withdrawing i and absconding, a lucky depositor can consume $i/E < i$. But it can be shown[46] that the bank will be able to pay the promised $\hat{c}$ to each of the $1 - \lambda^r$ epositors that do not run. Hence it cannot be optimal for lucky depositors to participate in a run.

In short, flexible rates implement the social optimum *uniquely*. In this model, dropping the commitment to a fixed exchange rate allows the central bank to provide assistance to the commercial bank in case of a run, and at the same time prevent the inefficient liquidation of the long-run assets of the economy. The latter ensures that domestic deposits will ultimately be honored, while the accompanying devaluation punishes early withdrawals. Rational depositors will then understand that it does not pay to run.

In a situation of potential for bank runs, flexible exchange rates appear to be a mechanism superior to fixed rates. But there are a number of qualifications to this statement. It applies only to a *regime* of floating, not to the sudden depreciation that typically happens when the authorities throw in the towel. And flexible rates "work" only if complemented by the appropriate monetary policy: in particular, the central bank must be willing to act as a lender of last resort.

These results also depend crucially on the assumption that deposits must be paid in pesos. If there are no local currency claims, movements in the nominal exchange rate cannot affect their real value. This is a reason to discourage, as Sachs (1997) has advocated, the "dollarization" of deposits. Notice that flexible rates cannot help in dealing with the panics of foreign creditors, since in practice foreign loans are denominated in foreign currency. The key operational question then is what are the proportions of foreign (dollar) and local (peso) claims on the local bank. If the latter are a sufficiently large share, flexible rates can be stabilizing.

9. And the Rest of the World?

We have tried to provide what Feldstein (1999) terms "a self-help guide for emerging markets." When analyzing the effect of different policies

---

46. To see this, note that in period 2 the bank will have $(1 - \lambda)R\hat{k}$ dollars available from its illiquid investments. Now, $(1 - \lambda)R\hat{k} - (1 - \lambda^r)\hat{c} = (1 - \lambda)(R\hat{k} - \hat{c}) + (\lambda^r - \lambda)\hat{c} > 0$, which means that the bank will be able to pay the promised $\hat{c}$ to each of the $1 - \lambda^r$ agents that did not withdraw in period 1.

on illiquidity and the potential for crises, we have asked not what the world can do for emerging economies, but what each emerging economy can do for itself.

But this does not mean that the rest of the world is off the hook. We have seen that the trade-offs faced by countries are unattractive and a policy regime, however stringent, is almost always vulnerable to a collapse of confidence by domestic and foreign investors. This means that there is much room for what is nowadays known as the *world financial architecture* to help nations help themselves.

The absence of an effective international lender of last resort is particularly serious. If financial crises such as those in East Asia were at least partially caused by self-fulfilling liquidity squeezes on banks, an international lender of last resort has a positive role in overcoming a financial system's international illiquidity. Funds from abroad to prevent unnecessary credit crunches and avoid costly liquidation of investment can increase welfare.

The usual (and valid) objection is moral hazard. But this need not be a rationale for policy paralysis. Fire insurance and bank deposit guarantees also risk inducing moral hazard, but the risk can be minimized by proper contract design and appropriate monitoring. No one advocates banning fire insurance simply because it leads some homeowners to be careless with their fireplaces. The same should be true of an international lender of last resort.

Appendix

A.1 AUTARKY

Consider a depositor who attempts to maximize long-run consumption, acting in isolation. She can, in period 0, borrow up to her credit limit and divide her total resources, $w \equiv a + f$, between the liquid and illiquid assets. Thus she faces the constraint (1) in the text.

We assume that it is optimal for initial investment in liquid assets to be enough to finance i. This requires

$$\lambda(R - r)w \geq [R - (1 - \lambda)]i, \tag{32}$$

which we assume. In that case we have

$$\tilde{b} = i, \tag{33}$$

since $R > 1$ implies that the depositor cannot profit from holding more liquidity than strictly necessary. Tildes denote autarky optimal values;

correspondingly, $\tilde{k} = w - i$. In that case, the agent's consumption will be $R\tilde{k} + \tilde{b} - f$ if lucky and $R\tilde{k} - f$ if not, which implies that her expected consumption will be

$$\tilde{c} = \lambda(R\tilde{k} - f) + (1 - \lambda)(R\tilde{k} + \tilde{b} - f) = R(w - i) + (1 - \lambda)i - f. \tag{34}$$

A.2 SHORT-TERM DEBT

Consider, first, the case of risk neutrality. As argued in the text, for small p the problem reduces to the determination of $\tilde{c}$. But the maximand in (18) is

$$\begin{aligned}
(1 - p)&[R\hat{k} - (1 + r_s)d_s - (1 + r_l)(f - d_s)] + pqi \\
&= (1 - p)R\hat{k} - (1 - p)(1 + r_s)d_s - (f - d_s) + pqi \\
&= (1 - p)R\hat{k} - f + pq[(1 + r_s)d_s + i] \\
&= (1 - p)R\hat{k} - f + p(\hat{b} + r\hat{k}),
\end{aligned}$$

where the first equality follows from the definition of r_l, the second from (17), and the third from the definition of q. It follows that the value of $\tilde{c}$ is the same for all d_s in $[0, f]$, as claimed in the text.

Consider now the case of risk aversion. For p small, the bank's problem is to maximize

$$(1 - p)u(c) + pqu(i) \tag{35}$$

subject to (17), (16),

$$\begin{aligned}
k + b &\le a + d_s + d_l, \\
d_s + d_l &\le f, \\
\lambda i &\le b, \\
c + (1 + r_s)d_s + (1 + r_l)d_l &\le Rk + b - \lambda i,
\end{aligned}$$

and incentive constraints. The function u is assumed to be strictly increasing, strictly concave, and continuously differentiable, and to satisfy $u(0) = 0$, $u'(0) = \infty$.

This is a standard constrained maximization problem, and the Kuhn–Tucker theorem applies. The first-order conditions for this problem can be written as

$$(1 - p)u'(c) = \mu_2,$$
$$\mu_0 - \theta - \mu_2(1 + r_s) + q_3[pu(i) + \gamma(1 + r_s)p] \le 0, \qquad =0 \quad \text{if } d_s > 0,$$
$$\mu_0 - \theta - \mu_2(1 + r_l) \le 0, \qquad =0 \quad \text{if } d_l > 0,$$
$$\mu_0 = R\mu_2,$$

$$-\mu_0 + \mu_1 + \mu_2 + q_1[pu(i) + \gamma(1 + r_s)p] = 0,$$
$$\gamma(1 - p + pq) = \mu_2 d_s + q_2[pu(i) + \gamma(1 + r_s)p],$$
$$k + b = e + f = w,$$
$$c + (1 + r_s)d_s + (1 + r_l)d_l = Rk + b - \lambda i,$$
$$\lambda i \le b, = b \quad \text{if } \mu_1 > 0,$$
$$d_s + d_l = f,$$

where $q = q(b, r_s, d_s)$ is given by (16) and θ, γ, and the μ's are nonnegative Lagrange multipliers. To simplify notation, we have assumed that $r = 0$; this is not essential as long as r is sufficiently small.

The interested reader can now verify that there is a solution of these conditions such that $d_l = f$ and $d_s = 0$. The key part is to check the first inequality in the preceding set; one may proceed as follows. If $d_l = f > 0$, then $\mu_0 - \theta = \mu_2(1 + r_l)$. Also, if $d_s = 0$, the fourth equality above yields $\gamma = 0$. Using these facts, the inequality in question reduces to

$$\mu_2(r_l - r_s) - q(1 + r_s)\frac{pu(i)}{i} \le 0, \tag{36}$$

which, after using (17) and $\mu_2 = (1 - p)u'(c)$, reduces to $u'(c) \le u(i)/i$. But this must hold, by the assumptions on u and the fact that $c \ge i$.

Finally, assume again risk neutrality, but suppose that there are many banks that take r_s, not (17), as given. The reasoning at the beginning of this appendix implies that each bank must choose d_s to maximize

$$(1 - p)R\hat{k} - (1 - p)(1 + r_s)(d_s - (f - d_s)) + p\frac{\hat{b}+r\hat{k}}{i + (1 + r_s)d_s}i. \tag{37}$$

Let $F(d_s)$ denote the above expression, as a function of d_s. Now,

$$F'(d_s) = -(1 - p)(1 + r_s) + 1 - \frac{piq}{i + (1 + r_s)d_s}(1 + r_s). \tag{38}$$

In equilibrium, (17) must hold, and inserting it in the above expression, we obtain

$$F'(d_s) = pq(1 + r_s)\frac{(1 + r_s)d_s}{i + (1 + r_s)d_s}. \tag{39}$$

The above expression is greater than zero for any $d_s > 0$. This implies that $d_s = f$ is an equilibrium, and that it is the only equilibrium with positive d_s. Finally, d_s cannot be zero in equilibrium. While the first-order condition (39) equals zero at $d_s = 0$, we have $F'' > 0$ for all d_s, as the reader can verify from (38). Hence $d_s = 0$ is a local minimum of F.

REFERENCES

Aghion, P., P. Bacchetta, and A. Banerjee. (1999). Capital markets and the instability of open economies. Studienzentrum Gerzensee. Working Paper 9901.

Bevilacqua, A., D. Dias Carneiro, M. Garcia, R. Werneck, F. Blanco, and P. Pierotti. (1998). The structure of public sector debt in Brazil. PUC-Rio. Manuscript.

Calvo, G. (1995). Varieties of capital market crises. Center for International Economics, University of Maryland. Working Paper 15.

———. (1998). Balance of payments crises in emerging markets: Large capital inflows and sovereign governments. University of Maryland. Manuscript.

Cárdenas, M., and F. Barrera. (1997). On the effectiveness of capital controls: The experience of Colombia during the 1990s. *Journal of Development Economics* 54:27–57.

Chang, R., and A. Velasco. (1998a). Financial fragility and the exchange rate regime. Cambridge, MA: National Bureau of Economic Research. NBER Working Paper 6469. Also available as RR. #98–05, C.V. Starr Center for Applied Economics, New York University.

———, and ———. (1998b). Financial crises in emerging markets: A canonical model. Cambridge, MA: National Bureau of Economic Research. NBER Working Paper 6606.

———, and ———. (1998c). The Asian liquidity crisis. Cambridge, MA: National Bureau of Economic Research. NBER Working Paper 6796.

———, and ———. (1999). Banks, debt maturity, and financial crises. Federal Reserve Bank of Atlanta and New York University. Manuscript.

Cooper, R., and T. Ross. (1998). Bank runs: Liquidity costs and investment distortions. *Journal of Monetary Economics* 41:27–38.

Corsetti, G., P. Pesenti, and N. Roubini. (1998a). What caused the Asian currency and financial crises? Part I: The macroeconomic overview. Cambridge, MA: National Bureau of Economic Research. NBER Working Paper 6833.

———, ———, and ———. (1998b). What caused the Asian currency and financial Crises? Part II: The policy debate. Cambridge, MA: National Bureau of Economic Research. NBER Working Paper 6834.

Demirguc-Kent, A., and E. Detragiache. (1998). Financial liberalization and financial fragility. International Monetary Fund. Working Paper.

Detragiache, E. (1996). Rational liquidity crises in the sovereign debt market: In search of a theory. *IMF Staff Papers* 43:545–570.

Diamond, D., and P. Dybvig. (1983). Bank runs, deposit insurance, and liquidity. *Journal of Political Economy* 91:401–419.

Díaz-Alejandro, C. F. (1985). Good-bye financial repression, hello financial crash. *Journal of Development Economics* 19:1–24.

Dornbusch, R. (1998). After Asia: New directions for the international financial system. MIT. Manuscript.

———, I. Goldfajn, and R. Valdés. (1995). Currency crises and collapses. *Brookings Papers on Economic Activity* 2:219–295.

Feldstein, M. (1999). A self-help guide for emerging markets. *Foreign Affairs*, March–April, pp. 93–110.

Furman, J., and J. Stiglitz. (1998). Economic crises: Evidence and insights from east Asia. *Brookings Papers in Economic Activity* 2:1–114.

Garber, P. (1996). Transition to a functional financial safety net in Latin America. Paper prepared for the Inter-American Development Bank Conference on "Safe and Sound Financial Systems: What Works for Latin America?" Washington.

Goldfajn, I., and R. Valdés. (1997). Capital flows and the twin crises: The role of liquidity. International Monetary Fund. Working Paper 97–87.

Ito, T. (1998). Lessons from the Asian currency crises. Hitotsubashi University. Manuscript.

Jeanne, O. (1998). The international liquidity mismatch and the new architecture. International Monetary Fund. Manuscript.

Kaminsky, G., and C. Reinhart. (1996). The twin crises: The causes of banking and balance of payments problems. Board of Governors of the Federal Reserve System. International Finance Discussion Paper 544.

Kenen, P. (1999). Comment on Radelet and Sachs. *Currency Crises.* Cambridge, MA: National Bureau of Economic Research, forthcoming.

Krugman, P. (1979). A model of balance of payments crises. *Journal of Money, Credit and Banking* 11:311–325.

———. (1998). Introduction. *Currency Crises.* Cambridge, MA: National Bureau of Economic Research, forthcoming.

———. (1999). Balance sheets, the transfer problem, and financial crises. MIT. Manuscript.

Larrain, F., R. Laban, and R. Chumacero. (1997). What determines capital inflows? An empirical analysis for Chile. Harvard Institute for International Development. Development Discussion Paper 590.

Montiel, P., and C. M. Reinhart. (1997). Do capital controls influence the volume and composition of capital flows: Evidence from the 1990s. Paper prepared for UNU/WIDER project on Short-Term Capital Movements and Balance of Payments Crises. Sussex.

Obstfeld, M. (1994). The logic of currency crises. *Cahiers Economiques et Monétaires* 34:189–213.

———, and K. Rogoff. (1995). The mirage of fixed exchange rates. Cambridge, MA: National Bureau of Economic Research. NBER Working Paper 5191.

Radelet, S., and J. Sachs. (1998). The onset of the Asian financial crisis. Harvard Institute for International Development. Manuscript.

Rodrik, D., and A. Velasco. (1999). Short-term capital flows. *Annual Bank Conference on Development Economics.* World Bank, forthcoming.

Sachs, J. (1997). Alternative approaches to financial crises in emerging markets. Harvard Institute for International Development. Development Discussion Paper 568.

———, A. Tornell, and A. Velasco. (1996a). The collapse of the Mexican peso: What have we learned? *Economic Policy* 22:13–56.

———, ———, and ———. (1996b). Financial crises in emerging markets: The lessons from 1995. *Brookings Papers on Economic Activity* 1:147–198.

Soto, M., and S. Valdés-Prieto. (1996). The effectiveness of capital controls in Chile. Catholic University of Chile. Manuscript.

Velasco, A. (1987). Financial and balance of payments crises. *Journal of Development Economics* 27:263–283.

————. (1992). Liberalization, crisis, intervention: The Chilean financial system 1975–1985. In *Banking Crises*, T. Baliño and V. Sundarajan (eds.). International Monetary Fund.

Wallace, N. (1996). Narrow banking meets the Diamond–Dybvig model. *Federal Reserve Bank of Minneapolis Quarterly Review,* Winter, pp. 3–13.

World Bank. (1998). *Global Economic Prospects and the Developing Countries 1998/99: Beyond Financial Crisis.* Washington, D.C.

Comment

ABHIJIT V. BANERJEE
Massachusetts Institute of Technology

This paper does three things: First, it builds a model of bank liquidity that is relevant for international lending; it accomplishes this by adapting the model of Diamond and Dybvig (1983) to recognize the fact that the assets and liabilities of the banking sector, and hence its liquidity position, are affected by real-exchange-rate movements. Second, it uses that model to argue that there is a potentially nasty interaction between banking crises and real-exchange-rate movements: The basic idea is that a banking crisis increases the likelihood of a real depreciation because it leads to a credit crunch, which in turn leads to a fall in the output of tradable goods. At the same time, a real depreciation leads to a loss of value in the nontradable sector, which increases the likelihood of a banking crisis (since, by assumption, loans to the nontradable sector are a part of the bank's more liquid assets). Third, the paper uses the model to analyze a host of policies. In particular, it emphasizes that this view of a banking crisis relies on real rather than nominal factors and is substantially independent of the exchange-rate regime and the denomination of the debt.

What makes the paper very useful is that it does all this in a simple and transparent model, which is nevertheless rich enough to allow for a wide range of policy experiments. Whether or not one agrees with the specific conclusions of the model, it is clear that Chang and Velasco's analysis sets a new standard for open-economy macro models of this class. That being said, I must also say that I have some reservations about the modeling approach. Most importantly, the paper says little about what is special about liquidity in an international context. The international part of the model comes from the fact that movements in the real exchange rate matter; but, as far as I can see, nothing fundamental in the model would be altered if we assumed a closed economy and looked at the effect of changes in some other relative price.

We clearly need better arguments for why the international context is important from the point of view of liquidity. For example, being a part of the world capital market may enhance liquidity because it is easier to sell the bank's assets when the bank needs cash. On the other hand, depositors and lenders in an open economy may be more footloose, so that it is easier to induce a liquidity crisis. More could also be done here to link country characteristics to the liquidity of the banking system. For example, people are reluctant to lend long-term to developing countries because they feel that there is more policy uncertainty, or because the level of macroeconomic volatility may be higher.

As a final point on modeling issues: This paper follows the work by Diamond and Dybvig in taking demand deposit contracts as the only form of the banking contract. In principle, of course, banks could have other contracts with depositors where the probability of being able to withdraw depends, for example, on the bank's liquidity position. There is, however, a more recent literature arguing that the demand deposit contract may be optimal precisely because it makes banks fragile, which improves their incentives (Calomiris and Kahn, 1991; Diamond and Rajan, 1998)— although it is not clear that these arguments go through once one takes account of the knock-on effects on the rest of the economy.[1]

Turning next to the specific story told in the paper about how a banking–currency crisis comes about, it is worth noting that the story is quite sensitive to the details of the model. For example, if most of the borrowing were in the nontraded-good sector (the opposite of what the paper assumes), then a banking crisis would lead to real appreciation. And if banks depend on the profits of the traded-good sector to remain liquid and able to finance the nontraded-good sector (once again, the opposite of what the paper assumes), a real appreciation would actually make the banks weaker and bring on a crisis. Alternatively, if nontraded goods are inputs into the production of traded goods, then a real appreciation leads to a squeeze on firm profits, which in turn could lead to a banking crisis, as all the firms draw on their credit lines.[2] Unfortunately there is not much reliable evidence about what happens to real exchange rates around the time of a crisis. The little that is known seems ambiguous for this story: Although there is usually both a real and a nominal depreciation in the course of a banking crisis, typically there is also a real

---

1. My sense is that the arguments will go through because individual banks do not internalize the effects on the rest of the economy. In other words, banks will choose to be more fragile than is socially optimal. This does however raise an interesting set of questions about banking regulation.
2. A related argument is in Aghion, Bacchetta, and Banerjee (1998).

appreciation in the runup to a crisis. What this model makes clear is that we really need more empirical research: We need to know whether exchange rates move in the direction predicted by the model and whether they move enough to cause a banking crisis. The latter also requires us to find out more about the term structure of bank lending to the tradable and nontradable sectors.

It is possible, however, to capture some of the flavor of the results in the paper without putting as much weight on the tradable–nontradable distinction. The key assumptions of such a model are:

1. Within a national market, price adjustments take time. It is well known that the convergence to purchasing-power parity is extremely slow. For example, Giacomelli (1998) estimates that it takes at least two years.
2. Nominal-exchange-rate adjustments are instantaneous.
3. Many developing-country firms borrow abroad in dollars but produce for the domestic market.

In the world described by these assumptions, a nominal depreciation hurts borrowers, which in turn can lead to a run on the banking system. The resulting contraction in credit leads to a fall in output. The fall in output, given the right assumption about money demand, can lead to a nominal depreciation. In other words, an expectation of a currency cum banking crisis can be self-confirming.

This mechanism, while superficially quite similar to the mechanism proposed by Chang and Velasco, has a number of quite different policy implications. Specifically, policies directed jointly towards the nominal exchange rate and the banking sector become very important. For example, a relaxed monetary stance, in a situation in which a currency crisis is threatened, may ease the pressure on the banks. This in turn allows the economy to avoid the credit crunch and the fall in output, thereby staving off the currency crisis (see Aghion, Bacchetta, and Banerjee, 1999, for a formalization). These different implications again underscore the importance of more empirical work. We need to determine whether real- or nominal-exchange-rate effects are central to most crises.

REFERENCES

Aghion, P., P. Bacchetta, and A. V. Banerjee. (1988). Capital markets and the instability of open economies. MIT. Unpublished.
———, ———, and ———. (1999). Monetary policy in the aftermath of a currency crisis. *European Economic Review,* forthcoming.
Calomiris, C. W., and C. M. Kahn. (1991). The role of demandable debt in

structuring optimal banking arrangements. *American Economic Review* 84: 320–331.

Diamond, D. W., and P. H. Dybvig. (1983). Bank runs, deposit insurance and liquidity. *Journal of Political Economy* 91:401–419.

Diamond, D. W., and R. G. Rajan. (1998). Liquidity risk, liquidity creation and financial fragility: A theory of banking. University of Chicago. Unpublished.

Giacomelli, D. (1998). Essays on consumption and the real exchange rate. MIT. Ph.D. Dissertation.

Comment

NOURIEL ROUBINI
NBER and New York University

1. Introduction

This is a very interesting and important paper, both in its positive results and in its normative implications. I am sure that it will be widely read and discussed. The main conclusion of the paper is simple: In an open economy where short-term assets are large relative to central-bank reserves, self-fulfilling international bank runs are a serious possibility. Unlike a closed economy, where the central bank can respond to a run by printing domestic money and serving as a lender of last resort, in an open economy the central bank is limited by its stock of foreign reserves and may not be able to prevent a run. A way to avoid such bank runs in an open economy is to have an international lender of last resort (ILLR) which is willing to provide unlimited resources to prevent an irrational bank panic.

While the authors stress modeling the "bank" aspects of a run, a self-fulfilling financial and exchange-rate crisis may also be triggered by the refusal of domestic and foreign investors to roll over other short-term assets, such as a country's public debt. Indeed, many authors have already emphasized the possibility of such self-fulfilling public-debt runs in models with multiple equilibria.

The authors also analyze a number of other interesting issues, including: (1) the relative likelihood of bank runs under fixed and flexible exchange rates; (2) the determinants of the probability of a run; (3) why debt is short-term in spite of the fact that this increases the possibility of a bank run; (4) the risks of financial liberalization and arguments for capital controls; (5) the links between government debt and deficits and runs on the public debt.

2. International Bank Runs and the Need for an International Lender of Last Resort

The usual rationale for an ILLR for countries that experience an attack in spite of their good economic policies is based on the possibility of *international bank runs*. This paper formalizes this rationale in a very elegant and interesting way. The model presented here is a version of Diamond and Dybvig's (1983) model of bank runs, expanded to address a number of new issues that are specific to an open economy.

Currency crises are formally analogous to, but more complex than, domestic bank runs. In a domestic context, depositors of a bank may suddenly lose confidence in the institution and seek to withdraw their funds *en masse*. In the face of a bank run, even a well-run bank will quickly exhaust its cash reserves. Since most bank investments are illiquid, the attempt to liquidate them prematurely will diminish their value. As a result, even strong banks can fail if a bank run occurs. And the failure of one bank can cause runs on others. This is the main message of the seminal Diamond–Dybvig model of bank runs.

Given the pivotal role that banks play within all modern economies, most governments provide deposit insurance to discourage bank runs as well as lender of last resort (LLR) facilities to assure banks ample access to liquidity. In addition, governments frequently rescue troubled financial institutions that are deemed "too big to fail," in order to mitigate the potential economic consequences of their bankruptcy.

Chang and Velasco extend the Diamond–Dybvig model to an open economy in order consider the possibility of international bank runs. In an open economy, with unrestricted capital markets, domestic banks are free to accept deposits from both domestic and foreign residents, in both domestic and foreign currency. In considering currency crises, however, other domestic institutions also have to be included. In general, any financial institution that issues short-term liabilities that can be converted into foreign currency can play a role in a currency crisis.

As in a closed economy, these liabilities are used primarily to fund longer-term, illiquid investments that cannot be readily converted to cash. If bank depositors—both foreign and domestic—seek to exchange their claims on financial institutions for foreign currency, an international bank run can result. In such an event, a rapid loss of reserves and extreme strain on the exchange rate are likely to ensue. The Korean experience in October 1997 suggests that such an outcome is more likely in the presence of large amounts of highly volatile short-term liabilities, such as interbank loans from foreign banks.

The provision of liquidity in a currency crisis poses a problem not faced in domestic bank runs. Both types of crisis begin with a widespread attempt to convert short-term claims into currency. In a closed economy, the central bank can satisfy these claims by issuing (in principle) an unlimited supply of domestic currency. In an open economy, on the other hand, the central bank can only provide foreign currency up to the extent of its stock of foreign reserves. Since all short-term domestic currency assets of the country (not just dollar deposits in banks) can in principle be converted into foreign currency during an attack, the domestic central bank may not be able to cover all potential claims. It is this fact that suggests the potential benefits of a precautionary facility for countries that have been unjustifiably hit by financial contagion.

In a closed economy, a bank run can be ruled out with deposit insurance and access to the central-bank discount window. In an open economy, the central bank may not have enough reserves to provide the LLR function; hence the potential need for an ILLR.

3. Causes of the Asian Crisis[1]

Before discussing in more detail the positive and empirical implications of the paper, it is useful to briefly assess the basic view of the paper that the Asian crisis can be understood and explained in terms of the idea of an international bank run.

The issue of whether the Asian crisis and other recent crisis episodes (Mexico, Russia, Brazil, Rumania, South Africa, Czech Republic) were due to fundamentals or self-fulfilling multiple equilibria (such as an international bank run) is very important for the policy implications of the paper, viz., the need for an ILLR. As we will discuss in detail below, if crises are triggered by fundamentals, the case for an ILLR is much weaker and an ILLR might actually be counterproductive.

The class of models with multiple equilibria (international-bank-run models, herd-behavior models, self-fulfilling panic models) represents one set of explanations of the crisis (see also Sachs and Radelet, 1998a, b). While these models differ in many important details, they are in spirit very similar in that they are all multiple-equilibrium models.

The main alternative explanation of the crisis (see Krugman, 1998) is based on the idea that implicit and explicit government guarantees, together with connected and directed lending, led to moral hazard, i.e., excessive international borrowing by domestic banks and lending to risky and unprofitable investment projects (see Krugman, 1998; Corsetti,

---

1. The discussion in this section follows Corsetti, Pesenti, and Roubini (1998, 1999a, 1999b).

Pesenti, and Roubini, 1998, 1999a, 1999b; and McKinnon and Pill, 1990). The investment boom led to large and growing current-account deficits that were financed primarily through the accumulation of a large stock of short-term, foreign-currency-denominated, and unhedged liabilities by the banking system. While actual budget deficits were apparently low, the implicit and explicit government guarantees of a bailout of the financial system in a crisis implied large and growing unfunded public liabilities that emerged once the currency crisis triggered a wider banking crisis.

At first sight, the view that the crisis was not due to fundamentals is supported by the fact that the Asian countries did not fit traditional models of economies prone to currency and financial crises. Currency and debt crises in the past (as, for example, in Latin America in the 1980s) typically occurred in countries sharing several common characteristics, including large public deficits and debt, high inflation as a result of deficit monetization, low economic growth, and low saving and investment rates. In Asia, in contrast, the crisis-afflicted countries had experienced low budget deficits, low public debt, single-digit inflation rates, high economic growth, and high saving and investment rates.

The absence of the macroeconomic imbalances typical of past crises is the reason why some academic studies have argued that the Asian crisis was due not to structural weaknesses. The "usual suspects" of currency crisis did not show up in Asia. These authors (including Chang and Velasco) argue that the crisis represented an essentially irrational but nevertheless self-fulfilling panic, akin to a bank run, fueled by hot money and fickle international investors.

Although the crisis might have been exacerbated by speculative capital flight, an alternative view (Corsetti, Pesenti, and Roubini 1998, 1999a, 1999b) is that, along with their many strong economic fundamentals, East Asian crisis countries also possessed some severe structural distortions and institutional weaknesses, especially in their financial systems. These vulnerabilities eventually triggered the crisis in the summer of 1997. In particular, the financial sectors of the crisis countries were prone to fragility due to the prevalence of corrupt credit practices, loans often being politically directed to favored firms and sectors. In addition, regulation and supervision of crisis-country banking systems were notably weak. Moreover, moral hazard derived from implicit or explicit government bailout guarantees of financial institutions. Such financial-sector weaknesses contributed to a lending boom and overinvestment in projects and sectors that often were risky and of low profitability, such as real estate and other nontraded sectors; excessive capacity accumulated in some traded-good sectors. Prior to the crisis, speculative purchases of assets in fixed supply fed an asset price bubble, with equity and real estate prices rising beyond levels warranted by fundamentals. Poor corporate governance and what has now come to be called "crony capitalism" exacerbated the distortions in this system and fueled the investment boom. Domestic and international capital liberalization may have aggravated the original distortions by allowing banks and firms to borrow more and at lower rates in international capital markets.

In spite of high saving rates, the excessive investment boom in the East Asian region led to large and growing current-account deficits, financed primarily through the accumulation of short-term, foreign currency-denominated, and unhedged liabilities by the banking system. Exchange-rate regimes entailing semifixed pegs to the dollar exacerbated the problem in two ways. First, they led to real currency appreciations (as a result of the 1995–1998 appreciation of the dollar) that worsened current account deficits. Second, the promise of fixed exchange rates led borrowers to discount the possibility of future devaluation, and thereby led them to underestimate the cost of foreign capital. Also, while budget deficits were apparently low, the implicit and explicit government guarantees of a bailout of the financial system in a crisis implied large and growing unfunded public liabilities that emerged once the currency crisis triggered a wider banking crisis.

In Korea, excessive investment was concentrated among the chaebols, the large conglomerates dominating the economy. The chaebols' control of financial institutions, together with government policies of directed lending to favored sectors, led to excessive and low-profitability investment in such traded-goods sectors as autos, steel, shipbuilding, and semiconductors. By early 1997, well before the onset of the won crisis, seven out of the thirty main chaebols were effectively bankrupt and the Korean economy was mired in a deep recession. High levels of corporate leverage were already prevalent in 1996, well before the currency crisis increased the burden of foreign debt. In Korea, the average debt-to-equity ratio of the top thirty chaebols was over 300% by the end of 1996; and by 1997 the return on invested capital was below the cost of capital for two-thirds of the top chaebols. By early 1997, nonperforming loans were a high 15% of total loans.

In Thailand, regulations restricted entrance into the banking system, but this led to the growth of unregulated, nonbank finance companies. Excessive borrowing by these finance companies fueled a boom in the real restate sector. Liberalization of capital-account regulations, for example through the establishment of the Bangkok International Banking Facility, led Thai banks and firms to borrow heavily abroad, in foreign currency, at very short maturities. Fifty-six of these finance companies that had borrowed excessively from abroad in foreign currency were distressed even before the Thai baht crisis, and were eventually closed after the onset of the crisis.

In Indonesia, a large fraction of all bank credit consisted of directed credit, channeled to politically favored firms and sectors. Although Indonesia had already suffered a banking crisis in the early 1990s, such practices remained prevalent. Moreover, most of the borrowing took place in foreign-currency terms, compounding debtors' inability to repay when the local currency depreciated. In Indonesia, a large fraction of foreign banks' lending was directly to the corporate sector rather than being intermediated through the domestic banking system.

Empirical studies confirm that the return to capital fell sharply in the East Asia region as the result of this excessive investment. For example, Pomerleano (1998) finds a rapid buildup of fixed assets throughout Asia between 1992 and 1996, with particularly rapid growth in Indonesia and Thailand. Since most of the growth was financed with debt (especially in Thailand and Korea), high levels of corporate leverage were already prevalent in 1996, well before the currency crisis increased the burden of foreign debt. At the same time, moderate to low profitability severely impaired the ability of many Asian firms to meet their interest payment obligations.

Exogenous disturbances contributed to make the East Asian countries vulnerable to crisis. These included a slowdown of export growth among many Asian countries in 1996 and a worsening of the terms of trade, deriving from factors including a slump in the world price of semiconductors; the persistent stagnation of the Japanese economy in the 1990s; the weakness of the yen, which caused a real appreciation of Asian currencies that were effectively pegged to the U.S. dollar; and the emergence of China as a major regional competitor.

In 1997, the bubble burst. Stock markets dropped (in some cases accelerating a reversal that had started before 1997), and the emergence of wide losses and/or outright corporate sector defaults revealed the low profitability of past investment projects. Nonperforming loans, already on the rise prior to the currency crisis, escalated, threatening bankruptcy of many East Asian financial institutions. In addition, the firms, banks, and investors that had heavily relied on external borrowing were left with a large stock of short-term, foreign-currency-denominated, and unhedged foreign debt that could not be easily repaid. The ensuing exchange-rate crisis exacerbated this problem, as currency depreciation dramatically increased the domestic-currency value of the debt denominated in foreign currency, provoking further financial crisis for banks and firms. The free fall of currencies was intensified by the sudden rush of firms, banks, and investors to cover their previously unhedged liabilities in foreign currency. Thus, accelerated depreciation aggravated the original foreign-currency debt problem, creating a vicious circle.

The concern of private investors about governments' commitment to structural reforms exacerbated the policy uncertainty, contributing to widespread capital outflows. While fundamentals likely triggered the crisis, currency and stock markets may also have overreacted, with panic, herd behavior, and a generalized increase in risk aversion producing a sudden reversal of capital flows that exacerbated the crisis.

If we accept the "fundamentals" explanation of the Asian crisis, then we must be skeptical of the ability of the theoretical analysis in the paper to explain the crisis. Moreover, the main policy implication of the paper, the need for an ILLR, can also be seriously questioned if we believe in a "fundamentals" model. I thus move to discuss in more detail the case for an ILLR.

4. Problems with an ILLR

Let us consider now in more detail one of the main policy implications of the paper, viz., the need for an ILLR. In a domestic context, the LLR role played by central banks and institutions such as deposit insurance is aimed at preventing self-fulfilling bank runs. However, such insurance creates moral-hazard incentives: If banks' deposits are insured and/or liquidity support is guaranteed in the case of a run, banks will have an incentive to make more risky loans than they would in the absence of insurance. The solution to this problem is strong capital adequacy standards and prudential supervision and regulation of banks.

In the international context, the expected provision of official liquidity may also lead to distorted incentives: Expectations of official emergency financing may lead international investors to lend carelessly and domestic governments to engage in risky policies. Moral hazard in the international context can also be mitigated if insolvent banks can be distinguished from illiquid ones. Ideally, in the international context, precautionary financial support should be given to countries with good policies—innocent bystanders in episodes of contagion—and be withheld from countries with weak policies. Drawing this distinction is obviously considerably more difficult among countries than among banks. There is a spectrum of crises, from those that stem primarily from poor policies to those that stem primarily from contagion. In practice, most fall somewhere in the middle. A regime for crisis response should provide for some combination of financial assistance and policy changes. The provision of large-scale official international finance also raises difficult questions: What criteria should be used for access to large-scale assistance, and on what terms? How should it be linked to private-sector involvement? And where will the required resources come from?

However, just as there is a role for the government to intervene to prevent a domestic financial crisis from destabilizing the domestic financial system, there is a role for the international community to intervene in an international financial crisis to help limit contagion and global instability. The current crisis has demonstrated that the official community needs, at times, to be able to provide huge financing packages to quell potential contagion and instability. A proposed new IMF precautionary facility (the Contingent Credit Line) allows large-scale international assistance for those cases where problems stem more from contagion than from poor policies. It may make sense in today's world of large and sudden liquidity needs for more official money than is provided by traditional IMF programs to be available up front in return for more up-front policy changes.

5. Are Runs Due to Self-Fulfilling Equilibria or to Fundamentals?

One should also be careful about pushing the argument that an ILLR is needed to prevent irrational, self-fulfilling runs on a country. Even in a domestic context, while a purely irrational run on a healthy bank is possible in theory, in reality all known runs have occurred on banks that had some serious fundamental weaknesses. Investors are not irrational and do not attack banks just for the fun of it. The large literature on the causes of systemic banking crisis confirms that crises are always the outcome of severe problems of the banking system: excessive lending, high levels of nonperforming loans, moral-hazard distortions, connected and directed lending, a weak macroeconomic environment, poorly designed deposit insurance, weak institutions, or poorly managed liberalization in the presence of distorted incentives (see Dziobek and Pazarbasioglu, 1997; Honohan, 1997; Goldstein and Turner, 1996; Demirgüç-Kunt and Detragiache, 1997; Caprio, 1998).

Moreover, in technical terms, the multiple-equilibrium literature is conceptually somewhat weak in that, once an economy is in the region where such bad equilibria may occur, nothing in the model explains why investors focus their expectations on the bad equilibrium rather than the good one. Each outcome is as likely as the other. Relying on sunspots, as this paper and others do, to nail down the probability of a run is just a technical solution with little economic or empirical content. In reality, instead, the probability of ending up in the bad equilibrium should depend on fundamentals; if fundamentals are weak, the probability that agents attack is higher. In the bank context, it is weak banks that are attacked; solid, healthy banks are almost never attacked. If one takes this analogy to countries, then the message is clear. It is unlikely that a country that has good fundamentals would be attacked, save for extreme cases of contagion that such countries should be able to deal with on their own. Countries that are attacked are usually countries that, in some dimension or the other, have weak fundamentals. If that is the case, such countries should in general not prequalify for an ILLR facility and would therefore get little benefit from the existence of such a facility. For such countries, traditional conditionality or, at most, a variant of it (e.g., early and substantial disbursements of funds conditional on a strong fundamentals adjustment) would be the sensible policy prescription.

Moreover, in a domestic context, the moral-hazard problems created by deposit insurance and LLR support are (or should be) compensated with strict regulation and supervision of the banking system and strong capital adequacy standards. When the latter are not effectively implemented, we repeatedly observe systemic bank crises that are very costly (fiscally and in terms of the output loss that a financial crisis triggers). However, in the international context sovereignty implies that we cannot directly regulate an economy or impose capital adequacy standards. The most we can do is to give some incentives for good behavior and expect countries to follow them. This means that the carrot of an ILLR cannot be directly linked, as in the domestic context, to the sticks of regulation of banks or countries. The best that one can do is to design an ILLR facility available to countries that qualify on the basis of some *ex ante* criteria.

6. Private-Sector Bail-in and ILLR

One important question in recent debates on financial architecture has been how to constructively *bail in* rather than bail out private (foreign) investors. The general issue is the one of how to constructively ensure private-sector involvement in crisis prevention and resolution and in burden sharing. Some concerns have been expressed that large IMF rescue packages may be used to bail out rather than bail in private creditors. Indeed, in Asia in 1997–1998 official financing effectively replaced part of the private capital that fled the region.

In this context, an important issue is whether an ILLR will clash with the objective of having private-sector involvement in crisis prevention and resolution. Specifically, if an ILLR will automatically bail out investors, how can we bail them in? A mechanical and indiscriminate ILLR

that would not distinguish countries that may be deserving unconditional ILLR support from those that have weak fundamentals and deserve support only subject to traditional IMF conditionality would have
perverse effects. Countries that should not be bailed out would be, and
there would be no room for constructive bail-in of private investors.

There are many (some controversial) suggestions on how to bail in the
private sectors, differing in their degree of coercion. These include

1. Collective action clauses to allow orderly workouts
2. Moral suasion to ensure rollover of loans and bonds
3. Rollover options in loan and debt contracts
4. Capital controls on outflows (or inflows)
5. Private contingent credit facilities (as in Mexico, Argentina, Indonesia)
6. Conditioning public ILLR on the existence of private contingent
   credit lines
7. Conditioning sovereign debt rescheduling by official creditors on
   rescheduling by private-sector creditors, including bondholders
8. Domestic and foreign debt restructuring
9. Debt service suspensions sanctioned by the IMF and supported by
   the IMF policy of "lending into arrears"
10. Orderly debt workout procedures

To see why an ILLR may conflict with the goal of bailing in the private
sector, consider one problem posed by the Asian crisis and by previous
financial crisis episodes: Once a financial crisis occurs, usually cross-
border interbank loans end up being guaranteed *ex post,* even if they were
not *ex ante.* For example, in Korea, all foreign liabilities of the private
banking system were guaranteed by the government after the crisis
erupted, as a condition for getting the rollover, and eventual stretching of
maturities, on such interbank liabilities. In Thailand, foreign liabilities of
the bankrupt finance companies were similarly guaranteed *ex post.* In
general, one of the lessons of Asia may be that, given concerns about the
stability of the banking system, creditor banks engaging in cross-border
interbank loans were not bailed in but rather bailed out.

In a domestic context, the logic of guaranteeing deposits is based on
the idea that small depositors do not have the resources to monitor what
the bank is doing with their deposits. To avoid irrational panic, we thus
insure their deposits. The same does not hold for large investors, who
can and should be careful about the actions of banks that are borrowing
funds. That is why there are limits to the amount of deposit insurance.
In an international context, it is not clear why foreign depositors in the

domestic banking system should be insured. More specifically, since a large fraction of the foreign-currency liabilities of commercial banks in emerging markets are short-term cross-border interbank loans, there is no good reason why such large investors should be insured. In reality, even without formal insurance, such liabilities have often ended up being insured *ex post,* exacerbating moral-hazard issues.

Now, if we believe that "no guarantee of foreign liabilities of the banks" is a worthwhile policy objective, then it is important that an extensive ILLR facility might undermine that effort. If a country can borrow from such a facility, international investors (as well as domestic ones) can be sure that they can liquidate their positions in the banking and financial system of emerging markets with no loss, assuming the exchange rate remains fixed. Even under flexible exchange rates the loss would be limited, because a country that dips into that facility will do so to use the funds to limit currency depreciation and thus allow investors/ depositors who do want to get out to do so effectively risk-free. Then, how can we design an ILLR facility that does not lead to implicit or explicit bailouts of interbank cross-border loans? There is no simple answer, and we may end up exacerbating the moral-hazard problem rather than mitigating it.

How would an ILLR enhance the objective of making sure that the private sector participates constructively to crisis prevention and resolution? One simple, but mistaken, argument would be that since a full and credible ILLR would prevent international bank runs from occurring in the first place, there is no issue with having to bail in private investors. Such investors will not rush to the door if they know they are insured. Reality is, of course more complex, as countries with fundamentals out of line will not and should not get unlimited and unconditional resources. If they did, the funds lent by an ILLR facility would be used by domestic and foreign investors to liquidate domestic assets and turn them into foreign ones, eventually exacerbating a crisis driven by weak fundamentals. This is also the reason why, in a domestic context, it would be destabilizing to give extensive LLR support to banks that are in serious financial distress or bankrupt. Giving more funds to such banks leads to moral hazard, i.e., "gambling for redemption," as the S&L crisis and many other episodes suggest. This is also why the correct response of a central bank to a banking crisis caused by poor behavior of the banking system is to provide emergency support (to avoid panic) in exchange for a very strict control of the financial institution under distress. Bank managers may be fired, the government may take effective control of the distressed banks, and the bank may be eventually closed or merged with others if it cannot be appropriately restructured. Since in an international context the idea of taking over countries, closing them down, and merging them with others is obviously meaningless, the policy implications are threefold. A country in severe distress because of fundamental weaknesses should not receive unconditional ILLR support: such support would bail out investors and eventually fail to prevent a crisis. Second, if support has to be given to provide incentives for reform and adjustment, then the support should be of the strict-conditionality form that comes with IMF packages. Third, to bail in private investors, the amount of support should be lower than the amount of total domestic assets that could be potentially converted into foreign currency, i.e., official financing support should be partial, for otherwise investors end up being fully bailed out. Note also that even countries that may prequalify for some ILLR support would not have access to unlimited funds: realistically, such a facility would not have enough funds to fully finance all potential cases of a bank run.

Recent research also suggests that there are many complex issues and difficulties in designing a system that provides official support while at the same time constructively bailing in the private sector. Three recent studies (Jeanne, 1999; Zettelmeyer, 1999; and Goldfajn and Valdes, 1999) show the problems with designing an ILLR while ensuring private-sector bail-ins. For example, consider the implication of the fact that the resources available to an ILLR will be limited, so that partial rather than full bailout will be the norm. If the amount of resources available to an ILLR is limited and full financing of a bank run is not feasible, a partial bailout may be worse than no bailout at all. For example, Zettelmeyer (1999) shows that limited crisis lending may be counterproductive by financing a run rather than avoiding one. Specifically, a limited bailout could lead more investors to run in a crisis, and even trigger a crisis if there is a large investor or a coalition of investors. Similarly, Goldfajn and Valdes (1999) show that if partial financing is provided, the ILLR does not necessarily reduce the probability of financial runs and banking cum exchange-rate crises, if its existence leads to more reserves being available at the initial exchange rate in case of a crisis.

Semicoercive private-sector involvement can also be counterproductive. It is known that capital controls (on outflows) that are unexpected can be effective in the short run in postponing a run (see Goldfajn and Valdes, 1999, for a recent modeling of this). However, it is also well known that expected capital controls can cause a run and have perverse effects. In this context, for example, part of the contagion from Russia to Brazil and other emerging markets in the summer of 1998 can be explained by the increased subjective probability of capital controls being imposed, following the decision by Russia and Malaysia to impose them in August 1998. Also, as shown by Goldfajn and Valdes (1999), private-sector participation conditions can increase the probability of financial runs if a large proportion of foreign investors expect to withdraw their investments without a loss.

Even rollover options that automatically lengthen the maturity of foreign debt (such as those suggested by Buiter and Sibert, 1999) are not without problems Jeanne (1999) shows that, in a model where short-term foreign lending is an equilibrium discipline device for governments subject to a deficit bias, rollover options may have counterproductive effects.

Private contingent credit lines (such as those arranged by Mexico, Argentina, and Indonesia with their creditors) may or may not work. They should provide funds to a country whose reserves are under pressure because of capital flight or contagion, and thus dampen market concerns about a country's ability to withstand a flight episode. But the amounts that are being mobilized are often small relative to the size of capital outflows. Moreover, it is not obvious that such a credit facility truly provides new net resources to a country above what creditors would have otherwise provided. Creditors can use derivatives and dynamic hedging strategies if they want to ensure that their net exposure to a country is not increased by the provision of such contingent credit lines.

7. The Endogenous Distribution of Bank Debt Maturity

An important issue in financial crises is why banks and domestic agents borrow short-term if this makes them vulnerable to a bank run. In the model presented in the paper, a large stock of short-term debt relative to foreign reserves is a necessary condition for the existence of an international bank run. The paper provides some interesting insights, but leaves open a number of issues. Chang and Velasco show that if domestic residents are risk-neutral, they are indifferent to the maturity structure of the bank debt, while if they are risk-averse, they will not borrow short-term at all. This leaves open the question of why so much debt is short-term. The authors suggest that to get an equilibrium with short-term debt one needs to introduce a market failure. The authors suggest four alternative reasons why such a market failure can exist. The last two are: "the expectation of a bailout, whether rational or not, encourages reckless behavior; reckless behavior may indeed make a bailout more likely, thereby having external effects."

Indeed, the authors come to agree that, in order to explain the bias towards short-term debt that is necessary for their theory of international bank runs, it may be necessary to rely on the moral-hazard distortions deriving from implicit and explicit government guarantees, as stressed by fundamentals explanations of the crisis (see Krugman, 1998; Corsetti, Pesenti, and Roubini, 1998, 1999a, b; and McKinnon and Pill, 1990).

8. Implications for the Choice of the Exchange-Rate Regime

An interesting stylized fact is that most currency and financial crises in the 1990s have occurred under regimes of relatively fixed exchange rates (e.g., ERM, 1992–1993; Mexico and the tequila crisis, 1994–1995; the Asian crisis, 1997–1998; Russia, 1998; Brazil, 1999). Chang and Velasco study the role of exchange-rate regimes in financial crises and find a number of interesting results. For example, they find that under a regime of fixed exchange rates with no capital controls, international bank runs are even a bigger problem because all the short-term assets of the country, whether denominated in foreign or in domestic currency, can be converted into foreign assets and thus become claims against central bank reserves. Flexible exchange rates suffer less from this problem, but with two big caveats. First, attempts to purchase foreign assets that lead to a run on reserves under fixed rates will lead to sharp exchange-rate depreciation under flexible exchange rates. Second, we cannot rule out international bank runs under flexible exchange rates. If short-term foreign-currency-denominated assets of a country are high relative to reserves, a self-fulfilling no-rollover crisis may occur. Thus, a financial crisis or banking crisis may also occur under flexible exchange rates.

So we have an explanation in the paper of why international bank runs more likely to occur under fixed rates. There are however alternative explanations of such twin crises. First, currency crises may often occur because the fixed parities are not consistent with the underlying fundamentals. Twin crises can be then understood by observing that fixed exchange rates are an important element of the moral hazard created by governments. If banks and firms are promised a pegged parity, they will borrow too much in foreign currency, as the cost of capital is biased by the promise of a fixed parity. Then, the implicit public liability of the fixed-rate promise can become very large once a devaluation leads to a collapse of the banking system and financial distress for corporations. Thus, fixed rates create moral hazard and lead to financial fragility and vulnerabilities in the corporate and financial system.

What is the policy implication of such an analysis? In one view that is becoming increasingly popular, emerging markets should either let their currency float or pick fixed-rate regimes that are truly credible and sustainable (specifically, currency boards supported by strong fundamentals). Fixed but adjustable peg regimes may be the worst of all, as they do not provide either policy credibility or enough exchange-rate flexibility.

9. Conclusion

As I said at the outset, this is a very interesting and important paper that will be widely read. It discusses in a unified and sophisticated analytical framework a set of important positive and normative issues. I am not convinced, though, by the paper's conclusion that the recent twin crises episodes were mostly due to self-fulfilling international bank runs. While overshooting of asset prices driven by sudden reversals of capital flows may have played a role in recent crisis episodes, an alternative explanation centered on structural weaknesses of the financial sector and distortions caused by government policies appears to provide a better interpretation. The issue of whether twin crises are due to funda- mentals or to multiple-equilibrium runs and panics is central for the validity of one of the main policy implications of the paper, i.e., the need for an international lender of last resort. Designing and implementing an ILLR is difficult and may result in perverse effects in cases where crises are triggered by weak fundamentals.

The views presented in the paper are solely those of the author and do not represent the views of any institution with which the author is affiliated.

REFERENCES

Buiter, W., and A. Sibert. (1999). UDROP or you drop: A small contribution to the new international financial architecture. Cambridge University. Unpublished.
Caprio, G. Jr. (1998). Banking on crises: Expensive lessons from recent financial crises. World Bank. Unpublished Working Paper.
Corsetti, G., P. Pesenti, and N. Roubini. (1998). Fundamental determinants of the Asian crisis: A preliminary assessment. Yale University. Unpublished.
———, ———, and ———. (1999a). What caused the Asian currency and finan- cial crisis? *Japan and the World Economy* 11(3):305–373.
———, ———, and ———. (1999b). Paper tigers? A model of the Asian crisis. *European Economic Review* 43(7):1211–1236.
———, ———, ———, and C. Tille. (1999). Trade and contagious devaluations: A welfare-based approach. Cambridge, MA: National Bureau of Economic Research. NBER Working Paper W6889.
Demirgüç-Kunt, A., and E. Detragiache. (1997). The determinants of banking crises: Evidence from industrial and developing countries. World Bank. Un- published Working Paper.
Diamond, D., and P. Dybvig. (1983). Bank runs, deposit insurance, and liquidity. *Journal of Political Economy* 91:401–419.
Dziobek, C., and Pazarbasioglu, C. (1997). Lessons from systemic bank restructur- ing: A survey of 24 countries. International Monetary Fund. Working Paper.

Goldfajn, I., and R. O. Valdes. (1999). Liquidity crises and the international financial architecture. International Monetary Fund. Unpublished.

Goldstein, M., and P. Turner (1996). Banking crises in emerging economies: Origins and policy options. Bank of International Settlements. Working Paper.

Honohan, P. (1997). Banking system failures in developing and transition countries: Diagnosis and prediction. Bank of International Settlements. Working Paper.

Jeanne, O. (1999). Sovereign liquidity crises and the global financial architecture. International Monetary Fund. Unpublished.

Krugman, P. (1998). What happened to Asia? MIT. Unpublished.

McKinnon, R., and H. Pill. (1990). Credible liberalization and international capital flows: The "overborrowing syndrome." In *Financial Deregulation and Integration in East Asia,* T. Ito and A.O. Krueger (eds.). Chicago: The University of Chicago Press.

Pomerleano, M. (1998). Corporate finance lessons from the East Asian crisis. World Bank. Unpublished.

Sachs, J., and S. Radelet. (1998a). The onset of the East Asian financial crisis. Cambridge, MA: National Bureau of Economic Research. NBER Working Paper 6680.

———, and ———. (1998b). The East Asian financial crisis: Diagnosis, remedies, prospects. Harvard University. Unpublished.

Zettelmeyer, J. (1999). The case against partial bail-outs. International Monetary Fund. Unpublished.

Discussion

Andrés Velasco replied to Abhijit Banerjee's comments by saying that the modeling approach suggested by Banerjee is not fundamentally very different from theirs. In particular, there is a difference in the definition of the real exchange rate, but otherwise the mechanisms are quite similar.

Rick Mishkin agreed with Nouriel Roubini in expressing reservations about the application of the Diamond–Dybvig framework in the context of emerging markets. The Diamond–Dybvig approach ignores moral-hazard issues, he noted, which are pervasive, particularly when there are explicit or implicit bailout guarantees by developing-country governments. He also raised the general issue of foreign-denominated debt in developing countries. The option of devaluation looks much less attractive when it increases the domestic-currency value of foreign debts and bankrupts firms and financial intermediaries.

Sebastian Edwards said he was concerned about the ability of developing countries to control short-term capital inflows. He noted that the historical record is not very promising; since the 1950s there have been 50–55 crises in Latin America, despite significant controls on both capital inflows and outflows. Edwards specifically questioned the efficacy of the

Chilean system, which imposes what amounts to a 600-basis-point implicit tax on short-term capital inflows. Despite this system, he said, since 1996 an average of 50% of Chile's international debt has been due within a year, a shorter maturity structure than that of Mexico, which does not restrict short-term flows. Velasco responded that capital restrictions which penalize short-term borrowing, such as those instituted by Chile, could still be helpful by lengthening the maturity of the debt. While recognizing that capital controls also entail costs, he emphasized the need to find the right tradeoff between their costs and benefits.

Martin Feldstein approved of the paper's emphasis on international illiquidity, which must be clearly distinguished from problems of insolvency. Bagehot taught us how to deal with illiquidity: by lending freely against good collateral. Whether this is feasible in the international context is an open question. The IMF has disbursed large loans but has not been a true lender of last resort; in particular, it neither lends freely nor takes collateral. An interesting question is whether it is possible in some cases for private lenders to step in and provide international liquidity against collateral: An example is Mexico's pledging of its oil export earnings as collateral. Feldstein conceded that relying on private lenders for liquidity had many problems, but thought it still might be an approach worth exploring. Velasco agreed with the comments, but noted that the emphasis of their paper was on "self-help" by small countries rather than on the international financial architecture. Feldstein also wondered whether countries might be able to increase liquidity on their own by borrowing large quantities of reserves in advance of the crisis, as opposed to relying on current-account surpluses to build reserves. The cost of such a policy might be reduced by holding higher-yielding securities than T-bills, although this implies potential issues of risk and illiquidity.

Anil Kashyap defended the Diamond–Dybvig model by saying that one could model a collapse of working-capital lending and a general credit crunch within this framework. In general, if banks create net liquidity they must be exposed, and if they have to retrench there must be consequences somewhere in the economy. Kashyap also suggested that looking at where the credit crunch hit in Asia would be useful. He encouraged the authors to extend their Table 1 to include Singapore, Hong Kong, Taiwan, and other emerging-market economies that survived the crisis to see whether their experiences confirm the liquidity story. Velasco noted that one important difference between their approach and the Diamond–Dybvig model is that some people who legitimately need a capital infusion cannot get it when there is a bank run, and this imposes real costs. This feature seems consistent with Kashyap's observation.

Ben Bernanke asked how the model accommodates contagion. Does the authors' model do a better job than a story based on fundamentals in explaining why crises appear to jump from one country to another?

Pierre Gourinchas noted the implication of Table 1 that the *level* of the ratio of short-term debt to international reserves determines whether there will be a crisis, as opposed to changes in this variable. An important question not addressed by the paper is how long a country can survive in the "danger zone." Gourinchas also suggested that it is important to look at the converse of the question studied in the paper, i.e., do banking or currency crises always follow a lending boom partly financed by international capital? He said that his work with Rodriguez and Valdez suggested otherwise.

Velasco responded that being in the danger zone appeared to be necessary but not sufficient for a crisis. His reading of the empirical literature on contagion is that fundamentals help to explain crises but that there are large unexplained residuals, suggesting that there may be self-fulfilling elements to crises. He disagreed with Roubini's suggestion that depositors do not run on solvent banks, arguing that the health of balance sheets after the crisis, when the economy is weak and asset prices have collapsed, can be misleading. If the crisis had not taken place, asset values would be higher, working-capital flows would be uninterrupted, and the bank's balance sheet might look very different. Hence, to conclude for example that the high cost of Mexico's bank bailout implies that all the banks were insolvent is incorrect.

Michael Mussa and Miguel Savastano
INTERNATIONAL MONETARY FUND

The IMF Approach to Economic Stabilization

1. Introduction

When the International Monetary Fund makes resources available to a member country to assist with adjustment of its balance of payments, it does so under an agreed arrangement (or *program*) specifying the conditions governing that support. These conditions, known as *IMF conditionality*, include both policies a member may need to carry out prior to approval of the arrangement (by the IMF's Executive Board) and disbursement of the initial tranche of support, as well as policy undertakings that must be met for disbursement of subsequent tranches over the life of the arrangement (usually one to three years).

Of necessity, the IMF's approach to economic stabilization has vital quantitative features. Projections must be made for key macroeconomic variables (national output, the price level, the current account balance, and so on), under the policies to be adopted under the program. Particular attention must be paid to the likely availability of external financing to assure that viability is restored to the country's external payments position. As a central element of conditionality, IMF programs contain quantitative "performance criteria" for key variables related to macroeconomic policies, which typically include ceilings for the fiscal deficit and the central bank's net domestic credit, and floors for net international reserves. These performance criteria, which must be agreed by the na-

The authors are, respectively, the Economic Counsellor and Director of the Research Department, and a Deputy Division Chief, in the Research Department of the International Monetary Fund. The opinions expressed in this paper are solely those of the authors and do not represent the views of the International Monetary Fund. The authors are grateful to Shailendra Anjaria, Ben Bernanke, Stanley Fischer, Mohsin Khan, Leslie Lipschitz, Paul Masson, Julio Rotemberg, Ratna Sahay, and colleagues in the Research Department for helpful comments and suggestions.

tional authorities and the IMF, are calculated using a flows-of-funds framework known as *financial programming*. Thus, in a general consideration of quantitative approaches to economic stabilization, the approach employed by the IMF merits particular scrutiny.

Over the years as well as recently, the IMF approach to economic stabilization and especially IMF conditionality have been the subject of much controversy. IMF programs are often characterized as unnecessarily damaging to growth, harmful to the poor, unduly inflexible and unresponsive to the differing needs and circumstances of member countries, and based on rigid application of outmoded and discredited economic principles. Some of these criticisms can and should be dismissed as factually inaccurate.[1] Others are based on the wishful thinking that there are easy policy choices or that there should be virtually unlimited concessional official financing (or grants) for countries with severe balance-of-payments problems—problems often due, at least partly, to the countries' own policy mistakes. Other criticisms clearly merit substantive consideration. In individual cases, while recognizing that undertaking adjustment to correct external imbalances is necessary and difficult and that there are limits to official support, the degree of tightening of macroeconomic policies and the balance between adjustment and financing are always debatable issues.

This paper is not primarily concerned with the latter type of criticisms, which can only be addressed on a case-by-case basis, but rather with two more specific critiques that relate to the quantitative character of the IMF approach to economic stabilization. First, because IMF-supported programs employ a similar quantitative framework across a very wide array of cases, there is the accusation that the IMF approach to stabilization is rigid and unresponsive to the particular situations of different members and to changing conditions over time. Second, because of the common practice of setting quantitative performance criteria for fiscal and monetary policy in virtually all IMF-supported programs, there is the indictment that the IMF approach is based on outmoded economic models and principles that fail to take account of the complexity and uncertainty

---

1. Chief among these are the claims that IMF-supported programs seldom pay attention to the effects of adjustment on the poor, that they all contemplate a fiscal retrenchment of approximately the same size and composition which relies heavily on regressive tax rate hikes and undue compression of public investment, and that they (almost) invariably require a large exchange-rate devaluation. The evidence contained in numerous studies, conducted inside and outside the Fund, shows that all those claims are unfounded. Some, but certainly not all, of the studies that provide (or refer to) that evidence include Bernstein and Boughton (1993), Burton and Gilman (1991), Gupta et al. (1998), Heller et al. (1988), International Monetary Fund (1997), IMF Assessment Project (1992), Johnson and Salop (1980), Killick (1995, Chapter 3), Nashashibi et al. (1992), and Schadler et al. (1993, 1995).

of key macroeconomic relationships. These accusations, we intend to show, largely reflect misconceptions about how the IMF approach operates in reality, misconceptions that are partly due to the way the IMF describes its programs.

To understand the IMF approach to economic stabilization and especially how it functions in its quantitative aspects, it is first essential to understand the *process* of an IMF-supported program, described in Section 2. A typical IMF-supported program is not set in stone at its inception, either to proceed subsequently in exact accord with the initial plan, or to be terminated because of some minor deviation. A program begins with an explicit request from a member. IMF staff then prepares a *blueprint* of a program that is used as the basis for negotiations. When agreement is reached, often after hard bargaining over key elements of the program, the arrangement has to be cleared by IMF management and then approved by the IMF Executive Board. Thereafter, disbursements proceed automatically if all the performance clauses are met as initially specified. This rarely happens all the way through an arrangement. Instead, if various conditions are not met, deviations may be accommodated with *waivers*, projections revised, and numerical targets changed. Those who participate in the process of IMF-supported programs, from both sides, do so with full awareness of their fundamentally iterative, open-loop character.

With an understanding of this process, the economics of IMF programs is addressed in Section 3. At their core, IMF-supported programs in countries facing actual or prospective balance of payments (the main focus of this paper) need to emphasize the country's actions in three areas: (1) securing sustainable external financing; (2) adopting demand-restraining measures consistent with available financing; and (3) proceeding with structural reforms to promote growth and adjustment in the medium and longer term. The country's more basic objectives of high output growth, alleviating poverty, and so forth are not explicitly among those core areas. This does not imply unconcern with these objectives, but rather the priority that a country experiencing severe extended payments difficulties must assign in the shorter term to ameliorating these difficulties and correcting the macroeconomic and structural imbalances at their root, in order to achieve more basic objectives in a sustainable manner over the longer term.

Beyond this, a good deal of misconception concerning the inflexibility and dogmatism ascribed to IMF programs probably derives from the superficial similarity that those programs exhibit in terms of the specification of quantitative performance criteria for fiscal and monetary policies. Once account is taken of the *process* of IMF-supported programs, however, it becomes apparent that there is a great deal of flexibility to respond both to differences in circumstances and to changes in conditions in individual cases. In fact, properly understood, the intellectual doctrine associated with IMF financial programming is primarily a recognition of basic accounting identities supplemented with a small number of behavioral relationships and forecasts of key economic variables, the latter two being subject to revision as new evidence becomes available. This is topped with a reasonable discretion in judging both the size of the required macroeconomic adjustment and the relative effectiveness of the policy instruments available to the authorities to undertake it.

Before turning to the main subject of the paper, five further points deserve clarification and emphasis. First, as an international organization, the International Monetary Fund must serve the interest of and be accountable to its membership, within an established set of policies, procedures, and practices that assure reasonable equality of treatment, with due recognition of differences in circumstance. In short, not everything goes. A degree of conservatism in Fund arrangements is not only inevitable, but also desirable.

Second, under its legal charter, the Articles of Agreement, IMF financial support to members is supposed to serve a particular purpose, as specified by Article I(iv):

To give confidence to members by making the general resources of the Fund temporarily available to them under adequate safeguards, thus providing them with the opportunity to correct maladjustments in their balance of payments without resorting to measures destructive to national or international prosperity.

Plausible assurance that a member's use of the Fund's resources will be temporary requires a reasonable expectation of a member's sufficiently early return to external-payments viability (so that the member will be able to repay the Fund). Indeed, the primary legal justification for conditionality, as provided in Article V of the Articles of Agreement, is to impose "adequate safeguards" that render that plausible assurance. No one may reasonably argue that the IMF should ignore this constraint in its conditionality. Moreover, the IMF has no authority to write down claims against members who fall into arrears on their obligations to the Fund; in the end, those members become outcasts of the international community with prolonged and dire consequences. In the application of conditionality, prudence to contain the risks of such situations is clearly essential.

Third, while we do not review them here, empirical studies that have evaluated the macroeconomic effects of IMF-supported programs have generally found that they do best what they are primarily designed to do, namely, improve the current-account balance and the overall balance of payments of countries experiencing external payments difficulties. And the most careful studies, which attempt to correct for a variety of econometric difficulties, confirm that this association is something more than the usual tendency for things to get better when they are very bad to start with.[2] Other macroeconomic effects associated with IMF-supported programs—on output growth, on inflation, and so forth—are more difficult to pin down, especially when proper account is taken of all the other factors that influence the outcome of a program. If anything, the results tend to show negative initial effects on output, while the effects on inflation are often not statistically significant.

Fourth, for exchange-rate policy (not discussed in detail in the rest of the paper), it is *not* the case that the IMF imposes its views on all members, or that those views (almost) always entail a devaluation and abandonment of currency pegs for "more flexible" regimes. True, discussions about exchange-rate policy and, in particular, the dismantling of exchange restrictions (an area that falls under the direct purview of the IMF as stated in Article VIII of the Articles of Agreement) are important and at times central aspects of program negotiations. Moreover, in some cases the reform of the foreign exchange system or an exchange-rate devaluation become preconditions ("prior actions") for Board approval of an IMF arrangement. But this is hardly the norm. As in other areas, negotiations over exchange-rate policy give considerable weight to the views and desires of the member country. The many arrangements approved for countries in the CFA franc zone in the years prior to the January 1994 devaluation of the CFA franc (a period when IMF staff voiced repeatedly, though subtly, its concerns about the harmful effects of maintaining the old parity) attest to this fact. So does the evidence from a large number of Fund arrangements approved in the 1980s that is reported in an external evaluation of IMF conditionality and that led the authors to conclude, with some surprise, that: "perhaps the strongest tendency of IMF conditionality was to leave existing exchange-rate policies intact" (IMF Assessment Project, 1992, p. 39).[3] That substantial deference is given to national authorities in

2. The empirical literature on the macroeconomic effects of IMF-supported programs is quite extensive. However, the question is difficult to address and the methodologies employed (particularly the earlier ones) have serious shortcomings, especially with the so-called "problem of the counterfactual"—i.e., ascertaining what would have been different in the absence of an IMF program—see Goldstein and Montiel (1986), Khan (1990), and Dicks-Mireaux et al. (1995). See Haque and Khan (1998) for a recent survey of this literature.
3. In the 1990s, views of country authorities have continued to play a key role in shaping exchange-rate policy in IMF-supported programs. For example, Argentina made its own

their exchange-rate and other economic policies is a reflection both of the right of members to determine their own policies, and of the experience showing that IMF programs tend to perform best when their associated policies are most closely "owned" by the national authorities in charge of implementing them.

Fifth, substantial deference to national authorities, however, still means that Fund arrangements impose tangible constraints on economic policies. This implies that there is an unavoidable political-economy component to IMF conditionality. National authorities may modify policies to comply with IMF conditionality when it would be difficult to find domestic political consensus in the absence of external pressure. On behalf of the international community, the IMF attaches conditions that the ultimate providers of IMF resources might find difficult to request and enforce on a bilateral basis. Thus, the IMF and its conditionality become a "scapegoat" on both sides of the bargain (see James, 1998). That such a scapegoat can be useful in securing necessary or desirable, but unpopular, policy adjustments is clear. That the IMF might actually be counterproductive because of the political consequences of its conditionality and the hostility associated with its scapegoat function is also at least a debatable issue (see Shultz, 1995, and Feldstein, 1998). We will not attempt to resolve this debate. We note, nonetheless, that the IMF is the creature of its members and is accountable and responsive to them; the IMF cannot, in broad terms and over a sustained period, pursue policies which the members do not generally approve.

2. The Process behind IMF-Supported Programs

IMF programs are, in practice, quite flexible. An IMF-supported program is *not* the initial agreement negotiated with a member. A Fund-supported program is a process. It evolves along a multiplicity of poten-

---

decision to adopt a currency board in early 1991, and received support from an IMF arrangement only in July of that year. When the peg came under intense pressure in the tequila crisis of 1995, a new program supported by the IMF helped Argentina sustain its decision to preserve its currency board. In mid-December 1994, Mexico devalued the peso and then moved to a floating rate before reaching any agreement with the IMF. Also outside any Fund arrangement, Brazil adopted the Real Plan in mid-1994 and defended it against intense pressures in the tequila crisis and from the Asian crisis beginning in October 1997. When Brazil requested, negotiated, and agreed on a program supported by the IMF in November 1998, the decision to continue with the Real Plan was fundamentally a decision of the Brazilian authorities. As market pressures intensified in mid-January 1999, the decision to devalue the real and subsequently to let it float was again a decision of the Brazilian authorities, although with knowledge that the IMF and the international community probably would not continue to support an exchange-rate policy that had become unviable.

tial pathways, driven by exogenous economic events, by policy actions of the national authorities, and by the responses of the IMF staff, management, and Executive Board, within the general framework of the Fund's policies governing assistance to members. Those who work on IMF programs, inside the Fund or with the national authorities, generally understand the iterative and open-loop nature of the process.

The process involves two main parties: a country facing external payments problems rooted in macroeconomic and/or structural imbalances, and the IMF with a mandate to offer financial and technical assistance to members that undertake economic adjustment. From the country's side, the process is delimited by the authorities' capacity and willingness to implement the measures needed to resolve their external payments problems. From the IMF's side, the process is governed by policies and procedures that regulate the access to, and uses of, IMF financing—i.e., by IMF conditionality. These policies and procedures have evolved over five and a half decades from a few general guidelines to a more complex body that reflects the major changes in the international monetary system during this period and the effects of those changes on an expanding and more heterogeneous IMF membership—see Polak (1991) and Guitián (1995). Notwithstanding its increased complexity (reflected also in a growing number of facilities tailored to the needs of particular groups of countries), the core process underlying IMF-supported programs has proved to be remarkably resilient in its main features. Indeed, with relatively minor differences across the various types of facilities, that process comprises six broadly defined phases: inception, blueprint, negotiation, approval, monitoring, and completion (Figure 1).

2.1 INCEPTION

IMF programs get underway when the authorities of a member request financial assistance from the IMF. The request need not be written; normally an oral communication from the authorities to IMF staff and/or management suffices. Prior discussions with staff or management sometimes precede a request, but the decision to request support rests with the country's authorities. Indeed, in the regular process of IMF surveillance, staff or management may impress upon the authorities the need to adopt measures to redress actual or potential external or other macroeconomic imbalances, but it is up to the country authorities whether and when to take up that advice (see Mussa, 1997). Often, authorities delay required adjustment, and domestic and external imbalances worsen significantly before a request for assistance from the IMF (see Santaella, 1996, and Knight and Santaella, 1997). As a consequence, IMF programs

Figure 1 PHASES OF IMF PROGRAMS

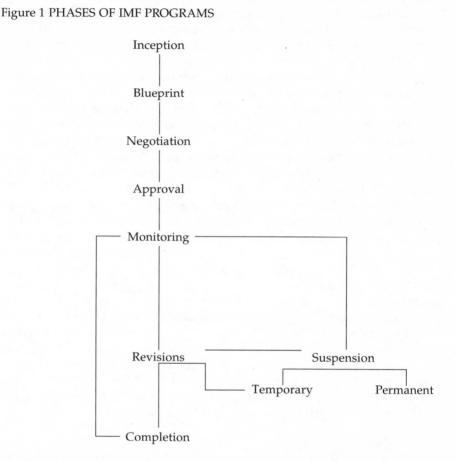

often start with crisis or near-crisis conditions in the balance of payments, necessitating rapid policy responses to normalize external payments and correct underlying macroeconomic imbalances.

2.2 BLUEPRINT

When a request for IMF assistance is made, IMF staff from the area department responsible for relations with the member prepare a blueprint of an adjustment program. The blueprint takes account of key characteristics of the country—e.g., membership in a currency union, size of the public sector, depth and soundness of the financial system, access to international capital markets—features that the IMF staff knows well from its regular surveillance and preprogram discussions with the authorities. The blueprint also contains a preliminary assessment of the proximate and underlying sources of the aggregate imbalances that have caused the deterioration of the country's balance of payments, gauges the size of the external disequilibria, evaluates the authorities' response to the unfolding crisis, and outlines the central elements of an adjustment program that could warrant financial support from the IMF. The staff then makes proposals regarding the type of financial arrangement, the size of the IMF loan, and the time profile of the disbursements that appear compatible with the country's external financing needs (the *access* and *phasing* under the arrangement), and the key policy measures that it would be advisable to have in place before providing any IMF financing (*prior actions*).[4]

A briefing paper summarizing the blueprint and containing a first attempt at gauging its quantitative implications in terms of a simple flow-of-funds accounting framework of key macroeconomic relationships is then prepared and circulated for comments to other (non-area) departments of the IMF. The flow-of-funds framework uses the latest annual estimates for the country's main macroeconomic variables and preliminary projections for at least one year ahead that incorporate the expected effects of the proposed adjustment measures. Consistent with the primary (and often pressing) goal of restoring balance-of-payments viability, the projections emphasize the expected evolution of international reserves, the current account, domestic credit growth, and the public-sector balance during the adjustment period; the rates of inflation and of output growth, the ultimate objectives of all adjustment programs, play a central role in the short-run projection exercise but are not regarded as formal targets of the prospective arrangement. A revised blueprint incorporating comments from departments is then submitted to IMF management for clearance. Management evaluates the blueprint and decides on the prior actions that should be sought from the authorities, as well as on the access and phasing proposals made by the staff.

2.3 NEGOTIATION

After the briefing paper is cleared by management, a mission visits the member to start negotiations (though sometimes negotiations may be held at Fund headquarters or in some other location). Normally, the mission's first task is to revise its estimates of external disequilibrium and of underlying macroeconomic imbalances and assess whether the adjustment effort envisaged in the blueprint remains broadly adequate. Even if revisions are not substantial, which they often are, the mission makes it

4. For a description of the various types of Fund arrangements and facilities and of the terms and conditions of IMF lending (as well as of the peculiar Fund terminology) see International Monetary Fund (1998).

clear to the authorities that negotiations will be conducted *ad referendum*, and that no agreement is final until the program is cleared by IMF management and approved by the IMF's Executive Board. In general, when agreement is reached, it represents a compromise between the blueprint in the staff's briefing paper and the initial negotiating position of the country's authorities.

Negotiations over some key aspects of the program can be contentious, though rarely openly confrontational. Disagreements about goals are not as common as disagreements about the policies necessary to attain those goals. Typically, country authorities tend to advocate less tightening of fiscal and monetary policies and a slower pace of structural reforms than those suggested by the staff, but there are cases where it is the staff who stands for an easing of the policy stance or some rebalancing of the policy mix. When the staff requests that certain actions—e.g., the dismantling of exchange restrictions, the lifting of interest-rate ceilings—be taken before Board approval of the program and disbursement of the first tranche of the IMF loan, the scope for disagreements and dispute tends to increase.

Program negotiations often take place over the course of several missions. If a serious impasse is reached, program discussions are put on hold. Typically, when negotiations resume (and they normally do), the country's situation has worsened markedly, requiring revisions to the staff's blueprint. Once the authorities and the staff reach agreement on the policies needed to underpin the adjustment effort, they negotiate the more technical features of the Fund arrangement. Those features comprise the mode and frequency of monitoring performance under the arrangement (i.e., macroeconomic and structural performance criteria, structural benchmarks, midterm reviews) and the relation between those performance clauses and the provision of IMF financing. Discussion of these features usually involves updates of the basic macroeconomic framework in the IMF staff's blueprint. This iterative procedure, the hallmark of financial programming, enables the staff and the authorities to assess in simple quantitative terms the interactions between the policy measures agreed on and the main targets of the adjustment program.[5] After reaching agreement on numerical values for the main objectives of the program, normally for at least one year ahead, authorities and staff negotiate numerical values for the quarterly path of a small set of macroeconomic variables used to monitor the authorities' adjustment effort. Two such *intermediate variables* on which almost all IMF programs

5. See Robichek (1985) and Polak (1997) for discussions of financial programming as practiced by IMF staff. See also Section 3.

focus are the public-sector deficit and creation of domestic credit by the central bank. Typically, the behavior of those variables during the first 6–12 months of the arrangement become formal performance criteria, while the numerical values for the outer dates are *indicative targets* subject to revision in the program's midterm reviews.

The outcome of the negotiations is summarized in a *letter of intent*. The letter and its attachments spell out the main objectives of the program, the policy actions and reforms that the authorities have taken and intend to take under the arrangement (especially those for the first year), and the modality and frequency of the performance clauses and monitoring techniques agreed on with the staff. The letter of intent signed by the country authorities is their formal request for IMF financing and marks the end of the (initial) negotiation phase.

2.4 APPROVAL

Back at headquarters, the mission team prepares a *staff report* containing an account of discussions with the authorities and of the policy understandings reached with them. The report is accompanied by a detailed macroeconomic framework, which typically includes a full set of projections of the country's fiscal, monetary, and balance-of-payments accounts covering at least the first full year under the IMF arrangement, as well as a medium-term scenario showing the progress toward external viability envisaged over a five-year period. The report also includes an appraisal by the staff of the main risks and uncertainties (of both external and domestic nature) surrounding the proposed adjustment program, and a summary of the technical features of the financial arrangement (i.e., duration, access and phasing of the IMF loan, and the performance clauses ascribed to the various tranches).

The staff report and the letter of intent are then circulated for comment to several non-area departments, which check that the proposed program remains broadly consistent with the blueprint in terms of the adjustment effort, the attainability of the program's primary goals, and the application of IMF conditionality. Departments also offer their views about the risks of the proposed arrangement—views which may not coincide fully with those of the originating area department. A revised draft of the staff report is then submitted to management for clearance. Management makes the final decision on the size and phasing of the IMF loan but generally makes no changes to the projections and other technical features of the arrangement or to the policy understandings agreed by the mission. Increasingly, especially in important cases, management's view and guidance are provided on a continuous basis throughout the negotiating process.

When cleared by management, the staff report and letter of intent are distributed to the IMF Executive Board, and a date is set for Board discussion of the proposed arrangement, with the actual meeting sometimes made contingent on implementation of prior actions by the authorities. Management must recommend approval of all IMF programs as a requirement of consideration by the Executive Board. Although there often are expressions of concern or even occasional abstentions, management's recommendations have invariably been accepted by the IMF Board. However, the views of Executive Directors and of the national authorities they represent have substantial importance. The Board meeting is the occasion when Executive Directors, representing the 182 member countries, *could* reject the proposed program, and that fact provides an incentive for IMF management and staff to take to the Board only programs that they expect will command its support. Board meetings signal the international community's endorsement of the adjustment program. Executive Directors use Board meetings to indicate to IMF management and staff, and to the representatives of the borrowing country, the aspects of the adjustment strategy they consider essential for the attainment of the program's goals—and therefore for the continuation of their support for the arrangement. Through this process the Executive Board exerts, over time, considerable influence on IMF conditionality.

Table 1 reports the number of IMF arrangements approved by the Executive Board in five year intervals, and by type of facility, from 1973 to 1997, as well as the number of countries that received IMF financing during that period, broken down by region. The figures in the table can be interpreted in many ways. However, the sheer fact that in the last twenty-five years the Fund has approved a total of 615 arrangements for 126 (developing) countries that have confronted all types of balance-of-payments difficulties is prima facie evidence that the process leading to the approval of IMF programs possesses enough flexibility to respond to the different and evolving needs of a heterogenous membership. Board approval leads to the release of the first tranche of the IMF loan. What happens thereafter, and in particular what determines the disbursement of remaining tranches of an IMF loan, is decided in the following (fifth) phase of the process.

2.5 MONITORING

Monitoring is the longest and probably most important phase of IMF-supported programs, covering a one- to three-year period when the bulk of the IMF loan is usually scheduled to be disbursed. Monitoring involves much more than periodically checking compliance with the numerical and structural performance criteria and benchmarks of the arrangement;

it entails a *continuous* assessment by the staff of developments in the borrowing country and of their implications for the attainment of the main goals of the program. Monitoring requires keeping track of the timely implementation of the policy measures agreed by the authorities and of the behavior of variables beyond the authorities' control that impinge on the macroeconomic projections on which the arrangement was based.

Monitoring acquires a formal dimension at the so-called *test dates* at which performance criteria need to be met in order for tranches of the IMF loan to be disbursed. Test dates are typically set at quarterly intervals (though recently some Fund arrangements have used monthly test dates) and can be of two types: those where performance is assessed in an essentially backward-looking manner, mainly in terms of numerical performance criteria, and those which, in addition, require the satisfactory completion of a program review that assesses the forward-looking potential for the program to meet its primary objectives. Both monitoring techniques share "the positive function of ensuring a member's access to Fund resources when the conditions are met, and the negative function of interrupting access when the country has failed to meet them" (Polak, 1991, p. 14).

Performance of a country under an IMF-supported program can follow four possible tracks (Figure 1): (1) The country may comply with all performance clauses established at the beginning of the arrangement and with relatively minor updates of the clauses made in program review(s) and hence be eligible to receive all the disbursements from the IMF loan according to the original schedule. (2) The country may be unable to comply with one or more performance clauses at some point during the arrangement, but a waiver of the unmet criterion may be granted or a modification in the program may be rapidly agreed on which allows the arrangement and its disbursements to proceed without interruption. (3) Substantial deviations from performance clauses may lead to a situation where it is not possible to agree rapidly on a modification of the program and on policy actions to bring the program back on (modified) track, thereby prompting the interruption of disbursements from the IMF. In many of these cases, following a new round of negotiations, a revised program can be agreed on and disbursements can be resumed; sometimes, the amounts of disbursements, their phasing, and the length of the arrangement are modified. (4) The country may be unable to comply with one or more performance clauses at some point during the arrangement, and in the ensuing negotiations the staff and the authorities may not reach agreement on a revised program; the arrangement then becomes inoperative and disbursements cease.

Programs that comply fully with all the initial performance clauses are

Table 1 IMF ARRANGEMENTS 1973–1997[a]

	1973–77	1978–82	1983–87	1988–92	1993–97	Total	No. of countries
Number of arrangements approved during the period (cumulative flows)							
Total	85	124	139	126	141	615	126
Standby	82	99	110	75	75	441	
Extended Fund facility	3	25	7	10	18	63	
SAF/ESAF			22	41	48	111	
Number of arrangements, by type of country							
Total	85	124	139	126	141	615	126
Industrial countries	6	2	1			9	5
Developing countries, by region:							
Africa	19	60	84	55	46	264	45
Asia	25	20	16	14	17	92	20
Central and eastern Europe	2	5	3	17	33	60	17
Central Asia and other				1	16	17	8
Middle East and Europe	4	5	3	3	8	23	6
Western hemisphere	29	32	32	36	21	150	25
Amounts committed under arrangements (SDR billion) (cumulative flows)							
Total	9.1	29.5	29.2	35.5	73.4	176.6	
Stand-By	8.3	13.8	18.8	15.8	53.9	111.1	
Extended Fund facility	0.8	15.7	9.2	15.4	13.2	54.2	
SAF/ESAF			1.2	4.3	6.3	11.8	

Countries with nine or more Fund arrangements approved between 1973 and 1997, by region

Country	No. of programs		No. of programs
Africa:		Asia:	
Kenya	12	Pakistan	13
Senegal	12	Philippines	12
Madagascar	11	Korea	9
Congo, Dem. Rep. of	10		
Mauritania	10	Western Hemisphere:	
Togo	10	Panama	13
Liberia	9	Haiti	12
Malawi	9	Jamaica	12
Morocco	9	Uruguay	12
Uganda	9	Costa Rica	10
Zambia	9	Guyana	10
		Argentina	9

Source: IMF, *Transactions of the Fund* (1998).

ªIncludes standby arrangements, EFF arrangements, and arrangements under the SAF and ESAF. Excludes STF arrangements and drawings under the first credit tranche and the CCFF.

not the norm. The majority of IMF arrangements follow one of the three other tracks. This is not surprising, when one considers the assumptions about the behavior of external and domestic variables and about the timeliness of policy implementation that need to be made when setting numerical values for the intermediate variables chosen as performance criteria and agreeing on the pace of structural reforms. Indeed, recognizing the need to give Fund arrangements sufficient flexibility to withstand departures from their initial assumptions, IMF conditionality became gradually equipped with a number of technical provisions—e.g., adjustors, waivers, rephasing, modifications, extensions—that facilitated making midcourse revisions to the arrangements approved by the Executive Board (see Polak, 1991, and International Monetary Fund, 1998).

Typically, revisions of IMF programs are triggered by the authorities' (actual or imminent) failure to comply with one or more performance clauses. When large deviations are detected or foreseen, a mission travels to the borrowing country to negotiate possible revisions to the arrangement, based on an updated blueprint that outlines the conditions that would justify maintaining or resuming lending from the IMF. Key issues are whether deviations were caused primarily by slippages in the implementation of agreed policies or by factors beyond the authorities' control, and what remedial policy measures are needed to correct the situation. If the staff and the authorities agree on a revised program, the staff (with management approval) presents a report to the Executive Board indicating the revisions to the arrangement. The country becomes eligible to resume access to the IMF loan immediately after the Board's approval of the report. If the staff and the authorities are unable to reach agreement, however, disbursements from the IMF loan remain suspended and the arrangement stays permanently off track, until it expires.

The data in Table 2 show that more than a third of all Fund arrangements approved between 1973 and 1997 ended with disbursements of less than half of the initially agreed support. In a few of these cases, the program was so successful (or conditions improved so rapidly) that the member needed to use only a fraction of the committed IMF financing. Mainly, however, these were cases where the program went off track because policies deviated significantly from those agreed with the IMF and subsequent negotiations failed to reach agreement on a modified program. Cases where 50 to 75% of the initially agreed support was disbursed (17.6% of all IMF arrangements) are more of a mixed bag: some highly successful, some canceled programs that were followed rapidly by new arrangements, and some that went permanently off track. Cases where 75% or more of the IMF loan was disbursed (45.5% of all arrangements) are generally those where the authorities adhered

Table 2 FRACTION OF IMF LOAN ACTUALLY DISBURSED UNDER EACH ARRANGEMENT, DISTRIBUTION BY QUARTILES

(x=fraction of total IMF loan disbursed under each arrangement)[a]

| | Percent of Total Arrangements | | | | | |
	$x<0.25$	$0.25≤x<0.50$	$0.50≤x<0.75$	$0.75≤x<1.0$	Fully disbursed ($x=1.0$)	Number of arrangements
All arrangements[b]						
1973–1977	36.5	7.1	5.9	5.9	44.7	85
1978–1982	19.4	16.1	10.5	12.9	41.1	124
1983–1987	12.9	15.8	19.4	7.9	43.9	139
1988–1992	17.5	15.1	20.6	14.3	32.5	126
1993–1997[c]	27.0	19.1	26.2	11.3	16.3	141
Full period (1973–1997)[c]	21.6	15.3	17.6	10.7	34.8	615
of which:						
Stand by[c]	23.1	13.4	15.0	9.5	39.0	441
EFF[c]	33.3	22.2	19.0	15.9	9.5	63
SAF/ESAF[c]	9.0	18.9	27.0	12.6	32.4	111

Source: IMF, Transactions of the Fund (1998).
[a] Calculated as the ratio of the total purchases made to the full amount of IMF resources committed under each arrangement.
[b] Includes standby arrangements, EFF arrangements, and arrangements under the SAF and ESAF. Exludes STF arrangements, and drawings under the first credit tranche and the CCFF.
[c] The distribution of the ratio x for the 1993–1997 period is biased (downward) by the inclusion of arrangements with expiration date posterior to 1997. The bias is also present in the distributions reported for the full period (1973–1997).

more closely to the policies they agreed to over the course of the arrangement. Even among these cases, however, rare were the instances where every performance criterion and numerical objective of the program was met as originally envisaged. The "success" of IMF programs in these cases signifies that it was possible to sustain an adjustment effort acceptable to both the countries' authorities and the IMF during the program period, not that programs attained the numerical targets of the original arrangement.

2.6 COMPLETION

Formally, IMF programs are completed when the borrowing country becomes eligible for the last tranche from the IMF loan. Because of revisions during the course of the program, that date may be later than the original expiration date of the arrangement and the disbursement may add to a total that can be higher or lower than the amount contemplated in the original arrangement. Table 3 provides a general indication of the relative frequency of these outcomes. For the total of all 615 Fund arrangements, 73 were extended beyond their original durations. By and large, these were cases where substantial progress was made toward the main program objectives but more time was allowed for the adjustment effort. The 70 arrangements that were canceled early but were followed promptly by a successor arrangement are most likely cases where weak policy implementation or large unforeseen shocks rendered unattainable the original program objectives, but where it was possible to reach understandings fairly rapidly on a new adjustment blueprint. The 44 arrangements that were canceled before their expiration date and were not soon followed by a new arrangement, represent mainly a subset of the programs that went permanently off track during the monitoring phase.

Completion of an IMF arrangement does not usually imply that the numerical targets for the main economic objectives of the country's program originally approved by the Executive Board were met. Completion does not even ensure that the country met the revised numerical targets agreed on at the last program review. Completion of an IMF-supported program does imply that, in the IMF's view, the country made substantial and satisfactory progress toward the primary objectives of its adjustment program (especially toward external viability), and that the policies of the authorities were broadly in line with the (often revised) understandings reached with the IMF during the life of the arrangement.

The relationship between the IMF and the borrowing country following completion of a Fund arrangement generally depends on the progress in eliminating the macroeconomic and structural imbalances that gave rise to the expiring IMF program and on the external environment

Table 3 DURATION OF IMF ARRANGEMENTS

	Number of arrangements	Original duration (average, in months)	Program extensions		Early cancellations		
			Number of extensions	Extension length (average, in months)	Number of early cancellations	Length of cancelled segment (average, in months)	o.w.: followed by successor arrangement (no. of arrangements)[a]
By type of arrangement (1973–1997):							
Standby	441	13.8	33	5.3	63	2.2	43
Extended Fund facility	63	29.3	7	16.2	28	9.7	16
SAF	38	30.7	2	9.3	10	9.9	10
ESAF	73	40.0	31	6.5	13	5.2	1
Total	615		73		114		70
By subperiod (all arrangements):							
1973–77	85	12.4	—	—	7	3.9	7
1978–82	124	15.2	—	—	36	1.0	26
1983–87	139	17.8	10	1.0	28	1.9	13
1988–92	126	24.7	38	13.2	14	8.1	13
1993–97	141	24.6	25	9.7	29	0.8	11

Source: IMF, Transactions of the Fund (1998).
[a]Successor arrangement approved up to one month following the cancellation of a prior arrangement.

at the time of completion. When progress has been substantial and the external environment is not seen as a threat, monitoring of the country's performance usually reverts to the preprogram mode—i.e., to IMF surveillance. When conditions are less favorable the country authorities may request a successor arrangement to help consolidate the (partial) gains from the previous program. Because of the recurrent nature of the shocks affecting many members and the gravity of their structural imbalances, such requests are not uncommon (see Table 1, lower panel). Typically, a successor arrangement will have a medium-term orientation and a goal of deepening structural reforms initiated during the previous program. The authorities' request for a successor arrangement sets in motion a multistaged process very similar to that followed in their prior request for IMF support.

3. The Economics of IMF-Supported Programs

3.1 CORE COMPONENTS

Despite differences imparted to IMF programs by country-specific characteristics, blueprints of adjustment prepared by Fund staff contain important common elements. These elements are closely linked to the IMF mandate established in the Articles of Agreement, and range from eligibility criteria for securing access to IMF resources—i.e., a situation of actual or potential balance-of-payments need—to priority in the programs for orderly restoration of external viability (see Guitián, 1995). In their practical application over time, these common elements have produced a three-pronged approach for confronting external payments problems: (1) securing sustainable external financing; (2) adoption of demand-restraining measures—especially in the early stages of a program; and (3) implementation of structural reforms (see Schadler et al., 1995). The relative importance of those components depends crucially on the specific circumstances of the member country. The blueprint for a country whose international reserves are depleted as a result of unsustainable fiscal imbalances will place considerably more (initial) emphasis on demand-restraining measures than that for a country whose balance of payments was adversely affected by external shocks. Likewise, the blueprints for countries with less pressing balance-of-payments problems often place more emphasis on structural measures aimed at hastening the pace of output growth.

Care should be taken, however, not to exaggerate the degree of substitutability among the three core components of the approach. In the midst of an external payments crisis the scope for, say, relying more heavily on additional external financing than on restraint of aggregate demand, or for further delaying structural reforms likely to have a bearing on the success of the stabilization program, is usually quite limited. Hence, it is often more appropriate to regard the three components of the general IMF approach to economic stabilization as complements, especially in the early stages of a program. As noted, once the crisis has been contained and confidence restored, external financing constraints often become less pressing and the macroeconomic policy stance can become more supportive of domestic demand and of structural reforms. It should be stressed, however, that the role of the IMF is to contribute to design the adjustment strategy, help the country secure external financing, and monitor the progress in overcoming the external crisis, but that it is up to the country's authorities to implement in a timely and credible manner the policy measures contemplated in the strategy.

The availability of external financing, the first component of the strategy, determines the magnitude and pace of the necessary adjustment effort. The amount and terms of the new foreign borrowing obtainable by a country experiencing balance-of-payments problems are largely predetermined—and typically scarce and onerous—at the outset of a program. Hence, in practice, there is little scope for treating the prospective external financing from official and private lenders as a "slack variable" when preparing the blueprint of the adjustment program, as has been suggested by some IMF critics (e.g., Killick, 1995, and Harrigan, 1996). Financial support from the Fund, of course, can help reduce the country's financing gap for a limited period. However, limits on the Fund's resources—limits which the membership establishes as reasonable and prudent in view of the IMF's mandate and which place upper bounds on IMF support to individual countries[6]—significantly constrain the extent to which the Fund can substitute for other sources of financing. Indeed, in the large financial support packages arranged for Mexico in 1995 and for Thailand, Indonesia, and Korea in 1997, the IMF provided less than half the announced funding, with the rest being promised by the World Bank, the regional development banks, and bilateral sources. And notwithstanding these exceptionally large packages, the four countries nonetheless had to make large and rapid adjustments to meet the pressures of their external financing constraint.

Precisely because the external financing constraint is often severe, Fund-supported programs aim at restoring the country's access to a sustainable flow of foreign financing as rapidly as possible. Gauging that sustainable flow, as well as the time it may take to secure it, is a

6. For a discussion of the access limits applicable to the various IMF facilities and of the criteria regulating access by individual member countries see International Monetary Fund (1998).

matter of judgement. General conditions in international financial markets and those specific to the program country (the level, composition, and maturity of its external liabilities, its debt service profile, and its access to private capital markets) play an important role. Of necessity, however, the estimates of net external financing incorporated in the (initial) adjustment program are tentative, are subject to considerable uncertainty, and undergo significant revisions over the course of an arrangement. That uncertainty is much higher in countries where the lion's share of foreign borrowing is undertaken by the private sector (including private banks), a situation that has become increasingly common in the 1990s.

The main guidelines of the approach followed by IMF staff when gauging the prospective external financing date back several decades, but have been applied more systematically and uniformly since the debt crisis of the 1980s (see Finch, 1989). Those guidelines require that the country not show an ex ante external financing gap, that it remain current in its debt service commitments, and (with some exceptions in special circumstances) that it eliminate external debt arrears it may have accumulated prior to the program approval. In practice, the guidelines require the staff to produce "reasonable" estimates of net financing flows from official and private sources, and to assume a coordinating role with the country's creditors in various fora—i.e., the Paris Club, the London Club, and special consultative groups of donors. This "concerted lending approach"—which required several modifications to the Fund's guidelines on foreign borrowing, notably the policy of *financing assurances*[7]—proved instrumental in dealing with the debt crisis of the 1980s, and continues to be useful for countries with limited access to private capital markets. However, the concerted approach has proved less useful for dealing with the complex external debt problems posed by a more diversified set of lenders and borrowers in countries with relatively unrestricted access to global capital markets—for example, for producing "reasonable" forecasts of redemption rates of domestic bonds and equities or of rollover rates of foreign credit lines to private-sector borrowers. Recent experience with these problems has generated calls for more effective ways of involving the private sector in forestalling and ameliorating financial crises, but no comprehensive solution, such as a world bankruptcy court, seems likely in the near future.

7. The policy of financing assurances reduced the Fund programs' reliance on judgmental estimates of voluntary financing from foreign creditors—which often failed to materialize—and made the securing of a critical mass of commitments of external assistance from the country's creditors a prerequisite for an IMF arrangement (see Polak, 1991, and Guitián, 1995).

Demand-restraining measures, the second component of the approach, comprise the macroeconomic policies that seek to restore and preserve viable equilibrium between aggregate expenditure and aggregate income in the program country. These measures are probably the best-known ingredient of IMF-supported programs, and are typically regarded as the cornerstone of the "traditional IMF package."[8] The measures normally contemplate a tightening of fiscal and monetary policies by an amount deemed necessary to bring aggregate demand in line with the staff's estimates of prospective output and available external financing and, hence, with a sustainable current account. Sometimes, though not as often as is commonly thought, the measures also contemplate changes in the (level or rate of crawl of the) nominal exchange rate as a means to facilitate external adjustment.

Conceptually, ascribing to fiscal and monetary policies the key task of restoring and preserving viable external balance can be readily understood in terms of a large class of theoretical models based on, or consistent with, the *absorption approach*—e.g., the dependent-economy model, the Mundell–Fleming model, and the monetary approach to the balance of payments.[9] In this regard, the macroeconomic policies normally recommended by the IMF are not significantly different from what most economists would recommend to countries experiencing severe balance-of-payments problems, allowing for differences over the specific advice in particular situations.[10] This is especially so when a large fiscal imbalance and/or excessively rapid credit expansion are at the heart of a country's balance-of-payments difficulties, and when a large exchange-rate devaluation or the adoption of an unfettered floating-rate regime are not seen as desirable means for adjusting the external payments position. In contrast, as in the recent Asian crisis, when an unsustainable fiscal position is not the main underlying problem, but a loss of confidence combined with domestic financial weaknesses induces sudden reversals of

8. This characterization can be found in numerous studies and accounts of IMF programs. See, for example, Edwards (1989), Killick (1995), and Feldstein (1998).

9. The absorption approach is discussed in (almost) every textbook of international economics. The interested reader is referred to the seminal article by Alexander (1952) and to the insightful (and complementary) presentations of the approach in Kenen (1985), International Monetary Fund (1987), Buiter (1990), and Cooper (1992).

10. In this connection, the well-known (and often cited) conclusion reached by Richard Cooper at a 1982 conference on IMF conditionality, namely, that any five people chosen randomly from the diverse group of participants at the conference would, if confronted with an external crisis from a position of authority, produce an adjustment program "that would not differ greatly from a typical IMF program," seems as pertinent and valid today as it was then (see Williamson, 1983). The assessment of the Fund's macroeconomic advice in a recent survey article by Anne Krueger (Krueger, 1998), seems to support this conjecture.

capital flows and domestic capital flight, leading to a *currency crash*, the macroeconomic policy emphasis should not be on tighter fiscal policy but on a temporary tightening of monetary policy. Although controversial, a monetary tightening in those circumstances would help resist massive currency depreciations that themselves tend to crush the domestic economy and induce a huge turnaround in the current account.

The third component of the general framework in the design of IMF-supported programs is the understandings on structural reforms. These comprise all types of policies aimed at reducing government-imposed distortions and other structural and institutional rigidities that impair an efficient allocation of resources in the economy and hinder growth. The reforms cover a wide spectrum of activities beyond the domain of macroeconomic policy, including measures related to trade liberalization, price liberalization, foreign exchange market reform, tax reform, government spending reform, privatization, pension reform, financial-sector reform, banking system restructuring, labor-market reform, and the strengthening of social safety nets.[11] Moreover, in many cases, and increasingly so in recent years, Fund arrangements are designed in close coordination with programs of the World Bank and/or the regional development banks.[12] As a result, the conditionality on structural aspects of IMF-supported programs often relates to issues that are under the more direct purview of other international financial institutions, but are included in the Fund arrangement to give a comprehensive picture of the reform effort.

Of course, the specific structural reform content in any arrangement depends on the characteristics and circumstances of the country requesting IMF support. One reason for this is the wide differences in levels of income and stage of development among member countries. For example, in the Asian crisis, the structural reform content of Fund-supported programs focused particularly on the financial sector because this was a critical problem area (Lane et al., 1999); in the arrangements for transition economies, privatization and the building of basic institutions of a market economy were key structural priorities (de Melo et al., 1996); and arrangements under the ESAF normally attach structural conditionality on a number of areas where distortions are particularly damaging (International Monetary Fund, 1997). Growing emphasis on structural issues

11. For general discussions of the rationale for structural reforms see International Monetary Fund (1987), Williamson (1990), and Krueger (1993). For an overview of the record on structural reforms in recent Fund arrangements see Schadler et al. (1995) and International Monetary Fund (1997).
12. This happens not only for arrangements under the ESAF (the Fund's concessional facility for low-income countries), where such coordination is formally required, but for other Fund arrangements as well.

in IMF-supported programs also reflects the (not so linear) evolution of the profession's views about the prerequisites for a well-functioning market economy.[13] Moreover, structural reforms differ from the other core components of IMF programs in the difficulties for monitoring progress in implementation, in their long gestation periods, and in their particularly strong political-economy ramifications. The confluence of these factors has resulted in a gradual but steady rise in the structural-reform content of IMF programs, a trend that has sparked strong, but often disparate, criticisms from many quarters.[14]

3.2 CRITICISMS OF THE IMF APPROACH

There is no shortage of criticisms of the basic IMF approach, some many years old, others relatively new. Some focus on one of the core components of the approach, others take issue with all of them. Not surprisingly, the number, diversity, and intensity of the criticisms increase when the international financial system faces a crisis, as with the breakdown of the Bretton Woods system, the debt crisis of the 1980s, the collapse of the centrally planned economies of Eastern Europe and the (former) Soviet Union, and, most recently, the financial crises in Mexico and Asia.

A driving force behind most criticisms of the IMF approach is the *visible disjunction* between its three core elements and what virtually everyone sees as the desirable objectives of economic policy. As noted before, those objectives normally include a high rate of growth and a low rate of inflation, alleviating poverty and avoiding social unrest, and ensuring an adequate supply of public goods. These broad objectives are relevant for program design (in terms of what should be achieved in the medium and long term), and so is the goal of minimizing damage to the international community from a balance-of-payments adjustment in any given country. But it cannot reasonably be argued that the immediate effect of IMF-supported programs is (or should be) always positive in all the desirable dimensions of economic policy and performance. Economic adjustment and reform are costly and difficult endeavors, and especially so in the crisis or near-crisis conditions in which member countries normally come to the Fund to request support (see Santaella, 1996). In those circumstances, there will generally be no quick and easy

13. Compare, for instance, the structural reform policies discussed in International Monetary Fund (1987) and Williamson (1990) with those stressed by Williamson (1994) and Burki and Perry (1998).
14. Polak (1991) and Killick (1995) document the increase in the structural-reform content of IMF programs; see also Schadler et al. (1995), International Monetary Fund (1997), and Lane et al. (1999).

solutions that will make everyone everywhere feel a lot better both immediately and forever after.

A (slight) variation of this general criticism is the view that the *macro-economics* underlying the IMF approach to stabilization is fundamentally wrong. This is the position taken, often without much analysis, by many critics of the Fund in several nongovernmental organizations and in the popular press. Some academics, such as Lance Taylor and other neostructuralists (Taylor, 1988, 1993), also advance this criticism. In response, one should stress that any country experiencing severe balance-of-payments difficulties and a shortage of external financing must, eventually, confront and redress its aggregate imbalances. This in turn generally requires a contraction of domestic spending, usually facilitated by a tightening of fiscal and monetary policies; in addition, when external disequilibria are large, a real depreciation of the currency may be needed. The analytical and empirical support for these basic facts of economic adjustment is overwhelming. To be sure, there are serious issues concerning whether, in specific cases, the policies recommended by IMF staff are the most appropriate, taking account of all of the relevant circumstances and constraints; these issues deserve to be debated, and it should not be expected that the professional consensus will always be that the Fund got it exactly right. But it is simply wishful thinking to believe that there *generally* is some better and easier way to secure, or avoid, macroeconomic adjustment in the midst of an external payments crisis.

Another common criticism stems from the belief that IMF-supported programs not only contain the same *type* of policy recommendations, but that they actually contemplate an adjustment of (approximately) the same *size* for all countries. This perception is surprisingly widespread, even among academics, but is also absolutely false. As noted before, every cross-country analysis of the experience with IMF-supported programs, conducted either by IMF staff or by outsiders, shows unequivocally that the size of the adjustment in those programs—as measured by the projected decline in the fiscal deficit, the projected improvement in the external current account, or the projected fall in the rate of inflation—varies considerably across programs and is, by and large, a monotonic function of the size of the (preexisting or prospective) imbalances.[15] For example, in several of the debt-crisis countries of the 1980s, massive and unsustainable fiscal deficits were major problems and lay at the heart of balance-of-payments difficulties and chronic inflation; objec-

15. For evidence on this point see the references cited in footnote 1; see also Lane et al., 1999.

tives for fiscal consolidation in Fund-supported programs, correspondingly, had to be very ambitious. This was much less so for the programs with Mexico and Argentina in the tequila crisis and for those with Indonesia and Korea in the Asian crisis, but was again a more critical issue in recent arrangements with Russia and Brazil.

Other criticisms take issue with the *structural-reform* component of Fund-supported programs. Here, the focus has shifted over time; whereas the debates in the 1980s revolved around IMF conditionality in trade reform, exchange-rate unification, and interest-rate liberalization, those of the 1990s have dealt mostly with privatization, pension reform, and, most recently, capital-account convertibility and banking-sector reform. There are, however, common themes to the criticisms. Prominent are those related to the "ownership" of the reforms; the horizon, sequence, and pace of their implementation (especially as they are seen as conflicting with the relatively short duration of Fund arrangements); and the lack of expertise, and mandate, of Fund staff to impart advice and design conditionality on structural issues.[16] We believe that it is pertinent to highlight two facts often forgotten in discussions of these issues: First, the inclusion of structural reforms in Fund-supported programs was largely a response to requests from the IMF membership for a broadening of the scope (and duration) of Fund arrangements to make them more suitable for tackling structural impediments to sustained growth and external viability (see International Monetary Fund, 1987, and Polak, 1991). Second, Fund condionality typically takes account of the difficulties and delays inherent in a process of structural adjustment, most notably by monitoring "progress" in these areas, mostly through periodical assessments of the authorities' willingness and (oftentimes constrained) capacity to comply with specific measures, rather than in terms of the realization of the benefits expected from full implementation of the reforms.

Yet another strand of criticisms questions whether the *intellectual doctrine* underlying Fund-supported programs is sufficiently responsive to changing conditions in the global economy and the evolution of professional thinking. Specifically, in dealing with the collapse of the centrally planned economies of Eastern Europe and the (former) Soviet Union, and with the financial crises of Mexico in 1995 and Thailand, Indonesia, and Korea in 1997–1998, many critics argued that the "traditional IMF approach" was ill suited for the (widely different) challenges posed by these

16. Recent studies by Killick (1995), Calomiris (1998), Feldstein (1998), and James (1998) discuss these themes in some length. For earlier criticisms see Group of Twenty-Four (1987), Dornbusch (1991), and Cooper (1992).

fundamentally new types of problems.[17] That the IMF approach to these recent problems was in fact quite different from earlier IMF-supported programs seems to have escaped notice. For example, the Fund arrangements for Mexico during the debt crisis of the 1980s consisted mostly of sizable fiscal adjustments, modest official financing, and concerted roll-over of commercial bank credits, whereas the 1995–1996 standby arrangement involved modest fiscal adjustment and very large official financing.

The controversy about the recent Fund arrangements for Thailand, Indonesia, and Korea is a prime example of the accusation that IMF programs are based on a misguided and dogmatic approach to macroeconomic stabilization. Interestingly, given other differences among the critics, a sort of consensus emerged that the fiscal and monetary policies recommended—or, as some critics prefer to say, imposed—by the Fund in those countries was "too tight." For fiscal policy, as documented in the study by Lane et al. (1999) and in the IMF's *World Economic Outlook* of December 1997 and May 1998, the adjustment called for in the initial programs was fairly small for Indonesia and Korea, and was moderate, by Fund standards, for Thailand. The economic assumptions for these initial programs—which the authorities were reluctant to see downgraded—envisioned slower but still significantly positive growth for all three countries in both 1997 and 1998 and contemplated only moderate exchange-rate depreciations. Under these assumptions, the initial fiscal policy prescriptions were reasonable and were accepted as such by the authorities. For Thailand, which entered the crisis with a current account deficit of 8% of GDP (much larger than the current-account imbalances of Indonesia or Korea), a larger fiscal effort seemed appropriate. As it became clear, to the Fund and everyone else, that the crises would be much deeper than originally expected, programs were revised and prescriptions for fiscal policy shifted from small or moderate restraint to significant stimulus, including the provision of social safety nets. This shift did not involve a change in Fund dogma, but rather a normal application of the flexibility to respond to unforeseen events embedded in the process described in Section 2.

---

17. Developments in the Asian and subsequent emerging market crises of 1997–1998 have given rise to a broad debate about reforming the "architecture" of the international monetary and financial system; see Eichengreen (1999) for an excellent overview of the issues. See also Minton-Beddoes (1995), Calomiris (1998), Krueger (1998), and Folkerts-Landau and Garber (1999). Although most of the issues in this debate do not directly concern the subject matter of this paper—the Fund's approach to economic stabilization—it is interesting that many of the reform proposals that do touch on this subject run counter to many criticisms of Fund conditionality. In particular, suggestions for reform generally push for less financing from the Fund and/or stricter conditionality for members accessing Fund resources.

In the case of monetary policy, the IMF advice at the outset of those programs stressed the need for a significant initial and temporary tightening to arrest excessive exchange-rate depreciations that threatened both an acceleration of domestic inflation and the spread of contagion to other countries. Some prominent economists have argued that the weak financial systems and faltering domestic demand in those economies called for an easing rather than a tightening of monetary policy; some have even suggested that an easier monetary policy would have led to a nominal appreciation of those currencies. Clearly there are circumstances where the tightening of monetary policy to resist some (perhaps significant) exchange-rate depreciation is not desirable, for example, after the United Kingdom exited from the Exchange Rate Mechanism in September 1992 or for Singapore and China in 1997–1998. Also, even when monetary tightening is appropriate to resist massive and unwarranted exchange-rate depreciations, the "right" degree and duration of monetary tightening is a difficult issue of judgement. Nevertheless, when a currency suddenly loses half its value amidst massive capital outflows and collapsing confidence, as was the case for Indonesia, Korea, and Thailand, monetary easing is not a sensible policy, and some significant temporary tightening is generally warranted. The ill effects of high interest rates on a weak economy and a fragile financial system must be weighed against the probable consequences of a large depreciation on the burden of foreign-currency indebtedness and on the unleashing of inflationary pressures.

In fact, in Thailand and Korea, where the IMF advice on monetary policy was followed after some initial hesitation, exchange rates were stabilized and subsequently recovered to more reasonable levels, and nominal interest rates were then progressively reduced to below pre-crisis levels. There was nothing bizarre in these cases suggesting a perverse relationship between monetary policy and the exchange rate; the behavior observed followed the pattern seen in earlier episodes of severe exchange-rate pressures, such as Mexico in 1995 or the Czech Republic in 1997 (see Lane et al., 1999, Chapter 6). In Indonesia, monetary policy was tightened only briefly before massive injections of liquidity to banks facing deposit runs, along with policy switches, political uncertainty, and social unrest, led to a massive 80% depreciation of the rupiah and to widespread default on private-sector debts. Again, the pattern was what one would expect from the large body of empirical evidence on the relation between monetary policy and the exchange rate. All things considered, the notion that in the context of the Asian crisis easings of monetary policy would have induced exchange-rate appreciations is nonsense.

3.3 WHY FUND PROGRAMS TEND TO LOOK ALIKE

Although many criticisms of the Fund lack a firm basis, there remains the impression that the IMF approach to economic stabilization is too rigid and dogmatic to accommodate the differing and changing circumstances of member countries that encounter balance-of-payments difficulties. This impression is not entirely without foundation. The IMF is a highly disciplined bureaucracy that operates in accord with well-established, and only gradually evolving, policies and procedures. Key IMF staff involved in program operations typically have long tenure in the Fund. There is a legal framework for IMF operations, based on the Articles of Agreement and established policies of the Executive Board, which imposes constraints on what is and what is not acceptable in Fund arrangements. All of this imparts a degree of conservatism to the IMF approach which is both bad and good. Bad because it implies a lesser degree of flexibility in Fund conditionality than would be desirable in some ideal world. Good because IMF members that may wish to make use of the Fund's resources or members who may be called upon to supply those resources have expressed a desire to have a reasonable understanding of the circumstances, conditions, and terms under which IMF financing may be made available. There must be reasonable assurance of equality of treatment; members encountering similar balance-of-payments problems and willing to undertake similar adjustment measures should have similar access to Fund resources. The IMF cannot act with unbridled discretion. As with any powerful institution, there is an unavoidable tension between giving to (and asking from) the IMF too much or too little flexibility.

The general impression of inflexibility in the Fund's actions, policies, and doctrine, however, is seriously exaggerated, in part because of the way in which the IMF has described its own activities. When Fund arrangements are announced (or leaked) to the public, they appear to present a rigid blueprint for a country's economic policies and for their expected results, including numerical performance criteria for key macroeconomic aggregates. All arrangements contain numerical targets for output growth, the inflation rate, and the current account for one to three years ahead; and all contain quantitative performance criteria for fiscal and monetary policy variables, usually for quarterly test dates covering the first six to twelve months of the arrangement.[18] The natural, but incorrect, perception for many outsiders is that if the quantitative

---

18. Interestingly, numerical performance criteria were not always a component of Fund arrangements, and their general adoption in the 1960s was in large part a response to the *borrowing countries'* demand for more predictability in the access to the (phased) IMF resources allocated in support of their adjustment programs—see Finch (1989).

criteria are met, the program is on track and disbursements of IMF resources continue, whereas if the criteria are not met, the program is off track and disbursements cease. The flexible process described in Section 2, with the possibility of waivers or modifications of performance criteria or of revisions and renegotiations of the adjustment blueprint to strengthen policy actions and minimize the interruptions to the flow of Fund disbursements, is not normally presented or perceived as an integral part of IMF arrangements—even though the member and the Fund fully understand these possibilities.

The impression of unreasonable uniformity in the macroeconomic conditionality of Fund-supported programs is reinforced by the apparent similarity in the numerical performance criteria in the critical areas of fiscal and monetary policy. Specifically, the main fiscal performance criterion in Fund arrangements is normally specified as (quarterly) ceilings on the nominal value of the fiscal deficit or on the portion of that deficit financed with domestic credit.[19] For monetary policy, performance criteria are typically specified as (quarterly) ceilings on the expansion of net domestic credit of the central bank and as (quarterly) floors on net international reserves (see Guitián, 1994).

On the substance of these performance criteria, it is straightforward to see why an upper limit on the fiscal deficit (or on credit to finance it) should generally be an element of IMF conditionality. For a country facing balance-of-payments difficulties, external credit to the government (as well as to the private sector) is usually tightly constrained. Resort to domestic credit to finance the government also has limits, particularly when credit conditions are tight and when additional monetary financing to the public sector (from the central bank or the banking system) may unleash inflationary pressures. Furthermore, in many cases a tightened fiscal stance is important, even central, to assist in redressing imbalances in the external current account. Of course, the degree of fiscal tightening should and does vary greatly across individual cases, depending not just on the size of the initial fiscal disequilibrium but also on the (expected) availability of sustainable and noninflationary means of deficit financing. Mistakes in setting fiscal targets will be made in individual cases, especially when the key assumptions on which a program is based are falsified by actual developments. But this cannot reasonably be an argument that Fund arrangements should refrain from an explicit requirement for fiscal restraint, especially considering that the arrangements place more emphasis on the adoption of policy measures that appear necessary to redress the existing fiscal imbalance than on

19. The rationale for this specification is explained in Tanzi (1987) and Guitián (1995).

attaining a given deficit target. By and large, if the measures adopted are judged appropriate but the bottom line is missed for reasons beyond the authorities' control, compliance with fiscal conditionality is often granted, provided that performance in other areas remains satisfactory.

While the rationale for fiscal conditionality may be recognized, greater controversy surrounds monetary-policy conditionality, especially the standard procedure of specifying quarterly quantitative targets on domestic credit and on the stock of net international reserves. The conceptual basis for this procedure is perceived to be deeply rooted in the monetary approach to the balance of payments, a theory of the adjustment process in an open economy that IMF staff contributed to developing.[20] Much criticism of IMF prescriptions for monetary policy in program countries has centered on the theoretical underpinnings and empirical validity of the monetary approach to the balance of payments and, in particular, of the "Polak model." Specifically, critics have emphasized the large body of evidence that documents the pervasive instability of money demand and the poor performance of operational frameworks for monetary policy that depends on targeting of monetary aggregates, especially over the short horizons used for setting performance criteria in Fund arrangements.[21] Notwithstanding these criticisms, the specification of monetary policy in IMF-supported programs has remained essentially unaltered. Until recently, the few justifications for this resilience that were given by Fund staff consisted either of highlighting the "encompassing character" of the monetary approach[22] or of restating the "strong association that is known to exist between an excess of domestic credit and an excess of aggregate spending over aggregate income." With some basis, those arguments were regarded by critics as symptoms of denial and dogmatism.[23] Nonetheless, when account is taken both of

20. The studies by Polak (1957) and Prais (1961) are widely regarded as modern precursors of the monetary approach, a theory that was further formalized and brought to the forefront of the academic debate by a group of economists from the University of Chicago in the 1970s. See Frenkel and Johnson (1976); see also International Monetary Fund (1977).
21. For these and other critiques to the (alleged) reliance of Fund programs on the monetary approach to the balance of payments see Dell (1982), Taylor (1988), Edwards (1989), Dornbusch (1991), Jager (1994), and Killick (1995).
22. For example, when discussing the design of monetary policy in Fund-supported programs, International Monetary Fund (1987) states that "[the monetary] approach can be considered a relatively general theory of long-run behavior that encompasses a variety of models of short-term adjustment. The fundamental equation . . . is thus an outcome of an adjustment process, not a description of the channels through which the policy variables affect changes in net foreign assets" (p. 18).
23. Two articles by Manuel Guitián, former director of the Monetary and Exchange Affairs department and distinguished IMF official, illustrate this point. There is in fact no substantive change in the theoretical justification he provides for focusing on domestic

the economic situation with which Fund arrangements are typically designed to deal and of the institutional process associated with those arrangements, there is a rationale for setting numerical performance criteria in terms of floors on net international reserves and ceilings on net domestic credit.

The primary rationale for setting a performance criterion for the floor on net international reserves actually has little to do with monetary policy, or especially with the monetary approach to the balance of payments. When a member requests a program, it usually has run down its international reserves and is anticipating continued downward pressures. Even if the exchange rate has been devalued or allowed to float, further substantial declines in reserves are usually undesirable. The policies associated with IMF arrangements are supposed to address this problem by reducing the external payments imbalance and helping to restore confidence; and the financial support of the IMF provides a desired supplement to the member's (gross) international reserves. Fund-supported programs, however, do not always make rapid progress towards their agreed objectives, and oftentimes this reflects (at least partly) the failure of the member to tighten its macroeconomic policies with sufficient resolve. In such situations, if substantial reserve losses continue, there is a clear signal that the adjustment program is not working as intended in an area of critical importance to the IMF. A performance criterion that sets a floor on net international reserves hence assures that when those reserves fall below an agreed threshold, a reconsideration of the program is triggered, with the range of possible outcomes described in Section 2. The legal mandate for IMF arrangements and the associated responsibility of the Fund to not put at (too much) risk the revolving character of its resources thus provide a distinct rationale for conditionality focused on the level of reserves.

Quantitative performance criteria for monetary policy come into play primarily in the setting of ceilings on net domestic credit of the central bank (or the banking system).[24] In the balance sheet of the central

---

credit as an indicator of monetary policy in IMF programs between his 1973 seminal article on the subject (Guitián, 1973) and an article written more than twenty years later (Guitián, 1994), at a time when many IMF members had abandoned fixed exchange rates, and financial innovation and capital-market integration had wreaked havoc with the stability of monetary aggregates in many industrial and emerging market economies. Tellingly, the conference discussant of the second paper, Henk Jager, expresses uneasiness and surprise at Guitián's unqualified presentation of the monetary approach to the balance of payments as a suitable framework for analyzing monetary policy in the short and medium term in the 1990s (Jager, 1994).

24. Whether the ceilings are set on net domestic credit from the central bank or from the banking system is a decision that depends, primarily, on the degree of financial

bank, the sum of net domestic credit and net international reserves determine, as fact of accounting, the quantity of base money.[25] Hence, given the floor on net international reserves set by the performance criterion on this component of the monetary base, setting a ceiling on net domestic credit establishes a quasiceiling on base money. Base money can be above this quasiceiling and still be in conformance with the performance criteria, but only to the extent that net international reserves are above their specified floor. Why should quantitative performance criteria for monetary policy be set in this way? Many times the reason a country gets into balance of payments difficulties and suffers reserve losses and exchange-rate pressures is that monetary policy has been too expansionary; base money has been allowed to expand too rapidly relative to the growth of sustainable demand, and net domestic credit of the central bank has grown at an even faster rate to offset (sterilize) losses of reserves. In other cases—for example when there is a sharp reversal of foreign capital inflows or a sudden bout of capital flight—reserve losses may not derive primarily from excessive money creation, but central banks typically will resist a large monetary contraction by sterilizing reserve losses through an offsetting expansion of net domestic credit. In either circumstance, under a Fund arrangement it is important to provide some assurance that expansionary monetary policy will not continue to be, or become, a problem that undermines external viability.

A performance criterion that sets ceilings on net domestic credit of the central bank is an admittedly crude way of attempting to provide such assurance. The ceilings are typically set by first estimating (or guessing) a reasonable path for base money under the program's assumptions regarding output growth, inflation, exchange rates, seasonal factors, and the behavior of velocity and the money multipliers.[26] Subtracting the floor on net international reserves yields the ceiling on net domestic

---

development of the country requesting Fund support. Ceilings at the banking-system level are considered more appropriate in countries where the financial system is relatively underdeveloped and the central bank resorts to direct controls or other distortionary means to influence credit conditions. Ceilings at the central-bank level are generally used in countries where the authorities rely on indirect instruments of monetary control—see International Monetary Fund 1987 and Guitián 1994. The discussion that follows is confined to the latter cases; however, the thrust of the argument also applies to the other cases.

25. Suitable definitions of these aggregates, with adjustments for other items on the balance sheet and other factors affecting reserves (which comprise what Fund staff calls "other items net"), assure that this statement is true.

26. For a fuller discussion see International Monetary Fund (1987) and Polak (1997); see also Fischer (1997).

credit that is consistent with this path for base money.[27] Notably and desirably, this procedure does not impose a ceiling or a floor on the monetary base.[28] The rationale for this is quite clear. If the demand for base money turns out to be higher than projected, putting upward pressure on the currency and international reserves, the central bank can accommodate the higher demand by allowing the international-reserves component of the monetary base to expand. Granting this flexibility, what about the uncertainties in forecasting the demand for base money? Here, there is no escape from assuming some degree of predictability of the demand for money, in accord with some quantifiable model. In particular, the numerical quasiceiling for base money will normally require a judgement about how the demand for money will behave over the coming two to four quarters, given program assumptions about the course of national income, capital flows, the price level, interest rates, the exchange rate, and (very importantly in most cases) seasonal factors. This involves, at least implicitly, numerical values for the short-run point elasticities of money demand. The estimates of what will happen to money demand must then be translated into judgements about base money by taking account of the likely behavior of the money multiplier relationships, which are often unstable in environments of economic and financial difficulty. The result is essentially an educated guess about how the economically appropriate supply of base money should be expected to evolve over the following six to twelve months, given the program's economic and policy assumptions. This educated guess, embodied in the performance criteria, is typically an outcome of the negotiations with the authorities, not the result of rigorous statistical estimation.

Admittedly, forecasts of the demand for base money obtained from this procedure can be far off the mark. But the saving grace is the flexibility in the process behind Fund-supported programs. Breaching the ceiling on net domestic credit or the floor on net international reserve triggers a reconsideration and possible revision of the Fund arrangement, not its termination. What happens depends on an assessment of why the performance criterion was breached, on implications going forward,

27. In some cases, the baseline path for net international reserves used to calculate the path for net domestic credit may lie above the performance criterion for the floor on net international reserves. The issue then arises of the extent to which discrepancies between the baseline and the floor should be sterilized through increases in net domestic credit.

28. A number of Fund arrangements have in fact included as performance criteria ceilings on the monetary base rather than on domestic credit. The staff's evaluation of monetary policy in those arrangements, however, by and large has followed the same logic as the one described in the text—particularly when reducing inflation was not the primary goal of the Fund arrangement and the rate of disinflation envisaged in the program was not particularly large.

and on the capacity to agree on suitable policy adjustments. While this process does not guarantee perfection, it is surely very different from a rigid application of a simplistic version of the monetary approach to the balance of payments.

To ensure minimal consistency among the numerical performance criteria for fiscal, monetary, and external-debt policy contained in every Fund arrangement it is necessary to employ a quantitative framework. As mentioned before, the framework that IMF staff developed and continues to use for this purpose is called *financial programming*. Financial programming is not a formal economic model, but rather a simple flow-of-funds framework that combines basic macro-accounting identities and balance-sheet constraints which the staff uses to gauge the size of the adjustment effort required from a country experiencing balance-of-payments difficulties, *given* assumptions about prospective external financing, output growth, inflation, and exchange rates.[29] Even in its simplest form, financial programming does involve a small number of behavioral equations and arbitrage conditions—e.g., a demand for money, a demand for imports, uncovered interest parity. Furthermore, the solution for the values of key performance criteria requires (approximate) knowledge of several key elasticities and policy multipliers. However, values for these key parameters are generally not estimated by formal econometric techniques. Because of the predominance of unstable relationships and unreliable data in the countries requesting Fund support, the estimates that are used mainly represent plausible judgements, based on rough statistical work.

In view of the errors that inevitably infect this process—or any alternative process for setting numerical performance criteria—the usefulness of financial programming depends not so much on the accuracy of its forecasts as on the *flexibility* for revising the main numerical targets as new information becomes available. In fact, all performance criteria in Fund-supported programs are set *conditional* on assumptions about the behavior of a number of variables. The assumptions are rarely kept unchanged for the duration of the program. During the monitoring phase, assumptions are revisited using the latest information for the key exogenous variables, projections about their future behavior are modi-

---

29. The seminal pieces on financial programming were written by E. Walter Robichek, former director of the IMF's Western Hemisphere Department (Robichek, 1967, 1971, 1985). Oral tradition and training manuals prepared by the IMF's Institute (e.g., International Monetary Fund, 1981, 1996) helped disseminate the financial-programming methodology. Working papers of Fund staff (e.g., Chand, 1987; Barth and Chadha, 1989; Mikkelsen, 1998) have served the same purpose. For a critique of the increasing, and in his view unwarranted, "sophistication" of financial programming in many of the latter pieces see Polak (1997).

fied, and, if necessary, numerical performance criteria are revised. The scope that this open-loop feature of the approach affords for exercising judgement when assessing the country's performance under the Fund arrangement is what explains why IMF financial programming has proved so resilient. The superficial uniformity that financial programming imparts to all Fund arrangements is hence a far cry from the view that portrays it as a standard and rigid economic model that is mechanically applied to all program countries.[30]

3.4 IMF PROGRAMS IN ACTION: MEXICO, 1995–1996

The Fund-supported program for Mexico in 1995–1996 provides a notable example of how the process of IMF programs works in practice. During 1994, Mexico was running a current-account deficit of 8% of GDP and suffered large reserve losses (which were sterilized by the Banco de Mexico) when a variety of internal and external disturbances helped to undermine confidence (see Annex I in the May 1995 *World Economic Outlook*). The Mexican authorities did not approach the Fund for an arrangement until after the peso had been devalued and subsequently allowed to float. At the insistence of the authorities, the arrangement agreed in January 1995 was based on economic assumptions that were quite optimistic, especially in hindsight. Real GDP growth was projected to slow from 3.5% in 1994 to 1.5% in 1995 and then recover. Exchange-rate depreciation was assumed to be contained with the assistance of moderately tight monetary policy. Inflation, on a December-to-December basis, was projected to rise from 7% to 19% and then decline. With support from fiscal measures to improve the primary government balance by 1.1 percentage points of GDP (very modest by the standards of earlier Fund arrangements with Mexico), the current account deficit was projected to shrink from 8% to 4% of GDP—a deficit assessed to be financeable with capital inflows and moderate use of official reserves. Performance criteria for the initial program were set on the basis of these assumptions.

Confidence, however, was not restored by this initial program. Massive capital outflows, especially by holders of *tesobonos*, led to large reserve losses and pushed the peso down to half its precrisis value by early March. Inflation soared; the December-to-December rate reached 52%.

---

30. In a recent paper dealing with the legacy of "his" model, Jacques Polak explains why it is mistaken to portray financial programming as a fully specified economic model; specifically, he notes that "the Fund has had to forego the comfort of its old model and base its conditionality on a set of ad hoc instruments that seemed plausible in the circumstances. . . . *Without much of a model to go by*, the Fund has in recent years tended to adopt an 'all risk' policy . . . reserving for periodic reviews a judgment as to the need for additional . . . action" (Polak, 1997, pp. 15–16; italics added).

Figure 2 Mexico: Domestic Credit (NDA) and International Reserves (NIR) in the 1995–1996 Standby Arrangement: Program Targets and Outcomes (In billions of pesos)

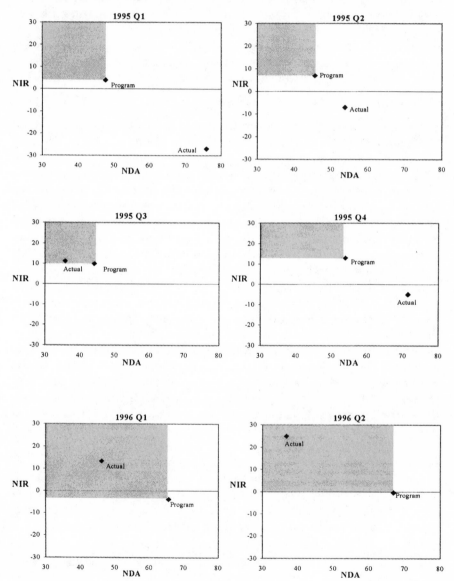

Sources: Fund staff estimates.

Output crashed; real GDP ultimately fell 7% in 1995, and real domestic demand fell more than double that amount. The current account improved by 7.6 percentage points of GDP, reaching near-balance by year end. To contain the depreciation of the peso and regain monetary control, in March the Banco de Mexico had to raise overnight interest rates temporarily above 80%.

What of the program's performance criteria? The fiscal targets were met scrupulously, despite the unexpectedly deep recession. In fact, the March 1995 program review tightened the annual fiscal target, and this target was more than met. For the monetary program, base money ran significantly below its quasiceiling through most of 1995, reaching the ceiling at year end. However, as illustrated in Figure 2 (where the shaded areas show the acceptable range of performance), the actual performance criteria for the floor on net international reserves and the ceiling on net domestic credit were both very badly breached on the test dates corresponding to the ends of the first, second, and fourth quarters of 1995. At the Fund, it was understood that in the face of very large and unexpected capital outflows and reserve losses, the Banco de Mexico had to expand net domestic credit well beyond the agreed ceiling to avoid a catastrophic decline of base money. Given the determination shown by the Mexican authorities in the fiscal area, in interest-rate policy, and in the behavior of base money, violations of the performance criteria for net international reserves and net domestic credit during 1995 were waived. The program proceeded without interruption. By late 1995 confidence was clearly recovering. In 1996 growth jumped to 5%, and inflation fell by 25 percentage points. All performance criteria of the program for the first half of the year were met, by wide margins in the monetary area, and Mexico regained access to private capital markets and decided not to draw the remaining tranches of the IMF loan.

4. Conclusion

The example of Mexico illustrates how IMF-supported programs work in practice, in accord with the iterative process described in Section 2 and involving the substantive elements and quantitative approach to macroeconomic policymaking discussed in Section 3. In this particular case, given the urgency of the situation, the phases of inception, blueprint, negotiation, and approval proceeded very rapidly and concluded with an agreement on a Fund arrangement that involved an exceptionally large financial support. However, the economic assumptions of the initial program proved overly optimistic, and the quantitative performance criteria for net domestic credit and net international reserves were seriously breached. In the monitoring phase of the arrangement this was handled, first, by revising the main assumptions of the 1995 program and, more substantively, by granting waivers for the breached performance criteria, as it was judged that the policy efforts of the Mexican authorities had been forceful and appropriate to meet the extremely adverse circumstances they confronted.

Other IMF-supported programs follow somewhat different courses. For instance, in the recent Fund arrangements for Thailand and Korea, initial program assumptions envisioned slowdowns in growth but not the severe recessions that actually ensued. During the monitoring phase, prescriptions for fiscal policy needed to be substantially modified, from moderate restraint to significant support. With these and other agreed modifications, the programs proceeded without interruption. In the case of Indonesia, in contrast, the efforts of the authorities to meet the macroeconomic and structural performance requirements of the initial program approved in November 1997 and of the revised program agreed on with the staff in February 1998 were judged to be inadequate, and the Fund arrangement went off track. Subsequent agreement with a new government on a substantially modified program has proved much more successful and has generally proceeded without serious delay. In the case of Brazil, the interval between inception (involving internal discussions of Fund staff and management) and approval of the IMF program in November 1998 was somewhat longer than in the other cases. The initial program featured significant fiscal consolidation to boost confidence in the continuation of the Real Plan and to contain and curtail a rapidly rising public-debt ratio. When the exchange-rate policy proved unsustainable in the face of large reserve losses, the arrangement went off track. A revised program, still with fiscal consolidation at its core but with a flexible exchange rate and a monetary policy geared toward low inflation, has so far proved more auspicious.

Other cases show an even wider range of experience with the actual evolution of Fund-supported programs through their six operational phases. Indeed, while the IMF maintains a general policy of uniformity of treatment of its members, the fact is that Fund-supported programs are far from uniform—notwithstanding their superficial resemblance. The reason for this is simply that IMF members have quite different economies, face different problems necessitating adjustments in their balance of payments, and display a variety of policy regimes and different ability and willingness to implement policies to correct external payments imbalances and their underlying causes. IMF programs need to be, and are, flexible instruments for addressing those problems, within a general framework that has a quantitative dimension and imposes a necessary degree of consistency and discipline across users of Fund resources.

REFERENCES

Alexander, S. (1952). Effects of a devaluation on a trade balance. *IMF Staff Papers*, 2(April):263–278.

Barth, R., and B. Chadha (1989). A simulation model for financial programming. Washington: International Monetary Fund. IMF Working Paper WP/89/24.

Bernstein, B., and J. Boughton. (1993). Adjusting to development: The IMF and the poor. IMF Paper on Policy Analysis and Assessment 93/4.

Buiter, W. (1990). Some thoughts on the role of fiscal policy in stabilization and structural adjustment in developing countries. In *Principles of Budgetary and Financial Policy,* W. Buiter, (ed.). Cambridge, MA: MIT Press, pp.407–448.

Burki, S., and G. Perry. (1998). *Beyond the Washington Consensus,* World Bank Latin American and Caribbean Studies. Washington: The World Bank.

Burton, D., and M. Gilman. (1991). Exchange rate policy and the IMF. *Finance and Development* 28(3):18–21.

Calomiris, C. (1998). The IMF's imprudent role as lender of last resort. *The Cato Journal* 17(3, Winter):275–294.

Chand, S. (1987). Toward a growth-oriented model for financial programming. Washington: International Monetary Fund. IMF Working Paper WP/87/10.

Cooper, R. (1992). *Economic Stabilization and Debt in Developing Countries.* Cambridge, MA: MIT Press.

Dell, S. (1982). Stabilization: The political economy of overkill. *World Development* (Oxford) 10(August):597–612.

de Melo, M., et al. (1996). Patterns of transition from plan to market. *World Bank Economic Review* 10(3):397–429.

Dicks-Mireaux, L., et al. (1995). The macroeconomic effects of ESAF-supported programs: Revisiting some methodological issues. Washington: International Monetary Fund. IMF Working Paper WP/95/92.

Dornbusch, R. (1991). Policies to move from stabilization to growth. Washington: The World Bank. World Bank Research Report.

Edwards, S. (1989). The International Monetary Fund and the developing countries: A critical evaluation. *Carnegie-Rochester Conference Series on Public Policy* 31:7–68.

Eichengreen, B. (1999). *Towards a New International Financial Architecture.* Washington: Institute for International Economics.

Feldstein, M. (1998). Refocusing the IMF. *Foreign Affairs* 77(2):20–23.

Finch, C. (1989). The IMF: The record and the prospect Princeton University. Princeton Essays in International Finance 175.

Fischer, S. (1997). Applied economics in action: IMF programs. *American Economic Review, Papers and Proceedings* 87(2):23–27.

Folkerts-Landau, D., and P. Garber. (1999). The new architecture in official doctrine. In *Global Markets Research.* London: Deutsche Bank.

Frenkel, J., and H. Johnson. (1976). *The Monetary Approach to the Balance of Payments.* London: Allen & Unwin.

Goldstein, M., and P. Montiel. (1986). Evaluating Fund stabilization programs with multicountry data: Some methodological pitfalls. *IMF Staff Papers* 33 (June):304–344.

Group of Twenty-Four. (1987). *The Role of the IMF in Adjustment with Growth*, Report of Working Group. Washington: Group of Twenty-Four.

Guitián, M. (1973). Credit versus money as an instrument of control. *IMF Staff Papers* 20(November):785–800.

———. (1994). The role of monetary policy in IMF programs. In *A Framework for Monetary Stability*, J.A.H. de Beaufort Wijnholds et al. (eds.). Dordrecht, The Netherlands: Kluwer Academic Publishers, pp.185–209.

———. (1995). Conditionality: Past, present, future. *IMF Staff Papers* 42(4, December):792–835.

Gupta, S., et al. (1998). *The IMF and the Poor*, IMF Pamphlet Series 52. Washington: International Monetary Fund.

Haque, N., and M. Khan. (1998). Do IMF-supported programs work? A survey of the cross-country empirical evidence, International Monetary Fund. IMF Working Paper WP/98/169.

Harrigan, J. (1996). Review article—the Bretton Woods institutions in developing countries: bêtes noires or toothless tigers? *The World Economy* 19(2):765–779.

Heller, P., et al. (1988). The implications of Fund-supported adjustment programs for poverty: Experiences in selected countries. Washington: International Monetary Fund. IMF Occasional Paper 58.

IMF Assessment Project. (1992). *IMF Conditionality 1980–1991*. Arlington, VA: Alexis de Tocqueville Institution.

International Monetary Fund. (1977). *The Monetary Approach to the Balance of Payments*, Washington: International Monetary Fund.

———. (1981). *Financial Programming Workshops: The Case of Kenya*, Washington: IMF Institute.

———. (1987). Theoretical aspects of the design of Fund-supported adjustment programs. Washington: International Monetary Fund. IMF Occasional Paper 55.

———. (1996). *Financial Programming and Policy: The Case of Sri Lanka*. Washington: IMF Institute.

———. (1997). The ESAF at ten years: Economic adjustment and reform in low income countries. Washington: International Monetary Fund. IMF Occasional Paper 156.

———. (1998). *Financial Organization and Operations of the IMF*, IMF Pamphlet Series 45, 5th ed. Washington: International Monetary Fund.

Jager, H. (1994). Comment on Manuel Guitián: The role of monetary policy in IMF programs. In *A Framework for Monetary Stability*, J.A.H. de Beaufort Wijnholds et al. (eds.). Dordrecht, The Netherlands: Kluwer Academic Publishers, pp.217–220.

James, H. (1998). From grandmotherliness to governance: The evolution of IMF conditionality. *Finance and Development* 35(4):44–47.

Johnson, O., and J. Salop. (1980). Distributional aspects of stabilization programs in developing countries. *IMF Staff Papers* 27(March):1–23.

Kenen, P. (1985). Macroeconomic theory and policy: How the closed economy was opened. In *Handbook of International Economics, Vol. 2*, R. Jones and P. Kenen (eds.). Amsterdam: North-Holland, pp.625–677.

Khan, M. (1990). The macroeconomic effects of Fund-supported adjustment programs. *IMF Staff Papers* 37(June):195–231.

Killick, T. (1995). *IMF Programmes in Developing Countries: Design and Impact*, London and New York: Routledge.

Knight, M., and J. Santaella. (1997). Economic determinants of IMF financial arrangements. *Journal of Development Economics* 54:405–436.

Krueger, A. (1993). *Political Economy of Policy Reform in Developing Countries.* Cambridge, MA: MIT Press.

———. (1998). Whither the World Bank and the IMF? *Journal of Economic Literature* 36(December):1983–2020.

Lane, T., et al. (1999). *IMF-Supported Programs in Indonesia, Korea, and Thailand: A Preliminary Assessment.* Washington: International Monetary Fund. IMF Occasional Paper 178.

Mikkelsen, J. (1998). A model for financial programming. Washington: International Monetary Fund. IMF Working Paper WP/98/80.

Minton-Beddoes, Z. (1995). Why the IMF needs reform. *Foreign Affairs* 74(3): 123–133.

Mussa, M. (1997). IMF surveillance. *American Economic Review, Papers and Proceedings* 87(2):28–31.

Nashashibi, K., et al. (1992). The fiscal dimensions of adjustment in low-income countries. IMF Occasional Paper 95.

Polak, J. J. (1957). Monetary analysis of income formation and payments problems. *IMF Staff Papers* 5(November):1–50.

———. (1991). The changing nature of IMF conditionality. Princeton Essays in International Finance 184. Princeton University.

———. (1997). The IMF monetary model at forty. Washington: International Monetary Fund. IMF Working Paper WP/97/49.

Prais, S. J. (1961). Some mathematical notes on the quantity theory of money in an open economy. *IMF Staff Papers* 8(May):212–226.

Robichek, E. W. (1967). Financial programming exercises of the International Monetary Fund in Latin America. Rio de Janeiro. Manuscript.

———. (1971). Financial programming: Stand-by arrangements and stabilization programs. Washington: International Monetary Fund. Manuscript.

———. (1985). Financial programming as practiced by the IMF. Washington: The World Bank. Manuscript.

Santaella, J. (1996). Stylized facts before IMF-supported macroeconomic adjustment. *IMF Staff Papers* 43(September):502–544.

Schadler, S., et al. (1993). Economic adjustment in low-income countries: Experience under the enhanced structural adjustment facility. Washington: International Monetary Fund. IMF Occasional Paper 106.

———, et al. (1995). IMF conditionality: Experience under stand-by and extended arrangements. Parts 1 and 2. Washington: International Monetary Fund. IMF Occasional Papers 128, 129.

Shultz, G. (1995). Economics in action: Ideas, institutions, policies. *American Economic Review, Papers and Proceedings* 85(2):1–8.

Tanzi, V. (1987). Fiscal policy, growth, and the design of stabilization programs. In *External Debt, Savings, and Growth in Latin America*, A. Martirena-Mantel (ed.). Washington: International Monetary Fund, pp.121–141.

Taylor, L. (1988). *Varieties of Stabilization Experience.* Oxford: Clarendon Press.

———, ed. (1993). *The Rocky Road to Reform.* Cambridge, MA: MIT Press.

Williamson, J., ed. (1983). *IMF Conditionality.* Cambridge, MA: MIT Press.

———. (1990). What Washington means by policy reform. In *Latin American Adjustment: How Much Has Happened?*, J. Williamson (ed.). Washington: Institute for International Economics.

Williamson, O. (1994). The institutions and governance of economic development and reform. In *Proceedings of The World Bank Annual Conference in Development Economics.* Washington: The World Bank, pp.171–197.

Comment

MARTIN EICHENBAUM
Northwestern University, NBER, and Federal Reserve Bank of Chicago

This paper will be of value to anyone interested in IMF stabilization
programs. But it is not an easy paper to discuss, as it contains neither a
theoretical model nor new empirical results. Instead the paper exposits
and defends, in broad terms, the IMF approach to economic stabilization. By this the authors mean the Fund's short-term tactics for stabilizing currency crises. The paper succeeds in defending the Fund from a
subset of its critics. My main criticism of it is that it does not address the
Fund's most serious critics: those who charge that the IMF's short-term
tactics for stabilizing currency crises raise the likelihood of future crises.
My comment lays out one version of this critique and urges the authors
to reply in future research.

As laid out by the authors, the objectives of their paper are to (1)
summarize the process by which IMF programs are set up, (2) explain
why the IMF conditions aid on various monetary and fiscal policy targets, and (3) defend the IMF from charges that its programs are excessively rigid and based on an outmoded economic model. To varying
degrees the paper succeeds in accomplishing all three objectives.

A little more than half of the paper is devoted to (1). I have little to add
here. Surely describing the details of how the Fund sets up its programs
is the authors' comparative advantage, not mine. Also, with one important exception, I have little to argue with regarding (2). The exception is
that I would like to see *much* more detail about how the Fund calculates
its monetary and fiscal targets. After all, God is in the details. And I
don't understand the details of these calculations any better having read
the paper.

Turning to the paper's third objective, I come to my major complaint.
The paper never grapples with the charge that the IMF's successful
short-term tactics for stabilizing currency crises increase the likelihood of
future crises occurring. The Fund has many critics. Some deserve to be
taken seriously. Others don't. In the latter group I include those who
charge that (1) the IMF staff blindly applies the same simplistic formula
to all crises, (2) the IMF should abandon conditionality, and (3) the IMF

has perversely encouraged countries that are in the throes of a currency crisis to pursue contractionary monetary and fiscal policy. The evidence against the first charge is overwhelming. The second charge is tantamount to urging the IMF to abandon its charter. Finally, there is no firm scientific basis for criticizing the Fund on the basis of the third charge. In the midst of a currency crisis, one way or another, you need to stabilize a country's current account. In practice this means securing sustainable external financing for the country and generating current-account surpluses. The most effective way to do that is contractionary monetary and fiscal policy. Like the authors, I don't know of any evidence to the contrary.

By focusing on the Fund's least persuasive critics, the authors have missed a valuable opportunity to defend the IMF from its most persuasive ones, whose position I summarize as follows.[1] In its search for a post-Bretton Woods mission, the IMF is trying to become an international lender of last resort. The Fund cannot successfully play this role. Even if the IMF had the mandate and the resources to move decisively in the midst of a crisis, it would not have the regulatory powers normally associated with successful lenders of last resort. Anticipating this problem, the Fund has tried to develop new forms of conditionality which involve detailed structural and institutional reforms in client countries. Increasingly these pertain to the structure of the financial sectors in those countries.

There are at least two reasons to be skeptical of these new forms of conditionality. First, it is far more difficult for the Fund to monitor and regulate the financial sector of sovereign states than it is for central banks. Given political realities and the limited enforcement mechanisms at its disposal, the Fund is unlikely to be able to reform a banking system *before* a crisis occurs. Second, banking reforms take longer to implement than the horizon of a typical IMF program period. So IMF funds are inevitably disbursed after a crisis occurs but before reforms actually happen.

According to the critics, because the Fund cannot credibly impose structural reforms on client countries, it has become an unwilling participant and facilitator of bank bailouts and loan guarantee schemes—the proximate causes of many, although not all, of the post-1980 currency crises. True, the IMF does not directly bail out banks or countries. But it does provide loans at below-market rates. More importantly, the Fund helps provide the political cover for governments to raise the resources required to pay off loans and carry out bank bailouts. Unfortunately, the people who benefit from the bailouts aren't the ones whose taxes are

1. See for example Calomiris (1998), Chari and Kehoe (1998), and the references therein.

ultimately raised. So, at least indirectly, the Fund contributes to the moral-hazard problems that are pervasive in the financial sectors of emerging (and other) market economies.

To the extent that one takes the previous critique seriously, the key question becomes: How can the Fund achieve the benefits of short-term interventions without exacerbating the perverse incentives faced by lenders in emerging markets and their foreign creditors? Presumably the answer to the previous question depends on what causes currency crises. According to many of the Fund's critics, the quasiliberalization of world financial markets that has occurred has led to new kinds of currency crises, of a type not anticipated by standard macroeconomic models. Some believe that these "new" currency crises are essentially self-fulfilling prophecies unrelated to moral-hazard issues or the fundamental health of the countries involved (see for example Chang and Velasco, 1999). From this perspective, the Fund's actions in Asia punished the victims of the crime, not the perpetrators. Tight monetary and fiscal policy just damaged otherwise sound financial systems.

Other researchers argue that the roots of many recent currency crises can be traced to moral-hazard problems associated with financial deregulation, the end of capital controls, and ongoing implicit guarantees to corporations, banks, and their foreign creditors. In fact, substantial evidence supports the view that banking crises have become increasingly severe and are now more closely linked to currency crises. Since 1982, there have been over ninety episodes of severe banking crises. The worst of these involve losses to taxpayers of unprecedented magnitude. For example, in more than twenty of the post-1982 cases, bailout costs exceeded 10% of the affected country's GDP. In roughly half of those cases, including the recent Southeast Asian episodes, the losses have been in the range of 25% of GDP.[2] Finally, currency crises are more correlated with banking crises in the post-1980 era than in the pre-1980 era.[3]

The increase in the rate and severity of banking crises reflects three factors: currency controls were far less pervasive in the post-1980 era, governments didn't subsidize risktaking by banks nearly as much as they do now, and international agencies, like the IMF, didn't help to insulate foreign creditors from default risk as much.

But why should banking crises be linked to currency crises? Here there are at least two possibilities: fundamental shocks to the banking sector, and self-fulfilling expectational links. To illustrate the first channel, sup-

---

2. To put this figure into perspective, the losses to U.S. taxpayers from the savings-and-loan crises was roughly 3% of U.S. GDP. Losses from bank failures during the Great Depression years of 1930–1933 equaled roughly 4% of U.S. GDP. See Calomiris (1998).
3. See Kaminsky, Lizondo, and Reinhart (1998) and Kaminsky and Reinhart (1999).

pose that real shocks to an economy cause higher bankruptcy rates in the banking sector that trigger large fiscal obligations on the part of the government. These shocks could reflect shifts in either the supply or the demand for the products of the banks' customers. One concrete example is provided by Thailand, where banks made substantial loans to firms that invested heavily in real estate projects that began to yield negative rates of return prior to the currency crises. Under these circumstances a banking crisis could lead to a currency crisis because of large *prospective* deficits associated with implicit bailout guarantees to failing banks. To the extent that market participants expect that future deficits will be financed, at least in part, by higher seignorage revenues, future monetary policy would be perceived as being inconsistent with the maintenance of fixed exchange rates. This would lead to a currency crisis before the deficits actually begin to be monetized.[4] From this perspective, government guarantees are the key conduits by which real shocks transform a banking crisis into a currency collapse.

The second connection between banking and currency crises is that the presence of government guarantees opens up the possibility of self-fulfilling twin banking–currency crises. Suppose that for extraneous reasons market participants come to expect that the government will pursue a monetary policy that is inconsistent with the maintenance of fixed exchange rates. These beliefs can be self-fulfilling in the sense that they lead to a successful currency attack and a future monetary policy that actually is inconsistent with the maintenance of fixed exchange rates.

To see how this might work, suppose that because of government guarantees, banks are unhedged against exchange-rate risk. Burnside, Eichenbaum, and Rebelo (1999) argue that a bank's optimal strategy is to be unhedged when its foreign creditors are insulated from the default risks associated with a devaluation.[5] Many banks would therefore go broke after a devaluation. This in turn triggers the government's obligations to banks' creditors. Under these circumstances, the government would have to meet its fiscal obligations, at least in part, via seignorage revenues. So if market participants believe that the government will

4. Burnside, Eichenbaum, and Rebelo (1998) argue that this connection between banking and currency crises was operative during the recent Thai and Korean currency crises.
5. In fact, in their model, it is optimal for banks to magnify exchange-rate risk by entering into forward positions which lose money when there is a devaluation. See also Mishkin (1996) and Obstfeld (1998), who argue that a government's promise to maintain a fixed exchange rate is often interpreted by the financial industry as an implicit guarantee against the adverse consequences of a devaluation. Consistent with this hypothesis, many researchers argue that firms and financial intermediaries borrow extensively from abroad prior to the onset of a currency crises but do not completely hedge exchange-rate risk. See for example, IMF (1998, p. 17) for a discussion of the recent crises in Indonesia, Korea, and Thailand.

meet future fiscal obligations by seignorage revenues, then they will take actions that trigger these fiscal obligations and the need to raise seignorage revenues. So there will be a self-fulfilling, apparently rational run on the currency, followed by a devaluation, a banking crisis, transfers to bank creditors, and a partial monetization of the debt. Indeed, the attack may set off a chain of self-fulfilling attacks on different currencies, i.e. contagion.

Note that under either the fundamental or the self-fulfilling-expectations scenario discussed above, currency crises are tightly linked to banking crises. Actions taken by domestic governments or international agencies that exacerbate the moral-hazard problem faced by banks raise the probability of future currency crises. To the extent that one takes this problem seriously, the task confronting the IMF is to assess the extent to which their successful short-run strategies for stabilizing currency crises affect the likelihood of future crises. On this issue Mussa and Savastano's paper is silent. That is a pity. No doubt they have much to say on this, *the* critical issue confronting policymakers at the Fund.

I conclude by reiterating that I learned a lot from this paper. The fact that I've urged the authors to write a sequel doesn't detract from what they have done. They have forcefully responded to a subset of the Fund's critics. The reader must wait for the sequel to see how the authors respond to the other critics.

REFERENCES

Burnside, C., M. Eichenbaum, and S. Rebelo. (1998). Prospective deficits and the South East Asian currency crises. Cambridge, MA: National Bureau of Economic Research. NBER Working Paper 6758.
———, ———, and ———. (1999). Hedging and financial fragility in fixed exchange rate regimes. Cambridge, MA: National Bureau of Economic Research. NBER Working Paper 7143.
Calomiris, C. (1998). The IMF's imprudent role as lender of last resort. *The Cato Journal* 17(3):275–294.
Chang, R., and A. Velasco (1999). Liquidity crises in emerging markets: Theory and policy. Cambridge, MA: National Bureau of Economic Research. NBER Working Paper 7272.
Chari, V. V., and P. Kehoe. (1998). Asking the right questions about the IMF. *The Region*, 1998 Annual Report Special Issue. Federal Reserve Bank of Minneapolis.
International Monetary Fund (1998). *International capital markets: developments, prospects, and key policy issues*. Washington, DC: IMF.
Kaminsky, G., S. Lizondo, and C.M. Reinhart. (1998). Leading indicators of currency crises. *International Monetary Fund Staff Papers* 45(1):1–48.
———, and C. M. Reinhart. (1999). The twin crises: The causes of banking and balance-of-payments problems. *American Economic Review* 89(3):473–500.

Mishkin, Frederic. (1996). Understanding financial crises: A developing country perspective. In *Annual World Bank Conference on Development Economics 1996,* Michael Bruno and Boris Pleskovic (eds.) Washington, DC: World Bank.

Obstfeld, Maurice. (1998). The global capital market: Benefactor or menace? *Journal of Economic Perspectives* 12:9–30.

Discussion

In reply to the comments of the formal discussants, Michael Mussa emphasized that the scope of their paper is the IMF approach to economic stabilization, which is why they did not address issues relating to moral hazard and the international-lender-of-last-resort function. He noted, however, that the problem of fragility of financial systems in emerging market economies had led, even prior to recent crises, to attempts by international institutions to create a set of standards that countries would be encouraged to adopt. Morris Goldstein of the IMF led this effort in 1996, and the Bank for International Settlements took over the project subsequently. This initiative illustrates that the IMF was trying to act preemptively on financial fragility and not just after the fact.

Mussa also expressed skepticism about the heavy weight being attached to the moral-hazard issue. He noted that in Mexico the problem was not just banking instability but the possibility of default on the tesobonos. If Mexico had defaulted on the tesobonos, it would have lost access to international capital markets on a sustained basis, imposing large costs on the country. The IMF's efforts to avert sovereign default in Mexico were thus necessary, even though creditors were also helped. He added that the IMF is not paying for the Mexican banks' losses and that the Mexican taxpayers are stuck with that bill. Mussa also used the examples of Thailand and Indonesia to point out that external creditors have not been made whole in every case. The decision to stop providing bailouts to Russia should have sent the powerful message that, no matter how important a country is, international support including IMF loans is conditional on reasonable policy performance and in any case is not unlimited. It is thus incorrect to characterize the IMF as being excessively prone to bailing out countries and institutions in trouble.

Martin Feldstein said that issues pertaining to the denomination of private debts were not mentioned in the paper. He noted that the typical problem of countries seeking IMF help is a current-account deficit that needs to be reduced, and the traditional formula is to devalue and deflate. However, devaluation is actually very contractionary in countries like Thailand in which corporate foreign-currency borrowing has been so massive that corporations (and ultimately also their creditor banks) find themselves bankrupt when there is a large devaluation. Feldstein added that in such a case the last thing that is needed is contractionary fiscal and monetary policies to further reduce aggregate demand. He asked whether the IMF explicitly takes into account the deflationary impact of devaluation through the foreign-debt channel when designing its programs. Mussa responded by saying that debt issues of this type are viewed as central to Fund programs. For example, getting the international banks to roll over Korean external debt was essential to the success of stabilizing the won and bringing it back to a reasonable level. Indeed, financial weakness in Asia was a major motivation for the Fund's recommendations to raise interest rates, because rate increases help to prevent devaluation by reducing capital outflows.

Michael Hutchison commented that in Korea many people think that some of the restructuring in IMF programs seems to be more relevant to the government's own agenda for change than to the need for macroeconomic reforms. Essentially, the government uses IMF backing to push through programs that otherwise do not have domestic political support. Mussa agreed that the IMF sometimes effectively plays what amounts to a political role, but added that governments should not be viewed as unitary actors. For example, the IMF often works with the finance ministries and central banks against the spending ministries and other constituencies. In the case of Korea, independently of domestic political concerns, corporate restructuring was a concern of the Fund because high precrisis corporate leverage ratios had made the Korean financial system extremely fragile. The Fund pursued corporate restructuring because it was viewed as being very important for avoiding future difficulties.

Takeo Hoshi and Anil Kashyap
GRADUATE SCHOOL OF INTERNATIONAL RELATIONS AND PACIFIC
STUDIES, UNIVERSITY OF CALIFORNIA, SAN DIEGO; AND GRADUATE
SCHOOL OF BUSINESS, UNIVERSITY OF CHICAGO, FEDERAL RESERVE
BANK OF CHICAGO, AND NBER

The Japanese Banking Crisis: Where Did it Come from and How Will it End?

1. Introduction

Japan's financial system is in the midst of a major transformation. One driving force is deregulation. The reform program that has come to be known as the *Japanese Big Bang* represents the conclusion of a deregulation process that began more than 20 years ago. By the time the Big Bang is complete, in 2001, banks, security firms, and insurance companies will face a level playing field on which unfettered competition can occur. At that time, Japanese financial markets will be at least as liberalized as the U.S. markets.

A second (and we will argue related) driving factor is the current huge

We thank Ben Bernanke, Ricardo Caballero, Menzie Chin, Peter Cowhey, Mitsuhiro Fukao, Mark Gertler, Peter Gourevitch, Yasushi Hamao, Masahiro Higo, Michael Hutchison, Tomohiro Kinoshita, Hugh Patrick, Joe Peek, Julio Rotemberg, Ross Starr, Robert Uriu, and Yaacov Vertzberger along with the participants in the presentations at the University of Chicago Graduate School of Business Brown Bag Lunch, the NBER Japan Group, the Bank of Japan, the Bank of Italy, the UCLA conference on the "Political Economy of the Japanese Financial Crisis," the Federal Reserve Bank of San Francisco, and IR/PS at University of California, San Diego for helpful comments. We thank Raghu Rajan for providing data from the National Survey of Small Business Finance, Itsuko Takemura of the Institute of Fiscal and Monetary Policy at the Japanese Ministry of Finance for providing data from *Hojin Kigyo Tokei*, and Simon Gilchrist, Kenji Hayashi, and Sumio Saruyama for helping us with other data issues. We thank Fernando Avalos, Yumiko Ito, John McNulty, and Motoki Yanase for excellent research assistance. Kashyap's work was supported through a grant from the National Science Foundation to the National Bureau of Economic Research. Hoshi's work was supported by a grant from Tokyo Center for Economic Research. The views expressed in this paper do not necessarily reflect those of the Federal Reserve Bank of Chicago or the Federal Reserve System.

financial crisis. As of September 1998, the estimates of bad loans in Japan remain at 7% of GDP (see Section 4 below for further details). This crisis has included the first significant bank failures since the end of the U.S. occupation of Japan. In policy circles, the banking problems are widely identified as one of the key factors for the poor performance of the Japanese economy over the last couple of years.[1] A growing academic literature suggests that the problems in the banking sector are now creating a serious drag on the economy's ability to recover.[2]

The Japanese government during the 1990s has taken a number of steps to address the financial problems. Starting with the loan purchasing program set up in early 1993, followed by the establishment of banks to buy out failed credit cooperatives and the *jusen,* and culminating in the reforms that reorganized the supervision authority for banks and earmarked over ¥60 trillion for bank reorganization and capitalization, there have been a nearly continuous set of attempts to fix the banking problem.[3]

In the latest attempt, the Long-Term Credit Bank of Japan (LTCB) and Nippon Credit Bank (NCB) were nationalized in late 1998, and three regional banks were put under receivership in the first half of 1999. Their balance sheets are supposed to be cleaned up so that they can be sold. Meanwhile, in March 1999, 15 large banks applied for a capital injection and received ¥7.4592 trillion of public funds. These banks are also required to carry out restructuring plans that will include eliminating 20,000 workers, closing 10% of their branches, and increasing profits by 50% over the next four years.[4] Nevertheless critics, including the U.S.

1. For example, both the International Monetary Fund (IMF) (1998a) and the Organization for Economic Cooperation and Development (OECD) (1998) country reports on Japan for 1998 point to the banking problems as a key factor in causing the post-November 1997 slowdown in growth. The Japanese government's 1998 Economic White Paper also identifies problems in the financial sector an important factor in prolonging the recession (Economic Planning Agency, 1998).
2. For instance, Bayoumi (1998) finds that fluctuations in asset prices played an important role in recent Japanese business cycles and that the shocks were mostly transmitted through bank lending. Without associated changes in bank loans, asset price fluctuations would not have affected the real economy very much, he argues. Likewise, Ogawa and Kitasaka (1998) report that small firms were especially hard hit by the decline in bank loans in the 1990s and that small- and large-firm investment differentials have emerged as the slow growth has continued. Motonishi and Yoshikawa (1998) find that the index of (firms' perception of) banks' willingness to lend (loose or tight) in BOJ's *Tankan* survey worsened substantially from late 1997 and contributed to slow growth, especially at small firms. Finally, Woo (1998) argues that since 1997 there has been a marked shift in bank-loan supply that has contributed to the weak growth in 1997 and 1998.
3. For a discussion of the loan purchasing program by the Cooperative Credit Corporation see Packer (1998). For a review of the *jusen* problems see Milhaupt and Miller (1997).
4. For more details on the restructuring plans, see Choy (1999). Individual restructuring plans in Japanese can be downloaded from the Financial Reconstruction Commission Web site (www.frc.go.jp).

Treasury, have argued that these steps have been inadequate.[5] In the latter half of 1999, two more regional banks were shut down and ¥260 billion of public funds were injected to re-capitalize four other regional banks. As of this writing there is still widespread pessimism about whether the banks have turned the corner.

We believe that a recurring problem with the Japanese government's attempts to overcome the crisis has been the lack of a clear vision for the future of the Japanese banking system. For instance, the debate that culminated in the passage of the Financial Reconstruction Bill in the fall of 1998 was drawn out because the ruling Liberal Democratic Party (LDP) and the major opposition party (the Democrats) haggled over two competing plans. On the surface, the negotiation seemed to center on what should happen to the Long-Term Credit Bank, which had been rumored to be insolvent for almost 4 months. At a deeper level, however, the two plans represented competing views about the current condition of the Japanese banking system.

LDP leaders believed that the major banks could not be allowed to fail. To them, the biggest problem with the Japanese banks was they were not strong enough to support (supposedly) healthy customers. Thus, the desired solution was to inject public funds into the major banks as they did in March 1998, to prevent a credit crunch. In the event of a failure, protecting solvent borrowers, by transferring the failed bank's business to a bridge bank, was given the highest priority.

The Democrats argued instead that giving public funds to the weak banks was a waste of taxpayers' money. Weak banks should be nationalized and restructured. Through this process, the Japanese banking sector would reemerge smaller but healthier.

In the end the LDP and the Democrats reached a compromise and passed the Financial Reconstruction Act. This law allows the newly created Financial Reconstruction Commission to choose between nationalization and a bridge bank scheme when a bank fails. However, shortly thereafter, over the objections of the Democrats, the LDP also formed a coalition with the Liberal Party and managed to pass the Prompt Recapitalization Act to help recapitalize supposedly healthy banks.[6]

Thus, the struggle in the Diet during the fall of 1998 amounted to a battle over whether the Japanese banking sector has too little capital or

5. For instance, Lawrence Summers, while he was U.S. Deputy Secretary of the Treasury, was reported to have suggested to Hakuo Yanagisawa, chairman of the Financial Reconstruction Committee, that another round of capital injections may be necessary (*Nikkei Net Interactive*, February 26, 1999.)

6. See Fukao (1999) for a summary and an analysis of the two laws, and Corbett (1999a) for a more complete history of the policies leading up to the fall 1998 legislation.

whether Japan is currently overbanked. To settle this issue one needs to ask what the banking sector will look like once the current crisis is over and the deregulation is complete. This question has attracted little attention. For instance, although there is now some discussion of how many large banks might be viable, aside from Moody's (1999) and Japan Economic Research Center (1997) (which we discuss in detail below) we are unaware of any attempts to determine how many *assets* will remain in the banking sector.[7]

More importantly, the mergers and closures that have occurred thus far (including the fall 1999 megamergers) have not reduced capacity in the industry. If the overbanking hypothesis is correct, these adjustments alone will probably not help. Similarly, the March 1999 capital injection required the 15 banks that received funds to reduce their general administrative expenses by ¥300 billion, but at the same time to increase loans to prevent a so-called "credit crunch." We believe that one needs a clear vision of the future of the industry to evaluate this situation.

One of the primary contributions of this paper is an attempt to make some educated guesses about the future size of the industry. We hope that by providing these estimates we can inform the debate over how much assistance it is reasonable to provide now. We believe that it is impossible to determine the appropriate level of resources to earmark for rescuing the existing banks without taking a position on what role the banks will play in the post-Big Bang economy.

To answer this question about the future, it is necessary to review the recent history of the financial system. In particular, we need to know how the Japanese banking system got into so much trouble. Having determined the cause of the current trouble we can then ask what will have to occur in order for the banks to get out of trouble. Based on our diagnosis, we can then assess what the financial system, particularly the banking system, will look like once the crisis is over.

The story that emerges from our investigation points to the nature of the deregulation leading up to the Big Bank as playing a major role in the banking crisis. During the Japanese high-growth era, usually dated from the mid-1950s through the mid-1970s, the financial system was regulated to steer both savers and borrowers towards banks. As growth slowed in the mid-1970s a gradual deregulation process started. By the late 1980s this deregulation had eliminated many of the restrictions regarding large corporations' options for financing. During the 1980s these key bank clients began sharply reducing their dependence on

---

7. For example, Atkinson (1998) argues that there will be only two to four major banks in Japan. We believe it is more important to focus on the size of the sector than on the number of banks.

bank financing. By the 1990s large Japanese firms' financing patterns had begun to look very similar to those of the large U.S. firms.

Meanwhile, innovation and the deregulation of the restriction on households' investment moved much more slowly. Most Japanese savings into the late 1990s continued to flow into banks. The banks therefore remained large but had to search for new lending opportunities. [The same type of argument is emphasized by Gorton and Rosen (1995) in their discussion of the U.S. banking crisis.] The new lines of business that they entered turned out badly.

We conclude that the lopsided nature of the financial deregulation, combined with maturing of the Japanese economy and slow growth starting in the mid-1970s, created a disequilibrium situation that has lasted to date. To eliminate the disequilibrium, further deregulation of the financial system will be inevitable. Once the deregulation is complete, the Japanese allocation of savings and the investment financing patterns will move further towards the patterns seen in the United States. We show this will imply a substantial decline in the prominence of the banks.

To paint this picture we divide the discussion into five parts. First, we review the regulatory conditions that prevailed prior to the Big Bang, focusing on the banking regulation that has governed the system over the last two decades. We argue that the regulation in Japan and the United States is converging and that the United States provides a sensible benchmark to use in forecasting what might happen in Japan. Section 3 provides some empirical support for this proposition. We show how past deregulation in Japan has altered firms' borrowing patterns and banks' activities. In Section 4 we describe the current state of the banking industry. This brief section aims to clarify some common misperceptions about the current crisis and explain why there are so many different estimates of its scope. In Section 5, we look ahead and ask how much lending will be required if Japanese firms' borrowing patterns move closer to those seen in the United States. Our calculations suggest that this will imply a sizable contraction in the traditional banking sector. Finally, in the conclusion we briefly discuss several scenarios for the transition between the current system and the eventual system.

2. Financial Regulation in Japan

To understand the current conditions and to put the current rules in context it is necessary to review briefly some background information. Until the 1920s, the Japanese banking system was characterized by free competition with little regulation. The Bank Act of 1890, for instance, set no minimum capital level for banks. A series of banking crises in the

1920s, especially the banking panic of 1927, led the Japanese government to change completely its attitude toward regulating banks, and tight regulation of the banking sector began. Government regulation and control of the financial system intensified under the wartime economy.

This pattern continued during the U.S. occupation of Japan. Indeed, some reform measures implemented during the occupation, such as the Glass–Steagall-style strict separation of commercial and investment banking, helped perpetuate the government's strong role in the financial sector. The financial system was also highly segmented. The regulatory framework that was completed during the occupation period stayed more or less in place until the mid-1970s.[8]

During the high-growth era from 1955 through 1973, banks dominated the financial system. Bond markets were repressed, and equity issuance was relatively uncommon.[9] In the 1970s this all began to change.

One big change was slower aggregate growth. Up until this time household savings were mostly channeled through banks to finance business investment. With lower growth the corporate funding requirements fell. The success of the Japanese economy in the rapid-economic-growth period also helped the corporations accumulate internal funds. This intensified the decline in the borrowing requirements of the companies.

A third feature of the economy in the 1970s was that the government began to run a sizable deficits. The deficits arose because of a combination of slower tax revenue growth, a policy decision to engage in deficit spending to try to spur the economy, and an expansion of the Social Security system. To finance the deficits, the government significantly ramped up its bond issuance.

2.1 CHANGES AFFECTING SAVERS

The increase in the government bond issues changed the financial system. Previously, the limited amounts of debt that were issued were sold almost exclusively to financial institutions. The coupon rates were low, but the banks and other buyers tolerated this because the total amount issued was small and other government regulation was protecting them from competition. Moreover, it was customary for the Bank of Japan to periodically buy up the government bonds from the financial institutions as a way to keep money-supply growth in line with aggregate growth. But the soaring debt issuance would have impaired the banks' profitability if they had been forced to absorb all the low-yielding government bonds.

Thus, the Ministry of Finance was compelled to open a secondary

---

8. See Patrick (1967, 1971, 1972) and Hoshi and Kashyap (1999a) for further details.
9. For instance, Patrick (1972) examined financial intermediation in this period and found that the "capital issue markets played a relatively minor role" (p. 112).

market for government bonds in 1977, and to start issuing some bonds through public auctions in 1978. The opening of the secondary market for government bonds, combined with accumulation of financial wealth by households during the rapid economic growth of the 1960s and the early 1970s, increased the demand for bonds. Moreover, many of the restrictions in the bond markets that had been put in place to ration funds during the high-growth era now started to look out of date.

The expansion of the secondary market for government bonds undermined the interest-rate controls that had been a prominent feature of the postwar financial system. Since the government bonds were now traded at market prices, investors were able to stay away from the other financial assets, such as deposits, whose interest rates were set at artificially low levels. Thus, opening up the government bond market led to the liberalization of interest rates in many other markets. For example, interest rates in the interbank lending market, the *tegata* market, and the *gensaki* market were all freed from any regulation by the late 1970s.[10] All the other interest rates except deposit rates were fully liberalized by the end of the 1980s. Starting with large deposit accounts, the deposit rates were gradually decontrolled during the 1980s and the 1990s, and were completely unrestricted by April 1993.

In addition to the interest-rate deregulation, there were several other steps that gave savers better options. Money-market mutual funds slowly began to appear, and investing in other new instruments such as commercial paper eventually became possible. However, there was a lag between the time when bond financing and commercial-paper issuance became commonplace and when savers could easily hold these securities. A summary of the major changes is contained in Table 1. The key conclusion from this table is that options for savers *gradually* changed and many restrictions survived into the late 1990s. As we will see, these changes lagged the changes that benefited borrowers and in several respects were not nearly as dramatic.

2.2 CHANGES AFFECTING BORROWERS

Probably the biggest development for borrowers was the emergence of vibrant bond markets both at home and abroad. In the domestic market, until the mid-1970s firms seeking to issue bonds had to secure approval from a body known as the Bond Issuance Committee. This group determined not only who would be allowed to issue bonds but also how much each issuer could raise. Firms seeking to issue bonds had to satisfy

10. In a *gensaki* transaction, a seller sells a security to a buyer with an agreement to repurchase the same security at a certain price on a certain future date. The *gensaki* market is open to all corporations. In a *tegata* transaction, a seller sells a bill before its maturity to a buyer at a discount. The *tegata* market is restricted to financial institutions.

Table 1   SIGNIFICANT EVENTS AFFECTING THE CHOICES AVAILABLE
TO JAPANESE SAVERS

1979	Negotiable CD market set up.
1981	Maturity-designated time deposits introduced (up to 3 yr); new type of loan trust fund (called "big") accounts introduced by trust banks.
1982	Money-market dealers allowed to begin buying bills; securities companies banned from selling foreign-currency zero-coupon Euro bonds to residents (ban lifted subject to certain restrictions in February 1983)
1983	Banks start over-the-counter sale of government bonds to the general public; government-bond time deposit account introduced; medium-term government-bond time deposit account introduced; postal insurance system permitted to invest in foreign bonds; banks authorized to sell long-term government bonds and medium-term government bonds over the counter.
1984	Short-term Euro–yen loans to residents liberalized; domestic trade in CDs and CPs issued abroad permitted.
1985	Initial relaxation of time-deposit rates (for deposits over 1 billion yen) and money-market certificate (MMC) rates (interest-rate ceiling of 0.75% below weekly average newly issued CD rate); bankers' acceptance market created.
1986	Treasury bill auction begins.
1987	Freely determined interest rates permitted for time deposit accounts over ¥100 million.
1988	Postal savings system allowed to progressively increase foreign investments and to diversify domestic investments (no longer obligated to place all its funds with the Trust Fund Bureau).
1989	Introduction of small-lot MMCs (minimum lot ¥3 million); unregulated interest rates for time deposits over ¥10 million.
1990	Interest-rate ceilings for money-market certificates removed; residents allowed to hold deposits of up to ¥30 million with banks overseas without prior authorization.
1991	Unregulated interest rates for time deposits over ¥3 million; pension funds and investment trusts allowed to buy securitized corporate loans.
1992	Securities houses allowed to offer money-market funds (minimum deposit of ¥1 million provided that more than half of such funds are invested in securities).
1993	All time-deposit rate ceilings removed.
1994	All major interest-rate restriction have been removed.
1997	Security houses allowed to handle consumer payments for their clients; restriction on minimum sales unit of commodity funds removed.
1998	OTC sales of investment trusts by banks and insurance companies.
1999	Liberalization of brokerage commissions for stock trading.

Sources: Takeda and Turner (1992); Ministry of Finance, *Banking Bureau Annual Report,* various issues; Ministry of Finance, *Securities Bureau Annual Report,* various issues.

a set of financial conditions relating to size, profitability, and dividend payments. In addition, bonds had to be issued with collateral.

The first step towards liberalization came in 1975 when the Bond Issuance Committee adopted a policy of honoring the requested amount of bond issues by every company. The collateral requirements also became gradually less important. In 1979, unsecured straight bonds and unsecured convertible bonds were permitted, but the bond issue criteria were so stringent that only two companies (Toyota Auto and Matsushita Electric) were qualified to issue. The criteria for unsecured bonds were gradually relaxed during the 1980s.

Several of the key developments played out in international markets. This first became possible because of the reform of the Foreign Exchange and Trade Control Act in 1980. Foreign exchange transactions, which were "forbidden in principle" under the old rule, were made "free unless expressly prohibited." The internationalization was further advanced in 1984 by the abolition of the "real demand principle," which required foreign exchange transactions to be backed by "real" demand for foreign exchange, such as foreign trade. Following the suggestions in the Yen–Dollar Commission report, the euro market was substantially deregulated and the Tokyo offshore market was opened in 1986.

The foreign bond markets were attractive for Japanese firms because they made it possible to bypass the Bond Issuance Committee.[11] Perhaps most importantly, no collateral was required in foreign markets. This led to high levels of issuance in foreign markets. Warrant bonds, which were introduced in 1981 and allowed the holders to have an option to buy shares at a prespecified price during a certain period, were a leading example. Throughout the 1980s many warrant bonds were issued outside Japan, even though these securities did not prove to be very popular in the domestic market.

Liberalization also proceeded in the domestic market. By 1987 the domestic commercial-paper market was created, giving firms another nonbank source of funding. By the late 1980s firms began to be able to avoid the bond issuance criteria if they were rated. Finally in 1996 all rules regarding bond issues were lifted.

---

11. However, some self-regulation by the security houses continued, so that firms in the 1980s were still forced to satisfy versions of the bond issuance criteria in order to be able to issue debt abroad. Although Japanese banks technically could underwrite foreign bond issues by Japanese corporations through the banks' foreign subsidiaries, the *three-bureaus agreement* of 1975 suggested that banks should "pay due respect to the experience gained by and the mandate given to the Japanese securities firms" (Rosenbluth, 1989, p.152). In practice, the three-bureaus agreement has been interpreted to prohibit subsidiaries of Japanese banks from becoming the lead underwriters of bond issues by Japanese corporations. Thus the Japanese banks did not have much say about the self-regulation of foreign bond issues.

Over this period regulations regarding stock markets were also changed. Listing requirements were eased, and commissions were eventually deregulated. These changes made equity issuance more attractive, although initial public offerings were typically more underpriced in Japan than elsewhere (see Jenkinson, 1990).

The key changes regarding the opening up of capital markets are collected in Table 2. Comparing this table and the previous one shows that the financing options for bank borrowers opened up much faster than the options for savers. As we document below, by the end of the 1980s many of the banks' traditional clients had already migrated to cheaper bond financing. One striking statistic is that during the decade the number of firms permitted to issue unsecured domestic bonds grew from two to over 500.

The third leg of deregulation dealt with changes in bank powers. The major changes are shown in Table 3. We draw three important lessons from the list. First, bank powers were expanded very slowly and gradually. While the banks' main borrowers were able to get quickly into the bond market, the banks had their hands tied in many respects. For instance, securitizing loans was not even possible until 1990. Second, many new types of businesses, particularly fee-generating activities, did not become available until relatively recently. For example, through 1998 Japanese banks were still prohibited from collecting fees by offering loan commitments. Thus, banks in Japan were essentially forced to continue to try to make money through conventional deposit-taking and loan-making during the 1980s. [Gorton and Rosen (1995) point out that similar problems were present in the U.S. Furthermore, the absence of an active takeover market for banks likely exacerbated the problems in both countries.] Finally, even up until the end of 1990s there were significant barriers which continued to keep investment banking and commercial banking separated in Japan.

The culmination of the deregulation is the Big Bang.[12] When the government first proposed the program in the fall of 1996, it was heralded as drive to make Japanese financial markets "free, fair and global." As we describe more completely below, the result will be that banks, insurance companies, and securities dealers will be able to compete directly.

2.3 COMPARISONS WITH THE UNITED STATES

As we look ahead we see these changes pushing the Japanese financial system to become more similar to the U.S. system. In fact, ever since the U.S. occupation of Japan there has been a certain degree of similarity

---

12. There are many good summaries of the provisions of the Big Bang. Two recent guides are Craig (1998) and Toyama (1998).

Table 2 SIGNIFICANT EVENTS IN THE LIBERALIZATION OF
CAPITAL MARKETS

1975   Bond issuance committee begins to honor requested amounts for firms
        that pass the criteria.
1976   Official recognition of *gensaki* (repurchase agreement) transactions.
1977   First issue of 5-year government bonds; first issue of Euro–yen bonds
        by a nonresident; secondary trading of government bonds permitted.
1978   First issue of medium-term coupon government bond (the first to be
        issued by auction; 3-year bonds on this occasion, followed by 2-year
        bonds in June 1979 and 4-year bonds in June 1980).
1979   Unsecured straight bonds and unsecured convertible bonds permitted.
1980   Foreign Exchange and Trade Control Act amended so "free unless pro-
        hibited" replaces "forbidden in principle."
1981   Warrant bonds introduced.
1982   Criteria for the issuance of unsecured bonds by Japanese residents in
        overseas market clarified.
1983   Eligibility standards for issuing unsecured convertible bonds relaxed.
1984   "Real demand rule" for foreign exchange lifted; swap agreements and
        hedging of forward foreign-exchange transactions allowed; collateral re-
        quirement for nonresident issue of Euro–yen bonds dropped; freer issu-
        ance of yen-dominated CDs in Japan; standards for issuing *samurai
        bonds*[a] by private companies eased.
1985   First unsecured straight corporate bond issued; bond futures intro-
        duced; first *shogun bond*[b] issue; first Euro–yen straight bond issued.
1986   The credit rating system in the qualification standard fully introduced
        for Euro–yen bonds issued by nonresidents; floating-rate notes and cur-
        rency conversion bonds introduced for Euro–yen issued by residents;
        first issue of short-term government bonds (TB); public issue of 20-year
        government bonds; Japan offshore market opened (minimum deposit
        ¥100 million; minimum time 2 days).
1987   Introduction of credit rating system in the qualification standards for
        Euro–yen bond issues by residents; packaged stock futures market es-
        tablished on the Osaka Stock Exchange, ending a ban introduced in
        1945; commercial-paper market created.
1988   Restrictions on samurai CP issues by nonresidents relaxed.
1989   Tokyo International Financial Futures Exchange established; rating crite-
        ria for bond issuance added.
1990   Accounting criteria for bond issuance removed.
1992   Bond issuance restrictions eased: more companies allowed to issue
        bonds overseas, and restraints on samurai bonds relaxed.
1995   Deregulation on OTC (JASDAQ) market, creating a new market to facili-
        tate fundraising for startups.
1996   All bond issuance restrictions have been removed.
1998   Introduction of medium-term notes; relaxation of rules governing asset-
        backed securities.

Sources: See Table 1.
[a] Yen-dominated public bonds which are issued in Japan by non-Japanese residents.
[b] Foreign-currency-denominated bonds issued in Japan by nonresidents.

Table 3 SIGNIFICANT EVENTS RELATING TO THE RANGE OF
PERMISSIBLE ACTIVITIES FOR BANKS

1979	Banks permitted to issue and deal in CDs; banks permitted to introduce short-term *impact loans* (foreign-currency loans to residents) subject to certain conditions.
1980	Foreign exchange banks allowed to make medium and long-term impact loans.
1982	Japanese banks permitted to lend yen overseas on a long-term basis to borrowers of their choice (earlier priority system for overseas yen lending is abolished).
1983	Banks started over-the-counter sale of government bonds to the general public; banks authorized to affiliate with mortgage securities companies.
1984	Securities licenses granted to subsidiaries/affiliates of some foreign banks with branches in Japan (equity stakes limited to 50%); permission for foreign and Japanese banks to issue Euro–yen CDs with maturities of 6 months or less; banks allowed to deal on their own account in public bonds.
1985	Foreign banks allowed to enter trust banking business; banks began trading in bond futures; medium and long-term Euro–yen loans to nonresidents liberalized.
1986	City banks authorized to issue long-term mortgage bonds; banks' overseas subsidiaries authorized to underwrite and deal in CP issues abroad.
1987	Banks allowed to engage in private placement of bond issues; banks begin underwriting and trading in the domestic CP market; banks allowed to deal in foreign financial futures.
1988	Banks allowed to securitize home loans.
1989	Banks begin brokering government-bond futures; banks allowed to securitize loans to local governments.
1990	Banks allowed to securitize loans to corporations; banks allowed to enter the pension trust business through their investment advisory companies.
1992	Financial System Reform Bill passes the Diet, allowing banks to set up subsidiaries to enter the securities business (effective April 1993).
1993	Three bureaus agreement ends, allowing banks to be lead underwriters in foreign bond issues; IBJ, LTCB, Norin Chukin Bank, Sumitomo Trust, and Mitsubishi Trust establish their subsidiary security firms.
1994	Major city banks establish their subsidiary security firms.
1998	Ban on financial holding companies lifted.
1999	Banks, trust banks, and securities houses can enter each other's markets; banks allowed to issue straight bonds.
2001	Banks and securities houses will be allowed to enter the insurance business.

Sources: See Table 1.

between the financial systems in the two countries. A key reason for the similarity is that Article 65 of the Securities and Exchange Act was passed in March of 1947 with the intent of mimicking the U.S. Bank Act of 1933 (Glass–Steagall). Both laws mandated a separation of investment and commercial banking. This separation has constituted a defining feature that differentiates the two financial systems from those in Europe and has shaped the evolution of both systems. In what follows, we argue that not only has the evolution been similar, but the banks in the two countries are going to become even more similar in the future.

The Japanese banks have traditionally been more successful than the U.S. banks in their attempts to participate in investment banking. For instance, the banks were able to play the role of trustee of collateral in the bond underwriting process in Japan, while they were mostly shut out in the United States. Similarly, Japanese banks were able to take limited equity positions in the firms to which they were lending. However, as Dale (1992) points out, like the U.S. banks, the Japanese banks were "excluded from market-making in and the public distribution of corporate securities." This constraint kept the Japanese banks from becoming full-fledged, German-style universal banks. Instead the Japanese financial system, like the U.S. system, was fragmented, with banks, insurance firms, and securities firms each maturing while facing little direct competition from each other.

Within the banking system in each country there was further segmentation. In the United States, cross-border branching was restricted until recently so that banks could not compete on a nationwide basis. Similarly, in Japan, competition between city banks, trust banks, regional banks, long-term credit banks, and other small banks such as credit unions has traditionally been restricted by legal measures and administrative guidance by the Ministry of Finance.

Beyond the segmentation, there are further similarities in the ways that the bank powers in the two countries changed over time. In both countries, the drive by the commercial banks to reenter investment banking has taken more than 50 years. During this period the deregulation process has been slow and incremental. In the United States, for example, banks were allowed to enter investment banking through subsidiaries only in 1987, as regulators began to reinterpret Section 20 of the banking laws that prohibits banks from having affiliates that are "principally engaged" in nonbanking activity. Over time the permissible fraction of bank income accruing from the so-called "Section 20 subsidiaries" has slowly risen.

In Japan, the financial system reform in 1993 made it possible for banks to enter the securities business through subsidiaries, but the actual establishment of bank-owned securities subsidiaries was only gradually permitted over the next couple of years. The range of securities services that these subsidiaries can provide is still limited, but the limitations will be incrementally removed between now and 2001.

Importantly, as banking deregulation proceeded in Japan, there was discussion over whether a shift toward permitting universal banking would be desirable. In March 1989 the Ministry of Finance convened an advisory group dubbed the Second Financial System Committee of the Financial System Research Council. This group described five possible routes towards permitting more integration of commercial and investment banking: separated subsidiaries, multi-functional subsidiaries, holding companies, universal banks, and a piecemeal approach (Second Financial System Committee, 1989). According to the Committee, "the sight of banks pushing out in every direction in pursuit of high returns, even at high risk, might shake people's faith in them." Thus, the Committee recommended against a universal banking approach. Ultimately, in 1993, the separated-subsidiary approach was adopted. Later, in 1997, relaxation of Section 9 of the Anti-Monopoly Act made it possible to establish a financial holding company.

As the turn of the century approaches, firms trying to offer one-stop financial shopping are facing fewer and fewer barriers in both countries. In Japan, as a result of the Big Bang, it is already possible to create a holding company that can span the securities and insurance industries. By April 2001 it will be possible to bring banking into the same holding company. In the United States legislation to repeal Glass–Steagall was finally passed, allowing the banking, securities underwriting, and insurance businesses to be integrated. Thus, in the near future the regulatory conditions in the two countries will be very similar.

Once the deregulation in both countries is complete, a transition featuring competition among entrenched securities firms, insurance companies, and banks will begin. In the previous version of this paper, Hoshi and Kashyap (1999b), we tabulated all the major alliances in the Japanese financial services industry that were announced in 1998 and early 1999. This very long list of tie-ups suggests that a scramble is already underway to provide much broader services than have been available in the past, and that the same sort of tie-ups are occurring in the United States and in Japan. Finally, the list also shows that foreign institutions are aggressively entering the Japanese market.

Collectively these patterns suggest that banks in the two countries are going to face the same types of competitive pressures and will have some sort of options available to respond to the pressures. Although the Japanese banks start from a much weaker capital position than the U.S.

banks, it is hard to see why the bank activities in the two countries will not become similar.

3. An Empirical Look at the Fallout from the Deregulation

To support our contention that Big Bang is going to push the financial system in Japan to look more like the U.S. system, we examine several pieces of evidence. For organizational purposes it is convenient to separate the discussion into the responses of the borrowers, savers, and lenders. We will see that the behavior of large and small borrowers turns out to be quite different. On the bank side we will distinguish between the portfolio adjustments that were made and the new business opportunities that were missed. For the savers we will see that the deregulation prior to the Big Bang has not made a big difference.

Throughout most of our discussion we will emphasize the importance of regulatory shifts. This choice does not mean that we doubt the importance of other factors such as macroeconomic conditions. In fact, it is quite reasonable to assume that the deregulation may have contributed to the fast growth of lending in the late 1980s that preceded the long recession of the 1990s. However, for the purposes of looking ahead we do not believe that it is necessary to separately identify the role of macroeconomic factors. Our basic point is that the past deregulation did have some independent effects and that based on the responses to past deregulation it is reasonable to expect that the Big Bang will have a large effect as well. Thus, our empirical work is aimed at showing that regulatory shifts have clear, independent influences on borrowers, savers, and banks.[13]

3.1 THE RESPONSE OF BORROWERS TO FINANCIAL-MARKET DEREGULATION

It is widely recognized that part of the reason why banks in Japan got into trouble is that they lost many of their best borrowers in a very short period of time.[14] As mentioned earlier, between 1983 and 1989 the Japa-

---

13. There are several studies that focus on drawing a more comprehensive picture of what caused the current banking problem in Japan. Cargill, Hutchison, and Ito (1997) list both macroeconomic conditions generated by loose monetary policy in the late 1980s and reduced corporate dependence on bank financing, on which we focus, as contributing factors to the problem. They also list other factors such as government deposit guarantees and regulatory forebearance. Cargill (1999) gives a similarly comprehensive list. By estimating some cross-section regressions, Ueda (1999) confirms the importance of both macroeconomic conditions and financial deregulation in bringing about the banking problem.

14. For instance, see Cargill, Hutchison, and Ito (1997), Cargill (1999), Ueda (1999), Lincoln (1998), Hutchison (1998), and Hoshi and Kashyap (1999a).

nese bond market blossomed, permitting many internationally known companies to tap the public debt markets for the first time. While this story is well known, we are unaware of any attempts to compare the bank dependence of large Japanese and U.S. firms before and after the deregulation. We provide evidence that the Japanese deregulation has permitted the largest Japanese firms to become almost as independent of banks as their U.S. counterparts.

A major challenge in conducting this investigation is the limited availability of comprehensive data on bank borrowing by firms. In Japan there are essentially two types of data that can be used. For exchange-traded firms, the corporate financial statements that are publicly available generally break out bank borrowing. This means that for these (typically) large firms one can get fairly good data. As an example, the Japan Development Bank Database provides this type of information on over 2000 firms for 1997.

To learn anything about unlisted companies one must rely on survey data. The most comprehensive survey that we know of on this topic is conducted by the Ministry of Finance and published in the *Hojin Kigyo Kiho* (*Quarterly Report of Incorporated Enterprise Statistics*). The cross-sectional coverage of these data is excellent. All nonfinancial corporations with book *capital* of ¥1 billion ($8.33 million using the exchange rate of 120 ¥/$) are included in the survey.[15] The remaining (small corporations) are randomly sampled with sampling factors that depend on their size. Only very tiny firms (those with less than ¥10 million in capital) are completely excluded. We believe that the survey is sufficiently comprehensive that it essentially sidesteps the selection problems associated with using listed data.[16]

The main drawback with the survey information is that data for firms with similar amounts of capital are aggregated, so that no firm-level statistics are accessible. Unfortunately, all the size thresholds used in the MOF data are based on *nominal* thresholds, so that over time (as the price level rises) firms drift into the upper grouping, even if their size measured in constant prices is unchanging. We discuss the effect of this limitation in the places where we believe it might be important.

In our analysis we focus on the ratio of (the book value of) bank debt to (the book value of) total assets as the basic measure of the importance of bank financing. We scale by assets to eliminate pure size differences.[17]

---

15. In what follows we use this exchange rate. We use GDP deflators when it is necessary to convert nominal amounts into real amounts.
16. For example, the 1997 fourth-quarter survey was sent to 23,475 firms, and the response rate was over 80% (19,007).
17. This ratio can also be thought of as the product of the bank-debt-to-total-debt ratio and

Below we also show some results which distinguish among different industries. The industry comparisons can be motivated in many ways, including as an attempt to correct for industry-level differences in risk and collateralizability of assets.

Table 4 shows the ratio of the bank debt to total assets based on the MOF data for different-sized Japanese firms over time. The data pertain to the second quarter of each year between 1980 and 1998. In addition to showing data for all industries, the table also displays separate series for manufacturing, wholesale and retail trade, and all other firms. The largest firms which are separately identified in the sample are those with a book value of equity greater than ¥1 billion in current prices. In the second quarter of 1998 the 5363 firms in this category had average assets of ¥112 billion.[18]

The table reveals a consistent pattern of large Japanese firms scaling back their bank borrowing. The shift has been most pronounced among manufacturing firms, where the ratio of bank debt to assets has dropped by almost 50%. Moreover, the shift was effectively complete by 1990—since then the ratio has been roughly constant. This timing suggests that the banks lost many of their traditional clients soon after the opening up of the bond market.

There was also a substantial drop in bank dependence for the trade firms. In publicly available versions of the survey all trade firms are shown together, but the Ministry of Finance provided us with unpublished data for selected years which allow us to separate wholesale trade companies from the retail trade companies. From the unpublished data we learned that the drop in bank dependence is more pronounced for retail trade firms than for wholesale trade firms. For instance, between 1980 and 1998 the large retail trade companies cut their bank-debt-to-asset ratio from 0.35 to 0.26, while the wholesale firms cut theirs from 0.35 to 0.30.

---

the total-debt-to-total-asset ratio. This decomposition distinguishes the total amount of leverage from the sources of financing for borrowers. For our purposes we believe this distinction is not very helpful, since the banks presumably care about their total lending. To a first approximation it probably does not matter if they are losing business *over the kind of long periods that we are studying* because of overall deleveraging as opposed to more competition from other funding sources. We also checked that using book-value data would not paint a misleading picture. A quick comparison of data on national income accounts in Japan and the United States suggested that the gap between the current value of assets (the analog to market value) and the historical value was similar in the two countries. Thus, we see no obvious biases from using book-value data for both countries.

18. Of the 5363 large firms, 2192 were in manufacturing, 941 were in trade (wholesale or retail), and the remaining 2230 were in other industries. There were 1,161,179 small firms in the 1998 survey, with 232,313 in manufacturing, 363,707 in trade, and 565,159 in the other industries.

Table 4 HOJIN KIGYO TOKEI DATA ON THE RATIO OF BANK DEBT TO ASSETS FOR JAPANESE FIRMS
(Large firms have book value of equity greater than 1 billion yen.)

	All Industries		Manufacturing		Wholesale and Retail		Other	
Year	Large Firms	Small Firms	Large Firms	Small Firms	Large Firms	Small Firms	Large Firms	Small Firms
1978	0.3786	0.3332	0.3654	0.3294	0.3818	0.2929	0.4007	0.3847
1979	0.3587	0.3282	0.3372	0.3009	0.3689	0.2897	0.3890	0.3984
1980	0.3431	0.3214	0.3181	0.2860	0.3486	0.2892	0.3833	0.3908
1981	0.3484	0.3329	0.3193	0.2954	0.3628	0.3015	0.3886	0.4048
1982	0.3473	0.3649	0.3122	0.3081	0.3650	0.3109	0.3947	0.4833
1983	0.3513	0.3600	0.3041	0.3178	0.3847	0.3059	0.4073	0.4433
1984	0.3420	0.3634	0.2806	0.3230	0.3762	0.3113	0.4197	0.4487
1985	0.3219	0.3754	0.2577	0.3257	0.3755	0.3184	0.3853	0.4705
1986	0.3281	0.3884	0.2560	0.3417	0.3910	0.3341	0.3938	0.4721
1987	0.3304	0.4039	0.2487	0.3613	0.3992	0.3373	0.4011	0.4912
1988	0.3202	0.4161	0.2179	0.3436	0.3865	0.3604	0.4050	0.5040
1989	0.3022	0.4311	0.1819	0.3438	0.3605	0.3543	0.4069	0.5364
1990	0.2901	0.4130	0.1614	0.3438	0.3106	0.3475	0.4174	0.4933
1991	0.2907	0.4225	0.1584	0.3350	0.3176	0.3367	0.4158	0.5225
1992	0.2867	0.4147	0.1645	0.3537	0.3092	0.3443	0.3971	0.4899
1993	0.2934	0.4342	0.1786	0.3837	0.3049	0.3621	0.3981	0.5033
1994	0.2925	0.4346	0.1800	0.3783	0.3145	0.3953	0.3915	0.4878
1995	0.2846	0.4317	0.1756	0.3878	0.2995	0.3891	0.3826	0.4827
1996	0.2797	0.4336	0.1658	0.3641	0.2857	0.3682	0.3850	0.5081
1997	0.2732	0.4224	0.1595	0.3653	0.2827	0.3775	0.3801	0.4773
1998	0.2761	0.4257	0.1647	0.3527	0.2876	0.3978	0.3796	0.4773

Source: Ministry of Finance, Hojin Kigyo Tokei. The survey includes all the corporations with book capital of ¥1 billion ($8.3 million using the exchange rate of 120 ¥/$) in all nonfinancial industries. The rest (small corporations) are randomly sampled with sampling factors depending on their sizes. The average value of assets for the large firms is ¥112 billion ($934 million) in 1998. There were 5,363 large firms and 1,161,179 small firms in the 1998 survey. The firms in the "other" category are all those which are not in manufacturing, wholesale trade, or retail trade.

Table 4 also indicates that remaining large firms hardly changed their bank borrowing.

To explore the effect of the nominal thresholds we also looked at other data for listed firms. In Table 5 we report analogous statistics in which we define large firms to have real assets (measured in 1990 prices) to be greater than ¥120 billion ($1 billion). Using this consistent size definition, the manufacturing firms show an even more pronounced shift away from bank debt. The larger drop is partly expected, since the nominal size thresholds in the MOF survey data will cause some smaller firms (which are presumably more bank-dependent) to drift into the large firm category over time.

The third and fourth columns in Table 5 show the patterns for large, listed wholesale and retail firms. The retail firms show the same general pattern as the manufacturing firms, although the drop in bank dependence is less pronounced. For the listed wholesale trade firms the bank-debt-to-asset ratio drifted up noticeably in the 1980s, before beginning to decline in the 1990s. This nonmonotonic decline can be traced to the behavior of the nine large general trading firms and is not representative of other wholesaling companies. The trend disappears when these nine firms are omitted, and the aforementioned unpublished MOF data showed a slight overall drop in bank dependence.[19] The final column in the table shows that the remaining large listed firms have also cut their bank borrowing.

The two tables together show a clear pattern of rapid adjustment by the large firms (except for possibly a few wholesale trade companies). Notice in Table 5 that for all the sectors where bank dependence was falling, the bank-debt-to-asset ratios in 1990 and 1998 were about the same, so that in fact much of the adjustment had occurred before the onset of slow aggregate growth.

In contrast, among the small firms there has been no clear reduction in bank dependence. Indeed, Table 4 shows that in each of the major sectors the smaller firms have become somewhat more bank-dependent as the deregulation has progressed, although in manufacturing and in the "other" sector small firms' bank dependence is below the peaks that occurred in the late 1980s and early 1990s. As we discuss below, we

19. The nine companies in question are Mitsui Bussan, Itochu, Kanematsu, Sumitomo and Company, Tomen, Nissho Iwai, Nichimen, Marubeni, and Mitsubishi and Company. When they are excluded, the ratio of bank debt to assets is much lower in most years (e.g. 0.248 in 1998 as opposed to 0.431), and in 1998 it is slightly lower than in the early 1970s. We have heard several anecdotes suggesting that this discrepancy arises because the large trading companies took on considerable bank debt in the 1980s in order to set up subsidiaries to enter the real estate business.

Table 5   RATIO OF BANK DEBT TO ASSETS FOR PUBLICLY TRADED
JAPANESE FIRMS
(Large firms are defined to have book value of assets $> ¥120$ billion
at 1990 prices.)

Year	Manufacturing	Wholesale	Retail	Nonmanufacturing Excluding Wholesale and Retail
1970	0.3621	0.3006	0.3019	0.3605
1971	0.3655	0.3207	0.3153	0.3620
1972	0.3891	0.3438	0.3486	0.3848
1973	0.3758	0.3590	0.3919	0.3961
1974	0.3388	0.3170	0.4367	0.3864
1975	0.3606	0.3513	0.4371	0.3860
1976	0.3809	0.3804	0.4378	0.3912
1977	0.3712	0.3902	0.4022	0.3863
1978	0.3650	0.4121	0.3640	0.3796
1979	0.3471	0.3970	0.3180	0.3691
1980	0.3157	0.3641	0.2922	0.3677
1981	0.3043	0.3745	0.3046	0.3595
1982	0.2970	0.3665	0.3142	0.3688
1983	0.2949	0.3989	0.3369	0.3788
1984	0.2736	0.4050	0.3239	0.3813
1985	0.2446	0.4003	0.3122	0.3793
1986	0.2380	0.4348	0.2975	0.3173
1987	0.2316	0.4503	0.2600	0.3107
1988	0.2031	0.4800	0.2134	0.3069
1989	0.1654	0.5242	0.1900	0.2976
1990	0.1269	0.5079	0.1726	0.2745
1991	0.1333	0.4784	0.1820	0.2757
1992	0.1386	0.4884	0.1830	0.2806
1993	0.1452	0.4983	0.1986	0.2755
1994	0.1496	0.4865	0.1915	0.2861
1995	0.1431	0.4768	0.2042	0.2878
1996	0.1311	0.4523	0.1943	0.2850
1997	0.1256	0.4311	0.1841	0.2899

Source: Authors' calculations using the Japan Development Bank Database of companies listed on the major Japanese stock exchanges.

believe that some of these patterns are attributable to the fact that the banks themselves did not shrink much as the deregulation proceeded.

One question raised by these patterns is what they imply for the future of relationship financing in Japan. The data in Tables 4 and 5 clearly show that even before the Big Bang had taken place, the large

Japanese firms had cut their bank dependence. Tight dependence of large firms on their banks was probably the most unusual aspect of the Japanese financial system.[20] A growing literature (e.g., Petersen and Rajan, 1994; Berger and Udell, 1995) shows that relationship financing for small firms is quite prevalent also outside of Japan. It appears that any relationship financing that will continue in Japan will be more like what is observed elsewhere in the world.

To put the size of the shift in behavior of the large firms in perspective, we offer a comparison with financing patterns in the United States. This effort is complicated because of the absence of completely comparable data for the United States. Contrary to the conventions followed in Japan, there are no standard sources that provide firm-level information on firms' bank borrowing. U.S. firms do sometimes identify bank lending in the footnotes to their financial statements, but databases such as Compustat do not report such information. So we cannot report data which would be comparable to Table 5.

The only broad-based U.S. data on bank borrowing patterns come from a survey conducted by the Census Bureau called the Quarterly Financial Report for Manufacturing, Mining, and Trade Corporations (QFR).[21] The QFR contains the financial statistics for corporations aggregated by industry and by size. Like the MOF survey, the size thresholds are based on nominal thresholds, although the QFR size cutoffs are based on assets rather than capital. The coverage of the QFR for manufacturing industries is outstanding. All the corporations with total assets of $250 million and over are included in the survey. Smaller firms are randomly sampled with sampling factors ranging from $\frac{1}{2}$ to $\frac{1}{160}$, depending on their sizes.

Unfortunately the QFR coverage beyond manufacturing is quite limited. For firms in three industries (mining, wholesale trade, and retail trade) all the corporations with total assets $250 million and over are included, but small corporations are intentionally excluded. Since 1988 the definition of "small" has been set so that no corporations with total assets under $50 million are included; previously, between 1981 and 1987, this threshold has been $25 million in current prices. This prevents us from examining the financing pattern of small firms outside manufacturing. Moreover, for industries that are not covered by the QFR (trans-

20. See Aoki and Patrick (1994) for a comprehensive study of the tight dependence of Japanese firms on banks. There is no contradiction in saying that the past relationships for the large firms may have been valuable but were not sustained after deregulation. This will be the case if, as capital markets improved, the costs of being tied to the banks was rising. See Hoshi and Kashyap (1999a) for further discussion on this point.

21. See Gertler and Gilchrist (1994) for more discussion of the QFR.

portation, communication, services, construction, etc.), we cannot get data even for large firms.

It is fairly straightforward to find a breakpoint in the QFR data that can be compared with the *Hojin Kigyo Tokei Kiho* data described in Table 4. Recall from Table 4 that the average asset size of the large Japanese firms was $934 million in 1998. According to QFR for 1998, the average size of total assets for manufacturing corporations with assets $10 million or above was $1020 million. Thus, it appears that "large" firms in Table 4 are roughly comparable to QFR data for firms with total assets of $10 million.

Table 6 shows data on the bank-debt-to-asset reported in the QFR from 1979 through 1997. Columns 2 through 4 show data on all manufacturing firms and then on large and small manufacturing firms respectively. We draw three conclusions from this part of table. First, and most importantly, the time-series variation in bank dependence in the U.S. data is much less noticeable than in the Japanese data. Second, for the large firms there has been a slight upward drift in the bank-debt-to-asset ratio. Consequently the bank dependence of the U.S. and Japanese large firms is much closer now than in the 1980s—we explore this further below. Third, the small manufacturing firms in the two countries do not seem to be converging in their borrowing behavior. The small U.S. manufacturing firms have held steady with a ratio of bank debt to assets between 16% and 19%. In contrast, the small Japanese firms' ratio has crept up from about 29% to 35%.[22]

The remainder of Table 6 provides information on borrowing patterns by wholesale and retail trade firms. Interpreting these figures requires some care, since the universe of firms included in the sample has changed greatly across the years—see the footnotes to the table for details. Despite these changes, it seems safe to conclude that very large nonmanufacturing firms in the United States are still much less bank-dependent than similar firms in Japan.

One potential concern with Table 6 is that the nominal size thresholds may be responsible for some of drift upwards in the large manufacturing firms' bank dependence. Unfortunately, we were unable to obtain any unpublished data from the U.S. Census Bureau to check this directly. However, based on the checks which we were able to perform using published data, this does not seem likely to be too much of an issue. For instance, it is possible to study manufacturing firms with more than $1 billion in assets. Within this sample, the firms which drift

---

22. Toward the end of the 1990s, however, the bank dependence of the small Japanese manufacturing firms did decline. We expect this pattern to continue after the Big Bang.

Table 6   QUARTERLY FINANCIAL REPORTS DATA ON THE RATIO OF BANK DEBT TO ASSETS FOR U.S. FIRMS
(Large manufacturing firms are defined as having nominal assets > $10 million.)

Year (4th Quarter)	All Manufacturing	Large Manufacturing	Small Manufacturing	Wholesale	Retail	All Industries
1979	0.0660	0.0550	0.1642	0.1777	0.1255	0.0919
1980	0.0680	0.0575	0.1688	0.1882	0.1206	0.0937
1981	0.0665	0.0568	0.1676	0.1844	0.0637	0.0850
1982	0.0712	0.0617	0.1695	0.2383	0.0546	0.0829
1983	0.0644	0.0542	0.1710	0.2028	0.0524	0.0746
1984	0.0754	0.0652	0.1860	0.1995	0.0553	0.0839
1985	0.0731	0.0632	0.1867	0.1825	0.0681	0.0820
1986	0.0796	0.0714	0.1878	0.1773	0.0797	0.0882
1987	0.0830	0.0751	0.1892	0.1865	0.0922	0.0932
1988	0.0950	0.0875	0.2045	0.1886	0.1296	0.1064
1989	0.1004	0.0944	0.1988	0.1937	0.1434	0.1130
1990	0.1032	0.0976	0.2009	0.1868	0.1417	0.1146
1991	0.0954	0.0899	0.1954	0.1771	0.1287	0.1064
1992	0.0924	0.0875	0.1831	0.1786	0.0968	0.1007
1993	0.0863	0.0814	0.1771	0.1671	0.0916	0.0945
1994	0.0850	0.0798	0.1868	0.1676	0.0932	0.0940
1995	0.0862	0.0809	0.1934	0.1703	0.0993	0.0961
1996	0.0834	0.0782	0.1910	0.1623	0.1026	0.0932
1997	0.0877	0.0834	0.1794	0.1513	0.1089	0.0966

Source: Quarterly Financial Report for Manufacturing, Mining, and Trade Corporations (QFR) produced by Bureau of Census. For manufacturing firms all corporations with total assets of $250 million and over are included in this survey. Smaller manufacturing firms are randomly sampling with sampling factors ranging from 1/2 to 1/160, depending on their sizes. We define large firms to be those with nominal assets greater than $10 million. The sampling rules governing the inclusion of wholesale and retail trade firms has changed over time. In the 1979 and 1980 surveys, the rules for these sectors were the same as that for manufacturing. From 1981 to 1987, only firms with assets above $25 million were included. From 1988 on, firms had to have assets above $50 million to be included.

into the category should already be quite large and have a low level of bank dependence. This sample of firms shows the same basic patterns as in Table 6: bank dependence rises in the late 1980s and then falls in the 1990s, but remains at a higher level than in 1980.

Comparing Tables 4 and 6, we find that the bank dependence of the large Japanese firms has become closer to that of comparable-sized U.S. firms, particularly in manufacturing industries. The convergence, however, still looks incomplete. One possible reason for this may be cross-country differences in the industrial structure. Average bank-debt-to-asset ratios vary considerably across industries. For instance, in the 1998 MOF data shown in Table 4, the range of bank-debt-to-assets ratios varies between 0.09 and 0.42 across manufacturing industries (using two-digit SIC codes to identify industries). This type of variation is not surprising, given the differences in riskiness and collateral of different industries. Such variation will probably persist even after the Big Bang. Therefore one would only expect convergence in the bank-debt-to-asset ratio for the entire manufacturing sector if the asset distribution across industries were the same in both countries. This suggests that it is advisable to study the borrowing patterns at the two-digit industry level (or finer).

One problem with looking to industry-level data is that there is less detail on the size distribution of firms within industries. The published QFR data only show separate information for firms with assets above and below $25 million. The published Quarterly Report of Incorporate Enterprise Statistics includes no information on different-sized firms in each industry. By getting unpublished data from Japan we were able to make some very rough comparisons.[23] The Japanese data cover firms with capital above ¥1 billion, so there is a slight size mismatch in the comparison.[24] The overlap in industrial classification definitions allows us to match 14 industries (food; textiles; pulp and paper; printing and publishing; chemicals; petroleum and coal products; stone, clay and glass; iron and steel; nonferrous metals; fabricated metal products; machinery; electrical and electronic machinery; transportation equipment; and precision machinery).

Table 7 reports information on how large Japanese firms' bank dependence has compared with U.S. firms' bank dependence over time. For the Japanese firms we show the bank-debt-to-asset ratio in 1980 and

23. We thank Itsuko Takemura for providing these data.
24. The ¥1 billion cutoff is closer to a $10 million cutoff. However, using the published data on all manufacturing firms, we verified that the firms with between $10 and $25 million in assets are of limited importance. Thus, we believe that the size mismatch is not likely to mislead us about the general trends in bank dependence in the two countries.

Table 7   INDUSTRY-LEVEL COMPARISONS OF BANK-DEBT-TO-TOTAL-ASSETS RATIO FOR LARGE U.S. AND JAPANESE MANUFACTURING FIRMS

Industry	U.S. 1998	Japan 1980	Japan 1998	Japan 1980 minus U.S. 1998	Japan 1998 minus U.S. 1998
Food	0.1216	0.1925	0.1369	0.0709	0.0153
Textiles	0.2014	0.3828	0.2465	0.1814	0.0451
Pulp and paper	0.1167	0.4372	0.3535	0.3205	0.2368
Printing and publishing	0.0860	0.0808	0.0852	−0.0052	−0.0008
Chemicals	0.0758	0.3145	0.1649	0.2387	0.0891
Petroleum and coal	0.0240	0.5836	0.4168	0.5596	0.3928
Stone, glass, and clay	0.1531	0.3708	0.1941	0.2177	0.0410
Iron and steel	0.1138	0.3924	0.2647	0.2786	0.1509
Nonferrous metals	0.0726	0.4458	0.3599	0.3732	0.2873
Metal products	0.1788	0.3150	0.1738	0.1362	−0.0050
Machinery	0.0725	0.2415	0.1568	0.1690	0.0843
Electronic machinery	0.0497	0.1542	0.0919	0.1045	0.0422
Transportation durables	0.0393	0.1479	0.1096	0.1086	0.0703
Precision machinery	0.1551	0.1647	0.1020	0.0096	−0.0531
Average	0.1043	0.3017	0.2040	0.1974	0.0997

Source: See text.
Note: Large U.S. firms are defined as those having assets >$25 million.

1998. Since there is no noticeable trend in the U.S. data, we report only the 1998 levels for the U.S. industries—using other years or an average of several years made no difference in what follows. The last two columns of the table show the difference for each of 14 industries in two periods. In 1980, the difference was diffusely distributed between 0 and 0.56. For the industry average the difference was 0.197. The table shows that by 1998 the distribution had become much more concentrated around zero. By 1998, for ten out of fourteen industries, the Japanese bank debt ratios are within 10 percentage points of the U.S. ratios. Moreover, for these ten industries the distribution of differences in bank dependence is more symmetric, with three of the ten Japanese industries appearing less bank-dependent than their U.S. counterparts.

Interestingly, the four industries where convergence has not occurred (pulp and paper, nonferrous metals, petroleum, and iron and steel) are all cases where a significant portion of the Japanese firms have performed poorly.[25] We believe that for these depressed industries the effects of

25. We thank Bob Uriu for pointing this out.

Table 8   INDUSTRY-LEVEL COMPARISONS OF THE RATIO OF BANK
DEBT TO TOTAL ASSETS FOR SMALL U.S. AND JAPANESE
MANUFACTURING FIRMS

Industry	U.S. 1998	Japan 1980	Japan 1998	Japan 1980 minus U.S. 1998	Japan 1998 minus U.S. 1998
Food	0.2637	0.3945	0.4877	0.1308	0.2240
Textiles	0.1971	0.3300	0.3460	0.1329	0.1489
Pulp and paper	0.2334	0.2591	0.3910	0.0257	0.1576
Printing and publishing	0.1958	0.3115	0.2600	0.1157	0.0642
Chemicals	0.1775	0.2095	0.2874	0.0320	0.1099
Petroleum and coal	0.1763	0.3917	0.2576	0.2154	0.0813
Stone, glass, and clay	0.2246	0.3068	0.4302	0.0822	0.2056
Iron and steel	0.1910	0.2818	0.4137	0.0908	0.2227
Nonferrous metals	0.1977	0.2727	0.4078	0.0750	0.2101
Metal products	0.1814	0.2720	0.4000	0.0906	0.2186
Machinery	0.1865	0.2622	0.3671	0.0757	0.1806
Electronic machinery	0.1771	0.2390	0.2632	0.0619	0.0861
Transportation durables	0.1795	0.2504	0.3271	0.0709	0.1476
Precision machinery	0.1295	0.2039	0.3236	0.0744	0.1941
Average	0.1937	0.2847	0.3545	0.0910	0.1608

Source: See text.
Note: Small U.S. firms are defined as those having assets <$25 million.

deregulation are likely being masked by the poor profitability of the firms; going to public debt markets is always hard for financially troubled firms. Overall we read the industry-level comparisons as further suggesting that large Japanese and U.S. manufacturing firms have become fairly similar in their bank dependence.

Table 8 shows a comparable set of industry differences for small manufacturing firms. The contrast with the previous table is striking. For the small firms there is no sign of convergence, and if anything the differences are larger than in 1980. However, the differences were even larger in 1993, so the relative gap is now closing. Nevertheless, there is still a long way to go.

3.2 SAVERS' RESPONSE TO THE DEREGULATION

An obvious question is why the small and large borrowers fared so differently. We believe that the key to understanding the difference comes from looking at the behavior of the banks' depositors. Japanese households have historically held the dominant part of their financial

Table 9   RATIOS OF BANK DEPOSITS TO GDP FOR SELECTED
         YEARS—G7 COUNTRIES

Country	Year	(Demand Deposits)/ GDP[a]	(Time Deposits)/ GDP[b]	(Total Deposits)/ GDP[a]	(Nonbank Deposits)/ GDP[b,c]	Addendum: (Total Deposits)/ Wealth[d]
Canada	1983	0.09	0.55	0.63	0.58	0.35
	1996	0.17	0.62	0.79	0.75	0.33
France	1983	0.18	0.43	0.61	0.46	0.57
	1996	0.20	0.45	0.65	0.68	0.36
Germany	1983	0.11	0.40	0.50	0.72	0.55
	1996	0.18	0.42	0.60	0.93	0.43
Italy	1983	0.31	0.36	0.67	0.59	0.35
	1996	0.27	0.25	0.52	0.51	0.33
Japan	1983	0.21	1.36	1.58	1.50	0.67
	1996	0.28	1.78	2.06	1.43	0.62
U.K.	1983	0.10	0.25	0.35	0.85	N/A
	1996	N/A	1.06	1.06	0.91	N/A
U.S.	1983	0.11	0.46	0.57	0.74	0.25
	1996	0.11	0.31	0.42	0.50	0.16

[a]International Financial Statistics, International Monetary Fund. This information includes all institutions that accept deposits, not only commercial banks.
[b]*Bank Profitability: Financial Statements of Banks, Statistical Supplement*, Organization for Economic Cooperation and Development, several issues.
[c]For United Kingdom the data correspond to 1984. For United Kingdom and Japan, nonbank deposits include interbank deposits.
[d]*Financial Accounts of OECD Countries*, Organization for Economic Cooperation and Development, several issues.

assets in bank deposits. The conventional explanation for this (e.g., Hamada and Horiuchi, 1987) was the relatively low overall level of financial assets held by the households along with the high transactions costs of operating in immature capital markets. Table 9, which shows the ratios of bank deposits to GDP for G7 countries, suggests that at the onset of deregulation in 1983 Japan had far more bank deposits (relative to GDP) than any of the other G7 countries. The total deposit-to-GDP ratio in Japan stood at 1.58, more than double the ratio for Italy, the next highest country.

The table also shows that by 1996 the picture had hardly changed. Japan still looks anomalous in its deposit/GDP ratio. Figure 1 shows yearly data for the city banks and confirms that there were no unusual breaks in the pattern and that even the large commercial banks were

Figure 1 HOUSEHOLDS' DEPOSITS AT CITY BANKS RELATIVE TO GDP
(1975–1997)

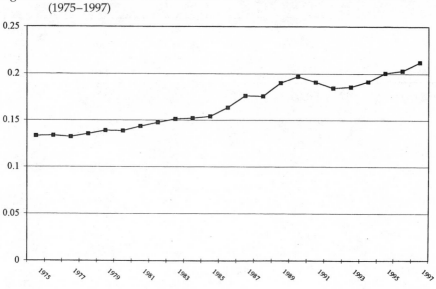

Source: Bank of Japan, *Economic Statistics Annual,* various issues.

gaining deposits (relative to GDP) in the last two decades. The fact that deposits at the city banks account for only about 10% of the deposits recorded in the IMF data is one way of seeing the importance of postal savings accounts. As we discuss below, forecasts of the future of the banking system need to be conditioned on what will happen to the postal savings accounts.

Why didn't the Japanese savers prune their bank deposits? One answer is that the deposit-to-GDP ratio may not tell the complete story. The last column in Table 9 shows that the ratio of deposits to *wealth* fell from 67% in 1983 to 62% in 1996. So from the households' perspective they did cut back slightly on their use of banks. Nevertheless, there does seem to be a puzzle as to why the banking reliance remained so strong, particularly since there were so many steps taken to liberalize financial markets during this time.

We believe that there were several features of the deregulation process that kept savers from pulling their money out of the banks. First, the deregulation process was very slow in allowing individual investors easy direct access to capital markets. For example, participating directly in the stock market remained expensive for individuals until very recently. Up until April 1998, commissions on trades as large as ¥50 million were still fixed and regulated. Only in October 1999 were all commissions fully deregulated. Similarly, a range of activities including stock options trading by individuals, over-the-counter trading of equity-related derivatives, and trading non-listed stocks through securities firms were prohibited until December 1998. So prior to the Big Bang it was very costly for individual investors to participate in capital markets directly.

But the limited direct access only partially explains individuals' strong attachments to bank deposits. One obvious question is why investment trusts (which have existed for many years) didn't draw money away from banks. Here again regulation was important. Until 1998, investment trusts in Japan were limited to contract-type funds, and company-type funds (i.e., U.S.-style mutual funds) were not allowed. Furthermore, any investment trust had to be sold to more than 50 investors, precluding the possibility of establishing funds specialized for a few rich investors, like many hedge funds, vulture funds, and LBO funds in the United States.

More importantly, entry into the investment trust business was limited by other regulations. This protection muted some of the incentives to improve the returns on investment trusts. Since almost all the investment trust companies were subsidiaries of securities companies, they were often interested in churning all the accounts they managed to collect the high commissions for their parents. Consequently the investment trusts had a poor track record, generally underperforming market indices by large margins (Cai, Chan, and Yamada, 1996; Ohmura and Kawakita, 1992, Chapter 7; Yonezawa and Maru, 1984, p. 31).

Other financial services companies were barred from offering investment trusts until the 1990s. But even in the 1990s, when the entry barriers finally started to be removed, the investment trust companies were still required to get government approval each time they set up a new investment trust fund. The restriction remained until December 1998 and stifled competition in introducing innovative products.[26]

We believe these factors together significantly limited the options of savers and led them to keep much of their money in the banks. Notice that our explanation does not emphasize any attempts by banks to attract funds to take advantage of their deposit insurance guarantees. This does

---

26. When a career official at the Ministry of Finance was arrested on corruption charges, the most important favor that he supposedly provided to the security firms was quickly approving the prospectuses of new investment funds that they proposed (*Nihon Keizai Shimbun*, March 6, 1998, evening edition).

Figure 2 CORPORATE BOND PURCHASES BY SECTOR (1981–1990)

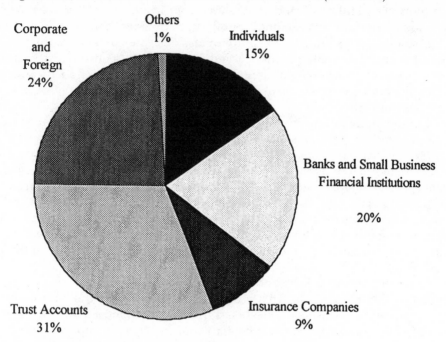

Source: Flow-of-funds accounts; see text for details.

not imply that we completely dismiss the moral-hazard stories that have been emphasized by others (e.g., Cargill, Hutchison, and Ito, 1997; Hutchison, 1998). Rather, we believe that our complementary explanation stressing the limited degree to which savings options were deregulated has been overlooked.

Of course, one might still wonder who ended up buying all the bonds that the companies issued. Figure 2 shows the distribution of bond purchases during the 1980s.[27] Consistent with our account, direct individuals' purchases were relatively small. Given the aforementioned impediments, we do not find this surprising. Instead, it appears that various types of financial institutions (most notably insurance companies, com-

27. These statistics are built up from flow-of-funds data that show owners of domesticity issued corporate bonds including convertibles and warrant bonds. The corporate bonds held by government financial institutions are excluded from the total to isolate the corporate bonds held by the private sector. Since the privatization of NTT in 1985 and JR in 1987 reclassified their bonds from public bonds to corporate bonds, the number includes NTT (JR) bonds that were issued before 1985 (1987) and had not been retired as of the end of 1990 in addition to the net purchases of corporate bonds.

mercial banks, and trust banks) were major purchasers, along with corporations and foreigners.[28]

We draw two further conclusions from this reading of the evidence. First, the Big Bang is likely to be more important in generating new options for savers than for borrowers, who by 1990 had already gained important alternatives to bank financing. Second, we believe that the historical record gives us little quantitative guidance as to how the households will respond to the Big Bang. It is clear that the banks will face significant new competition for funds, but there is too little evidence for us to make any strong predictions about which competitors will be the most threatening to the banks. Banks themselves are now allowed to sell investment trusts over their counters (since December 1998). This means that when we make our projections about the future size of the banking industry, our calculations will not rely on any specific assumptions about the future supply of funds to the industry. Instead, as a plausibility check we will see what our forecasts imply about future changes in household portfolio decisions.

3.3 BANKS' RESPONSES TO THE DEREGULATION

Our account of the savings behavior suggests that banks had a bit of a windfall in that they were able to hold on to many of their deposits despite the deregulation. But the windfall was not big enough to offset the adverse fallout from deregulation, and by the end of the 1990s the banks were in bad shape. While our story clearly gets the timing of events right, it may not correctly characterize the causation. For instance, one alternative explanation is that the Japanese banks are suffering now purely because of the poor performance of the overall Japanese economy in the 1990s. While we believe that macro conditions played an important role in shaping the fate of the industry, the question we care about is whether macro factors were all that mattered. To assess this question we offer several pieces of evidence.

The starting point for our exploration is to see how the banks responded under the constraints of the prevailing regulations. As mentioned above, Japanese banks prior to the Big Bang were not really able to move into the nontraditional areas of banking that many of the other global banks have pursued. To gauge the significance of these restrictions we compare the recent profitability and income sources for large U.S. and Japanese banks.

---

28. At the aggregate level corporate borrowing was rising, since the large firms were tapping the bond markets and the smaller firms were increasing their bank borrowing. The savings that were funding this seem to have previously been going towards financing the government deficit, which was falling in the late 1980s.

Table 10 PROFITABILITY AND NONINTEREST INCOME: MAJOR U.S. BANKS, 1976–1996

Year	Noninterest Income[a]	ROA[b]	ROE[c]
1976	0.1053	0.0055	0.0919
1977	0.1024	0.0058	0.1013
1978	0.0967	0.0062	0.1106
1979	0.1377	0.0065	0.1185
1980	0.1294	0.0049	0.0889
1981	0.1171	0.0036	0.0297
1982	0.1271	0.0041	0.0481
1983	0.1431	0.0049	0.0634
1984	0.1093	0.0055	0.0759
1985	0.1325	0.0071	0.1287
1986	0.1448	0.0065	0.1040
1987	0.1506	0.0003	−0.0135
1988	0.1513	0.0071	0.1468
1989	0.1472	0.0041	−0.1150
1990	0.1527	0.0023	0.0534
1991	0.1864	0.0056	0.0783
1992	0.2213	0.0104	0.1384
1993	0.2465	0.0131	0.1684
1994	0.2373	0.0127	0.1691
1995	0.2246	0.0128	0.1645
1996	0.2535	0.0146	0.1670

Notes: Data are taken from the December call report for each year. Each entry is the average over the top 1% institutions (according to total assets) of the ratio for the year. All the variable names in the footnotes are extracted from the instructions for submitting call reports, 1976–1996.
[a]Mean ratio of noninterest income to total income. Before 1984, noninterest income is computed as total income minus interest income, which is the sum of riad4000, riad4020, riad4025, riad4063, riad4065, and riad4115. From 1984 onward, there is a specific item that keeps track of nininterest income (riad4107). Thus, from 1984 onward, we define noninterest income as riad4000 minus riad4107.
[b]Mean return on assets, computed as net income (riad4340) divided by total assets (rcfd2170).
[c]Mean return on equity, computed as net income (riad4340) divided by total equity capital (rcfd3210).

Table 10 shows data on the U.S. banks. Unfortunately, the regulatory reports from which these data are compiled do not directly provide information on revenue sources by line of business. As a crude measure of the income from nontraditional activities one can look at noninterest income. The table shows that noninterest income (relative to total income) has doubled since the early 1980s. This ratio has climbed steadily, and most banking experts use these figures to argue that U.S. banks are successfully pushing into new lines of business.

The table also shows that U.S. bank profitability at the end of 1990s is

Table 11   INTEREST iNCOME, FEE INCOME, RETURN ON ASSETS, AND
RETURN ON EQUITY FOR JAPANESE CITY BANKS

Year	RINT[a]	RLINT[b]	RFEE[c]	ROCUR[d]	ROA[e]	ROE[f]	AROA[g]
1976	0.9317	0.7152	0.0359	0.0024	NA	NA	NA
1977	0.9314	0.6980	0.0375	0.0028	0.0013	0.0528	0.0028
1978	0.8967	0.6385	0.0415	0.0047	0.0012	0.0476	0.0026
1979	0.8965	0.5876	0.0451	0.0031	0.0012	0.0484	0.0026
1980	0.8987	0.5568	0.0347	0.0025	0.0007	0.0300	0.0013
1981	0.9292	0.5760	0.0286	0.0019	0.0009	0.0425	0.0017
1982	0.9320	0.5163	0.0298	0.0015	0.0022	0.1094	0.0047
1983	0.9388	0.5192	0.0308	0.0014	0.0020	0.1030	0.0047
1984	0.9362	0.5482	0.0323	0.0015	0.0024	0.1297	0.0053
1985	0.9380	0.5091	0.0288	0.0014	0.0023	0.1190	0.0051
1986	0.9236	0.5541	0.0319	0.0018	0.0022	0.1213	0.0044
1987	0.8965	0.5301	0.0337	0.0030	0.0026	0.1341	0.0059
1988	0.8463	0.4764	0.0323	0.0036	0.0030	0.1541	0.0070
1989	0.8338	0.4867	0.0310	0.0940	0.0036	0.1617	0.0031
1990	0.8690	0.4894	0.0267	0.0696	0.0027	0.1073	0.0009
1991	0.9075	0.5857	0.0236	0.0364	0.0019	0.0683	0.0014
1992	0.9103	0.6213	0.0242	0.0424	0.0014	0.0465	0.0022
1993	0.9205	0.6091	0.0313	0.0153	0.0008	0.0248	0.0023
1994	0.8482	0.5324	0.0355	0.0651	0.0007	0.0212	−0.0012
1995	0.8011	0.4679	0.0361	0.1224	−0.0002	−0.0046	−0.0045
1996	0.8074	0.3906	0.0363	0.0867	−0.0042	−0.1171	−0.0077
1997	0.7916	0.3710	0.0410	0.1188	−0.0001	−0.0040	−0.0024

Note: Data are from the Nikkei Database for the accounting year ending in March of each year.
[a]Proportion of interest income in the current income.
[b]Proportion of interest income on loans in the current income.
[c]Proportion of fee income in the current income.
[d]Proportion of the other current income, including realized capital gains on securities.
[e]After-tax net income divided by total assets from March of the previous year.
[f]After-tax net income divided by total capital (capital plus reserves) from March of the previous year.
[g]Adjusted ROA: (current profits − gains from sales of the securities + losses from sales from the securities + losses from revaluation of securities)/(total assets from March of the previous year).

at near-record levels. The U.S. banks successfully rebounded from their very poor performance in the late 1980s. The initial recovery may have been partly due to luck, because the steep U.S. yield curve made it very easy for banks to make money by taking in deposits and investing them in government securities. However, even as the U.S. yield curve has flattened out, U.S. bank profits have remained high, and during this time the percentage of noninterest income has continued to grow.

Table 11 shows similar data for large Japanese banks. Perhaps surprisingly, they have about the same fraction of revenue coming from fee-

Figure 3 PROPORTION OF LOANS TO SMALL ENTERPRISES (1973–1997)

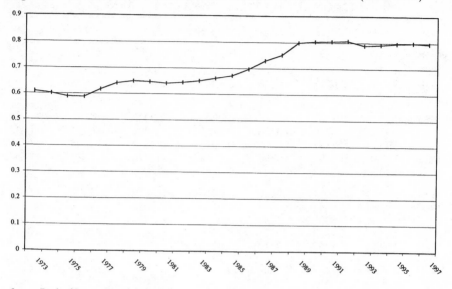

Source: Bank of Japan, *Economic Statistics Annual,* various issues.

based activities in the late 1990s as in the early 1980s. Although during the 1990s the banks have made a lower fraction of income from interest receipts, most of the decline has been due to an increase in capital gains realized by selling securities.[29] Put differently, the total of interest income and "other" income has hardly changed in Japan. The table also shows how profitability (measured by either return on assets or return on equity) has deteriorated in the 1990s (even more so than the U.S. banks in the late 1980s.) Interestingly, the raw ROA levels (shown in the third-to-last column) are typically higher than the adjusted ROA levels, which omit gains and losses from securities sales (and are shown in the last column).[30] Thus, it appears that the banks have tried to mask some of the performance deterioration by realizing capital gains on securities holdings.

While the Japanese banks have yet to expand much into nontradi-

29. This shows the practice referred to as *fukumi keiei,* hidden asset management. The Japanese banks and large firms often hold shares which were purchased long ago and therefore have unrealized capital gains. These firms sometimes try to smooth their earnings by selling the shares when operating profits are low. Table 11 shows this clearly. To protect their cross-shareholding the sellers often buy back the shares after realizing the capital gains.
30. The corrected return on assets is calculated as (current profits—gains from sales of stocks and other securities + losses from sales of stocks and other securities + losses from devaluation of stock holdings)/(total assets at the beginning of the period).

Figure 4 PROPORTION OF LOANS TO THE REAL ESTATE INDUSTRY
(1970–1997)

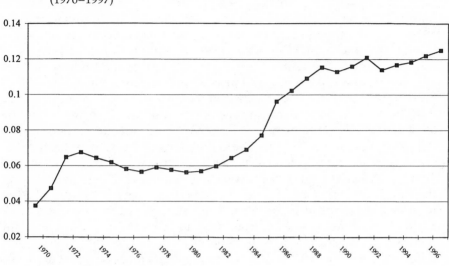

Source: Bank of Japan, *Economic Statistics Annual,* various issues.

tional lines of business, they did reorganize their traditional lending patterns. Figure 3 shows the proportion of bank loans to small enterprises.[31] The graph shows a dramatic increase in small business lending in the 1980s. As the banks started to lose their large customers to capital markets, they went after small firms. Most observers agree that previously the banks had not had close ties to many of these smaller borrowers. We return to this point below.

Figure 4 shows a second aspect of the banks' portfolio shift: increasing loans to the real estate industry. The proportion of loans to the real estate industry started to soar in the beginning of 1980s and soon surpassed the previous peak, which had occurred during the Japanese Archipelago rebuilding boom of 1972–1973. By the early 1990s, the proportion of loans to the real estate industry by banks had doubled from its level in the early 1980s.

A third change in the banks' behavior, which has been emphasized by Peek and Rosengren (1997a, b), was a noticeable increase in foreign

31. These data are taken from the *Bank of Japan Economic Statistics Monthly.* The small firms here are defined to be those that are not large according to the Bank of Japan definition: large firms are those firms which have more than ¥100 million in equity and more than 300 regular employees. The definition of small firms here roughly corresponds to that in the other tables in this paper.

lending. As they explain, in some cases this lending was done through separately capitalized subsidiaries so that not all the loans would show up on the parent bank's balance sheets. Peek and Rosengren's analysis shows that the foreign activity has dramatically slowed in the 1990s.

One way to evaluate the portfolio shifts and performance is to see if they might have represented a natural response to the underlying economic conditions. After all, land prices were soaring in the late 1980s, so perhaps the shift into property-based lending was simply in keeping with past practices. To explore how much of the banks' performance might be attributable to basic economic conditions, we ran several regressions.

The dependent variable for the regressions is the adjusted return on assets (AROA) for city banks, which was shown in the last column of Table 11. As a robustness check we also tried the same regressions using the raw ROA series and found the same basic patterns. The adjusted ROA series is graphed in Figure 5. The figure shows that Japanese bank performance slowly declined from the mid-1950s through the 1980s and then sharply deteriorated in the 1990s.

To determine the role of deregulation on performance one would like to include a proxy for deregulation in a full-blown model of bank profitability. Unfortunately, we lack not only a compelling theoretical model that makes tight predictions about the exact determinants of (adjusted) ROA, but also convincing proxies for the impact of deregulation. Given these limitations, we take the indirect and admittedly ad hoc approach of looking only to see whether the dynamics for ROA changed following deregulation. Operationally our strategy amounts to checking whether there is a stable relation between ROA and standard macroeconomic variables before and after 1983 (the date at which we argue the deregulation of the bond market began in earnest.) Thus, our modest goal is to provide evidence against a story that posits that macro factors can *fully* explain the banks' performance after the onset of deregulation.

We considered interest rates, land prices, stock prices, and GDP growth to be the baseline set of macroeconomic variables that could be plausibly justified as determinants of ROA. Intuitively, these variables allow for monetary policy, collateral, and general economic conditions to drive bank performance. Because we had just under 30 years of data and did not have much guidance about how many lags to allow for in the regressions, we did almost no experimenting with other variables. The one exception was inflation, which we measured using the GDP deflator; we found no independent effect of controlling for inflation.

Data limitations largely drove our choices of the specific proxies used in the regressions. In particular, the call rate (which measures the price of overnight credit between banks) is the only consistent interest-rate

Figure 5 CITY BANKS' ADJUSTED ROA (1956–1997)

Source: Ministry of Finance, *Banking Bureau Annual Report,* various issues, and Nikkei Database. Raw ROA has been adjusted for gains and losses due to sale or revaluation of equity holdings.

series that is available from the 1950s onward. We take the difference between the nominal call rate and the current year's inflation to form our real call-rate series.[32]

Similarly, the only consistent land price data come from a semiannual survey conducted by the Japan Real Estate Research Institute. One survey covers all land prices nationwide, and the other pertains to land prices in the six major metropolitan areas. The logarithmic differences in both series (again subtracting inflation) are graphed in Figure 6. This graph also shows the logarithmic difference of the TOPIX stock return index and inflation.

The figure shows three important things. First, the stock return series is much more volatile than either land price series. Large swings in stock prices routinely occurred throughout the period. Second, large changes in the relative price of land also had happened several times prior to the late 1980s. Furthermore, the land price changes were not always coincident with the swings in stock prices. This is important because it means that we have some hope of identifying the econometric connection between land prices, stock prices, and bank profits. Finally, the figure also

32. Using instead the nominal call rate along with a separate inflation variable made no difference in what follows.

Figure 6 PERCENTAGE REAL CHANGE IN LAND AND STOCK PRICES
(1957–1997)

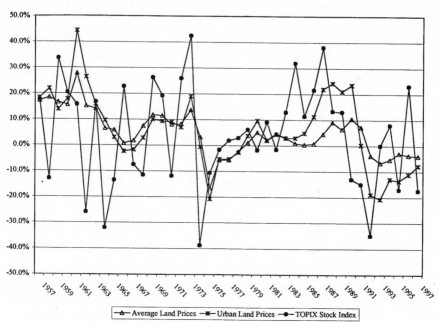

Sources: Japan Real Estate Research Institute and Tokyo Stock Exchange.

Note: All nominal data are converted to constant prices using the GDP deflator.

shows that the choice of which land price series to use could be potentially important. The late 1980s land price run-up was concentrated in the major cities.

Two representative regression specifications among those we tried are shown in Table 12. One key issue is how to account for the long-term decline in profitability documented in Figure 5. In the first pair of regressions (which differ only in which land price is used) we include a time trend in addition to the macroeconomic variables. We draw two conclusions from these regressions. First, and not surprisingly, the time trend is the most important variable in the equation. Second, aside from stock prices, which are of borderline importance, most of the macro variables appear to have no correlation with bank profitability.

The next two columns repeat the first specification except that a lagged dependent variable is added. The addition of the lagged dependent variable marginally improves the R^2 and wipes out the explanatory power of the time trend. The *t*-statistics of several of the macro variables

Table 12   REGRESSIONS RELATING BANKS' RETURN ON ASSETS AND
MACROECONOMIC VARIABLES
(Dependent variable is city banks' adjusted return on assets; sample
Period is 1957–1983.)

	Coefficient and (t-statistic)			
Variable	*Regression 1*	*2*	*3*	*4*
Intercept	0.01138 (5.833)	0.01182 (5.951)	0.00337 (0.990)	0.00413 (1.122)
Time trend	−0.00026 (−3.645)	−0.00028 (−4.039)	−0.00009 (−0.982)	−0.00010 (−1.018)
Real GDP growth	−0.00377 (−0.331)	−0.00359 (−0.295)	−0.00255 (−0.263)	−0.00020 (−0.018)
Real GDP growth $(t-1)$	0.00479 (0.456)	0.00343 (0.359)	0.01993 (1.893)	0.01432 (1.495)
Log change in real average land price	−0.00584 (−0.761)	— —	−0.01355 (−1.906)	— —
Log change in real average land price $(t-1)$	0.00646 (1.281)	— —	0.00861 (1.981)	— —
Log change in real urban land price	— —	−0.00299 (−0.654)	— —	−0.00634 (−1.487)
Log change in real urban land price $(t-1)$	— —	0.00241 (0.671)	— —	0.00369 (1.149)
Real call rate	0.00620 (0.518)	0.00501 (0.423)	0.01547 (1.442)	0.01166 (1.080)
Real call rate $(t-1)$	−0.00862 (−0.971)	−0.00983 (−1.039)	−0.00495 (−0.648)	−0.00725 (−0.864)
ROA $(t-1)$	— —	— —	0.53427 (2.693)	0.48948 (2.375)
Log change in real equity prices	0.00370 (2.088)	0.00362 (2.159)	0.00392 (2.608)	0.00343 (2.319)
Log change in real equity prices $(t-1)$	0.00248 (0.973)	0.00273 (1.089)	0.00201 (0.928)	0.00191 (0.857)
R^2	0.8259	0.8144	0.8826	0.8651

P-Values from Exclusion Tests for the Sum of the Coefficients on

GDP growth	0.9432	0.9916	0.2135	0.3381
Land prices	0.9274	0.8858	0.4271	0.4743
Interest rates	0.8467	0.6896	0.3743	0.6972
Equity prices	0.1113	0.0820	0.0756	0.0994

P-Values from Tests for the Equality of Coefficients after 1984

	0.0149	0.0241	0.0298	0.0658

Figure 7 ACTUAL VERSUS PREDICTED ADJUSTED ROA FOR CITY BANKS

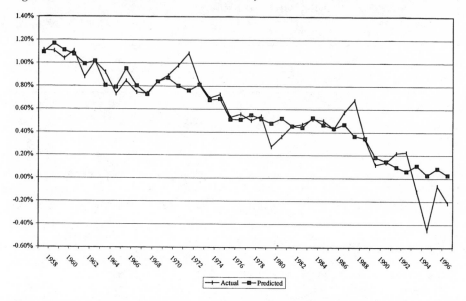

Source: Authors' calculations using regression coefficients from regression 1 in Table 12.

rise, but the tests on the statistical significance of the sum of the coefficients, shown at the bottom of the table, continue to indicate that only the stock price coefficients are likely to be different from zero. This same pattern turned up in all of the variations that we tried that included lagged dependent variables. From this we conclude that prior to the mid-1980s there was at best a loose link between macro variables and bank profitability.

For both specifications we then checked how they fit after 1983. Figures 7 and 8 compare the actual values and fitted values for the regression specification including average land prices (regressions 1 and 3 in the table). Importantly, the fitted values are one-step-ahead forecasts, so the actual values of the right-hand variables are being used in forming these predictions. By taking this approach rather than going with a full dynamic simulation we are giving the prediction equation its best chance at explaining the postderegulation events.

Our main conclusion from the figures is that the macro variables lead to an underprediction of bank ROA in the late 1980s and an overprediction in the 1990s. This is most clearly seen in Figure 7 (which shows the results when there is no lagged dependent variable), but even in Figure 8, where the lagged dependent variable keeps the forecasts

Figure 8 ACTUAL VERSUS PREDICTED ADJUSTED ROA FOR CITY BANKS

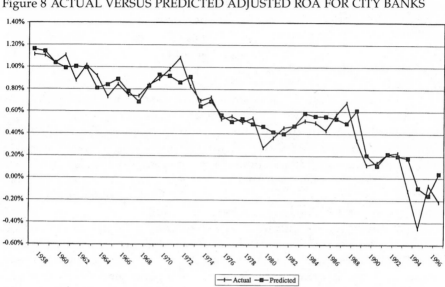

Source: Authors' calculations using the regression coefficients from regression 3 in Table 12.

more closely on track, the 1988 and 1989 peaks are underestimated and the last few years of the sample are overestimated. This evidence leads us to doubt stories which argue that the formation of the bubble and its bursting can *fully* explain the banks' performance over the last fifteen years.

An alternative way to judge the stability of the models is to check for a structural break in the coefficients. Having only 15 years of data in the deregulated era led us to suspect that this type of test would have very little power. Nevertheless, the tests for structural breaks shown in the bottom half of the table indicate that none of the four equations is stable across the two regimes. In each case we can decisively reject the hypothesis of no change in the coefficients. In addition to being statistically different across the two periods, the differences also appear to be large in terms of their economic implications. For instance, many of the coefficients reverse their signs and the magnitude of the coefficient on lagged dependent variable also moves noticeably. Overall the tests for coefficient stability also confirm the inability of a set of stable macro correlations to explain the recent ROA data.

While we view this evidence as suggestive, we recognize that there are clear limitations to how hard we can lean on the lack of a well-fitting time-series model for bank profitability. Our preferred interpretation of the Table 12 results is that the deregulation pushed the banks to alter their business practices so that their exposure to macroeconomic factors changed. But it is also possible that we have simply failed to control for the correct macro factors and that the poor specification of our model is masking the truth.

We believe a stronger test of the importance of deregulation can be conducted by looking at cross-bank differences in performance. If our story emphasizing the role of deregulation is correct, then those banks which relied more heavily on loans to customers who obtained access to capital markets should have underperformed after deregulation. To test this hypothesis we check whether bank performance in the postderegulation period is negatively correlated with the bank's preregulation dependence on bank loans to traditional customers.

In this analysis we continue to date the start of the deregulation period as fiscal year 1983. Our performance measure is again return on assets corrected for the gains and losses from stock sales and the revaluation of stock holdings. To measure postderegulation performance we use a time average of this variable. Time averaging allows us to avoid being too dependent on correctly specifying the exact dates of the adjustment period. However, it could also mean that we are including observations when the response to deregulation had yet to begin or was already complete. To guard against this possibility we consider two different averaging intervals. We first use the average return for 1991–1997. We then also use the average for 1984–1997 so that we pick up both the boom in the late 1980s and the stagnation in the 1990s.

We consider two types of prederegulation bank characteristics that could influence the postderegulation performance. One factor is a bank's reliance on income from traditional activities. We expect banks intensive in traditional activities to have fared (relatively) badly in the deregulation environment. As a proxy we use the proportion of current income coming from interest on loans. If this proportion is high, it indicates that the bank's performance was relatively dependent on traditional activities at the onset of the reforms.

A second factor relates to the bank's customer base at the onset of deregulation. Ideally we would like to know which banks had many customers that were eligible to shift to bond financing. Unfortunately, data on the the external financing options for the bank customers are not available. We were able to collect information on the proportion of loans made to listed firms and the proportion of loans made to manufacturing firms. Given that the listed firms are typically large and are required to release audited information on their performance, we think this is a fairly good proxy. We expect the banks that had a higher exposure to listed firms to have been at more risk of losing customers to the capital markets. We also know that the size-based standards of the bond issuance rules made it easier for manufacturing firms to go to the capital markets in the 1980s. Thus, we also expect the banks that had more clients in the manufacturing industry to have also been more likely to lose customers.

All the data except for the listed company loan shares come from Nikkei database on bank balance sheets and income statements. The data on the loan shares were collected from Keizai Chosakai's annual publication *Kin'yu Kikan no Toyushi*. The sample for the regressions includes 10 city banks, 3 long-term credit banks, 6 trust banks, 64 regional banks, and 60 second-tier regional banks.[33]

Table 13 shows the estimation results. Each column reports the coefficient estimates and their *t*-statistics for a different regression model. We draw several conclusions from this table. First, the proportion of interest on loans in the current income in 1983 is significantly negatively correlated with the postderegulation performance. The correlation seems to be robust, as it turned up in all the specifications that we considered. Second, the proportion of loans to listed firms is also negatively correlated with postderegulation performance, although the statistical significance of the coefficient is marginal when the average for whole postderegulation period (1984–1997) is used.[34] Finally, the proportion of loans to manufacturing industry in 1983 is also significantly negatively correlated with the postderegulation performance. We read these results as saying the firms that were more at risk because of the deregulation did seem to underperform after 1983.

Returning to the big picture, there are several ways to interpret the differences in the paths taken by the U.S. and Japanese banks. One interpretation is that the Japanese banks had a different vision of the future of the industry and pursued that vision. For instance, maybe

33. Nippon Trust and Banking was excluded from the analysis because its return on assets is dramatically lower than all the other banks in the sample for the 1990s. Including this bank noticeably changes the results, especially the ones concerning the effect of loans to listed firms. There are some other trust banks and long-term credit banks that experienced very low return on assets for the 1990s, but none of them individually influences the regression results in any significant way. When we ran the same set of regressions excluding all trust banks and long-term credit banks, we obtained qualitatively similar results.

34. One problem with using listed firms is that we do not know if they in fact qualified to issue bonds. For some of the smaller listed firms the bias in the bond issuance rules may have been a problem.

Table 13 CROSS-SECTION REGRESSIONS RELATING POSTDEREGULATION RETURN ON ASSETS WITH PREDEREGULATION BANK CHARACTERISTICS

Independent Variable	Dependent Variable Is Adjusted Return on Assets, 1991–1997				Dependent Variable Is Adjusted Return on Assets, 1984–1997			
	Model 1	2	3	4	5	6	7	8
City-bank dummy	0.00281 (1.165)	0.00042 (0.385)	0.00129 (0.942)	0.01114 (3.875)	0.00619 (3.432)	0.00246 (3.139)	0.00245 (2.604)	0.01034 (4.797)
Long-term credit dummy	0.00076 (0.269)	−0.00232 (−1.395)	0.00094 (0.353)	0.01181 (3.103)	0.00508 (2.413)	0.00066 (0.593)	0.00157 (0.933)	0.01041 (3.804)
Trust-bank dummy	−0.00155 (−1.002)	−0.00204 (−1.756)	0.01426 (2.410)	0.02019 (3.230)	0.00478 (4.277)	0.00317 (3.995)	0.00914 (2.206)	0.01448 (3.235)
Regional-bank I dummy	0.00904 (3.064)	0.00490 (7.003)	0.00375 (11.154)	0.01544 (5.319)	0.01065 (4.667)	0.00532 (10.306)	0.00460 (18.479)	0.01396 (5.994)
Regional-bank II dummy	0.00948 (2.863)	0.00407 (7.527)	0.00272 (10.591)	0.01526 (4.802)	0.01100 (4.342)	0.00462 (10.635)	0.00388 (19.752)	0.01399 (5.538)
1983 interest on loans relative to current income	−0.00898 (−2.092)			−0.01463 (−3.658)	−0.00927 (−2.833)			−0.01203 (−3.824)
1983 fraction of loans to manufacturing firms		−0.00828 (−2.882)		−0.00637 (−2.420)		−0.00434 (−2.078)		−0.00408 (−2.107)
1983 fraction of loans to publicly traded firms			−0.01589 (−3.165)	−0.01579 (−3.040)			−0.00612 (−1.719)	−0.00670 (−1.747)
Adjusted R^2	.479	.498	.509	.548	.345	.332	.326	.387

Dependent variable: return on assets adjusted for gains and losses of stock sales averaged over either 1991–1997 or 1984–1997. Mean of dependent variable: 0.001901 (average for 1991–1997); 0.003931 (average for 1984–1997). Independent variables are measured for accounting year ending in the March of 1983. The 143 observations include data for ten city banks, three long-term credit banks, six trust banks (excluding Nippon Trust), 64 regional banks, and 60 second-tier regional banks. Each column shows coefficient estimates for a separate regression model. Numbers in the parentheses below coefficients are t-statistics, calculated using a heteroskedastic consistent covariance matrix following White (1980).

the strong Japanese growth in the late 1980s led the banks to assess the profitability of various strategic options differently than U.S. banks (which were trying to recover from the bad loans they had extended in Latin America). We believe the regression evidence in the last two tables casts some doubt on this explanation, but perhaps a more complicated story involving incorrect future beliefs could explain the performance data. In this case, the fact the Japanese strategy may not have worked out is more of an accident than anything that was caused by the regulatory regime.

A second reading of the evidence is that the Japanese banks were constrained by the regulation from taking the path of the U.S. banks. Since many fee-generating lines of business were not available, the banks chose to move into property-related lending and lending more to small firms, perhaps knowing that this involved taking on more risk.[35] This was not the only option for the banks. When large customers started to leave bank financing, the banks could have started buying government bonds and other securities instead of lending to new customers. We know now both that this strategy looked relatively attractive and that few, if any, banks in Japan followed it. Regardless of what one decides about the rationality of the banks' responses, it seems clear that banks would never have chosen to search for new lines of business if their large customers had not shifted their financing patterns in response to the deregulation. In this sense, the regulatory mix seems to have mattered, and one interpretation of our findings is that the poor performance was partially due to the deregulation.

For the purposes of looking ahead, it may not matter whether we can separate these two alternatives. At this point the Japanese banks remain among the largest in the world, yet they are now among the least profitable. Moreover, the approach of sticking to traditional banking and focusing on new, smaller customers has failed. As Hoshi and Kashyap (1999b) show, foreign firms and nonbank financial firms are moving quickly to compete with banks for funds. It seems reasonable to conclude that the Japanese banks are going to be pushed by all of these considerations to shift their strategy and become more like U.S. banks. But the current conditions of the industry may place some constraints on which options are achievable. Thus, before making any forecasts, we briefly review the current conditions of the banks.

35. At least ex post, property lending was risky. For example, four major banks (Sanwa, Sumitomo, Dai-ichi Kangyo, and Tokyo-Mitsubishi) published data showing nonperforming loans broken out by the industry. For these banks, between 16% and 40% of total nonperforming loans are to the real estate sector, and for all the banks besides Dai-ichi Kangyo this is the leading sector for nonperforming loans.

4. The Bad-Loans Problem

While it is widely recognized that Japanese banks are in bad shape, there appears to be little consensus on the magnitude of the problems. For instance, in early February 1999 a top Ministry of Finance official (Eisuke Sakakibara) was quoted as saying that the financial crisis would be over within a matter of weeks. At the time private-sector analysts were arguing that conditions were deteriorating and that bold new steps were needed. Such conflicting opinions have been common for the last several years.

One problem plaguing the entire discussion is that there is no common standard for what people mean when they refer to "bad loans." One reason for this ambiguity is that the standards for determining which loans the banks identify as being at risk on their financial statements have varied over time. A second problem is that numbers from the bank balance sheets are only one of three types of estimates which are sometimes used to identify loans that are at risk. Unfortunately, these three types of estimates are not even intended to measure the same thing, and for each approach there are judgmental decisions that can swing the numbers considerably. As we now show, these considerations explain why, to a casual observer, there have been such divergent claims about the scope of the banking crisis in Japan. After having clarified the size of the problem, we then discuss its implications for the future.

4.1 ESTIMATES BASED ON DATA FROM BANKS' FINANCIAL STATEMENTS

Remarkably, Japanese banks did not disclose anything about the extent of their problem loans prior to 1993. This lack of disclosure made it impossible to say very much about the condition of the banks. Since 1993 the banks have included footnotes on their financial statements that classify loans according to the health of the borrowers. The decisions about which loans should be identified in the footnotes have been made by the Japanese Bankers Association (Zenginkyo). Importantly, these voluntarily disclosed data are not supposed to take account of differences in the chances the different loans might be repaid (say because of differences in the collateral associated with the loans). For example, if a borrower files for bankruptcy, all the loans made to the borrower are treated equivalently.

Table 14 shows these voluntarily disclosed data for 1993 through 1998. The first half of the table shows information for major banks (city banks, trust banks, and long-term credit banks), and the second part shows the comparable number for all banks (major banks plus regional banks).

From March 1993 to September 1995, the statistics covered only the loans to failed enterprises and the loans for which no payments had been made for at least 6 months. Thus, the figures did not include any restructured loans. Moreover, regional banks did not have to disclose (and many chose not to disclose) the loans with suspended payments. Under this reporting convention the amount of bad loans fluctuated around ¥12 trillion (roughly 3.5% of total loans) for major banks and ¥13.5 trillion (roughly 2.5% of total loans) for all banks.

For the major banks, intermittent data on loan write-offs are available for this period from the Web site of the Financial Supervisory Agency. These data, shown in the third column of the table, indicate that write-offs were quite low in these first couple of years of the banking crisis. The fourth and seventh columns of the table show that during this period the banks were also slow in increasing the amount of funds set aside to cover the bad loans. Although provisioning was increasing, the loan loss reserves were never sufficient to cover the expected losses. For instance, as of September 1995, the loan loss reserves covered only 52% of bad loans for major banks (and 60% for all banks). Analysts in the private sector repeatedly argued that the reported data grossly understated the true extent of the problems. For example, Ohara (1996) argued that as of March 1995 the bad loans for the major banks were more likely to be as large as ¥75 trillion, once all the restructured loans and future liabilities of the affiliated nonbanks were properly accounted.

Starting with the accounting data released in March 1996, a couple of changes were made. First, the regional banks were now instructed to classify any loans with suspended payments as bad. More importantly, the bad-loan definition was expanded to include loans for which the interest rates were cut to levels below the Bank of Japan discount rate at the time of the concession. These changes led to a sharp jump in the reported figures (with the totals rising to ¥20 trillion for major banks and almost ¥27 trillion for all banks). At the same time the amount of write-offs jumped.

The accounting data released in the following March included another change in definition, as loans to enterprises undergoing creditor-assisted restructuring were now included. Although the definition was expanded, the amount of bad loans declined slightly (to ¥18 trillion for major banks and ¥24 trillion for all banks). The amount of loan loss reserves also declined by ¥1 trillion for major banks and by ¥1.2 trillion for all banks. One contributing factor to the declines was an acceleration in the actual write-offs (which remove bad assets from the balance sheets). A second factor that probably helped was the brief recovery of the Japanese economy in 1996.

Table 14   PROBLEM LOAN STATISTICS FOR JAPANESE BANKS: 1993–1998 (BILLION YEN)

	Major Banks			All Banks		
Date	Bad Loans	Cumulative Write-offs[a]	Special Reserves for Loan Losses	Bad Loans	Cumulative Write-offs[a]	Special Reserves for Loan Losses
March 1993	11,730	424	3,699	12,685	N/A	4,876
September 1993	12,662	N/A	3,875	13,732	N/A	5,128
March 1994	12,472	2,514	4,547	13,659	N/A	5,967
September 1994	12,198	N/A	4,798	13,439	N/A	6,327
March 1995	11,637	5,322	5,537	12,961	N/A	7,305
September 1995	11,969	N/A	6,173	13,421	N/A	8,047
March 1996	20,357	10,812	10,345	26,831	11,602	13,469
September 1996	18,846	N/A	9,508	24,383	N/A	12,035
March 1997	18,447	14,488	9,388	23,987	15,918	12,299
September 1997	17,890	N/A	10,330	23,896	N/A	13,685
March 1998	21,978	17,988	13,601	29,758	19,911	17,815
September 1998	22,008	18,653	12,457	30,078	19,630	16,932
March 1999	20,250	22,256	9,258	29,627	24,620	14,797

Sources: Federation of Bankers Associations of Japan, *Analysis of Financial Statements of All Banks*, various issues. Federation of Bankers Associations of Japan, *Analysts of Interim Financial Statements of All Banks*, various issues. Financial Supervisory Agency (FSA), "The status of risk management loans held by all banks in Japan (as of the end of September, 1998)," press release, January 22, 1999 and FSA, "The status of risk management loans held by all banks in Japan (as of the end of March 1999)," press release, July 23, 1999.

Notes: Definitions of bad loans: From March, 1993 to September, 1995, for major banks, loans for failed enterprises and loans whose payment had been suspended for 6 months or more; for regional banks, only loans for failed enterprises. From March, 1996 to September 1996, loans for failed enterprises, loans whose payment had been suspended for 6 months or more, and loans with interest rates lowered below the BOJ discount rate at the time of the rate cut. From March 1997 to September 1997, loans for failed enterprises, loans whose payment had been suspended for 6 months or more, loans with interest rates lowered below the BOJ discount rate at the time of the rate cut, and loans for enterprises under restructuring. For March 1998, loans for failed enterprises, loans whose payment had been suspended for 3 months or more, and loans with relaxed conditions.

Coverage: From March 1993 to September 1995, the numbers are for 21 major banks (11 city banks, 7 trust banks, 3 long-term credit banks) and 151 banks in all (64 regional banks and 66 second-tier regional banks in addition to the major banks). Hyogo Bank, which was closed in 1995 and reopened with a new name (Midori Bank) and organization, is not included in the numbers for March 1996 and later. The merger between Mitsubishi Bank and Bank of Tokyo in April of 1996 (to form Mitsubishi Bank of Tokyo) reduced the number of city banks by one. Taiheiyo Bank (later Wakashio Bank) and Hanwa Bank failed in 1996 and dropped out of the sample, starting in March 1997. Hokkaido Takushoku Bank, one of the major banks, failed in 1997 and dropped out of the sample in March 1998. Tokuyo City, Kyoto Kyoei, Naniwa, and Fukutoku dropped out of the sample in September 1998. In March 1999, Long-term Credit Bank, Nippon Credit Bank, Kokumin, Koufuku, and Tokyo Sowa were eliminated from the coverage. As a result of these changes, the sample for March 1999 covers 17 major banks (9 city banks, 7 trust banks, and 1 long-term credit bank), as well as 121 other banks (64 regional and 57 second-tier regional banks) for a total of 138 banks.

[a] Cumulative direct write-offs (which include losses on sales of loans to other entities such as the CCPC and losses on support to other financial institutions) (billion yen).

In March 1998, the definition of bad loans was once again expanded. The new definition, which remains in place at this writing, identifies bad loans (now called "risk management credits") as loans to failed enterprises, loans whose interest payments have been suspended for 3 months or more, and loans with concessions (which cover loans with reduced interest rates and loans to corporations under reorganization). This expansion of the definition and the deterioration in the economy in 1997 sharply increased the stock of bad loans. Thus, as of March 1999, despite continued write-offs and removal of many banks which failed over the last couple of years, the official amount of bad loans for the major banks (all banks) stood at ¥20 trillion (¥30 trillion).[36] Overall, the bad-loan numbers quoted on the bank financial statements still tend to be low, since the banks need not identify loans to firms that are in trouble but where no restructuring or missed payments have yet been recorded.

4.2 ESTIMATES BASED ON SUPERVISORY GUIDELINES

For supervisory purposes, the regulators have always been aware of this problem so the Bank of Japan and Ministry of Finance [and now the Financial Supervisory Authority (FSA)] have focused on the chances that a loan will be collected. This means that both the condition of the borrower and the quality of collateral are relevant. Accordingly, loans to the same borrower can be classified into different categories if they are secured by different collateral and hence offer different expected levels of repayment. The coverage of assets which are considered is also slightly broader than the voluntarily disclosed data, since this assessment includes loanlike items such as securities loaned in addition to conventional loans.

Under this scheme, which is also used by U.S. regulators, loans are classified into four categories. Category 4 includes the loans that are noncollectable or of no value. These are the unsecured portions of loans made to failed firms. Category 3 is the set of loans that are seriously doubtful with regard to their ultimate collection. These include loans to bankrupt (or nearly bankrupt) companies that are secured, but where the market value of collateral is well below the book value. In practice these loans are expected to return little or nothing, unless the value of the collateral increases dramatically. The FSA describes Category 2 loans as "credits subject to specific risk management." These loans are not yet judged to be uncollectible but are

---

36. See the footnotes to Table 14 for a complete list of when various banks were dropped from the official statistics.

deemed to require attention; the popular press sometimes refers to the Category 2 loans as being in the "gray zone." Category 2 loans are sometimes further classified to separate those loans that require "special attention" from the others. For example, the Financial Reconstruction Commission's guideline on provisioning for nonperforming loans suggests two different provisioning ratios for these two subcategories. Finally, Category 1 covers the remaining loans whose repayment is not supposed to be in any doubt.

Because of the large number of Category 2 loans (which are mostly excluded from the numbers shown on the bank financial statements), this classification scheme generally produces much larger estimates of problem loans. In 1998, the government started to publish aggregate statistics on loans sorted according to these criteria. The banks' own assessments are reported in the top panel of Table 15. In December 1998 the FSA released its own estimates for the major banks (as of March 1998, based on their 1998 on-site examinations). These figures are shown in the bottom panel of the table. The FSA data suggest that the major banks in Japan had ¥57.4 trillion of bad loans (or 14% of total loans) as of March of 1998.

Converting these figures into the expected cost of cleaning up the bank balance sheets requires two more assumptions. First, one has to decide whether the supervisors have correctly identified all the problem loans at the banks. It is generally agreed that the banks' self-reporting has been fairly optimistic. For example, when Nippon Credit Bank (NCB) was nationalized, the FSA announced that it had problem loans of more than ¥3.7 trillion; NCB's own assessment put the losses at roughly ¥3.2 trillion. The same kind of underreporting was uncovered when the Long-Term Credit Bank (LTCB) was nationalized. Comparing the top and bottom panels in Table 15 shows that the FSA believed that the major banks had failed to identify roughly ¥7 trillion of risky loans. In April 1999, the FSA issued new guidelines that included detailed instructions on how to classify loans.

A second problem is determining the fraction of the Category 2 and Category 3 loans that will ultimately be lost. A study by the Supervision Department of the Bank of Japan (1997) found that 17% of Category 2 loans and 75% of Category 3 loans identified in 1993 became uncollectable within three years. Although the sample size used in the BOJ study was very small, the numbers provide an upper bound on the recovery rates for Category 2 and Category 3 of 83% and 25% respectively. Assuming that the Category 4 loans are worthless, but that Category 2 loans do return ¥83 against every ¥100 is owed and that Category 3 loans return ¥25 per ¥100, the data in Table 15 imply that the total expected loss

Table 15 DISTRIBUTION OF LOANS BY SUPERVISORY CLASSIFICATION

Banks' 1998 Self-Reported Data[a]

Sample	Date	Category 1	2	3	4	Total Loans
		Loans (billion yen)				
Major banks	Mar. 1998	371,607	45,157	4,808	125	421,697
All banks	Mar. 1998	544,814	65,488	6,065	130	616,495
Major banks	Sept. 1998	354,629	45,537	5,697	77	405,940
All banks	Sept. 1998	524,980	66,078	6,863	86	598,007

March 1998 Data for 19 Major Banks as Determined by FSA Audits[b]

Category 1	2	3	4	Total Loans
Loans (billion yen)				
364,332	48,971	7,756	637	421,696

There are four loan categories used by bank supervisors. Category 4 includes the loans that are noncollectable or of no value. Category 3 is the set of loans that are seriously doubtful with regard to their ultimate collection. In practice these loans are also expected to return nothing. Category 2 loans are "credits subject to specific management risk." These loans are not yet judged to be uncollectable but are deemed to require special attention. Category 1 covers the remaining loans, whose repayment is not supposed to be in any doubt. (See text for further details.)
[a]*Source:* Financial Supervisory Agency, "The status of risk management loans held by all banks in Japan (as of the end of September, 1998)," press release, January 22, 1999. The figures include loans of Long-Term Credit Bank and Nippon Credit Bank, but exclude those of Hokkaido Takushoku Bank, Tokuyo City Bank, Kyoto Kyoei Bank, Naniwa Bank, Fukutoku Bank, and Midori Bank.
[b]*Source:* Financial Supervisory Agency Web site (www.fsa.go.jp), published in December 1998. Note that these figures include loans of the Long Term Credit Bank and Nippon Credit Bank.

amounts to ¥14.78 trillion (which is about 3% of GDP or 3.5% of total loans).

Some private-sector analysts find this calculation very optimistic, because the calculation is based on the amount of problem loans reported by banks and FSA, and the figures in BOJ study overestimate the true recovery rates for problem loans. For example, Ohara (1998) estimates that the amount of bad loans at the major banks to be ¥73.4 trillion as of March 1998. Assuming a 25% recovery rate for the risk management loans and 62.5% recovery rate for the remaining bad loans, she arrives at ¥35 trillion (7% of GDP) as the estimated loss. Fiorillo (1999) estimated, as of February 1999, the size of loans for the major banks that will eventually be uncollectable to be ¥38 trillion, or 7.6% of GDP.[37] These estimates suggest (plausibly to us) that many more loans will have to be written off than have been disposed of so far.

37. Private-sector analysts also point out that there are probably large losses in financial institutions besides the banks.

4.3 ESTIMATES BASED ON THE DISCLOSURES MANDATED BY
THE FINANCIAL RECONSTRUCTION ACT

Since April 1999 another set of bad-loan estimates have been floating around. Section 7 of the Financial Reconstruction Act (FRA) requires each bank to report bad loans (as described below) to the Financial Reconstruction Commission and to publish the data. Unfortunately, the FRA definition of bad loans falls in between the two previously described definitions. In particular, the FRA highlights loans to failed enterprises and de facto failed enterprises, loans to near-bankrupt companies, loans whose interest payments have been suspended for more than three months, and loans with concessions. Essentially this means that the FRA definition includes the Category 3 and 4 loans according to the supervisory definition, but not all of the Category 2 loans. Instead the FRA definition focuses only on any remaining loans that would be counted in the banks' voluntarily disclosed data.

Given this reporting convention, the FRA estimates should be expected to lie in between the two prior sets of estimates. In the first round of disclosure, which covered the conditions as of March 1999, the amount of bad loans at all banks was ¥34 trillion. Based on data from the web sites of the FSA and FRC, this was about ¥4 trillion larger than voluntarily disclosed data, but far lower than the ¥64 trillion estimated by the supervisors. This is about ¥6 trillion larger than the voluntarily disclosed data, but far below the supervisory estimates (Fiorillo, 1999). For a further discussion of how the various sets of estimates compare see Iwahara, Okina, Kanemoto, and Narisawa (1999).

Overall, we conclude that there are three key considerations that must be kept in mind when evaluating different estimates of the size of the bad-loan problem. First, and most importantly, one must check whether the data are based on assessments of the collectability of loans or are taken from the bank financial statements. Second assuming that most people will want the collection-based estimates, it is necessary to determine whether the data have been self-reported by the banks or are based on supervisors' (or private-sector analysts') estimates. Finally, it is imperative to be clear about what assumptions are being used regarding the fraction of the gray-zone loans that will be collected.

To help put the Japanese bad loans problem in perspective, Table 16 shows the size of banking crises in other developed countries over the last two decades (see Corbett, 1999b, for a more comprehensive comparison). Clearly the Japanese crisis is much larger than the U.S. savings-and-loan crisis, and thus a full bailout would require significantly more resources than were deployed in the U.S. rescue. Discussions of what to

Table 16 REVIEW OF SELECTED COUNTRIES' BANKING PROBLEMS, 1980–1996

Country	Period	Non-performing Loans[a]	Fiscal Cost[b]	Comments
Argentina	1980–1982	9%	4%	
	1989–1990	27%	N/A	37% of state-owned banks were nonperforming. Failed banks held 40% of financial system assets.
	1995	N/A	N/A	45 of 205 institutions were closed or merged.
Australia	1989–1992	6%	1.90%	
Chile	1981–1987	16%	19%	8 banks intervened in 1981 (33% of outstanding loans, 11 in 1982–1983 (45% of outstanding loans).
Colombia	1982–1985	15%	5%	
Czech Rep.	1991–present	38%	12%	
Finland	1991–1994	13%	8%	Liquidity crisis in 1991.
France	1991–1995	9%	1%	
Indonesia	1992–1995	25%	2%	Nonperforming loans concentrated in state-owned banks.
Italy	1990–1995	10%	N/A	
South Korea	Mid-1980s	7%	N/A	
Malaysia	1985–1988	32%	5%	Loans loss equivalent to 1.4% of GDP.
Mexico	1982	N/A	N/A	Banking system nationalized.
	1994–present	12%	6%	
Niger	1983–present	50%	N/A	
Norway	1987–1993	6%	3%	
Philippines	1981–1987	30%	13%	
Sweden	1990–1993	18%	4%	
United States	1980–1992	4%	2%	1142 S&L institutions and 1395 banks were closed.
Uruguay	1981–1985	59%	31%	
Venezuela	1994–present	N/A	17%	

Sources: IMF (1998c) and Lindgren, Garcia, and Saal (1996).
[a]Estimated at peak of the crisis, as percentage of total loans.
[b]Estmated as percentage of annual GDP during the restructuring period.

do about a bailout are further clouded by the fact that the government is already running a large deficit (estimated to be more than 6% of GDP by the IMF, 1998b). On top of this, Japan faces a significant upcoming social security problem. This has led the government to try to rein in the deficits. For instance, the Fiscal Structural Reform Act passed in November 1997 required the government to bring the deficit below 3% of GDP by fiscal year 2003. The weakness of the economy led the government to first push back the goal by two years in May 1998 and then eventually suspend the Act completely in December 1998. There is still strong sentiment, however, within the government for trying to begin cutting the deficit as soon as possible.

We draw two conclusions from this assessment. First, the fiscal concerns suggest it is important to focus on the amount of funds that would be needed to keep a large enough banking sector in place to serve borrowers once the crisis is over and the deregulation has taken hold. By looking ahead, one can try to determine the minimum amount of public money that will be needed. We can then compare the minimum estimates with the various proposals that have been made.

Second, in assessing the options that the banks have in developing new strategies it is important to allow for their weak capital positions. The flip side of the problems documented in Tables 14 and 15 is that the Japanese banks have very low levels of capital and are likely to have trouble raising much money in the capital markets in the short run. For instance, Moody's rating agency gives most of the major Japanese banks a financial strength rating of E or E+ (the two lowest ratings on their scale). Such banks are expected to "require periodic outside support." As a consequence the banks are unlikely to be able to purchase other large firms in order to acquire expertise. Similarly, bankruptcy seems like a real risk that would become more imminent if they were to undertake any large investments that have long payback periods. With this in mind, we sketch one scenario for the future of the Japanese banking sector.

5. Quantifying the Impending Shrinkage of the Japanese Banking Sector

The evidence presented in Section 3 suggests that large Japanese manufacturing companies have already almost reduced their reliance on banks to about the level of bank dependence observed in the United States. If our conjecture that other firms will soon be following this lead is correct, it is natural to ask what that might imply for the future of Japanese banks. The purpose of this section is to explore this question quantitatively.

5.1 MAINTAINED ASSUMPTIONS AND CAVEATS

Before diving into the calculation it is important to recognize several caveats about the exercise. First, our approach should be thought of as only calibrating the eventual size of a possible reduction in loan demand. We will explore several different assumptions about potential shifts, but all of our scenarios will take years to play out, so that the numbers that follow can at best be thought of as medium-run forecasts. We discuss the timing issues further in the next section.

Second, we are implicitly assuming that loan demand will drive the size of banks. Although we believe this is the most reasonable assumption to make, it could fail for a variety of reasons. For instance, depositors may continue to stuff their money into the banks even after all the Big Bang reforms are complete. For the most part we have also ignored the presence of the huge Japanese postal savings system (PSS). But there is a continuing debate about whether the PSS should be reformed. It is easy to imagine PSS reforms that wind up pushing large savings flows back towards the banks. We will briefly discuss the plausibility of the size of the implied adjustment in deposits after we present our findings.

Another risk of basing our forecasts on loan demand is the possibility that the banks could shed loans but pick up enough new lines of business so that they would not have to shrink.[38] Given that the Japanese banks currently have very little expertise outside of traditional banking and limited capital to buy such expertise, this scenario may seem unlikely right now. However, if some of these banks end up being sold to foreign financial services firms, it becomes much more realistic. In view of the rapidly changing competitive landscape of the Japanese financial services industry, we view this as a genuine possibility.

A third complication is that, because we focus on the bank debt-to-asset ratio, one must take a stand on what will happen to the growth of corporate assets in order to draw any conclusions about the level of bank lending. Put differently, if corporate assets are growing, then forecasts of a declining bank debt-to-asset ratio need not imply that the level of bank loans will fall. However, there are several pieces of evidence which suggest that an assumption of zero growth of corporate assets is a reasonable forecast for Japanese firms over the medium run.

One consideration is the recent evidence on asset growth. The Hojin Kigyo Tokei data suggest that total assets for all industries grew only at 1.7% a year from 1993 to 1998. Since new firms are added to the survey

---

38. There are also factors that push in the other direction. For instance, these calculations ignore the possibility of foreign lenders taking away business from the Japanese banks.

each year, the number in fact overstates the true growth rate of corporate assets. If this trend were to continue, then asset growth would be sufficiently low not to matter much for our purposes.

Another factor, which has been emphasized by the Japan Economic Research Center (1997), is that Japanese corporations are expected to begin reducing their financial assets (especially low-return liquid assets) as their financial management skills improve. The dwindling of the banks' practice of requiring compensating balances, together with the winding down of cross-shareholdings, will further contribute to the reduction of financial assets. Thus, even if a business-cycle recovery leads Japanese corporations to start increasing their fixed assets, declining financial assets will be a significant offsetting factor. For these reasons we believe that a reasonable benchmark is to translate any forecast declines in the bank debt-to-asset ratio into one-for-one declines in bank lending.

Finally, we also recognize that this whole exercise ignores the potential general equilibrium feedbacks that could occur with large changes in intermediation. Partly this is out of necessity, since building a full model of the financial sector is not yet possible. However, this strategy can be partially justified if we maintain that the economic role of banks is tied to loan generation, particularly to smaller firms, and that for most other activities banks are redundant. Under this view, if the banks were to hold onto customers that might otherwise go to the capital market, the banks would have to match the capital-market rates. As these rates are increasingly determined by global forces, our assumption does not seem very unreasonable.

Keeping in mind all these caveats, we now explore what would happen if all Japanese corporations followed the lead of the large manufacturing firms that have already moved towards U.S. levels of bank dependence.[39] Since we want to consider several scenarios, we start by describing and defending the two basic assumptions that are common to all projections. After discussing these premises we outline the different scenarios that we consider.

The first key assumption is that loan demand for large and small firms can be aggregated within sectors. Thus, for each sector we treat all large firms and all small firms identically. We do not necessarily treat large firms and small firms symmetrically within or across sectors. Our main justification for this approach is the evidence in Table 6 regarding the relative stability of the bank borrowing patterns exhibited by the U.S. firms.

Our second key assumption involves the choice of sectors to be ana-

---

39. The whole exercise is very much in the spirit of Rajan and Zingales (1998).

lyzed. The only really reliable data that we have for the United States pertain to manufacturing. We also have some information for large firms in the wholesale and retail trade sectors. In all of our projections we model these three sectors separately, in some cases making finer assumptions about what is happening within manufacturing. Unfortunately, this means that we have no U.S. data to guide us for other industries. For this reason we aggregate the remaining Japanese industries into an "other" category.

5.2 IMPLICATIONS OF U.S. BORROWING PATTERNS FOR JAPANESE LOAN DEMAND

There are three basic inputs into the forecasts that we report. The first piece of information is the 1998 total amounts of borrowing done by large and small firms across our four sectors of the Japanese economy. These numbers come from the *Hojin Kigyo Tokei,* and we follow the convention from Table 4 of defining large firms to have a book value of capital above ¥1 billion. The second element in the calculation are the initial observed levels of bank dependence for the large and small firms in the different sectors. These numbers can also be computed directly using the unpublished data we obtained.

Table 17 shows the 1998 distribution of bank borrowing and bank dependence for Japanese firms. Table 4 has already shown the noticeable differences in large-and small-firm bank dependence across sectors. We draw three further conclusions from Table 17. First, the "other" category covers over half of the bank borrowing done by firms in the sample. Since we have no representative data for these firms in the United States, this means that a significant portion of our forecast will be based purely on imputations for what might happen to this large, unmodeled segment of borrowers.

Second, the table shows that Japanese banks are already serving primarily small borrowers. Adding up loans made to small firms across all four sectors reveals that small borrowers receive about 64% of the bank credit tracked in the *Hojin Kigyo Tokei.* One check on the plausibility of our forecasts will be to see if they imply reasonable splits between the aggregate amount of large- and small-firm borrowing.

Lastly, the table also indirectly shows the comprehensive coverage of the *Hojin Kigyo Tokei.* According to balance-sheet information for all banks, total lending should be about ¥450 trillion as of March 1998.[40] The

---

40. This figure excludes overdrafts. We believe that excluding overdrafts makes sense because such commitment lending is unlikely to be affected by the Big Bang. See Kashyap, Rajan, and Stein (1999) for theoretical support for this argument and empirical evidence showing that even in the U.S. the commitment business is dominated by banks.

Table 17   DISTRIBUTION OF THE 1998 QUANTITY OF BANK
            BORROWING AND THE RATIO OF BANK DEBT TO ASSETS FOR
            JAPANESE FIRMS

Sample[a]	Total Bank Borrowing (trillion yen)		Ratio of Bank Debt to Assets		Fraction of Category Borrowing by Small Firms
All firms, all industries	445		0.3567		0.6432
Large firms, all industries		159		0.2761	
Small firms, all industries		286		0.4257	
All firms, manufacturing	92		0.2372		0.5738
Large firms, manufacturing		39		0.1647	
Small firms, manufacturing		53		0.3527	
All firms, wholesale trade	65		0.3392		0.7160
Large firms, wholesale trade		19		0.3027	
Small firms, wholesale trade		46		0.3562	
All firms, retail trade	41		0.4110		0.8193
Large firms, retail trade		7		0.2559	
Small firms, retail trade		34		0.4746	
All firms, other industries[b]	247		0.4348		0.6207
Large firms, other industries		94		0.3796	
Small firms, other industries		153		0.4773	

Source: Ministry of Finance, *Hojin Kigyo Tokei.*
[a]Large firms are those that have book value of equity greater than ¥1 billion.
[b]All those which are not in manufacturing, wholesale trade, or retail trade.

coverage in our sample is ¥445 trillion. The close match actually masks two differences. One is that the survey includes borrowing from financial institutions such as credit unions that are not counted as banks. However, the survey also excludes borrowing done by truly tiny firms and individuals. It appears these two differences largely cancel.

The final ingredient needed for our forecasts is the assumed level of bank dependence that will prevail in the new steady state. Wherever possible we try to pin down these figures using the U.S. experience. Based on the QFR data from Table 6, we can get benchmarks for large and small manufacturing firms, large retail firms, and large wholesale firms. In fact, for the manufacturing sector we can do better and get two-digit-level data for the 14 industries. However, we have no solid data for the borrowing by U.S. firms in the "other" industries and therefore try several very different ways of calibrating the changes for these firms.

Since each hypothesized steady state requires eight assumptions about the bank debt-to-asset ratios (two types of firms in four sectors), there are endless simulation possibilities. To simplify the reporting, we focus on three different variations that we believe should bound the implied adjustments. Each of these variations amounts to setting a switch that pins down two or more of the eight bank debt-to-asset ratios.

The first set of alternatives involve differing assumptions about the behavior of Japanese manufacturing firms. Our simplest assumption is that the large and the small firms' bank dependence in Japan converge to the same levels that hold for the typical large and small manufacturing firms in the U.S. We call this case the *simple manufacturing assumption*. This assumption ignores the differences in industrial composition between the two countries. Therefore, we repeat the calculations assuming instead that large and small Japanese firms' bank dependence converge on an industry-by-industry basis to the U.S. levels. Here we have data for 14 industries (shown in Tables 7 and 8), and we form a fifteenth category for the remaining firms. Although we conduct the calculations at the industry level, the results are aggregated back to the total manufacturing level for reporting purposes. We denote this second case as the *industry-adjusted manufacturing assumption*.

A second pair of assumptions relate to the treatment of small firms in the wholesale and retail sectors. Although the QFR gives us some data on U.S. borrowing propensities for large firms, there are no QFR data for small firms in these sectors. The only available data that we know of describing small-firm borrowing patterns in the U.S. are in the 1993 National Survey of Small Business Finances (NSSBF). This survey, conducted for the Board of Governors of the Federal Reserve System and the U.S. Small Business Administration, covers a nationally representative sample of very small businesses.[41]

Petersen and Rajan (1994) have analyzed these data and were kind enough to provide us with some simple tabulations of the ratio of bank debt to assets for these firms. These tabulations suggest that for the NSSBF the total debt ratio was between 0.18 and 0.24 for the sector groupings that we are analyzing (on an asset-weighted basis). We also learned that banks supply about half of all loans to these firms. However, there are two factors that make us hesitant to rely completely on these numbers in our simulations. One concern is that the firms in the NSSBF are very small. For instance, the top decile of firms in this sample includes firms with as little as $2.3 million in assets. The "small" Japanese firms that we are studying appear to be about ten times bigger in terms of average assets.

41. The target population is all for-profit, nonfinancial, nonfarm business enterprises that had fewer than 500 employees and were in operation as of year-end 1992. The public data set contains 4637 firms and describes all the loans each firm has as of year-end 1992, as well as the institutions that these loans came from.

Secondly, we know that bank borrowing becomes more important once firms grow. For instance, within the NSSBF sample, both the fraction of firms with any debt and the fraction of firms' debt owed to banks rise with firm size. Thus, we suspect that U.S. firms which would be comparable in size to our sample of Japanese firms would be more bank-dependent in their financing than are the NSSBF firms. Nevertheless, it seems to us unlikely that this growth effect would be strong enough to push the firms' bank-debt-to-asset ratio much beyond the 35% (which is the upper end of the range for the total debt-to-asset ratio in the NSSBF).

With these numbers as a reference we consider two different scenarios for the small trade firms. The first approach plays off of the small-firm-to-large-firm borrowing ratio that is observed in U.S. manufacturing. We apply this ratio to the level of the QFR for large firms in each sector to get a target level of small firms in each sector. We describe this assumption as identifying small trade firms' bank dependence using U.S. manufacturing data. Given the data in Table 6, we can see that this will imply bank-debt-to-asset ratios of about 0.23 and 0.32 for small retail and wholesale firms respectively.

Are these numbers reasonable? In the NSSBF sample they are 0.24 and 0.20, respectively. Using the figures from Table 6, this suggests that the ratio of the NSSBF levels of bank dependence to the levels found for large retailers and wholesalers is in line with the approximate 2:1 ratio found in U.S. manufacturing. Thus, we believe that unless the NSSBF data significantly understate small firms' bank dependence, assuming the small and large firms' differences are about the same (in ratio terms) across sectors seems plausible.

Our second approach exploits the fact that we can observe both small and large firms' borrowing patterns for the Japanese trade firms. In this case we get the steady-state target level of small-firm borrowing for wholesalers by multiplying the ratio of small-firm to large-firm bank dependence of wholesalers in Japan by the level of bank dependence for large U.S. wholesalers. In essence this assumes that both large and small Japanese wholesalers will adjust by the same *percentage*. We carry out the same calculations for retailers, and describe this assumption as identifying small trade firms' bank dependence using existing Japanese borrowing patterns. Using these assumptions, the target levels of bank dependence are 0.20 and 0.18 for small retail and wholesale firms respectively. These targets are both below the levels found in the NSSBF and thus are likely to lead us to overstate the decline in bank dependence.

Our third and last set of cases involve the assumptions about the levels of bank dependence for the other industries such as transportation, communications, services, and construction, where we have absolutely no QFR data. Based on the Japanese data shown in Table 17, we can see that as of 1998 these firms are more bank-dependent than the wholesale and retail firms. However, these firms also have more of their bank borrowing being done by large firms than is the case for either wholesalers or retailers. Considering both these factors, we use the average proportional adjustment done by the wholesale and retail trade firms to come up with the required adjustment for the large and small firms in the other category. More specifically, we assume that the ratio of the target level to the current level of bank dependence for large (small) "other" firms is equal to the weighted average of the target-to-current ratio for large (small) firms in wholesale and retail trade industries. In the NSSBF data the *level* of bank dependence for other sector firms is close to the level of bank dependence for trade firms. Thus, for small firms this assumption (which does not force the levels to converge) seems conservative.

Given the amount of guesswork involved constructing this benchmark, we consider a second refinement in which we assume these other firms only adjust half as much as the similar-sized average trade firm. We describe this refinement as *halfway convergence* to distinguish it from the first case above, which is called *full convergence*. Halfway convergence is an attempt to trade off our ignorance about how the large firms in this sector are financed against the presumption that capital-market financing is likely to displace at least some bank lending.

We summarize the pairs of alternatives and introduce some shorthand notation for describing them in Table 18. Since the three alternatives are mutually exclusive, we have eight total cases to consider. By comparing the scenarios where two of the three factors are held constant, we will be able to take "derivatives" to determine which of the convergence assumptions are most powerful. Below, as a sensitivity check, we also explore what happens if we do not assume that the large Japanese firms in wholesale and retail trade go all the way to the levels seen in the United States.

Table 19 compares the eight alternative steady states for future loan demand with the current levels of borrowing by Japanese firms. We draw five main conclusions from the calculations. First and most importantly, under all the scenarios we explore, *the U.S. benchmark implies a large impending decline in loan demand by Japanese firms.* The smallest hypothesized contraction suggests a decline of more than 25% in bank-loan demand. Even recognizing that these calculations refer to medium-term adjustments, we find the implied drops to be quite large. We discuss the transitional implications of this kind of shift in the concluding section.

Second, the forecasts all seem reasonable in their implications for the

Table 18   ALTERNATIVE ASSUMPTIONS REGARDING LOAN DEMAND
USED FOR CALCULATING STEADY LOAN AMOUNTS

Sector(s) Directly Affected	Shorthand Name	Brief Description
Manufacturing	Simple manufacturing convergence	Large and small Japanese manufacturing firms' bank dependence converges to U.S. levels.
	Industry-adjusted manufacturing convergence	Within each of 15 manufacturing industries, large and small Japanese firms' bank dependence converges to the U.S. levels.
Wholesale and Retail Trade	Small trade firms' borrowing based on U.S. manufacturing	The ratio of bank dependence between U.S. large and small manufacturing is imposed to infer the target level of borrowing for small trade firms.
	Small trade firms' borrowing based on current Japanese patterns	The existing ratio of bank dependence between large and small firms within each sector is imposed to infer the target level of borrowing for small firms in each sector.
Other industries	Full convergence	Target levels for these firms are set to deliver an equal percentage adjustment in bank dependence for similar-sized trade firms.
	Halfway convergence	Target levels for these firms are set to deliver an equal percentage adjustment in bank dependence for similar-sized trade firms.

Table 19   IMPLIED REDUCTIONS IN LENDING FOR JAPANESE BANKS, ASSUMING U.S. BORROWING PATTERNS

Assumption for Manufacturing Firms	Assumption for Target of Small Trade Firms	Assumption for Target Level in Other Industries	Implied Decrease in Lending	Fraction of Total Lending to Small Firms
Simple convergence	Based on U.S. manufacturing	Full convergence	41.5%	70.6%
		Half convergence	29.8%	67.4%
	Based on current Japanese patterns	Full convergence	52.4%	63.8%
		Half convergence	37.5%	63.4%
Industry-adjusted convergence	Based on U.S. manufacturing	Full convergence	41.6%	71.3%
		Half convergence	29.9%	68.0%
	Based on current Japanese patterns	Full convergence	52.5%	64.7%
		Half convergence	37.5%	64.1%

Calculations assume that Japanese firms' borrowing patterns move towards U.S. levels. Benchmarks for the United States are taken from QFR for the 2nd quarter of 1998. For categories where the QFR data are not sufficient, the assumptions shown in columns 2 and 3 are used. These assumptions are described fully in the text and briefly in Table 18.

steady-state customer mix of the Japanese banks. The various scenarios all imply that small firms will account for between 62% and 72% of bank borrowing. These ranges seem to be plausible, and since this ratio was calculated endogenously, we find this to be a reassuring check on the methodology and our assumptions.

The other three conclusions concern which of the different assumptions appear to be quantitatively important. The different treatment for manufacturing firms does not appear to matter much. Holding constant our other assumption about the nonmanufacturing firms, the decision to take account of interindustry variation in manufacturing borrowing patterns only changes the implied level of borrowing by about 0.1%. The implied percentages of aggregate borrowing by small firms also do not move very much across these two assumptions.

In contrast, the other two assumptions make a big difference. These two assumptions interact, since the target levels assumed for the small trade firms also help determine the target level of borrowing by small firms in the other category. Whether or not the "other" firms adjust all the way or just halfway accounts for at least an 11-percentage-point difference in the total projected level of borrowing. Similarly, the two alternatives for the target levels of borrowing by small trade firms lead to an estimated difference of at least 7-percentage points. As predicted, the benchmark based on the patterns in U.S. manufacturing produces smaller declines. Overall, the large size of these effects suggests that further work to narrow the uncertainty over which assumptions to rely upon is needed.

5.3 PLAUSIBILITY CHECKS FOR THE IMPLIED SHRINKAGE IN THE JAPANESE BANKING SECTOR

Given the large magnitudes of the projected decline in lending, one would like to see if there are other implications of this forecast that can be verified or alternative assumptions might overturn the prediction. We briefly describe three plausibility checks that we have conducted.

Our first test is to see whether the sectoral implications for drops in loan demand are credible. Implicit in all the estimates shown in Table 19 is the assumption that firms in the trade sector fully converge to the levels of bank dependence in the United States. Given the sizable existing gaps between large firms' bank dependence in the two countries documented in Tables 4 and 6, this is a fairly strong assumption. Indeed, one might also question whether it is prudent to forecast that bank dependence among small manufacturing firms will converge.

To address these concerns we conducted another set of simulations that presume far less convergence than is built into our baseline scenario. In these simulations, we maintained that only large manufacturing firms would fully converge to the same level of bank dependence. For all the remaining firms, Japanese firms were posited to move halfway towards the level of bank dependence that is observed in the United States. We view these assumptions as being extremely conservative, and yet they still imply reductions in the bank-debt-to-asset ratio between 22% and 29% (depending on which of the various assumptions are used to pin down the target levels for the small trade and other firms).

From Table 17 one can see why a reduction of at least 20% seems inevitable. The key observation is that the 1998 borrowing patterns in Japan do not involve much bank credit going to large trade firms. So varying their bank dependence does not have much aggregate effect. But about 42% of total bank lending is going to small firms in retail trade and other industries which have very high bank-debt-to-asset ratios. Even modest adjustments by these firms, combined with a continued decline in bank borrowing by the numerous large manufacturing firms, will generate a large decline in the bank-debt-to-asset ratio.

A second plausibility check involves exploring what our forecast will imply for depositors. The evidence in Section 3 suggested that in the past Japanese individuals have not abandoned the banks. One obvious question is whether our medium-term forecast implies incredible shifts in the behavior of depositors.

Figure 9 shows how (as of June, 1998) Japanese households allocated their ¥1,200 trillion of financial assets. As we pointed out in Table 9, the Japanese households historically have heavily relied on deposits. Figure 9 indicates that currently 59% of household financial assets are in cash and deposits (including postal savings). A 30% rate of shrinkage for bank loans translates into ¥133 trillion reduction (using 1998 2nd-quarter data from *Quarterly Report of Incorporated Enterprise Statistics*). If we consider an extreme case, then deposits at these institutions also must fall by 30%. This would reduce the total amount of cash and deposits (including postal savings) by 18%, and its proportion in total financial wealth would fall to 48%. In the deposit-to-GDP ratio we would also expect a decline of 18%, which would reduce the ratio to 1.69.

Looking at Table 9, we note that a deposit-to-GDP ratio of 1.69 would still be higher than what is found in any of the other industrialized countries shown in the table. The prediction that the proportion of cash and deposits in the household financial assets will decline to 48% is also plausible—this would still leave Japan with more deposits relative to wealth than other G7 countries. Similarly, the Japan Economic Research Center (JERC) (1997) forecast that the proportion of cash and deposits in household financial assets will decline to 45% by 2010 and to 35% by 2020.

Their forecast is premised on a massive shift of household assets from deposits to investment trusts, which they see growing from their current level of 2.3% to 9.1% by 2010 and to 20% by 2020. In our scenario, if we assume all the decline in household deposits is matched by an increase in investment trusts, then we would expect the share of investment trusts to increase to 13%. Thus, our scenario also implies a huge boom for investment trusts.

Figure 9 JUNE 1998 DISTRIBUTION OF HOUSEHOLDS' SAVINGS ACROSS DIFFERENT INSTRUMENTS

Total wealth is ¥1,239,710 billion. (Category totals in billions of yen are shown in parentheses.)

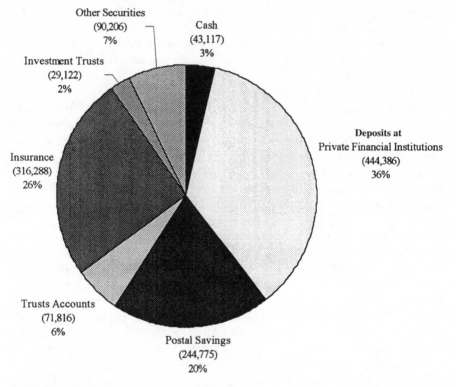

Other Securities
(90,206)
7%

Cash
(43,117)
3%

Investment Trusts
(29,122)
2%

Insurance
(316,288)
26%

Deposits at
Private Financial Institutions
(444,386)
36%

Trusts Accounts
(71,816)
6%

Postal Savings
(244,775)
20%

Source: Flow-of-funds accounts.

There are many other analysts who forecast similar gains for investment trusts. For instance, Naito (1999) argues that because of a 1998 change in regulation, investment trusts are the most appealing financial product for households. The 1998 change allowed "company-based" investment trusts, which are closer to U.S. mutual funds than are "contract-based" investment trusts, which have existed in Japan throughout the post-war period. Perhaps more importantly, the change allowed banks and insurance companies to sell investment trusts at their counters starting in December 1998. According to the Nihon Keizai Shinbum (November 12, 1999), the amount of investment trusts purchased through banks and insurance companies through October 1999 was already ¥2.4 trillion. The total amount of investment trusts outstanding also had increased to ¥53 trillion. Given these considerations, we do not find the implications of forecasts for bank deposits to be implausible.

Finally, we ask whether there are any methods one might use to estimate the future size of the banking sector that do not rely on assumptions about loan demand. Moody's (1999) offers a prediction based on profitability. It argues that a reasonable benchmark is to assume that Japanese banks will need to have the same ratio of tangible equity to assets as is found in other countries.[42] They estimate that as of March 1999 Japanese banks have a tangible-equity-to-asset ratio of 4.2%, while large U.S. banks have a ratio of around 6.5%. Assuming that equity issuance is not possible, this leads Moody's to forecast a reduction of over ¥100 trillion in risk-weighted assets to reach the U.S. level.[43] As they note, in the short run this can be done partially by securitizing loans. But ultimately this seems like another way to arrive at the conclusion that a large contraction in the sector is needed.

An alternative prediction is available from a long-term forecast published by the Japan Economic Research Center (1997). The JERC forecasts the levels of financial assets and liabilities for each sector identified by Bank of Japan flow-of-funds statistics. Although they do not reveal detailed assumptions behind their forecasts, some of their predictions are based on assumptions very similar to ours. For instance, they assume the Japanese corporate financing patterns will move toward the U.S. model. Looking at their forecasts for the market values of financial assets and liabilities, we find that their prediction implies that the bank-debt-to-asset ratio for the corporate sector will decline from 0.4461 in 1995 to 0.2395 by 2020. Since they use the market values, the numbers are not directly comparable to our numbers, but the magnitude of the decline in the bank-debt ratio (46% in 25 years) is as large as what our analysis implies.

Because they assume rather high rate of growth in assets (3.3% per year for 25 years), they forecast the level of bank loans to rise from ¥555 trillion in 1995 to ¥675 trillion in 2020 (0.76% growth per year). Assuming a more reasonable growth rate for assets, their prediction would imply a reduction in the absolute level of loans. For example, if the assets grew only at 1.5% per year, then bank loans would be projected to decline to ¥432 trillion by 2020, a 22% drop.

42. The ratio they consider is Tier 1 capital (as defined by the Basle banking accord) minus state capital minus preferred securities, divided by risk-weighted assets (see Moody's, 1999, p. 24 for details).
43. Loans are roughly ¥450 trillion, so if the reduction were made entirely by cutting loans, this would imply a 22.2% decline.

6. Conclusions

We have argued that the disequilibrium created by the gradual and lopsided deregulation in the Japanese financial system played an important role in the current banking crisis. The deregulation allowed large bank customers to quickly shift from bank financing to capital-market funding. Meanwhile, the deregulation did relatively little for savers, so banks continued to attract deposits. However, the deregulation of bank powers also was slow and gradual. This meant that if the banks were to keep lending they would need to seek out new customers. The banks did take on many new small customers. They also expanded their real estate lending. Ultimately these bets proved to be unprofitable.

In support of this story, we present a variety of evidence. One finding is that the banks' performance was worse in the 1990s than would be predicted just on the basis of macroeconomic conditions. Similarly, across banks, we find that the banks that were most at risk for losing customers to the capital markets performed worse than others. Both these results suggest the importance of the deregulation. We also document that large Japanese firms (particularly in manufacturing) are now almost as independent of bank financing as comparable U.S. firms.

We argue that once the Big Bang financial deregulation is complete, even the relatively small firms will start following the route already taken by the large firms by cutting their dependence on bank loans. By assuming other firms' financing patterns will also converge to the U.S. patterns, we calculated how much the Japanese banking sector must shrink in the steady state. Uniformly, the scenarios that we examined imply a massive contraction in the size of the traditional banking business in Japan.

While there are many reasons why one might quibble with the details of the calculations in Table 19, we think they at least provide a reasonable benchmark. To overturn the basic thrust of the calculations, one must argue that the basic U.S. benchmark is inappropriate. We believe we have made a compelling case that for the large firms the benchmark is reasonable. For the small firms, we concede that there is much more guesswork involved. But, even if we take our most conservative scenario where full convergence in bank dependence is only assumed for large manufacturing firms and all remaining firms move halfway toward the U.S. levels, we still end up projecting more than a 20% decline in loan demand. This forecast is comparable to the one Moody's (1999) arrived at by making quite different assumptions.

What would a 20% decline imply for the configuration of the banking sector? There are many possible ways that this could shake out. However, given the current debate over how much public money should be used to prop up the banks, one natural question to ask is how many weak banks would have to completely exit to eliminate the excess capacity in the industry. To pursue this, we took the ranking of 142 Japanese banks as of September 1998, put forward in the March 1999 issue of *Kin'yu Business*, and calculated the share of loans for each bank.[44] This allows us to examine how many banks must exit so that the cumulative shrinkage in loans is sufficient to bring the system to its new steady state.

We find that a 20% reduction in lending requires a complete exit of the lowest-rated 45 banks of a total of 142 banks. These include Long-Term Credit Bank (LTCB) and Nippon Credit Bank (NCB), which were nationalized in late 1998, and the regional banks that were put into receivership in the first half of 1999. Perhaps more importantly, this set of 45 banks would include 3 of the 15 major banks (Daiwa, Tokai, and Chuo Trust) that received a government capital injection in March 1999. If we consider a 30% shrinkage, which is closer to the average of the Table 19 estimates, the number of weak banks that would have to be eliminated jumps to 69, including three more (Yokohama, Asahi, and Toyo Trust) of the 15 banks which received government money. Even if the relatively healthy banks can somehow be convinced to cut back on some of their lending, it is hard to escape the conclusion that any transition looks like it will involve the exit of a number of major banks.

Because any assessment of banks' health is somewhat subjective, we also looked at the Moody's Investor Service (1999) rankings. They estimate the "financial strength" of 51 Japanese banks. Their ratings range from B (Shizuoka Bank) to E (10 banks including LTCB and NCB). Moody's assessment differs from the *Kin'yu Business* ranking in that it focuses on solvency and looks at not only obligations of the parent but also those of supported subsidiaries. Nonetheless, the *Kin'yu Business* ranking and Moody's rating identify very similar sets of weak banks. For

44. They rank ordinary banks (city banks and regional banks) and trust banks separately by looking at size (measured by the average amount of funds), profitability (measured by business-profits-to-asset ratio and interest margin), efficiency (measured by expense ratio and interest income per employee), and solvency (measured by capital ratio, nonperforming-loan ratio, provision ratio for nonperforming loans, and market-to-book ratio of securities holdings). In order to combine two separate rankings, we reranked city banks, trust banks, and a long-term credit bank (Industrial Bank of Japan) using eight of the nine indicators used by *Kin'yu Business*. The last indicator (market-to-book ratio of securities holdings) was not easily available. We established the rankings of trust banks and IBJ in the list of ordinary banks by comparing them with city banks included in the list. For example, we rank Sumitomo Trust after DKB (ranked 12 in *Kin'yu Business*) and before Fuji (ranked 28), since Sumitomo Trust is located more or less between DKB and Fuji according to the indicators we are looking at. Finally, we added the two banks that were nationalized in late 1998, Long-Term Credit Bank of Japan and Nippon Credit Bank, at the bottom of the ranking.

example, 10 of the 45 lowest-ranked banks in *Kin'yu Business* are rated by Moody's, and of those 8 have the lowest rating (E) and the other 2 are the next lowest rating (E+), Among *Kin'yu Business*'s 69 worst banks, 15 are rated by Moody's, and of those 9 have E and the other 6 have E+. Thus, the weakest banks in the *Kin'yu Business* ranking are also rated very low by Moody's.

Given this overlap, it is therefore not surprising that if we base our exit forecasts on the Moody's data we get a very similar picture. If we assume that 10 banks with E ratings will disappear, their cumulative loans amount to 11.5% of total loans in the banking sector. Three of 15 banks (Daiwa, Chuo Trust, and Mitsui Trust) that have received capital injections are included in this group. If all the banks with E ratings and E+ ratings were to exit, their cumulative loans would be 49% of total loans, suggesting a much bigger contraction than we expect. However, included in the set of E and E+ banks are 13 of the 15 banks that received government money, so it still seems like a nontrivial fraction of these banks may be redundant.

How long will it take for such a shift in the Japanese banking to be completed? The speed of adjustment will primarily depend on three factors: how fast corporations adjust their financing, how fast households shift their funds out of bank deposits, and how fast the banking industry is reorganized. The previous experience suggests that the adjustment by corporate borrowers will be fairly quick. Although the restrictions on corporate financing options were only gradually loosened, many firms adjusted quickly and most completed their adjustments in less than 10 years. The deregulation of the remaining restrictions on corporate financing will be rapid. Thus, we expect the adjustment on the corporate finance side to be complete well within 10 years.

How fast will the households move? Because the most significant elements of the liberalization of savers' options have started only very recently, this question is much harder to answer. As we saw above, the dependence on deposits by Japanese households starts from such a high level that even a modest change towards the patterns observed in other OECD economies would be sufficient to support our forecast. We believe that a modest shift can take place in ten years, but there is a considerable amount of uncertainty in this conjecture.

Finally, the shrinkage of bank loans will imply a substantial exit in the banking industry unless Japanese banks shift away from traditional banking business very aggressively. The speed of such a reorganization obviously depends on the government's policy stance toward bank failures. As we saw in Section 4, the Japanese government seems finally to have begun addressing the bad-loan problem. The next step will require more closures of insolvent banks. If the current tough stance of the FSA and the FRC continues, the days of the convoy system of rescues will be over.

Nevertheless, once the restructuring begins in earnest, we imagine that it will take several years for the doomed banks to exit. Importantly, the mergers among the largest banks in the fall of 1999 are not the kind of restructuring we have in mind, unless contrary to the initial descriptions of these alliances, they facilitate reductions in assets that would not otherwise be possible. Combinations of organizations that do not promote downsizing are likely to be counterproductive. A particularly salient benchmark is Hokkaido Takushoku which, although it has been dead for more than two years, still has most of its assets in the banking system. Our forecasts require that the assets of a failed institution be disposed of, not merely moved into other banks. The Hokkaido Takushoku experience suggests that the reorganization could take years, although we see no reason to expect it to take more than a decade. Thus, overall, we expect the transition to the new steady state to be fairly complete by the end of the next decade.

REFERENCES

Aoki, M., and H. Patrick. (1994). *The Japanese Main Bank System: Its Relevance for Developing and Transforming Economies*. Oxford University Press.

Atkinson, D. (1998). Nihon ni oote ginko ha 2–4 ko shika hitsuyo denai (Japan needs no more than 2–4 major banks). Goldman Sachs Investment Research.

Bank of Japan, Bank Supervision Department. (1997). Sin'yo risuku kanri no koudo-ka ni muketa jiko satei no katsuyo ni tsuite (Using self-examination to improve credit risk management). *Nihon Ginko Geppo,* October, pp. 1–16.

Bayoumi, T. (1998). The morning after: Explaining the slowdown in Japanese growth in the 1990s. Washington: International Monetary Fund. IMF Working Paper.

Berger, A., and G. Udell. (1995). Lines of credit and relationship lending in small firm finance. *Journal of Business* 68:351–381.

Cai, J., K.C. Chan, and T. Yamada. (1996). The performance of Japanese mutual funds. Columbia University, Center on Japanese Economy and Business. Working Paper 107.

Cargill, T. (1999). What caused the current banking crisis? Reno: University of Nevada. Manuscript.

———, M. M. Hutchison, and T. Ito. (1997). *The Political Economy of Japanese Monetary Policy*. Cambridge, MA: MIT Press.

Choy, J. (1999). Japan's banking industry: The "convoy" disperses in stormy seas. Japan Economic Institute. Report 10A.

Corbett, J. (1999a). Crisis, what crisis? The policy response to Japan's banking crisis. In *Why Did Japan Stumble? Causes and Cures,* C. Freedman (ed.). Edward Elgar.

———. (1999b) Japan's banking crisis in international perspective. In *Finance, Government, and Competitiveness,* M. Aoki and G. Saxonhouse (eds.). Oxford: Oxford University Press.

Craig, V. (1998). Financial deregulation in Japan. *FDIC Banking Review* 11(3):1–12.

Dale, R. (1992). *International Banking Deregulation: The Great Banking Experiment,* Malden: Blackwell Publishers.

Economic Planning Agency. (1998). *Keizai Hakusho (Economic White Paper).*

Fiorillo, J. (1999). Private correspondence.

Fukao, M. (1999). Re-capitalizing Japan's banks: The functions and problems of the Financial Revitalization Act and the Bank Recapitalization Act. Keio University. Mimeo.

Gertler, M., and S. Gilchrist. (1994). Monetary policy, business cycles, and the behavior of small manufacturing firms. *Quarterly Journal of Economics* 59:309–340.

Gorton, G., and R. Rosen (1995). Corporate control, portfolio choice, and the decline of banking. *Journal of Finance* 50:1377–1420.

Hamada, K., and A. Horiuchi. (1987). The political economy of financial markets. In *The Political Economy of Japan: Volume I. The Domestic Transformation,* K. Yamamura and Y. Yasuba (eds.). Stanford, CA: Stanford University Press, pp.223–260.

Hoshi, T., and A. Kashyap. (1999a). *Keiretsu Financing.* Manuscript in progress.

———, and ———. (1999b). The Japanese banking crisis: Where did it come from and how will it end? Cambridge, MA: National Bureau of Economic Research. NBER Working Paper. 7520, August.

Hutchison, M. (1998). Are all banking crises alike? Santa Cruz: University of California. Working Paper.

International Monetary Fund. (1998a). Japan selected issues. Washington: International Monetary Fund. IMF Staff Country Report 98/113.

———. (1998b). *International Financial Statistics.* Washington: International Monetary Fund.

———. (1998c). *World Economic Outlook May 1998.* Washington: International Monetary Fund.

Iwahara, S., Y. Okina, Y. Kanemoto, and K. Narisawa. (1999). Kin'yu kikan no furyo saiken no jittai to hatan shori sukiimu (The reality of bad loans at financial institutions and schemes to deal with failures). *Jurist* (Tokyo) 1151: 10–36.

Japan Economic Research Center. (1997). *2020 nen no Nihon no Kin'yu (Japanese Finance in 2020).* Japan Economic Research Center.

Jenkinson, T. J. (1990). Initial public offerings in the United Kingdom, the United States and Japan. *Journal of the Japanese and International Economies* 3(4):428–449.

Kashyap, A., R. Rajan, and J. Stein. (1999). Banks as liquidity providers: An explanation for the coexistence of lending and deposit-taking. Cambridge, MA: National Bureau of Economic Research. NBER Working Paper 6962.

Lincoln, E. (1998). Japan's financial problems. *Brookings Papers on Economic Activity* 2:347–385.

Lindgren, C.-J., G. Garcia, and M. I. Saal. (1996). *Bank Soundness and Macroeconomic Policy.* Washington: International Monetary Fund.

Milhaupt, C. J., and G. P. Miller (1997). Cooperation, conflict, and convergence in Japanese finance: Evidence from the "jusen" problem. *Law and Policy in International Business* 29:1–78.

Moody's Investors Service. (1999). *Moody's Banking System Outlook.*

Motonishi, T., and H. Yoshikawa. (1998). Causes of the long stagnation of Japan during the 1990s: Financial or real. Tokyo University. Working Paper.

Naito, K. (1999). Nihon-ban Big Bang ni yotte toujousuru kin'yu shohin no kojin kin'yu shisan unyo he no eikyo (The impact of new financial products introduced by the Japanese Big Bang on financial investments by individuals). Fuji Research Institute. Research Paper.

Ogawa, K., and S. Kitasaka. (1998). Bank lending in Japan: Its determinants and macroeconomic implications. Osaka University. Working Paper.

Ohara, Y. (1996). Japan's banking: The darkest hour before dawn. The future is in the hands of MoF. Columbia University, Center on Japanese Economy and Business. Working Paper 127.

———. (1998). *Ginko Sector One Point (Banking Sector One Point)*. SBC Warburg.

Ohmura, K., and H. Kawakita (1992). *Zeminaru Nihon no Kabushiki Shijo (Seminar Japanese Stock Markets)*. Tokyo: Toyo Keizai Shinpo-sha.

Organization for Economic Co-operation and Development. (1998). *OECD Economic Surveys 1998: Japan*. (Paris: OECD).

Packer, F. (1998). The disposal of bad loans in Japan: The case of CCPC. Federal Reserve Bank of New York. Manuscript.

Patrick, H. T. (1967). Japan, 1868–1914. In *Banking in the Early Stages of Industrialization*, R. Cameron, O. Crisp, H. T. Patrick, and R. Tilly (eds.). New York: Oxford University Press, pp. 239–289.

———. (1971). The economic muddle of the 1920s. In *Dilemmas of Growth in Prewar Japan*, J. W. Morley (ed.). Princeton, NJ: Princeton University Press, pp. 211–266.

———. (1972). Finance, capital markets and economic growth in Japan. In. *Financial Development and Economic Growth*, A. W. Sametz (ed.). New York: New York University Press, pp.109–139.

Peek, J., and E. Rosengren. (1997a). The international transmission of financial shocks: The case of Japan. *American Economic Review* 87(4):495–505.

———, and ———. (1997b). Collateral damage: Effects of the Japanese real estate collapse on credit availability and real activity in the United States. Federal Reserve Bank of Boston. Working Paper 97–5.

Petersen, M., and R. Rajan. (1994). The benefits of firm–creditor relationships: Evidence from small business data. *Journal of Finance* 49:3–37.

Rajan, R., and L. Zingales. (1998). Financial dependence and growth. *American Economic Review* 88(3):559–586.

Rosenbluth, F. M. (1989). *Financial politics in Contemporary Japan*. Ithaca, NY: Cornell University Press.

Second Financial System Committee of the Financial System Research Council. (1989). Interim report on "a new Japanese financial system." English translation by the Federation of Bankers Associations of Japan.

Takeda, M., and P. Turner. (1992). The liberalisation of Japan's financial markets: Some major themes. Bank of International Settlements. Working Paper.

Toyama, H. (1998). The monetary regulatory and competitive implications of the restructuring of the Japanese banking industry. Bank of Japan. Working Paper.

Ueda, K. (1999). Causes of the Japanese banking instability in the 1990s. Bank of Japan. Manuscript.

Woo, D. (1998). In search of "capital crunch": Supply factors behind the credit slowdown in Japan. Washington: International Monetary Fund. Working Paper.

White, Halbert (1980), A heteroskedasticity-consistent covariance matrix estimator and a direct test for heteroskedasticity, *Econometrica* 48:817–38.

Comment

MICHAEL HUTCHISON
University of California at Santa Cruz

Takeo Hoshi and Anil Kashyap have given an insightful and comprehensive account of the Japanese banking problem, and offer us a picture of an industry likely to be in continuous turmoil over the next decade or so as banking is downsized in favor of open financial markets. The authors make several important points. First, Japanese banks are under severe competitive pressure, mainly due to unbalanced financial regulation allowing large firms to go to open markets but not allowing banks to compete effectively. Second, the asset price bubble and subsequent recession are neither the only, nor perhaps the primary, reasons for banking distress in Japan. Third, the Big Bang in Japan will eventually lead the structure of Japanese finance to converge to the U.S. norm. Fourth, convergence to the U.S. norm implies that the demand for loans by Japanese firms will decline dramatically over the next decade or so, indicating a *huge* contraction in the Japanese banking sector.

I agree with most of the points made in the paper and believe the authors do an admirable job in supporting their arguments. It should be a key reference work for everyone interested in Japanese banking and finance. In my comments, I focus on two points: (1) the role of the asset price collapse and subsequent recession in explaining the banking problem in Japan, and (2) the extent to which bank-loan demand determines the size of the banking sector.

1. Banking Problems: Long-Run Decline in Competitiveness or Asset Price Collapse and Recession?

The question of what caused the banking problem is reviewed in the paper. An important part of the story is that banks have been under severe competitive pressure and have changed their principal business operations due to shifts in the flows of funds and unbalanced deregulation of the financial services industry. The response of borrowers is that large firms, but not small firms, have reduced their dependence on bank lending, at least up to 1990 (before the Big Bang). Savers in Japan, on the other hand, continue to be highly dependent on bank deposits as a major investment vehicle. Why have they stayed in low-interest deposits? The authors argue that the poor service of investment trusts and the slow introduction of new products are the major reasons. The upshot is that banks at present continue to have a large deposit base but have lost their primary function in financing large firms' investment projects. How have they utilized the funds? By pursuing other forms of lending outside their traditional customer base, such as real estate, private finance, and other relatively high-risk lending activities.

A major point of the paper is that long-run competitive pressure is an important factor in the decline in the return on assets (ROA) in the banking sector and in large part responsible for the banking crisis in Japan. The authors' view is that the present crisis and consolidation in the industry should be seen in the context of a longer-term trend towards contraction in the industry. Another explanation, perhaps complementary, would be that macroeconomic developments (viz., a lengthy and deep recession) and idiosyncratic temporary factors (viz., the asset price collapse) are primarily responsible for the banking crisis in Japan in the 1990s. The empirical section of the paper is important in that it provides evidence for the authors' contention that low ROA in the banking sector has a significant long-run trend component, and is likely to result in a large-scale contraction of the banking sector.

The authors present time-series evidence on this point. They estimate an equation with macroeconomic variables prior to the period of deregulation (1983 is the date the authors argue that deregulation of the bond market began in earnest) to see what helps explain the secular decline in the accounting rates of return. Data on the accounting rate of return (after-tax net income divided by total assets) reported by the firms are employed after adjusting for the sales (gains and losses) or revaluation of securities. Banks have generally tried to smooth their reported returns, however, using flexible accounting practices to push returns higher during bad times and lower in good times. Since bad times (good times) generally correspond with regressions (upturns), it is perhaps not surprising that cyclical fluctuations in the macroeconomic variables do not generally enter the regressions significantly. The smoothing of the ROA data can't hide the secular trend decline, however, and perhaps this is why the most significant explanatory variables in the regressions are the time trend and the lagged dependent variable.

The cross-section evidence is stronger. The idea is to see if banks that were more dependent on large firms or interest income *before* deregulation would be particularly hard hit, in terms of lower ROAs, during the period following deregulation. The maintained hypotheses are that banks (1) that lend to large firms (firms that were more able to take advantage of deregulation and find alternative forms of financing in domestic bond markets abroad), or (2) that are more concentrated in traditional lending operations (that would come under increasing competition with deregulation) would show particularly large declines in ROAs. The authors find fairly strong evidence of this effect on the decline in ROA in the 1990s, supporting their argument that the loss of traditional markets was an important contributing factor to the banking crisis.

2. Size of the Banking Contraction

Even accepting that deregulation and other forces are exerting long-term competitive pressures on banks, essentially forcing a contraction in the entire industry, the eventual steady-state size of the industry is still uncertain. The authors attempt to quantify the projected contraction of the Japanese banking sector by using the U.S. case as a benchmark model. The basic idea is that a falloff in loan demand by Japanese firms, bringing them more in line with firms in the U.S., will reduce the size of banks. Banking customers are anticipated to leave banks in favor of direct finance, with the decline in loan demand driving a reduction in the size of the banking sector. Making a number of simplifying assumptions, and given the constraints imposed by limited U.S. data, the authors consider several alternative scenarios about how large the reduction in bank loans might be over the *medium term*, as the Big Bang facilitates the development of more open and deeper financial markets. All of these scenarios indicate a large reduction in loan demand and contraction in the Japanese banking sector ranging from about 30% to over 50%.

These medium-term projections seem plausible, but there are a number of uncertainties and caveats surrounding the scenarios. The paper is really about declining loan demand and not about the size of the banking sector. There is an implicit assumption that Japanese banks will not be nimble enough to reinvent themselves in new lines of business— even, the authors argue, if they are able to keep the high share of deposits that they currently enjoy. This seems to be borne out by recent experience indicating that Japanese financial institutions continue to dominate the low-margin traditional areas such as retail banking, corporate lending, and straight corporate bond issuance. Foreign firms, by contrast, are rapidly growing in asset management and other areas that have higher margins.

The authors conjecture, however, that the Japanese banks that end up being sold to foreign financial institutions (with more expertise in new financial services and more capital) may be able to effectively pick up new lines of business while they shed loans. The issue appears to boil down to who owns the banks and, if the controlling interests are Japanese, whether they can marshal the capital and expertise to compete in new financial services. The decline in traditional banking business— where low margins have contributed to the current bank problem—need not signal the end of the prominent position of banks in Japan or a contraction of the banking industry. And the powers that banks have to enter investment banking, securities business, and insurance will be virtually complete by the year 2001. There is already a scramble in Japan to form new alliances and tie-ups to take advantage of these opportunities. The authors document over 60 tie-ups and mergers in the Japanese financial services industry announced in 1998 and early 1999. Banks, flush with funds from their huge deposit base, would seemingly have some advantage in entering these new markets. The prospect of a form of universal banking along Swiss and German lines may be real.

The 1980s was a dynamic period for Japanese banks, especially on the international front. Japanese banks grew rapidly, eventually topping the list of the world's largest banks, and Tokyo because a leading international financial center. The 1990s has been a decade of contraction, consolidation, and pessimism for the industry. The Big Bang has changed the playing field for Japanese finance in the new millennium, however, and some Japanese banks appear to be in a good position to take advantage of new opportunities. A 30–50% decline in loan demand need *not* translate into an equally gloomy projection of banking-sector decline, but clearly signals a new form of banking in Japan.

Comment

MARK GERTLER
New York University and NBER

This paper provides a thoughtful and exhaustive analysis of the banking problems that have plagued the Japanese economy over the last decade. It is a useful reference for anyone interested in the issue.

Two basic premises motivate the analysis.

The first is that the weak financial health of the banking system is a central factor underlying the prolonged stagnation of the Japanese economy. Over the past decade, heavy loan losses have seriously depleted the capital base of Japanese banks. Loan losses have amounted to about 7% of GDP, as compared to the roughly 2% experienced during the banking crisis in the United States. This extraordinary contraction of bank capital, in turn, has impeded the ability of banks to lend: Adequate capital helps banks both to guarantee their uninsured liabilities (thus allowing them to attract loanable funds) and also to meet regulatory minimum requirements on the ratio of capital to assets. If capital is insufficient, bank lending may be constrained. Bernanke and Lown

(1991) provide evidence that this kind of phenomenon played an important role in the 1990–1991 recession in the United States. In the present context, Woo (1998) has shown that depletion of bank capital was a significant factor in the 1997 recession in Japan.

The second underlying premise, which follows from the first, is that recapitalization of the banking system is critical to the recovery in Japan. This problem of how to recapitalize is complex, however. Due to informational problems and the like, it is expensive for banks to recapitalize simply by floating new equity issues. Retained earnings are the usual method by which banks rebuild capital, but this can be a long, drawn-out process. Typically, in situations like the one now prevailing in Japan, some kind of public intervention involving taxpayer funds is necessary. An expectation of public bailouts, however, may create adverse incentives for excessive risktaking.

The absence of a straightforward solution to the problem has prompted a heated debate in the Japanese Diet over the path of recapitalization. It is this debate that provides the paper's explicit point of departure. On the one hand, the Liberal Democratic Party (LDP) favors directly injecting public funds to prop up the existing system. On the other, the Democratic Party favors nationalizing and restructuring the system in a way that would likely involve a downsizing. As of this writing, a compromise approach has been adopted, with some tilt toward the LDP position.

The authors observe that the debate reflects fundamentally differing views of the future of the Japanese banking system. They interpret the LDP position as reflecting the belief that the postcrisis banking system will look a lot like the precrisis one, implying the need for large capital replenishment. The Democrats, they argue, envision a smaller system, implying less need for public injections of bank capital. Given this interpretation of the debate, the authors focus their analysis on providing a rough estimate of the future scale of the Japanese banking system, in order to get a sense of what the future capital needs may really be.

I agree that the kind of exercise the authors perform is central to resolving the issue. There is, however, another important dimension to the debate: namely, differing views on the incentive effects of public subsidies. At issue is not only how much capital is needed, but also what is the best mechanism by which to undertake the recapitalization. In this vein, I interpret the LDP position as being that injections of public funds will relax capital constraints and thereby stimulate bank credit extension and economic activity, with minimal bad side effects on risktaking incentives. On the other hand, the Democratic Party perceives the incentives for excessive risktaking as being a first-order problem, with the channeling of funds into risky, negative-present-value projects being the likely outcome of a bailout. In particular, in the Democratic view, for banks well below minimum capital standards, incremental injections of public funds are not likely to deter excessive risktaking, especially in the absence of fundamental reforms of the supervision and regulatory system.

Though it is not the focus of the paper's analysis, the issue of the incentive effects of the restructuring is central to the question at hand and at least as important as the matter of how much capital is needed. For both questions, the U.S. experience with banking problems is instructive.

The first question is: why such a mess? The answer: as before, but worse. As in the case of the United States, we can trace the beginning of the story in Japan to a major deregulation of financial markets that occurred in the late 1970s and early 1980s. To be clear, the problems did not simply evolve from deregulation, which in principle is a good thing. Rather, they evolved from the failure of the authorities to adjust the supervision and regulatory system adequately in light of the new environment. In particular, the opening up of capital markets and the emergence of nonbank intermediaries afforded by the deregulation led to greatly increased competition for commercial banks. Banks, as a consequence, lost high-quality borrowers. They responded by moving into riskier ventures, such as commercial real estate finance. The problem was that the implicit lender-of-last-resort protection of banking remained unaltered. As with the United States, this unadjusted protection served to encourage excessive risktaking in the face of increased competitive pressures.

But why was the Japanese debacle so much worse than what occurred in the United States? Here the authors provide a convincing answer: relative to the United States, capital markets before deregulation in Japan were far more heavily distorted in favor of banks. The authors make a convincing case that the powerful Japanese megabanks were the product less of greater efficiency than of basic regulatory distortions, in regard to both the financial instruments available to savers and the sources of funds available to borrowers. Everything else equal, accordingly, it is only natural that deregulation brought more additional competition for Japanese banks than for their U.S. counterparts.

Another important factor, I believe, involved regulatory forbearance, i.e., lax supervision. Here the problem was very much like the U.S. savings-and-loan crisis, where failure to enforce capital requirements led to sustained high-stakes gambling by zombie-like financial institutions. The scale of this type of behavior was simply much larger in Japan. Why? First, it is likely that the strong performance of the Japanese economy until the early 1990s masked the heavy underlying risk exposure in the banking system. The United States had the (perverse) luxury of the

S&L crisis to provide a wake-up call to regulators in the mid-1980s, who as a consequence were better positioned to address the subsequent problems in commercial banking. In Japan, in contrast, everything hit at once, beginning in 1993. The failure to anticipate the crisis, in conjunction with a weak overall system of supervision and regulation, is thus an important aspect of the crisis.

What role did macroeconomic factors play? I agree with the interpretation that the authors give in the revised version of the paper: Poorly planned deregulation raised the exposure of the banking system to macroeconomic shocks, such as the decline in asset prices and the overall poor performance of the economy. Further, given that Japanese banks hold equity directly, it is hard to believe that the stock-market crash did not have an important impact on bank capital. In this vein, I am concerned that the authors' inability to find a significant role for macroeconomic factors in recent years may reflect measurement problems. Their measure of bank profitability, return on assets, is an accounting concept rather than a market-based one. But in the current draft the authors offer a careful qualification of their findings.

What will happen in the future? To what level will the Japanese banking system converge? Here the authors undertake what I regard as an eminently sensible exercise. They begin with the premise that, given that the legal regulatory structures in the two countries are now reasonably similar, the banks in Japan should converge to the point where they are providing roughly the same fraction of overall firm financing as their counterparts in the United States. Given this benchmark, they proceed with a calibration exercise to compute the future equilibrium level of bank assets in Japan. They forecast a decline of something between 20% and 50% in the size of the Japanese banking system, depending on the scenario.

In the spirit of calibration, no standard errors are to be found. But overall, I find the forecast to be reasonable. The only quibble I would have is that the authors only consider directly held, i.e., on-balance-sheet, assets. In the United States, commercial banks have gone heavily into off-balance-sheet activities, which include providing backup lines of credit, derivatives trading, and so on. These off-balance-sheet activities entail risk, and banks are required to hold capital in proportion to their credit equivalents (i.e., the measure of on-balance-sheet assets that would entail equivalent risk; see Boyd and Gertler, 1994). Thus, any attempt to measure bank capital needs, in my view, should include off-balance-sheet activity as well as traditional on-balance-sheet assets.

Again, the U.S. example is instructive. Measures based simply on on-balance-sheet assets suggest that U.S. commercial banks are steadily declining in relative importance. I show in my work with John Boyd, however, that after allowing for off-balance-sheet activities, the reverse is in fact true: U.S. commercial banks have actually grown in relative importance. It is true that Japanese banks have been slow to move into these nontraditional lines of business. However, if the Japanese financial system evolves toward the U.S. system, as assumed here, then we should similarly expect to see a rise in off-balance-sheet business. Firms that issue open-market debt in the United States, for example, often secure this debt by obtaining backup lines of credit from commercial banks. We should also expect a similar reliance on backup credit lines at banks to support direct financing in Japan. I am not suggesting that allowing for nontraditional bank activities will reverse the authors' results, but I do think that it is important to do so in any debate over the future size of Japanese banking.

I conclude with one final message from the U.S. experience. The recovery of the U.S. banking system involved not only replenishment of capital, but also the adoption of a tougher supervision and regulatory system. In addition, macroeconomic policy, and monetary policy in particular, helped provide a stable climate for banks to operate. For Japan to succeed, it must follow the United States in these two important dimensions.

REFERENCES

Bernanke, B. S., and C. Lown. (1991). The credit crunch. *Brookings Papers on Economic Activity* 1991:2, pp.205–239.
Boyd, J., and M. Gertler. (1994). Are banks dead or are the reports greatly exaggerated? *Federal Reserve Bank of Minneapolis Quarterly Review,* Summer, pp. 2–23.
Woo, David (1998), In search of 'capital crunch': Supply factors behind the credit slowdown in Japan, Washington, International Monetary Fund. Working Paper.

Discussion

In his reply to the discussants, Anil Kashyap agreed that macroeconomic factors had probably played some role in the Japanese banking crisis. The authors' intention had not been to deny the role of macro factors, but to highlight the part played by deregulation, as well as the likely convergence of Japanese banking to U.S. norms. He noted that there was no fundamental disagreement between the authors and the discussants about the forecast of a large contraction in the Japanese banking sector. Kashyap conceded that it is possible, as Mark Gertler suggested, that expansion of off-balance-sheet activities might mitigate the shrinkage, but he also pointed out data in the paper showing that fee income relative to total income for Japanese banks is the same now as it was in 1979, implying little growth in such activities. The policy implication of their work, Kashyap said, was that funds should not be injected into the banking system indiscriminately, since many banks are unlikely to survive in any case.

Michael Mussa said that prior to 1995 no bank among the largest twenty banks in Japan had reported an annual loss and that, more generally, the short-run accounting numbers are not to be believed. This poses obvious econometric difficulties when one tries to estimate the sensitivity of the rate of return on bank assets to macroeconomic disturbances; one will find coefficients that are much too low. Mussa also commented that one of the key issues is who will ultimately be stuck with the bill for the losses that are on the balance sheets of the banks now. If taxpayers foot the bill, banks will be more able to expand into other businesses, but if the banking industry as a whole bears much of the cost, their competitive disadvantage will be increased. Mussa concluded that if the Japanese banks are handed the bill, the authors' estimates of the ultimate size of Japanese banking system may turn out to be too high.

Hoshi responded to Mussa's comment by saying that transactions in "hidden assets" are the most popular method used by Japanese banks to smooth out returns. Banks sell these securities in the market, realize accounting capital gains, and then buy back the securities at market prices. Hoshi said that the authors plan to subtract capital gains from the current income of the banks to obtain what might be a more accurate measure of profits from operations. On Mussa's second point, Hoshi thought that Japan has been moving toward increasing the contribution of taxpayers and reducing that of banks.

John Fernald asked whether financial and banking reforms were of great consequence in Japan. The usual argument is that the financial system's health affects the allocation of capital, but Fernald cited Michael Gibson's work which emphasizes the importance of corporate governance. Gibson has argued that many features of the Japanese corporate governance system insulate managers from shareholder pressure to a much greater extent than in the United States. Absent reform in this dimension, banking reform may not improve the allocation of capital. Moreover, if Japanese corporate governance differs radically from the U.S. case, the argument for convergence of the two banking systems is less compelling. Fernald also raised the issue of how exactly the downsizing will occur: he felt that layoffs, shutdowns, and attempts to diversify into new businesses would all prove difficult.

Nouriel Roubini commented that the banking crisis in Japan resembles the banking crises in the rest of Asia. In particular, in both cases deregulation, liberalization of the capital account, poor regulatory supervision, and poorly designed deposit insurance on the banking side, as well as poor corporate governance, led to excessively risky lending to the real estate and manufacturing sectors. As the number of nonperforming loans grew, policymakers compounded their errors by turning a blind eye, leading to further risktaking on the part of both lenders and borrowers. In short, Roubini agreed with Fernald that banking-system reform is only half of the story; the other half is reform of corporate governance and corporate restructuring. Hoshi agreed that there are similarities between Japan and other East Asian cases. A difference, however, is that in Thailand and Korea bad loans made as part of cozy bank–firm relationships were partly responsible for the crisis, whereas in Japan the issue was not relationship banking but rather its collapse, which happened before the crisis. He argued that corporate governance (as it evolved under the keiretsu and main bank systems) might have been better in Japan before deregulation, so that deregulation worsened governance.

Martin Feldstein suggested that, while U.S. banks began to take up liability management when they understood that their good lending opportunities were shrinking, the Japanese banks didn't worry about such issues because of their confidence that the government would protect them. In short, the market had not been allowed to work in Japan. Feldstein asked why the Japanese government had deregulated in the first place and whether U.S. influence was important. Kashyap downplayed possible U.S. influence on the decision to deregulate, emphasizing instead the 1974 recession that led the Japanese government to run big deficits. To place the resulting bonds the government had to liberalize the bond market, and once that had been done, political pressure increased to liberalize other financial markets as well. Feldstein responded that in the early 1980s there had been attempts by the U.S. government to get the Japanese to Americanize their financial system, because some U.S. officials apparently thought that this would help to improve the bilateral trade balance.

Rick Mishkin suggested that not only deregulation but also changes in information technology have made it easier to use nonbank finance. He also cited the need for more sophisticated supervision with, in particular, an emphasis on overall risk management rather than on the quality of individual loans or the level of accounting capital. Similar problems are likely to be encountered in Europe to those in Japan, Mishkin said, as changing markets and deregulation proceed but supervision doesn't keep up. Kashyap said that in 1998, when the Financial Supervisory Agency was formed in Japan, many people, including him, were pessimistic: The FSA had only 400 bank supervisors for all of Japan, and they were the same people who, as employees of the Ministry of Finance, had presided over the whole debacle in the first place. To Kashyap's surprise, however, the new FSA turned out to be vigilant, tough, and sophisticated. Michael Hutchison interjected that perhaps it should not be a surprise that institutional changes matter; in particular, having a separate FSA directly under the prime minister and with political support is a very different situation from what existed before. Hutchison added that after all the praise that had been heaped on the "Asian model," supposedly characterized by the close and willing cooperation of banks, government, and corporations, it was interesting to see how quickly many participants had left the system when the opportunity presented itself.

Ben Bernanke asked a question about the flow of funds. If the savers are still putting their money into deposits but suddenly the firms can go to the capital markets, where are the funds in the capital markets coming from? He suggested that retained earnings might be a major source of corporate financing, which if true suggests that the source of the decline in loan demand is not deregulation so much as a corporate sector that is increasingly self-financed. Julio Rotemberg added that, in light of Japan's large current-account surplus, somebody has to be acquiring claims on foreigners; perhaps this is being done through banks. Feldstein said that banks and insurance companies are large net purchasers of dollar-denominated bonds.

Bernanke said that, based on earlier work by the authors with David Scharfstein, he had the impression that close bank–firm relationships were beneficial in that they reduced information and incentive problems in lending. Yet when deregulation occurred, the big firms abandoned their bank relationships as quickly as they could. Why did that happen? Kashyap answered that the main bank system and the attendant regulation had benefits but also costs, such as reduced flexibility of financing options. Hoshi added that the benefits of relationship banking were relatively larger for small firms, so that when deregulation occurred large firms had the stronger incentive to leave their relationships.

Stephen Zeldes pointed out a common theme in this paper and Heaton and Lucas's paper in this volume, which is increased participation of consumers in financial markets. For example, as Japanese savers begin to hold diversified stock portfolios, perhaps Japanese stock prices will rise, as Heaton and Lucas argue happened in the United States. Higher stock prices would have the side benefit of helping the banks. Kashyap acknowledged the possibility, but reiterated the point that liberalization for savers has proceeded relatively slowly in Japan.

John Heaton and Deborah Lucas
NORTHWESTERN UNIVERSITY KELLOGG GRADUATE SCHOOL OF
MANAGEMENT AND NBER

Stock Prices and Fundamentals

1. Introduction

While stock returns in the United States this past century have exceeded
Treasury returns by an average of about 6% annually, in the last few years
they have done so by more than 12% annually. Commentators have suggested a variety of explanations for the dramatic stock-market run-up that
accompanied these high returns. The baby boom is entering peak savings
years, productivity has escalated worldwide due to technological improvements and political change, and stock-market participation rates are
on the rise. The growth of mutual funds has lowered transaction costs and
made diversification feasible. Public awareness of the benefits of stock-
market investing is high. On the other hand, irrational exuberance could
be fueling the price rise, with inexperienced investors expecting double-
digit returns to continue indefinitely or at least long enough to reap a
substantial gain.

Whether the price rise is due primarily to fundamentals or whether it
is the result of a bubble is important to policymakers concerned with
avoiding the real disruption a sharp stock-market decline could precipi-
tate. It is also important to the academic debate over the determinants of
stock valuations. Because this paper is about the relations between stock
prices and fundamentals, we emphasize three broad categories of explanations for the recent price rise: changes in corporate earnings growth,
changes in consumer preferences, and changes in stock-market participation patterns. The goal in qualifying the importance of fundamental
effects is to better understand whether a combination of fundamentals
and statistical fluctuation can plausibly explain the observed magnitudes, or whether a bubble is the likely cause of the price rise.

The paper has benefited from the comments of John Campbell, Annette Vissing-
Jørgensen, and participants of the 1999 NBER Macroeconomics Annual Conference. We
thank the National Science Foundation for financial support.

Although the paper touches on a variety of issues, its main contribution is to look more closely at how participation patterns have changed, and at how they are expected to affect required returns in a stochastic equilibrium model. We interpret participation broadly to include both the fraction of the population that holds any stocks, and the degree of diversification of a typical stockholder. To review the evidence, we use data from the Survey of Consumer Finances (SCF) to document changes in stock-holding patterns and reported attitudes toward risk from 1989 to 1995. Consistent with previous studies (e.g., Poterba, 1993; Vissing-Jørgensen, 1997), we see an increasing rate of stock-market participation over time. Participation rates among the wealthy, who own the majority of stock, however, have increased only slightly. Foreign participation changes may also influence required returns. Using data from the U.S. Treasury, we find that net purchases of stocks by foreigners have been relatively high in recent years, but small in comparison with total trading volume. Finally, flow-of-funds data show that diversification has increased markedly, with large outflows of individual stocks from household portfolios moving into mutual funds and other institutional accounts.

To quantify the potential impact of these changes, we calibrate an overlapping-generations model that allows for considerable heterogeneity in the cross section of nonmarketable income risk, preferences, diversification, and participation. This extends the analyses of Basak and Cuoco (1998), Saito (1995), and Vissing-Jorgensen (1997), all of whom consider the effect of participation when traded securities span income realizations. We use this framework to experiment with changes in stock-market participation rates, changes in background risk, changes in preferences, and changes in the expected dividend process reflecting changes in diversification. We find that for realistic changes in raw participation rates, expected stock returns change very little. Within the range of risk-aversion parameters normally considered, preference changes also have little effect on expected return differentials. Changing the rate of time preference has a significant effect on the level of all returns, but not on the differential between stock and bond returns. One factor that appears to have a significant effect on required returns is the degree of assumed diversification. This suggests that one fundamental reason for the stock price run-up may be the rapid growth of mutual funds and the accompanying large increase in diversification.

The remainder of the paper is organized as follows. In Section 2 we review the statistical evidence on whether the current stock price level is anomalous. In Section 3, we discuss some possible explanations for the stock price increase in the context of a simple discounted-cash-flow model, and present some evidence from the SCF and other sources on

changes in stock-market participation patterns. The influence of participation rates, extent of diversification, background income risk, and
preferences on stock prices is examined in Section 4 in an overlapping-
generations model. By considering a variety of scenarios reflecting simultaneous changes in several of these factors, we show that changes
in fundamentals can account for perhaps half of the observed increase
in price–dividend ratios in the model. Section 5 concludes.

2. Empirical Facts

Historically stocks have returned a substantial premium over bonds. Over
the period 1871 to 1998, the average annual (log) real return on a broad-
based index of U.S. stocks was 7.3%, compared to an average (log) real
return on bonds of about 3%.[1] The return on stocks over the last few years
has exceeded this historical average. For example, since 1991, the average
real return on stocks was 17% per year. This has led many observers to
question whether expected returns looking forward are lower than they
have been in the past.

A related issue is the composition of recent returns, which have been
mostly the result of capital gains rather than increased dividend payments. To illustrate this, Figure 1 plots the ratios of prices to dividends
and prices to earnings for aggregate U.S. stocks. (For the years since
1926 this is based on the S&P 500 index.) Notice that the price–dividend
ratio for this index has increased to an unprecedented level since about
1995. The increase in this ratio is significant because in a discounted-
cash-flow model of stock valuation, it indicates a reduction in the expected rate of return or an increase in the dividend growth rate (see
Section 3). Because dividends are discretionary and only one of the ways
in which corporations distribute cash to shareholders, it may be more
informative to look at price–earnings ratios. Figure 1 also shows the ratio
of prices to earnings. This ratio is also at a relatively high level, but the
change has not been as dramatic as for dividends.

A notable aspect of the rise in the price–dividend ratio is that there is
substantial evidence that a large value of the price–dividend ratio predicts lower stock returns in the future. For example, Table 1 reports the
results of regressing annual (log) stock returns on a constant and the log
of the price–dividend ratio lagged one year for the period 1887 to 1998.
Notice that the coefficient on the dividend–price ratio is negative. This is
consistent with a large body of evidence (e.g., Campbell and Shiller,
1988; Hodrick, 1992; Lamont, 1998). At the current high level of the

1. Source: Robert Shiller's data, available at http://www.econ.yale.edu/shiller/chapt26.html.

Figure 1 PRICE–DIVIDEND RATIO AND PRICE–EARNINGS RATIO,
1871–1998

__ Price-Dividend Ratio, ____ Price-Earnings Ratio

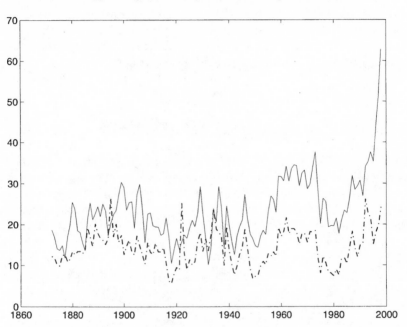

price–dividend ratio, this regression predicts a substantial decline in the
stock market over the next year. In fact, since 1995 this regression has
consistently predicted a decline in the stock market.

On the other hand, due to the substantial variability in stock returns, it
is possible that the recent returns are within the bounds of normal statis-

Table 1   REGRESSION OF ONE-
YEAR STOCK RETURNS
ON LAGGED P/D OVER
THE PERIOD 1871 TO 1998

Coefficient	Estimate	Standard Error[a]
α	0.28	0.02
β	−0.07	0.05

$\log R_{t+1}^{s} = \alpha + \beta \log(P_t/D_t) + \epsilon_t.$

[a]Corrected for conditional heteroskedasticity
and autocorrelation using the procedure of
Newey and West (1987) and two years of lags.

tical fluctuations, without any change in the underlying driving processes. For example, the standard deviation of the annual premium of stock returns over bond returns over the period 1871 to 1998 was 18%. Therefore, it is not improbable that one would observe several years of premiums in excess of 20% per year, even with no change in the underlying statistical process. Since there is not a statistically definitive answer to the question of whether returns have been abnormally high, we focus below on whether recent changes in various aspects of the economy are large enough to suggest a fundamental change in expected returns.

3. Possible Explanations

In this section, we discuss some of the potential explanations that have been offered for the stock price run-up, and begin to evaluate their likely quantitative importance in the context of a simple discounted-cash-flow model. We also present some evidence on changes in market participation patterns that may be influencing required returns.

3.1. GORDON GROWTH MODEL

The *Gordon growth model* is perhaps the simplest fundamentals-based approach to predicting stock prices.[2] In this model, stock prices are based on the discounted present value of future expected dividend payments. It is assumed that dividends grow, on average, at a constant rate, g, and investors discount dividends at a constant rate, r. Dividends, earnings, and growth are connected by two equations: $DIV = (1 - p)E$ and $g = p(ROE)$, where DIV is dividends, E is earnings, p is the proportion of earnings reinvested, and ROE is the marginal physical product of capital. If the marginal physical product of capital is constant, and if the fraction of reinvested earnings is constant, then, all else equal, dividend growth is constant. Then the price–dividend ratio equals $1/(r - g)$.

The model highlights two of the fundamental reasons that the price–dividend ratio can change. The first is due to changes in dividend growth, reflected in the choice of g. The second is due to changes in preferences that affect the subjective rate of time preference or the premium demanded for risk, reflected in the choice of r.

Expectations of g may be higher than in the past for several reasons. A major determinant of dividend growth is the availability of profitable investment projects. The potential for sustained economic growth in excess of historical precedent has been attributed to the opening and

2. This valuation model, a staple of market analysts, is described, for instance, in Brealey and Myers (1996).

integration of world markets, continuing technological advances, and an increasingly educated labor force. In fact, U.S. per capita GDP growth has been slightly higher than average in recent years, averaging 2.3% from 1995 to 1998, compared with 2.0% from 1947 to 1998.

Other considerations suggest that r may be lower than in the past. One possibility is that aggregate preferences have changed. Either a decrease in risk aversion or an increase in patience could contribute to the run-up in stock prices. Risk aversion could vary across generations due to their varying experiences and circumstances. For example, baby boomers do not share their parents' first-hand experience with the Great Depression. Some have argued that the economy is more stable, reducing the exposure to background risk, and possibly reducing the risk to dividends. Davis and Willen (1998) show, for example, that the income risk for households with various educational attainments has changed over time. Reduced transaction costs in financial markets make diversification easier, which, as discussed below, can reduce effective aversion to the risk of holding stocks as people hold more diversified portfolios.

It should be noted that these types of changes affect the risk-free rate as well as the expected return on stocks. Since the risk-free rate has been relatively stable over the period of the recent stock price run-up, in much of what follows we focus on factors that affect the equity premium, rather than the absolute level of rates.[3]

The Survey of Consumer Finances (SCF) is one of the few data sources that provides some direct survey evidence on peoples' attitude towards financial risk and how it has changed over time. Respondents to the SCF answer detailed questions, both quantitative and qualitative, about their financial situation. The survey is conducted by the Federal Reserve Board every three years, with different households in each survey year. Here we focus on the question:

Which of the statements on this page comes closest to the amount of financial risk that you (and your husband/wife) are willing to take when you save or make investments? If more than one box checked, code smallest category #.

1. *take substantial financial risks expected to earn substantial returns*
2. *take above average financial risks expecting to earn above average returns*
3. *take average financial risks expecting to earn average returns*
4. *not willing to take any financial risks*

---

3. See Blanchard (1993) for an analysis of historical trends in the equity premium and risk-free rate.

Table 2   AVERAGE RESPONSE BY AGE AND SURVEY YEAR TO
QUESTIONS ABOUT RISK AVERSION FROM THE SCF.

Year	Response[a]		
	Age < 35	35–65	>65
1989	3.14 (0.88)	3.32 (0.77)	3.63 (0.61)
1992	3.19 (0.84)	3.26 (0.81)	3.64 (0.60)
1995	3.07 (0.87)	3.18 (0.82)	3.58 (0.68)

[a]Implied population standard deviations in parentheses.

Table 2 reports the average response by age and survey year. The implied population standard deviation across responses is reported in parentheses. Since the population represented by the survey totals approximately 90 million households, the standard errors of the estimates of the means are quite small. Consistent with the idea that risk tolerance has increased, the average reported aversion to risk has decreased slightly for each age category over time. Older households own significantly more stock than younger households, and reported risk aversion increases with age in each survey year. When a similar tabulation (not reported here) is done conditional on households that own at least $500 in stocks, the same patterns emerge with respect to age and time. The average reported level of risk tolerance, however, is higher when we condition on stockholders. For instance, in 1995 the average risk attitude for stockholders over age 65 was 3.17, as compared to 3.58 for all households over 65. This suggests that those who already own stocks are more risk-tolerant as a group than nonparticipants. Hence, the entry of new stockholders may slightly decrease the average level of risk tolerance. One would expect this to mitigate the effect of wider participation in reducing the equity premium.

There are objective reasons why the underlying subjective rate of time preference also may be changing. Increases in life expectancy beyond retirement would likely increase the incentive to save and thereby reduce required returns. Mortality, for example, has declined at an average annual rate of 3.3% over the period 1900 to 1988 (Social Security Administration). Past improvements in health and life expectancy might understate expected improvements in these factors that are premised on continued medical progress.[4] As with the other explanations considered for the stock price run-up, however, it is hard to point to events that would

4. In fact, there is a lively debate in the demographic literature on these questions, with some authors claiming that a life expectancy at birth of 100 years will be realized early in the next century.

trigger a large change in aggregate preferences over the course of only a few years.

Calibrating the Gordon growth model gives a rough sense of how far earnings growth rates or stock returns would have to deviate from their historical averages to justify current price levels. This approach has the advantage that it allows one to avoid taking a definitive stand on the magnitude of technology or preference parameter changes. In the tabulations presented here, we focus on earnings-adjusted price–dividend ratios rather than actual price–dividend ratios because earnings are likely to be a more stable proxy for long-run payments to shareholders. Consistent with the average ratio of dividends to earnings over the period 1947 to 1997, we assume an average reinvestment rate of 50%. Hence, the adjusted price–dividend ratio is defined as twice the price–earnings ratio.[5]

Over the past century, real earnings growth has averaged about 1.4% annually, with a standard deviation of about 25%. Table 3 shows the required growth rate in the future to match current and historical adjusted price–dividend ratios, for various levels of required returns. For r ranging from 5% to 15%, column 2 reports the growth rate g that is consistent with the adjusted price–dividend ratio of 28 for the period 1872 to 1998. Column 3 reports the growth rate necessary to match the adjusted price–dividend ratio of 48 in January 1998 (the ratio in January 1999 is even higher at 58). For instance, to realize a real stock return of 7% (consistent with a 6% equity premium and a 1% real risk-free rate) and to match the average historical adjusted price–dividend ratio of 28 requires growth of 3.4%. To match the 1998 adjusted price–dividend ratio of 48, assuming a real risk-free rate of 3% and an equity premium of 6%, requires perpetual growth of 6.9%. This is a large number by historical standards, suggesting that, at least in this simple model, a plausible increase in the expected long-run growth rate is unlikely to be the sole explanation for the increase in stock prices.

The growth rate and required return enter symmetrically in these calculations. Therefore, another interpretation of the results in Table 3 is that if growth rates are expected to be similar to historical averages, the expected real return on the stock market is now less than 5%. Again assuming a risk-free return of 3%, this implies an equity premium below 2%. This large a change in expected returns also seems unlikely to have taken place over the period of only a few years.

One shortcoming of this model is the restriction that the expected

5. While stock prices depend on the long-run behavior of dividends, properly measured, in the short run dividends can vary due to temporary changes in payout policy (for instance, in response to changes in the tax law). Therefore, it is common to focus on the price–earnings ratio, adjusted for reinvestment rates, to approximate long-run price–dividend ratios.

Table 3   GROWTH RATES IMPLIED BY THE GORDON GROWTH MODEL

r^s	Long-Run g to Match Historical P/E	Long-Run g to Match 1998 P/E	Ten-Year g to Match 1998 P/E with 2% Tail
0.05	0.014	0.029	0.064
0.07	0.034	0.049	0.134
0.09	0.054	0.069	0.189
0.11	0.074	0.089	0.236
0.13	0.094	0.109	0.280
0.15	0.114	0.129	0.320

growth rate is constant. This assumption, however, can be relaxed quite easily. A minor variation on the model is to assume a higher growth rate for some number of years, followed by a return to a lower long-run growth rate. Column 4 of Table 3 reports, for each value of *r* in column 1, the growth rate over 10 years necessary to explain the adjusted price–dividend ratio in January 1998. The calculation assumes that the growth rate returns to the long-run average of 2% from year 10 onward. In this case achieving a 9% average rate of return requires a growth rate of 18.9% for ten years!

Although these calculations are admittedly primitive, more detailed analyses along similar lines produce qualitatively similar conclusions. For instance, Lee and Swaminathan (1999) estimate the value of individual stocks in the Dow Jones Industrial Average, projecting cash flows using accounting data and analysts' forecasts, and discounting using the CAPM. They conclude that the index is about 1.6 times the fundamental value predicted by their analysis.

Despite the apparently large changes in parameters necessary to explain current price levels, these results do not preclude a fundamentals-based explanation. It is possible that there have been a simultaneous increase in expected growth rates and a reduction in required returns. For instance, if the long-run growth rate is realistically expected to be about 2.4% and if expected returns fall to about 6.6%, current prices are in line with fundamentals. Our focus in the rest of the paper is on whether such a change in expected returns can be attributed to measurable changes in the economy, in the context of an equilibrium model. One factor of particular interest is the change in stock-market participation patterns, which is the topic of the next subsection.

3.2 STOCK-MARKET PARTICIPATION PATTERNS

It is well documented that a large fraction of the U.S. population holds little or no stocks (Bertaut and Haliassos, 1995; Blume and Zeldes, 1993) and that participation varies systematically with factors such as wealth and age (Gentry and Hubbard, 1998; King and Leape, 1987). As noted in several recent studies (e.g., Basak and Cuoco, 1998; Constantinides, Donaldson, and Mehra, 1998; Saito, 1995; Polkovnichencko, 1998; Vissing-Jørgensen, 1997), an increase in the stock-market participation rate has, in theory, the potential to decrease the required risk premium on stocks because it spreads market risk over a broader population.[6] Not only has the number of participants been rising, but the nature of participation has changed. A typical stockholder today has a more diversified portfolio than in the past, presumably due to the lower cost of diversification. Thus, the effective risk of the typical portfolio may have declined. In this subsection, we review some of the evidence on these changes.

The best source of data on market participation rates in the United States is perhaps the SCF, which reports detailed information about household wealth composition every three years. Using these data, Poterba (1998) reports that in 1995 there were approximately 69.3 million shareholders in the United States, compared to 61.4 million in 1992 and 52.3 million in 1989. There is also evidence that people are entering the market at a younger age. Poterba and Samwick (1997) show that baby boomers are participating more heavily in the market than previous generations at a similar age. Baby boomers are entering peak savings years and directing some of their savings into stocks. More generally, the aging of the population should result in a greater demand for stocks, since older people hold proportionally more of their wealth in the market than do younger people (see, e.g., Heaton and Lucas, 1998). Finally, foreign participation in the U.S. markets has increased, further spreading the risk across a broader population.

Market participants are also holding more diversified portfolios, which reduces their exposure to risk from their stockholdings. This is potentially important, since holders of diversified portfolios may demand a lower average return. Historical evidence on this phenomenon of improving diversification is summarized in Allen and Gale (1994). Friend and Blume (1975) found that a large proportion of investors had only one or two stocks in their portfolios and very few had more than ten. At the time, this lack of diversification in individual stockholdings could not be justified by the claim that these investors achieved diversification through unreported mutual-fund holdings. In fact, King and Leape (1984) found that

6. Bakshi and Chen (1994) note that to the extent that demographic changes have an effect on the demand for stocks, they will have a predictable effect on asset prices. Bodie, Merton, and Samuelson (1992) provide a theoretical justification for the demand for stocks to vary with age.

only 1% of investors' wealth was in mutual funds at around that time. In contrast, Poterba (1998) reports a sharp increase in the proportion of stock held in mutual funds over time and a reduction in directly held stocks. For instance, while the total number of individuals holding stock increased from 61.4 million to 69.3 million from 1992 to 1995, the number of individuals holding stock directly fell from 29.2 million to 27.4 million over the same period. In the calibrations presented below, we will look at whether this diversification effect is significant by comparing stock prices with different underlying assumptions about dividend volatility, where high assumed dividend volatility proxies for less diversification.

Although these statistics point to an increase in participation and a reduction in risk exposure, it is questionable how significant these effects are quantitatively. The change from 52 million to 69 million participants is a 33% increase, but when the numbers are wealth-weighted, the increase is much smaller. Now as in the past, the vast majority of stocks are held by wealthy individuals. For instance, Poterba (1998) finds that in the 1995 SCF, 82% of stock was held by households with a stock portfolio exceeding $100,000, and 54% of stock was held by households with annual income over $100,000. This suggests that stockholdings remain extremely concentrated. Figures 2 and 3 present a more complete picture of how the distribution of stockholdings vs. wealth and income has changed over the period 1989 to 1995 (see also Table 4). Using data from the SCF, we plot the share of stocks held against the share of income or wealth. Stockholding looks more democratic when measured relative to income than relative to wealth, since as noted in Vissing-Jørgensen (1997), lower-labor-income households own a larger share of the market than in the past. When the metric is wealth, however, there has been very little change—holdings were and are extremely concentrated.

Table 4   PROPORTION OF POPULATION THAT HOLDS STOCK BY WEALTH COHORT

Percentile Range (%)	*Range ($)*	*Proportion (%)*	*Range ($)*	*Proportion (%)*
<25	<801	2.3	<1101	4.7
26–50	801–40,051	13.0	1102–40,500	17.8
51–75	40,052–121,500	21.6	40,501–126,251	28.7
76–90	121,501–279,001	36.7	126,252–309,501	47.8
91–95	279,001–456,000	55.4	309,502–574,000	62.8
96–99	456,001–1,767,730	65.8	574,001–1,814,330	78.3
>99	>1,767,730	84.3	>1,814,331	82.0

Figure 2 PERCENTAGE OF STOCK HELD BY INCOME PERCENTILE

O: 1995, X: 1989

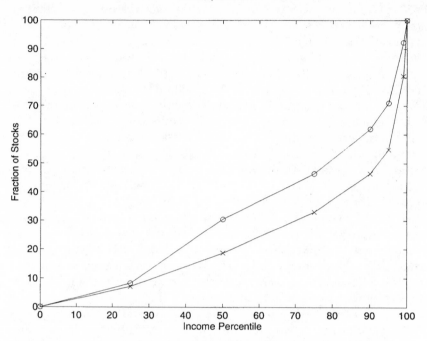

Figure 3 PERCENTAGE OF STOCK HELD BY WEALTH PERCENTILE

O: 1995, X: 1989

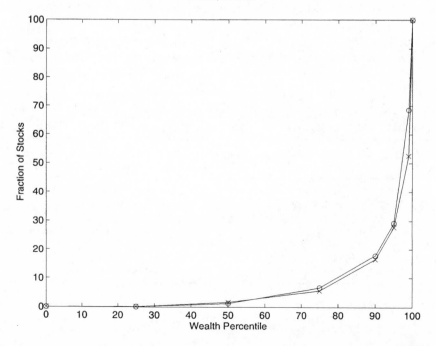

Table 5   NET PURCHASES OF STOCKS BY INDIVIDUALS

| | Purchases (billions of dollars) | | |
Year	Net	Through Mutual Funds	Outside Mutual Funds
1995	−116.1	91.3	−207.4
1996	−101.9	218.4	−320.3
1997	−179.0	190.2	−369.2

Ideally, one would like to measure the net investment in the stock market in recent years on behalf of households. If net inflows were large, one could perhaps conclude that the demand for stocks had significantly increased. The fact that aggregate savings rates are low is indirect evidence that these net inflows cannot be large. Still, there could be substitution out of money and bonds into stocks, increasing the net flow into stocks. According to the flow-of-funds accounts, U.S. Treasury securities are the only category of fixed-income investment that had a large net outflow from the household sector in recent years. Calculating flows into stocks directly is tricky because there have been large changes in the institutional structure of the investment industry. Table 5, using data from the Investment Company Institute, shows net purchases of stocks, purchases made through mutual funds, and purchases made outside mutual funds, by households, from 1995 to 1997. While purchases made through mutual funds increased significantly over the period, net purchases of equities by households were actually negative in each year. This is because households were net sellers of equities to institutions.

Changes in foreign participation in the U.S. market may also affect expected returns. Assuming that foreign participants are similar to U.S. stockholders in their attitude towards risk and their ex ante risk exposure, an increase in foreign participation should lower expected returns by increasing opportunities for diversification. Net foreign purchases of stock have spiked sharply in recent years (see Figure 4), and these inflows, over the period January 1988 to February 1999, have a correlation of 0.13 with monthly returns on the S&P 500. The average monthly net inflow between January 1996 and February 1999 is $3.8 billion, compared to only $349 million from the period January 1988 to December 1995. Although the inflows have increased significantly, they still represent a small fraction of total market transactions, which totaled approximately $479 billion per month in 1997 on the New York Stock Exchange alone.[7]

7. Data on foreign purchases and sales of U.S. stocks are from the U.S. Department of the Treasury's table "TIC Capital Movements, U.S. Transactions with Foreigners in Long Term Securities." S&P 500 monthly returns data are from Robert Shiller. Total trading volume is from the *NYSE 1997 Fact Book*.

Figure 4 FOREIGN NET INVESTMENT AND RETURNS

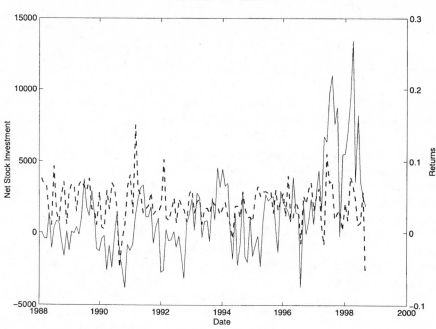

4. *An Overlapping-Generations Model*

In this section, we ask whether changing stock-market participation patterns and increased diversification can have a quantitatively important effect on stock prices in an equilibrium model. We calibrate an overlapping-generations (OLG) model in which agents face both aggregate and idiosyncratic income risk, and a variable subset of agents has limited access to financial markets.

The effects of limited participation in financial markets has been considered by a number of authors, including Basak and Cuoco (1998), Saito (1995), and Vissing-Jørgensen (1997). In these papers, aggregate consumption is completely traded in financial markets in the form of dividends. Only a limited number of agents can trade claims on this dividend flow directly. The other agents participate in financial markets only by trading claims to risk-free bonds. The result is incomplete sharing of aggregate risk, with stockholders often taking leveraged positions to accommodate the demand for bonds by nonparticipants. Because of this, a larger risk premium is necessary to induce those in the stock market to hold all of the aggregate risk. It is difficult to justify the magnitude of the observed equity premium in these models, however, unless one assumes very high risk aversion or very low participation rates.

One way to increase the effects of limited participation is to include other sources of uninsurable income risk. For instance, income from wages and/or privately held businesses constitutes the majority of income for most households (Heaton and Lucas, 1998). These income flows are difficult to contract upon, and a large component of this income risk is specific to each individual of household. We refer to the sum of labor income and privately held business income as *non-marketed income.* Potential differences in the properties of this income for participants versus nonparticipants are likely to influence the effects of limited participation on asset returns. This is consistent with the empirical observation that the consumption of stockholders is more volatile than that of nonstockholders (Mankiw and Zeldes, 1991). Polkovnichenko (1998) demonstrates how differential income risk and risk aversion can affect asset prices in a model with infinite-lived heterogeneous agents. He shows that a small fixed transaction cost that endogenously limits stock-market participation can interact with idiosyncratic risk to result in a bigger equity premium than in a representative agent model, although matching the observed premium is still elusive.

The model presented here allows us to examine the effect of participation and diversification while considering a greater degree of cross-sectional heterogeneity than in the previous literature, due to the simplifying assumption of two-period lives. Unlike the papers discussed above, which focus on whether limited participation can explain the historical equity premium, we focus on the question of to what extent observed *changes* in participation rates can explain the recent run-up in stock prices. We also emphasize the effect of changes in the degree of portfolio diversification.

4.1 STRUCTURE OF THE MODEL

At each time period, t, a generation of J "young" agents are born and live for two periods.[8] Let $C(j,t)$ be the consumption of agent j when young,

---

8. Storesletten, Telmer, and Yaron (1998) consider an OLG model in which the agents face nontradable idiosyncratic risk and live for a large number of periods. We limit ourselves to a smaller number of periods to make numerical solution of the model easier.

and $C^o(j,t + 1)$ be the consumption of agent j when old ($j = 1,2, \ldots, J$). The utility specification for agent j distinguishes between risk aversion and the elasticity of intertemporal substitution. We use the parametric form proposed by Epstein and Zin (1989) and Weil (1990):

$$U(j,t) \equiv \log C(j,t) + \frac{\beta_j}{1 - \alpha_j} \log E[C^o(j,t + 1)^{1-\alpha_j} \mid \mathcal{F}(t)], \tag{1}$$

where $\beta_j > 0$ and $\alpha_j > 0$. Here $\mathcal{F}(t)$ is the information available at time t and is assumed to be common across agents. As discussed by Epstein and Zin (1989), the parameter α_j is the coefficient of relative risk aversion. The elasticity of intertemporal substitution equals one. In the experiments considered below, changes in participation affect the equilibrium volatility of individual consumption in the second period. In general, this affects both the level of interest rates and the equity premium. By distinguishing between risk aversion and the elasticity of intertemporal substitution, the effect of the income process on the equity premium is to some extent separated from its effect on the risk-free rate.

Each agent $j(j = 1,2, \ldots, J)$ is endowed with random nonmarketed income $Y(j,t)$ at time t and random nonmarketed income $Y^o(j,t + 1)$ when old at time $t + 1$. The details of the individual income processes are described below. The agents trade in financial markets in an attempt to smooth consumption over time. There are two securities that can be traded: a stock and a risk-free bond. At time t the stock represents a claim to future dividends $\{D(t + \tau) : \tau = 1,2, \ldots \}$. The total supply of stock is normalized to one. The bond is assumed to be in zero net supply.

Each agent is exposed to nonmarketed income risk that has both an aggregate component and an idiosyncratic component. Aggregate nonmarketed income at time t is denoted by $Y^a(t)$, where

$$Y^a(t) = \sum_{j=1}^{J} Y(j,t) + \sum_{j=1}^{J} Y^o(j,t). \tag{2}$$

In equilibrium, this endowment plus dividends equals aggregate consumption at time t. The properties of individual nonmarketed income $Y(j,t)$ and $Y^o(j,t)$ will be potentially important in assessing the effects of changing participation and background income risk on equilibrium returns.

At time t each young agent maximizes utility (1) subject to a constraint that depends on the agent's access to financial markets. Let $P^s(t)$ be the price of the stock at time t, and $P^b(t)$ be the price of a bond that pays one unit of consumption at time $t + 1$ for sure. If agent j has access to both financial markets, then the agent's flow wealth constraints are

$$C(j,t) = Y(j,t) - S(j,t)P^S(t) - B(j,t)P^b(t), \tag{3a}$$
$$C^o(j,t + 1) = Y^o(j,t + 1) + S(j,t)[P^s(t + 1) + D(t + 1)] + B(j,t), \tag{3b}$$

where $S(j,t)$ gives the stockholdings of agent j, and $B(j,t)$ gives the bondholdings of agent j. A subset of the agents is assumed to have only limited access to financial markets and can trade only in bonds. In this case the constraints (3) are replaced by

$$C(j,t) = Y(j,t) - B(j,t)P^b(t), \tag{4a}$$
$$C^o(j,t + 1) = Y^o(j,t + 1) + B(j,t). \tag{4b}$$

An equilibrium is given by processes for stock and bond prices $\{P^s(t) : t = 0,1, \ldots \}$ and $\{P^b(t) : t = 0,1, \ldots \}$ such that

$$\sum_{j=1}^{J} S^*(j,t) = 1, \tag{5a}$$

$$\sum_{j=1}^{J} B^*(j,t) = 0, \tag{5b}$$

where $\{S^*(j,t), B^*(j,t)\}$ maximizes (1) subject to (3) if the agent can trade in both markets, or subject to (4) if the agent can trade only in the bond market.

We assume that nonmarketed income $\{Y^a(t) : t = 0,1, \ldots \}$ and dividend income grow over time in such a way that the growth rate of aggregate income is a stationary process. Consistent with this, we assume that at time t we have $Y(j,t) = y(j,t)Y^a(t)$ and $D(t) = d(t)Y^a(t)$, where $y(j,t)$ denotes the share of individual j's income in aggregate income, and $d(t)$ the dividend relative to aggregate nonmarketed income. Similarly we assume that $Y^o(j,t) = y^o(j,t)Y^a(t)$. This implies that one can look for an equilibrium in which the stock price also scales with aggregate income, so that $P^s(t) = p^s(t)Y^a(t)$. Finally, we assume that the face value of a bond purchased at time t is given by $Y^a(t)$, so that $B(j,t) = b(j,t)Y^a(t)$, where $b(j,t)$ gives the quantity of these "rescaled" bonds purchased by agent j.

4.2 CALIBRATION

In this subsection, we calibrate the model in order to revisit quantitatively some of the questions discussed in Section 3. How much do assumed changes in participation rates affect the predicted equity premium and expected returns (and hence prices)? How does the degree of portfolio diversification affect required returns? Can small changes in preference parameters, reflecting changes in patience or risk aversion, result in large changes in required returns? How important is heterogeneity in income risk? To answer these questions, the model is solved numerically using standard techniques. Although we assume considerable heterogeneity in the cross section, the fact that agents only live for two periods makes the problem numerically tractable.[9]

We begin by describing the parameterization of the income processes and preferences. Parameters are chosen to reflect limited stock-market participation, and to try to match gross features of the data with respect to stock returns, the risk-free rate, and the driving processes for non-marketed income and dividends.

As in most exercises of this type, the equity-premium puzzle remains a serious problem. For income and dividend processes and participation rates based on historical data, the model predicts an unrealistically small equity premium. We have increased the assumed volatility of aggregate income to increase the predicted premium, but want to emphasize that this may not be a neutral adjustment with respect to the other quantities of interest.[10]

4.2.1 Income and Preferences Let $\gamma(t) \equiv \log[Y^a(t)/Y^a(t-1)]$ be the growth rate of aggregate nonmarketed income at time t. Then the aggregate state of the economy is given by $z(t) \equiv [\gamma(t)\ d(t)]'$, which is assumed to be generated by a Markov chain. To calibrate a process for $z(t)$ we assume that a period corresponds to 25 years. The first period roughly corresponds to the working years between age 40 and retirement, and the second period is the time in retirement. Over the period 1889 to 1985, the average annual (log) growth rate in real aggregate consumption was 1.7% with a standard deviation of 3.5%. So that the model will produce a nonnegligible equity premium, we assume that the standard deviation of the aggregate growth rate in the model is 1.5 times the historical standard deviation of aggregate

---

9. The Matlab code is available upon request.
10. Recently Campbell and Cochrane (1998) suggested that time-varying habit provides a higher estimate of the equity premium in a model based on aggregate consumption. However, Cochrane (1997) claims that this preference specification cannot account for the recent run-up in stock prices.

consumption. For the same reason, we assume that annual income growth is independently and identically distributed over time, although in fact it is slightly negatively autocorrelated. This implies a 25-year average (log) growth rate of 42.5% with a standard deviation of 17.5%. This distribution is discretized by assuming that γ takes on the values 0.16 and 0.69 with equal conditional probability.

The capital share in total income averages approximately 30%. Consistent with the aggregate statistics reported in Heaton and Lucas (1998), we assume that only half of this capital income is actually tradable. The nontradable portion, generated by private business holdings, is accounted for in nonmarketed income. Since dividends in the model are scaled relative to nonmarketed income, this means that we require $d(t)$ to average 18%. In most of the calculations $d(t)$ is fixed at 18%. In other experiments described below, we assume a more volatile dividend process to proxy for a lack of diversification.[11]

The relative nonmarketed income of young agent j and of old agent k at time t are given by

$$y(j,t) = \epsilon(j,t)[1 - \eta(t)], \tag{6}$$
$$y^o(k,t) = \epsilon^o(k,t)\eta(t), \tag{7}$$

where

$$\sum_{j=1}^{J} \epsilon(j,t) = 1 \quad \text{and} \quad \sum_{k=1}^{J} \epsilon^o(k,t) = 1. \tag{8}$$

Under this normalization, $\eta(t)$ gives the share of old individuals' nonmarketed income in total nonmarketed income. The analysis is sensitive to this parameter because the amount of nonmarketed income influences agents' attitude towards the risk of investment income. For the basic analyis we assume that $\eta = 0.2$ for all t, reflecting the observation that noninvestment wealth is relatively small for retirees. In the sensitivity analysis, this parameter is varied to a maximum of 0.3.

The process for $\epsilon(j,t)$ and $\epsilon^o(k,t)$ captures idiosyncratic income risk across agents. We know from earlier work (e.g., Constantinides and Duffie, 1996) that asset returns are potentially sensitive to the persistence of idiosyncratic income shocks and to the correlation and conditional covariance of idiosyncratic and aggregate shocks. We assume a process for individual income risk based in part on the estimations re-

---

11. In constructing the total dividend series, we always normalize the level of dividends so that they average 15% of GDP.

ported in Deaton (1992) and adjusted for the assumed 25-year period length. Deaton reports a standard deviation of shocks for an MA(1) specification of individual income growth of 15%, and an MA coefficient of −0.4. Based on this, the idiosyncratic income shocks for both the young and the old are assumed to have a standard deviation of 45% over each 25-year period. The shock when young is assumed to be completely persistent, so that

$$\epsilon^o(j,t + 1) = \epsilon(j,t)\omega(j,t + 1),\qquad(9)$$

where $\omega(j,t + 1)$ is the further 45%-standard-deviation shock to relative nonmarketed income that agent j faces when old. In experiments below, we also consider the situation in which the idiosyncratic shocks of a subset of the population are correlated with dividends. This captures the possibility that certain classes of agents, such as business owners or executives who own large shares of stock in their own corporation, face risks that are more correlated with the market than a typical individual. Because preferences are homothetic, when agents are assumed to be homogeneous only the ω-shock affects prices and portfolio choice. When the wealth and income of participants and nonparticipants differ, however, the income distribution of the young can affect predicted returns.

For most of the analysis, preferences are parametrized with $\beta_j = 0.95^{25}$ and $\alpha_j = 5$ for all j. These parameters are also varied in the sensitivity analysis.

4.2.2 Varying Participation Rates   Table 6 shows what happens when the assumed participation rate in the stock market is varied between 30% and 100% of the population, assuming the preference specification and processes for individual and aggregate income described above. As one would expect, increased participation lowers the equity premium. Notice, however, that the effect is small in the region of participation rates that correspond to the data. For example, when participation increases from 50% to 80% of the population, the equity premium and the absolute level of equity returns are reduced by less than a tenth of a percent. Changing participation also has a small effect on the level of the risk-free rate, with an increase in participation increasing the average rate of return. This can be attributed to a precautionary effect that decreases when risk is spread more evenly over the population. Although small, this effect is in keeping with the observation that the risk-free rate has risen in recent years.

Consistent with the literature on the equity-premium puzzle, aggre-

Table 6 AVERAGE ANNUAL RETURNS AS A FUNCTION
OF PARTICIPATION

Percentage of Stockholders	Returns (%)		
	$E(r^b)$	$E(r^s)$	$E(r^s - r^b)$
100	4.42	5.47	1.05
90	4.40	5.48	1.08
80	4.38	5.49	1.11
70	4.37	5.50	1.13
60	4.35	5.51	1.16
50	4.33	5.52	1.19
40	4.32	5.53	1.21
30	4.32	5.55	1.23

gate income and dividend risk alone are not sufficient to generate a sizable equity premium. This is true even under the assumption of extremely limited participation, inflated aggregate risk, and nonmarketed income risk. Still, the premium predicted here is higher than in Mehra and Prescott (1985) by about 1%. Experiments not reported here indicate that this difference is due primarily to the assumption that aggregate risk is higher than that observed in the data, rather than to limited participation or exposure to idiosyncratic income risk.

In the experiments that follow, we examine other stochastic steady states based on different degrees of diversification, risk aversion, etc. Although looking across steady states does not allow one to watch returns gradually changing over time as parameters gradually change, it does provide an upper bound on the size of these effects. Thus, one can give a temporal interpretation to some of the experiments. For instance, we will compare the stylized historical past, with low diversification and low participation rates, to the stylized present, with greater diversification, more complete participation, and greater patience.

4.2.3 Increasing Diversification As a proxy for the increased diversification of a typical market participant over time, we vary the assumed volatility of the dividend process. It is an empirical fact that the variability of returns falls dramatically as diversification increases. Based on CRSP monthly data from 1962 to 1997, Table 7 shows the effect of diversification on a typical portfolio's annual standard deviation. In monthly data, we find an average individual stock standard deviation of 16% and an average pairwise covariance of 0.01. The portfolio standard devia-

Table 7   THE EFFECT OF DIVERSIFICATION ON
           PORTFOLIO VOLATILITY

| No. of | Standard Deviation (%) | |
Stocks	Monthly	Annual
1	16.0	55.4
2	11.7	40.4
3	9.8	33.9
4	8.7	30.2
5	8.0	27.7
10	6.3	21.9
20	5.3	18.3
100	4.3	14.9
500	4.1	14.1

tions reported in the table assume equal value weights on each stock. Monthly returns are annualized under the assumption that they are independent. These calculations show that holding a one-stock portfolio results in an annual standard deviation of 55%, while increasing holdings to five stocks decreases the standard deviation to 28%, and holding 500 stocks brings it down to 14%.

The above statistics on portfolio returns do not translate directly into parameter values, since the inputs into the model are income and dividend processes, whereas returns are endogenous. One assumption about dividends that produces returns consistent with those observed in CRSP data is that $d(t)$ is variable over time, taking on the values 0.11 and 0.25 with equal probability. This level of variation essentially brackets the variation in dividends' share in total income, based on the S&P 500 dividend flow and U.S. gross domestic product since 1947. We call this the case of *high dividend volatility*. It implies variation that is approximately consistent with a three-stock portfolio under the parametrizations we focus on.

Second, we consider a situation referred to as *correlated high dividend volatility*. Here the aggregate dividend is assumed to be correlated with nonmarketed income, taking on the value 0.11 in the low-nonmarketed-income state and 0.25 in the high-nonmarketed-income state. These first two cases bracket two views of the relation between dividend growth and income growth. The first is that there is very little correlation between income growth and dividend growth on an annual basis. The second is that over longer time periods, such as the 25-year periods considered here, there is a positive correlation between dividends and income.[12]

Finally, we represent the increased volatility in a poorly diversified portfolio by assuming a skewed distribution of dividends. The dividend share, δ, is fixed at 0.1865 for 95% of the time, but falls to 0.06 for 5% of the time, independent of the aggregate state. This *skewed dividend* case represents bankruptcy of a poorly diversified portfolio. It is further assumed that zero is an absorbing state for the value of a bankrupt portfolio after this small dividend is paid. To maintain stationarity, bankrupt shares are replaced by new shares in the new generation. These new shares are held in the portfolios of the young, but cannot be sold until the following period. The reason to consider a more skewed distribution of payoffs is twofold. First, although catastrophic outcomes are rare for the U.S. stock market as a whole, individual firms fail quite frequently. Secondly, the properties of the utility function suggest that skewed outcomes will have a much different effect on asset prices than a symmetric distribution with the same variance. In fact, the implied volatility of returns in this case is set to be similar to that in the case of high dividend volatility.

Table 8 is similar to Table 6, but reports results under the assumptions of high dividend volatility, correlated high dividend volatility, and skewed dividends. Panel A reproduces the predicted returns under the base-case set of assumptions for participation rates of 50% and 100%. Relative to panel A, assuming high dividend volatility (panel B) has the effect of decreasing the risk-free rate by 0.61% and 0.82% for participation levels of 100% and 50% respectively. It increases the equity premium by 0.71% and 0.97%, respectively, for the same participation rates. These results are consistent with the view that increased diversification has significantly reduced the required equity premium, although for these parameters it suggests only a slight decrease in the level of the required return on equities. For the case of correlated high dividend volatility (panel C), the effect on the equity premium of an increase in dividend volatility is even larger.

Notice that for high dividend volatility an increase in participation results in a larger decline in the equity premium than for low dividend volatility. This occurs in part because with high dividend volatility case there is more risk to be shared, and hence a greater benefit from spreading

---

12. As one would expect, predicted returns are sensitive to the assumed degree of correlation between dividends and nonmarketed income. It is not obvious, however, whether the dividends from a poorly diversified portfolio are likely to be more or less highly correlated with nonmarketed income than for a well-diversified portfolio. If, for instance, households own stock primarily in the companies for which they work (a common phenomenon), the correlation may be relatively high.

Table 8   AVERAGE RETURNS AS A FUNCTION OF PARTICIPATION AND
           THE DIVIDEND PROCESS

Percentage of Stockholders	Returns (%)		
	$E(r^b)$	$E(r^s)$	$E(r^s - r^b)$
A. Low Dividend Volatility			
100	4.42	5.47	1.05
50	4.33	5.52	1.19
B. High Dividend Volatility			
100	3.81	5.57	1.76
50	3.51	5.67	2.16
C. Correlated High Dividend Volatility			
100	3.38	5.87	2.49
50	3.36	5.95	2.59
D. Skewed Dividends			
100	1.54	6.17	4.63
50	0.47	6.93	6.46

this risk to new participants with no initial exposure to market risk. For correlated high dividend volatility, however, changes in participation have a smaller effect on the equity premium than for uncorrelated high dividend volatility. This is because the new entrants are less willing to bear stock-market risk when it is correlated with their nonmarketed risk.

Finally, the much more dramatic results in the skewed-dividend case are shown in panel D. The small risk of a catastrophic outcome reduces the risk-free rate to 0.47% and increases the equity premium to 6.46% with 50% participation. With 100% participation, the risk-free rate equals 1.54% and the equity premium is 4.63%. This assumption therefore allows one to match the historical equity premium. It also suggests that in this region of parameter space the premium is more sensitive to changes in participation rates. This points to changes in diversification as a potentially large factor in explaining changes in expected returns.

4.2.4 *Preference-Parameter Changes*   The potential effects of changing risk attitudes are explored by changing the coefficient of relative risk aversion, α_j. Recall that in all the results reported above α_j is set to 5. If α_j is increased to 10, with all else as in the high-dividend-volatility case and at a 50% participation rate, the equity premium rises by only 0.16%. The risk-free rate falls by 0.3%. It is clear that over the range of risk-aversion coefficients usually considered, a change in risk aversion does not account for large changes in stock prices in this model.

As discussed in Section 3, increases in life expectancy may affect the subjective rate of discount. Varying β_j is a proxy for these changes. Unlike in an infinite-horizon model, where β generally does not have a first-order effect on the equity premium, varying β_j here influences the equity premium as well as the general level of returns. The reason is that when β_j increases, the value of future dividends and nonmarketable income increases relative to the value of first-period income. This changes the share of capital in wealth and increases the importance of second-period income risk. For the parameters we consider, this results in a lower equity premium in levels, but a higher premium relative to the risk-free rate. For instance, increasing β from 0.95^{25} to 0.96^{25}, with 50% participation, high dividend volatility, α equal to 5, and η equal to 0.2, moves the equity premium from 2.16% to 2.02%, and the risk-free rate from 3.51% to 3.05%. We interpret the increase in the relative premium as a response to the increased exposure to market risk. The reduction in the absolute premium reflects the increased precautionary demand for savings with the increase in risk, which lowers all required rates of return.

Varying η, the share of nonmarketed income accruing to the elderly, similarly affects risk and hence returns. For instance, increasing η from 0.2 to 0.3, with β_j equal to 0.95^{25} and all else as in the case above, moves the equity premium from 2.16% to 2.49% and the risk-free rate from 3.51% to 4.14%.

4.2.5 Heterogeneity in Idiosyncratic Income Shocks   An interesting question is whether background income risk (i.e., nonmarketable risk) is different for stockholders and nonstockholders, and whether this difference interacts with the effect of participation changes on asset returns. In Heaton and Lucas (1998) we present evidence that many large stockholders depend more heavily on income from privately held businesses than on labor income. Business income is more volatile and more highly correlated with stock returns than is labor income. Hence, the equity premium is likely to fall more sharply if new entrants who are otherwise similar to stockholders depend predominantly on labor income. As discussed in Section 3.2, in recent years there has been an increase in participation by middle-income households, which are likely to contain wage earners. We investigate the potential quantitative effect of this change by assuming a different idiosyncratic income process for a subset of the stockholders and for nonstockholders.[13]

13. Ideally we would make participation endogenous and hence a function of the assumed income process, as in Polkovnichenko (1998). This tends reduce the risk-sharing capacity of new entrants, since the most risk-tolerant agents already hold stocks when entry

Table 9   AVERAGE RETURNS AS A FUNCTION OF PARTICIPATION AND
THE DIVIDEND PROCESS (HETEROGENEOUS INCOME RISK)

Percentage of Stockholders	Returns (%)		
	$E(r^b)$	$E(r^s)$	$E(r^s - r^b)$
A. High Dividend Volatility			
100	3.74	5.49	1.75
50	3.42	5.58	2.16
B. Correlated High Dividend Volatility			
100	3.32	5.79	2.47
50	3.28	5.85	2.57
C. Skewed Dividends			
100	1.18	6.12	4.94
50	0.17	6.82	6.65

To implement this, we assume that a fixed number of participants have nonmarketed income that is correlated with the dividend flow from stocks. New entrants to the stock market and nonparticipants have a less correlated income process. More precisely, we assume that 25% of the population receive idiosyncratic income when old, with a standard deviation of 67.5% and a correlation with dividends' share in aggregate income of 0.2. this group is always assumed to hold stocks.[14] The rest of the population receives idiosyncratic shocks that have a standard deviation of 45% as before, and a correlation with dividends of −0.1. This negative correlation is necessary to produce an average correlation that is consistent with data. In annual data, one does in fact see a slight negative correlation between labor income and stock returns.

Table 9 reports results under these assumptions for high dividend volatility (panel A), correlated high dividend volatility (panel B), and skewed dividends (panel C). In each case, the experiment is to move from a situation in which 50% of the stockholding population is exposed to high background risk to one in which 25% has this exposure. Changes in participation now have only slightly more effect than in Table 8 for high dividend volatility. The effect of a change in participation is slightly smaller for skewed dividends. The effect of an increase in participation on the premium relative to the risk-free rate is higher in each case,

---

is endogenous. For simplicity, and to put an upper bound on this effect, we assume that participation is completely exogenous.

14. These parameter assumptions are consistent with the estimates reported by Heaton and Lucas (1998).

however, because of the greater volatility of the nonmarketed income of stockholders. As in Table 8, the greatest effect of participation is in the case of skewed dividends, where the equity premium falls by 1.71% when participation increases from 50% to 100%.

4.2.6 Simultaneous Changes As discussed in the introduction, each of the factors that we have looked at individually has been suggested as a fundamental reason for the stock price run-up. We have seen that none of these factors alone is sufficient to produce a large change in required equity returns, and hence the large run-up in stock prices. Here we examine the best case for the model, simultaneously changing a number of parameters. The stylized historical past is characterized by a β of 0.95^{25}, dividends as described in the skewed-dividend case, and a participation rate of 50%. Income processes are heterogeneous as described in the previous subsection, so that 50% of stockholders have highly volatile income that is correlated with dividends. The risk aversion α is fixed at 5, and η is fixed at 0.2. The stylized present is described by a β of 0.96^{25}, reflecting an upward revision of expected life expectancy, low-volatility dividends as in Table 6 reflecting a considerable increase in diversification, and a participation rate of 80%. All else is as in the past. This results in a risk-free rate that rises from 0.17% to 3.73%, and an expected return on stocks that decreases from 6.82% to 4.84%. The equity premium is substantially reduced, from 6.65% to 1.11%. We conclude, then, that assuming reasonable changes in a number of variables simultaneously can account for changes in expected returns in keeping with what appears to be the case in the U.S. economy.

5. Conclusions

In this paper, we have looked at a number of potential fundamentals-based explanations for the recent stock price run-up. In particular, we focused on whether changes in market participation patterns or changes in portfolio diversification are likely to account for a substantial fraction of the rise in stock prices. We conclude that the changes in participation that have occurred over this decade are unlikely to be a major part of the explanation. This conclusion is based both on the data, which suggest only small changes in participation for wealthy households, and the model, which implies that participation changes have to be quite extreme to substantially affect expected returns. Increased portfolio diversification, however, is likely to have had a larger effect. There is empirical evidence that households have significantly diversified their portfolios, selling individual stocks and buying mutual funds. An important difference between poorly diversified portfolios and a market index is the likelihood of catastrophic outcomes. When this difference is reflected in model parameters, the expected equity premium falls by more than 4%.

More generally, we can construct scenarios that are loosely consistent with the data in which the required return on stocks falls by 2%. As shown in Section 3.1 using a calibrated Gordon growth model, this amount of change in expected returns goes at least halfway towards justifying the current high level of the price–dividend ratio in the U.S. market. We interpret this as quite a positive result, especially because it is difficult to produce much variation in the predicted equity premium in this class of models. The model also predicts an increase in the real risk-free rate, which also appears to be consistent with the data.

These results depend in an important way on changes in diversification and, to a lesser extent, on income heterogeneity. There is evidence that entrepreneurs and managers tend to be large stockholders who bear a sizable amount of undiversifiable risk in the form of their own businesses. Still, we do not have a complete picture of the income and wealth characteristics of large stockholders, and we are uncertain about the extent of their diversification. We also do not have a satisfactory understanding of how older stockholders, who own a substantial fraction of the market, view the risk of stock ownership. Looking even more closely at the characteristics of large stockholders remains a useful direction for future research.

REFERENCES

Allen, F., and D. Gale. (1994). Limited market participation and volatility of asset prices. *American Economic Review* 84:933–955.
Bakshi, G., and Z. Chen. (1994). Baby boom, population aging, and capital markets. *Journal of Business* 67:165–202.
Basak, S., and D. Cuoco. (1998). An equilibrium model with restricted stock market participation. *Review of Financial Studies* 11:309–341.
Bertaut, C., and M. Haliassos. (1995). Why do so few hold stocks? *The Economic Journal,* 105:1110–1129.
Blanchard, O. (1993). Movements in the equity premium. *Brookings Papers on Economic Activity* 2:75–138.
Blume, M., and S. Zeldes (1993). The structure of stockownership in the U.S. Wharton. Manuscript.
Bodie, Z., R. Merton, and W. Samuelson (1992). Labor supply flexibility and portfolio choice in a life-cycle model. Cambridge, MA: National Bureau of Economic Research. NBER Working Paper 6.
Brealey, R., and S. Myers (1996). *Principles of Corporate Finance,* 5th ed. New York: McGraw-Hill.
Campbell, J., and J. Cochrane (1998). By force of habit: A consumption-based explanation of aggregate stock market behavior. *Journal of Political Economy* 107:205–251.

Cochrane, J. (1997). Where is the market going? Uncertain facts and novel theories. *Federal Reserve Bank of Chicago Economic Perspectives* XXI(6):3–37.

Campbell, J., and R. Shiller. (1988). Stock prices, earnings, and expected dividends. *Journal of Finance* 43:661–676.

Constantinides, G., J. Donaldson, and R. Mehra. (1998). Junior can't borrow: A new perspective on the equity premium puzzle. University of Chicago. Manuscript.

———, and D. Duffie. (1996). Asset pricing with heterogeneous consumers. *Journal of Political Economy* 104(2):219–240.

Davis, S., and P. Willen. (1998). Using financial assets to hedge labor income risks: Estimating the benefits. Princeton University. Manuscript.

Deaton, A. (1992). Savings and liquidity constraints. *Econometrica* 59:1221–1248.

Epstein, L., and S. Zin (1989). Substitution, risk aversion and the temporal behavior of consumption and asset returns: A theoretical framework. *Econometrica* 57:937–969.

Friend, I., and M. Blume. (1975). The demand for risky assets. *American Economic Review* 65:900–922.

Gentry, W. M., and R. G. Hubbard. (1998). Why do the wealthy save so much? Columbia University. Manuscript.

Heaton, J., and D. Lucas (1998). Asset pricing and portfolio choice: The importance of entrepreneurial risk. Northwestern University. Manuscript.

Hodrick, R. (1992). Dividend yields and expected stock returns: Alternative procedures for inference and measurement. *Review of Financial Studies* 5:357–386.

King, M., and J. Leape (1984). Asset accumulation, information, and the life cycle. Cambridge, MA: National Bureau of Economic Research. NBER Working Paper 2392.

Lamont, O. (1998). Earnings and expected returns. *Journal of Finance* 53:1563–1587.

Lee, Charles M. C., and B. Swaminathan. (1999). Valuing the Dow: A bottom-up approach. Cornell University. Manuscript.

Mankiw, N. G., and S. Zeldes (1991). The consumption of stockholders and nonstockholders. *Journal of Financial Economics* 29:97–112.

Mehra, R., and E. Prescott (1985). The equity premium: A puzzle. *Journal of Monetary Economics* 15:145–161.

Newey, W., and K. West (1987). A simple positive semi-definite heteroskedasticity and autocorrelation consistent covariance matrix estimator. *Econometrica* 55:703–708.

Polkovnichenko, V. (1988). Heterogeneity and proprietary income risk: Implications for stock market participation and asset prices. Kellogg Graduate School of Management. Manuscript.

Poterba, J. (1993). Who owns corporate stock?: A report to the New York Stock Exchange. MIT. Manuscript.

———. (1998). Population age structure and asset returns: An empirical investigation. Cambridge, MA: National Bureau of Economic Research. NBER Working Paper 6774.

———, and A. Samwick. (1997). Household portfolio allocation over the life cycle. Cambridge, MA: National Bureau of Economic Research. NBER Working Paper 6185.

Saito, M. (1995). Limited market participation and asset pricing. Department of Economics, University of British Columbia. Manuscript.

Storesletten, K., C. Telmer, and A. Yaron. (1998). Asset pricing with idiosyncratic risk and overlapping generations. Carnegie Mellon University. Manuscript.

Vissing-Jørgensen, A. (1997). Limited stock market participation. Department of Economics, MIT. Manuscript.

Weil, P. (1990). Nonexpected utility in macroeconomics. *Quarterly Journal of Economics* 105:29–42.

Comment

ANNETTE VISSING-JØRGENSEN
University of Chicago

1. Introduction

During the period 1995–1998 the U.S. stock market experienced four consecutive years with real stock returns above 20%. Suppose as a rough approximation that annual real log gross stock returns are normally distributed and independent over time. With a mean and variance of this distribution equal to the historical values for the period 1871–1994, the probability of observing four years of above 20% returns is 0.4%.[1] The high returns have come primarily from capital gains driving price–dividend and price–earnings ratios to historical highs (the latest numbers from August 9 for the S&P 500 are P/D = 78.5 and P/E = 31.9). Thus, even taking into account statistical fluctuation, it is becoming increasingly unlikely that nothing has changed. The only period since 1871 with as impressive returns was 1924–1928, with five years of above 20% real stock returns. Over the three-year period following that event, real stock returns averaged −15.4% annually.

In the present paper Heaton and Lucas ask whether the recent stock-market boom can be explained by changes in economic fundamentals. Three candidates are considered: changes in corporate earnings growth, changes in consumer preferences, and changes in stock-market participation patterns. Participation is defined broadly as concerning both the level of stock-market participation and the amount of diversification among participants. Poor diversification is found to have large effects on equilibrium returns in an overlapping generations exchange economy. The main conclusion of the paper is that increased diversification by itself can explain at least half of the increase in the adjusted P/D ratio. This is an interesting finding, not only for interpreting the recent past but also seen in the context of the literature on the equity premium

---

[1]. Using the data from Robert Shiller's home page, the 1871–1994 mean and standard deviation of $\log(1 + r^{stock,real})$ are 0.067 and 0.17.

puzzle. Increased participation is found to have only small effects. For readers who attended the presentation of the paper at the NBER Macroeconomics Annual conference, I should mention that the part of the paper which concerns diversification is new and thus was not discussed at that time.

My discussion focuses first in Section 2 on whether the increase in diversification is sufficiently recent and sufficiently large for this to be considered the main reason for the recent stock-market boom. In Section 3 I turn to the overlapping-generations model to address whether the theoretical results regarding large effects of diversification and smaller effects of participation are likely to be robust. Section 4 comments on the authors' calibration of the Gordon growth model and contains current and historical data for analyst earnings forecasts to determine if high earnings growth expectations rather than lower required stock returns could be driving the stock-market boom. Section 5 concludes.

2. Is the Increase in Diversification Large and Recent Enough?

In the overlapping-generations model calibrated by Heaton and Lucas a shift from a three-stock portfolio to full diversification generates a decline in the mean real stock return of 1.41 percentage points for participation fixed at 50% (compare cases D and A in Table 8). This is in fact more than needed to explain current valuation ratios according to my calculations in Section 4 below. Should we conclude from this that increased diversification is the main reason behind the stock-market boom? From an empirical perspective it would need to be established that diversification has in fact increased from something close to the level of a three-stock portfolio to close to full diversification and that the timing of the increase coincides to a reasonable extent with the stock-market boom. The evidence presented below shows that the trend in diversification started long before the recent stock-market boom. Thus if diversification is as important as suggested, valuation ratios should have reached historical highs long before the 1990s. P/D and P/E ratios have trended upward since the early 1980s, but much of this was a return to normal levels from very low values in the beginning of the 1980s.[2]

2. In Vissing-Jørgensen (1998) I documented the upward trend in stock-market participation from around 6% of households in the beginning of the 1950s to around 41% in 1995. It is too early to say whether the trend in participation has strengthened significantly since then. It will be interesting to see the latest numbers when the 1998 Survey of Consumer Finances becomes available. However, the increase in participation since 1995 would have to be dramatic, since the effect of increased participation is likely to be

Figure 1 STOCK OWNERSHIP SHARES, 1952–1999, FLOW OF
FUNDS ACCOUNTS

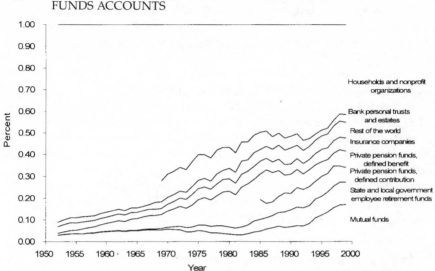

The values shown are for the end of the first quarter of the year, except for the last data point for the split of private pension plans between defined contribution and defined benefits, which is for the end of 1998. The data are not seasonally adjusted. Mutual funds include closed-end funds. The category "bank personal trusts and estates" was added in 1969. Before this it was lumped together with direct owner-ship by households and nonprofit organizations. Four small categories summing to less than 1.5% of the total for all years are left out of the graph for simplicity, but are included in the numbers given in the text. These are state and local governments, commercial banking, savings institutions, and security brokers and dealers. The measure of equity in the Flow of Funds Accounts is the total U.S. stock-market capitalization including closely held companies.

Figure 1 updates Table 5 of Poterba and Samwick (1995), which shows the proportions of the stock market owned through various channels. The source of the data is the Flow of Funds Accounts. Consistent with Heaton and Lucas's Table 4, the share of stocks held through mutual funds has increased over the period since 1995. However, direct stock ownership has declined steadily throughout the period. The correspond-ing increases are mainly in the shares for pensions and for mutual funds. Stockholding by private and governmental pension plans increased from a negligible share in the beginning of the 1950s to a maximum of 27.0% in 1986:1. It has been fairly stable since then. The upward trend in stockholding through mutual funds started around 1982 after a slight decrease in the 1970s. The increase was 8.9 percentage points from 1982:1 to 1995:1 and 4.9 percentage points from 1995:1 to 1999:1. The mutual fund share for 1999:1 was 16.5%.

nonlinear, with a bigger effect of a given increase in participation at initially low partici-pation levels. It seems more plausible that changes in participation have contributed to a gradual trend in returns than that they are responsible for the recent boom.

Up to the beginning of the 1980s the growth in stockholding through pension plans represented purchases by defined-benefit pension plans. It is likely that stock purchases by governmental defined-benefit plans represent a significant increase in risk sharing. The bearers of the investment risk in this case are the taxpayers. Thus stockholding by these pension plans spreads risk over a broad group of households and thus increases risk sharing.

Since defined-benefit plans are managed by investment professionals, one would expect them to be well diversified. It is however not clear that increased stock ownership by private defined-benefit plans has increased the diversification level of the typical stockholder to a significant extent. Consider a world with workers and capitalists where stocks are in unit net supply, and bonds are in zero net supply. Initially workers save for retirement out of wages. Workers do not like risk and save in the form of bonds issued by capitalists (directly or indirectly through company debt). Capitalists bear all output risk. A defined-benefit plan is then introduced. Workers must accept a reduction in wages in exchange for the pension benefits. The shareholders of each company take this part of wages and invest it in other companies. They pay workers a riskless stream when retired. Thus capitalists still end up bearing all the risk. Workers get riskless retirement benefits in either case. In the situation with a pension plan each shareholder is more diversified: He still only owns a small number of stocks directly, but now there is cross ownership of stocks by companies via the pension plans. Buying one share of a given company now gives you the right to a payment stream representing partly this company's earnings and partly other companies' earnings. However, with cross holding at most equal to the share of private benefit plans in total stock-market capitalization, this effect is small.

Since the introduction of individual retirement accounts (IRAs) in 1981 and 401(k) plans in 1978, there has been a shift from defined-benefit to defined-contribution plans. In these, individual beneficiaries fully or partially decide how to invest their assets. The increased share for 401(k)s and similar plans represents a significant increase in diversification, since these plans typically offer choices of stock portfolios rather than allowing employees to pick individual stocks.[3]

Overall, while the effects are hard to quantify, increased stock ownership by pension plans most likely contributed to increased diversification and risk sharing long before the recent stock-market boom.

The share of stocks held directly remains large. Thus it is important to

3. Since 1993, 401(k) providers have been required by law to include a broad range of equity funds in the investment choices. Large holdings of own-company stock remain an issue for diversification of 401(k) stockholdings.

consider whether diversification has increased significantly for stock-holders who hold all or most of their stocks directly. Table 1 gives various measures of diversification based on data from the Survey of Consumer Finances (SCF) for 1983, 1989, and 1995. The numbers for 1971 are from Blume and Friend (1978, Chart 2–5) and are based on a sample of 17,056 federal income tax forms. There is a clear trend towards increased diversi-fication of directly held stocks. The share of directly held equity which is held by households with less than 10 stocks has decreased from 56.5% in 1971 to 37.9% in 1995. For 1989 and 1995 the SCF contains information about how much equity is held in indirect form (mutual funds, pension plans, trusts, and managed investment accounts). If we assume that all such stockholdings are well diversified and that households with 20 or more directly held stocks are well diversified, then 73.8% of household-owned equity is owned by well-diversified investors, up from 60.8% in 1989.

Counting the number of directly held stocks overstates the level of diversification if portfolios are unbalanced. Blume, Crockett, and Friend (1974) found this to be important. Even for high-income households with on average 18.7 different stocks, the level of diversification only corresponded to an equal-weighted portfolio of about two stocks. The SCF contains information about holdings of stock in the company where household members work or have worked (I refer to these as *own-company stock*). The bottom part of Table 1 shows that own-company stockholding is likely to be a main cause of poor diversification. House-holds with positive holdings of own-company stock owned 40.2% of directly held equity in 1995. Of their direct stockholdings the mean percentage held in own-company stock was 47.8%. Even if one allows for indirect stockholding of these households, they still on average hold 30.8% of their equity portfolio in their own company [this number does not include own-company stockholdings via 401(k) or similar plans]. This suggests that a substantial share of the stock market remains owned by poorly diversified households. It furthermore emphasizes that under-standing why so many households hold substantial amounts of wealth in own-company stock is crucial for understanding the effects of poor diversification. Are the results driven by rich households holding large shares of companies they founded? Is delaying payment of capital gains taxes a key reason they do not sell part of these stocks and invest in a more diversified portfolio? Do rich households choose to hold large shares of few companies to have influence on company decisions? Or are people simply overly optimistic about their own company, in which case poor diversification would not warrant higher returns? A better understanding of these issues is crucial for determining the general equi-librium effects on asset returns caused by poor diversification.

Table 1   TRENDS IN DIVERSIFICATION OF DIRECTLY HELD EQUITY[a]

	Number of stocks	1971	1983	1989	1995
1. Percentage of equity held directly		—	—	59.5	41.4
2. Percentage of equity held in mutual funds		—	—	9.3	20.2
3. Percentage of directly held equity owned by households	3	18.3	18.0	15.9	15.2
with less than this number of stocks	5	—	26.1	24.4	22.8
	10	56.5	48.9	44.3	37.9
	15	—	60.9	55.3	51.7
	20	74.9	71.9	65.4	64.9
4. Percentage of equity held by households with half or	3	—	—	91.4	94.1
more of their equity holdings in indirect form or at	5	—	—	86.0	91.3
least this number of stocks	10	—	—	74.0	85.0
	15	—	—	66.8	79.6
	20	—	—	60.8	73.8
5. Own-company stock as percentage of directly held equity		—	23.4	17.1	19.2
6. Own-company stock as percentage of directly and indirectly held equity		—	—	10.2	7.9
Households with positive holdings of own-company stock:					
7. Percentage of directly held equity owned by these households		—	36.0	31.0	40.2
8. Percentage of directly and indirectly held equity owned by these households		—	—	23.1	25.7
9. Mean percentage of own-company stock in direct equity portfolio for these households		—	65.0	55.3	47.8
10. Mean percentage of own-company stock in direct and indirect equity portfolio for these households		—	—	44.1	30.8

Note: For the numbers based on the Survey of Consumer Finances (SCF) observations are weighted using SCF weights. For 1989 and 1995 the numbers shown are averages of the numbers obtained for each of the five SCF imputations. For 1983 the edited and imputed SCF data file is used. "Indirect stockholding" refers to stockholding in mutual funds (half of holdings in combined mutual funds are assumed to be equity), in IRAs, in thrift-type plans as defined in the SCF net-worth program, and in trusts, annuities, and managed investment accounts. In line 9 values are weighted by size of direct stockholdings; in line 10 values are weighted by size of direct and indirect stockholdings.
[a]Tax return sample 1971, Survey of Consumer Finances 1983, 1989, 1995.

In sum, the empirical evidence raises two concerns for the theory that the recent stock-market boom is due to increased diversification: firstly, that the trend in diversification started much earlier than 1995; secondly, that although diversification has improved, the share of equity owned through mutual funds is still only 16.5% and a substantial share of the stock market remains owned by poorly diversified households. It would be interesting to see how large effects on returns Heaton and Lucas's model generate for changes in diversification more in line with this.

3. Robustness of Theoretical Results from the OLG Model

I was surprised by the way the authors calibrate the poor-diversification cases (cases B–D). They first use firm-level return data to determine the effects of holding a larger number of stocks on the standard deviation of a portfolio (Table 7). The amount of idiosyncratic dividend risk (and for case D bankruptcy risk) is then chosen such that the model generates a stock return volatility equal to that observed for a typical three-stock portfolio. For this amount of volatility the expected stock return and the equity premium are much higher than in the full-diversification case (case A). But how do we know whether this is a reasonable amount of idiosyncratic dividend and bankruptcy risk? This could be checked against the firm-level data. In fact, a more standard approach would be to first use the firm-level data to determine the dividend risk and the bankruptcy probability for a typical firm, then assume that a portfolio of three such stocks was bought, and determine if the model generates a stock return (a return to such a portfolio) which is much higher than the one for full diversification.

It should also be emphasized that the assumption of risk aversion equal to 5 may be crucial for the large effects of diversification on the mean stock return. If risk aversion were set to 1, there would most likely be little or no effect on the mean stock return of either diversification or participation. To see this, consider the following special case of the model for which a simple closed-form solution for the stock price is available. Suppose there is no idiosyncratic labor income risk and no labor income when old. With risk aversion set to one (and thus equal to the assumed elasticity of intertemporal substitution), Epstein–Zin preferences specialize to CRRA preferences. Then each young agent consumes the constant fraction $a = \beta/(1 + \beta)$ of wages, independent of asset returns. Let λ denote the proportion who are stockholders, ω_t their portfolio share for stocks at time t, and P_{st} the stock price at t. The equilibrium conditions for the stock and the bond market at t are then as follows.

Stocks: $\lambda\omega_t(1 - a)(1 - d_t)Y_t = P_{st},$ (1)

Bonds: $\lambda(1 - \omega_t)(1 - a)(1 - d_t)Y_t + (1 - \lambda)(1 - a)(1 - d_t)Y_t = 0.$ (2)

Equation (2) implies $\lambda\omega_t = 1$. Inserting this in (1) gives $P_{st} = (1 - a)(1 - d_t)Y_t$. Thus in this special case the stock price is unaffected by the level of stock-market participation. Furthermore, the stock price is affected by diversification only because this is modeled by a stochastic aggregate dividend share (causing the wage share to be stochastic) rather than using several different stocks. In other words, for this special case increased participation [diversification] affects the equity premium only [mainly] via the bond rate, with no [little] effect on stock price and the stock return. Given this, I would expect much smaller effects of diversification on the mean stock return if risk aversion were set equal to 2 or 3 rather than 5 (in the end the right number may turn out to be 5 or higher, but given that we do not have precise knowledge about this parameter, sensitivity analysis is relevant).

The underlying reason that the stock price is unaffected by participation or diversification in the log utility case is that the model is an exchange economy. With log utility the propensity to save is the same for all households. The bond market therefore requires that stockholders in equilibrium be willing to lend to the nonstockholders as much as stockholders wish to save. This implies $\lambda\omega_t = 1$ and thus, along with a constant, leaves the stock price to be determined by the wage income of the young. In an exchange economy wages are exogenous to both participation and diversification. This suggests that an alternative way of generating a higher stock price upon entry or diversification, even in the log utility case, is to change the model to one in which the resources of the young can be affected by increased participation or diversification. In Vissing-Jørgensen (1998) I analyze an OLG model with production to study the general equilibrium effects of limited participation. In that model (for the log utility case) the riskless rate is unaffected by participation, and the full effect on the equity premium is due to a lower mean stock return. Wages, the capital stock, and the stock price are higher for higher levels of participation. I recalibrated the model to have similar amounts of output risk to Heaton and Lucas's low-dividend-volatility case. Increasing participation from 10% to 60% then decreases the mean stock return by around 0.5 percentage point.[4]

4. The model is fairly standard. The results are not sensitive to whether the production function is assumed to exhibit constant or decreasing returns to scale. One assumption which is central for the results is that in each period, factor input levels and wages are set before the realization of uncertainty. Factors are paid after output is realized. Thus the labor share of output is countercyclical, since workers do not take any of the output risk. Countercyclical labor shares are well documented in the business-cycle literature.

4. The Gordon Growth Model

Although I agree that a decrease in the required return is needed to explain recent valuation ratios, the authors' calculation based on the Gordon growth model to some extent overstates the necessary change.

The required stock return in the formula $P/E = 1/(r - g)$ is net of transaction costs, and these have declined significantly. While it is hard to evaluate costs of direct investment, Bogle (1991) finds that equity mutual funds underperformed the S&P 500 by an average of 2.1 percentage points over the period 1969–1989. Rea and Reid (1998) find that the sales-weighted average of total shareholder costs for equity mutual funds has decreased from 2.25% in 1980 to 1.49% in 1997. Indeed, declining transaction costs both for direct investment and for investment via mutual funds are likely to have been a key factor behind the increases in diversification and participation (the issue of lower transaction costs does not arise in the overlapping-generations model, since diversification or participation is changed exogenously). Assuming a 0.75-percentage-point decline in transaction costs, the change in $r - g$ needed to imply a movement in the adjusted P/D ratio from 28 historically to 48 at the end of the authors' sample is not $\frac{1}{28} - \frac{1}{48} = 0.015$ but 0.0075, or 0.75 percentage points. It is worth pointing out in this context that without transaction costs it is very difficult to reconcile the Gordon growth model with the historical-mean-adjusted P/D ratio. With a historical value of g around 2% the model implies a historical required real stock return of $\frac{1}{28} + 0.02 = 0.056$. The actual real stock return was much higher at 8.5% (arithmetic average) for 1871–1994, and 9.1% if we include the recent period up to 1998.

The authors' calibration of the Gordon growth model furthermore assumes that the riskless rate has increased by 2 percentage points. Therefore an increase in g of 3.5 percentage points (or a g of 13.4% for 10 years and 2% thereafter) is required to explain an adjusted P/D of 48 with a constant equity premium. The most relevant interest rate in this context is the real interest rate on long-term bonds. These rates are currently high (around 4% for long-term inflation-indexed U.S. Treasury bonds), but it may be premature to conclude that they are as much as 2 percentage points higher than their historical mean. Blanchard (1993) and the discussion of it by Siegel show that fluctuations in long-term real bond rates have historically been quite dramatic.

As for the dividend growth g, it has in fact been higher than its historical average lately. The geometric and arithmetic averages were 1.5% and 2.4%, respectively, for 1871–1994, but 3.9% and 4.0%, respectively, for 1995–1998.[5] An alternative to considering the recent past is to look at

5. The Gordon growth model assumes that g is nonstochastic and thus does not recommend whether to use geometric or arithmetic means. The numbers for real earnings

Figure 2 I/B/E/S TWO-YEAR-AHEAD EARNINGS GROWTH FORECASTS, 1982–1999

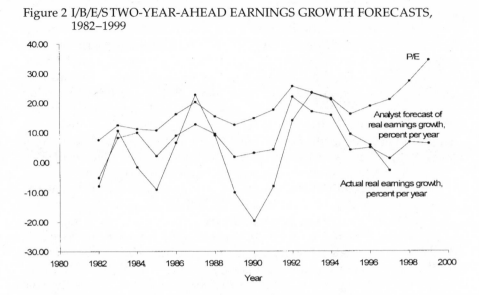

forecasts from market participants. It is well known that analyst earnings forecasts tend to be upward biased. Therefore it is useful to consider earnings forecasts for which historical data are available and focus on whether forecasts are higher than usual. Figure 2 shows I/B/E/S forecasts for two-year-ahead S&P 500 earnings growth for 1982–1999 as well as the subsequent realization and the P/E ratio at the time of the forecast. Forecasts for long-run growth were only available for a smaller number of analysts. The forecasts shown are *top-down* forecasts. This means that the analysts were asked for a single forecast for the index rather than forecasts for each of the companies which make up the index. The latest *bottom-up* forecasts for S&P 500 earnings growth are much higher than the top-down forecasts, but I do not have a time series to determine if they are higher than their previous values. The average number of analysts reporting per year is 10. The minimum number is 4. The forecasts plotted are the means across analysts. For each year the values are for the first month after the previous annual earnings realization is known, usually March. Thus the forecast value for 1999 shows the expected percentage increase in year 2000 earnings over 1998 earnings, right after 1998 earnings became known. The 1999 forecasts are from March. The analysts provide nominal earnings forecasts but no inflation forecasts. To convert the forecasts to real terms, I used the annual inflation rate over the previous five-year period.

---

growth are as follows. Geometric means: 1.9% for 1871–1994, 4.0% for 1995–1998. Arithmetic means: 5.0% for 1871–1994, 4.1% for 1995–1998.

Several points are worth noticing. First, analyst earnings growth fore-casts are quite good. The R^2 from a regression of the realized earnings growth rates on the forecasts is 0.59 for the real-earnings growth rates and 0.52 for the nominal-earnings growth rates. Second, until 1995 the correlation between the P/E ratio and the two-year-ahead real-earnings growth forecast is surprisingly high, 0.87. But third, this correlation breaks down after 1995. Earnings growth forecasts have stayed essen-tially constant while the P/E ratio has increased sharply. Thus, if the expectations of the analysts asked by I/B/E/S are representative of current market expectations, it looks like the stock market boom since 1995 ei-ther is driven by a sudden decrease in required returns or is a bubble.

In sum, the required change in $r - g$ to explain an increase in the adjusted P/D from 28 historically to 48 recently is around 0.75 percentage points. Dividend growth and (geometric) earnings growth has been higher since 1995 and thus might warrant an increase in the expected dividend growth rate. However, at least according to one source, market participants have not increased their dividend growth expectations. If, therefore, a change in the required real stock return is left as the sole factor explaining the increase in valuation ratios, the necessary change is around 0.75 percentage points. For given long-term real bond rates the necessary change in the equity premium is of the same size. If we believe long-term real bond rates will be higher in the future, the required de-crease in the equity premium is correspondingly larger.[6]

5. Conclusion

Heaton and Lucas address an important but difficult question: What caused the recent stock-market boom? They focus on changes in stock-market participation and diversification. Having worked on limited stock-market participation, I found the analysis of the related issue of diversification very interesting. The references given by the authors and the numbers in Table 1 above indicate that poor diversification is in fact a pervasive phenomenon which should be considered seriously in general equilibrium asset pricing models. Understanding why many households concentrate large amounts of wealth in own-company stock seems cru-cial in this respect.

More work is needed to determine exactly how large the effects on

---

6. The latest P/D ratio of 78.5 is higher than the value 48 used by Heaton and Lucas, suggesting that larger changes in $r - g$ are needed. This depends on how the P/D ratio is adjusted. Campbell and Shiller (1998) refer to studies suggesting adjustments to D/P of 80 basis points for 1996 and 1997. This would make the latest adjusted P/D equal to 48.2, close to the value 48 used in Heaton and Lucas's calibration.

equilibrium returns of poor diversification are. In the calibration of the OLG model in the present paper, a concern is whether the amount of idiosyncratic dividend and bankruptcy risk is consistent with the data. More analysis regarding sensitivity of the results to changes in risk aversion and the extent of poor diversification would also be useful. From an empirical perspective any explanation of the current boom which relies on changes in either participation or diversification will have difficulties with timing. The upward trend in both participation and diversification started long before the current boom, suggesting that valuation ratios should have reached historical highs much earlier. However, valuation ratios have historically fluctuated substantially, making it difficult to discern gradual trends. Aside from patiently awaiting more data for the United States, it would be interesting to consider evidence from other countries.

REFERENCES

Blanchard, O. J. (1993). Movements in the equity premium. *Brookings Papers on Economic Activity* 1993(2):75–118, 137–138.

Blume, M. E., and I. Friend. (1978). *The Changing Role of the Individual Investor: A Twentieth Century Fund Report.* New York: Wiley.

Blume, M. E., J. Crockett, and I. Friend. (1974). Stock ownership in the United States: Characteristics and trends. *Survey of Current Business* 54(11):16–40.

Bogle, J. C. (1991). Investing in the 1990s. *Journal of Portfolio Management,* 17(3):5–14.

Campbell, J. Y., and R. J. Shiller. (1998). Valuation rates and the long-run stock market outlook. *Journal of Portfolio Management,* 24(2):11–26.

Poterba, J. M., and A. A. Samwick. (1995). Stock ownership patterns, stock market fluctuations, and consumption. *Brookings Papers on Economic Activity* 1995(2):295–357, 368–372.

Rea, J. D., and B. K. Reid. (1998). Trends in the ownership cost of equity mutual funds. *Investment Company Institute Perspective* 4(3).

Vissing-Jørgensen, A. (1998). Limited stock market participation. Department of Economics, MIT. Ph.D. Thesis.

Comment

JOHN Y. CAMPBELL
Harvard University

1. Introduction

The dramatic bull market of the late 1990s has challenged economists to explain why stock prices are so high relative to historical valuation levels. John Heaton and Deborah Lucas begin their interesting paper by reviewing some facts and then using theory to interpret them; I shall organize my discussion in a similar fashion.

2. How High Is the Stock Market?

Popular commentary often uses the Dow Jones Industrial Average index (around 11,000 as I write) or the Standard and Poor 500 index (around 1,300) to track the level of stock prices. Of course, index levels can increase because of general price inflation, or growth in the real economy, or changes in the size of the publicly traded corporate sector relative to the economy, or changes in the size of index-included firms relative to other publicly traded firms. Intelligent analysis of stock index levels must begin by scaling them in some way.

Recognizing this point, Heaton and Lucas discuss price–dividend and price–earnings ratios for the S&P 500 index. Both ratios are high relative to historic norms, but the price–dividend ratio is far more extreme; it is almost two-thirds higher than its previous peak in the early 1970s, whereas the price–earnings ratio is close to levels reached earlier in this decade and in several previous decades.

Heaton and Lucas focus on the price–earnings ratio (scaled by the historical average payout ratio of dividends to earnings) rather than the price–dividend ratio. They claim that "earnings are likely to be a more stable proxy for long-run payments to shareholders" (Section 3.1) and that "in the short run dividends can vary due to temporary changes in payout policy (for instance, in response to changes in the tax law). Therefore, it is common to focus on the price–earnings ratio, adjusted for reinvestment rates, to approximate long-run price–dividend ratios" (footnote 5).

It is certainly true that changes in corporate financial policy can affect the price–dividend ratio. Most notably, a shift from paying dividends to repurchasing shares can permanently increase the price–dividend ratio. The Gordon growth model, discussed in the paper, says that the price–dividend ratio is the reciprocal of the difference between the discount rate and the growth rate of dividends per share. A share repurchase program causes the number of outstanding shares to shrink over time; this increases the growth rate of dividends per share and increases the price–dividend ratio. Share repurchases account for some of the increase in the price–dividend ratio over the last decade, although direct estimates of the effect are fairly modest. Cole, Helwege, and Laster (1996), for example, suggest that net repurchases have increased the growth rate of dividends per share by about 0.8%. Their calculation assumes that shares are issued and repurchased at the market price; to the extent that shares are issued at below-market prices as part of executive compensation, then the true repurchase effect is smaller.

Despite these difficulties with the price–dividend ratios, I do not agree that the price–earnings ratio is a superior measure of stock-market valuation. The problem is that earnings are subject to short-term noise arising from the business cycle. One can see the importance of this by inspecting Figure 1 in the paper. Previous peaks of the price–earnings ratio, close to levels today, were reached in the early 1990s, the mid-1930s, the early 1920s, and the 1890s. None of these were peaks in stock prices; instead, they were recession years when corporate earnings temporarily declined.

The issue of noise in current earnings has been recognized at least since the work of Graham and Dodd (1934), who in their famous textbook *Security Analysis* recommended that analysts should use an average of earnings over "not less than five years, preferably seven or ten years" (p. 452). Campbell and Shiller (1998) follow Graham and Dodd's advice and smooth earnings over ten years. They find that the ratio of price to smoothed earnings behaves more like the price–dividend ratio than like the conventional price–earnings ratio. It is currently far above its previous peak reached in 1929.

Heaton and Lucas use the Gordon growth model, adjusting the current price–earnings ratio for the long-run average payout ratio of dividends to earnings, to characterize combinations of earnings growth rates and discount rates that could rationalize the current level of stock prices. They conclude that real earnings growth of 2.4% (1% above the historical average) and a real discount rate of 6.6% (4.1% below the historical average) could do the job. In the rest of the paper, they use alternative theoretical models to try to hit this target.

The problem with this analysis is that the cyclical noise in earnings should lead earnings growth forecasts to be adjusted downwards at cyclical peaks when earnings are temporarily high, and upwards at cyclical troughs when earnings are temporarily low. Rapid earnings growth from a starting point in 1999, after many years of robust economic growth, is less likely than Heaton and Lucas admit.[1] Heaton and Lucas could correct for this problem by using the price–smoothed-earnings ratio instead of the conventional price–earnings ratio.

---

1. One factor that can produce higher long-run earnings growth is a reduction in the payout ratio. As Heaton and Lucas point out, the earnings growth rate should be the fraction of earnings that is retained (one minus the payout ratio) times the return on equity. If the payout ratio falls, earnings growth should be expected to increase. Unfortunately this effect also increases Heaton and Lucas's adjusted price–earnings ratio, so it does not make it easier to account for the level of stock prices.

Even though rapid earnings growth following a period of strong economic performance would be historically unusual, some commentators do appear to believe that it will occur. Interesting evidence on this point is provided by Steven Sharpe (1999). Sharpe studies the consensus forecasts of stock analysts, and finds that since 1994 forecasts of two-year nominal earnings growth have been high and stable (between 10% and 15%), even though realized two-year earnings growth has been declining. He also finds that forecasts of long-term (five-year) nominal earnings growth have increased from 10.5% in 1989 to over 13% in 1998. Over the same period forecasts of long-term (ten-year) inflation have decreased from 4.5% to 2.5%, implying a remarkable increase of 4.5 percentage points in the expected long-run growth rate of real earnings.

Of course, analysts' earnings forecasts are hard to interpret. It may be that they reflect a rational assessment of the prospects for a "new era" of corporate profitability in the twenty-first century. It may be, as Sharpe suggests, that analysts have failed to adjust their nominal earnings forecasts for the effects of declining inflation and thus are subject to a form of money illusion first proposed by Modigliani and Cohn (1979). Finally, a cynic might say that Wall Street analysts do not have incentives to produce the most accurate earnings forecasts, but rather to produce forecasts that justify the current level of stock prices.

3. Modeling Declining Discount Rates

While reasonable people can disagree about the prospects for future earnings growth, it is almost impossible to rationalize the current level of stock prices without some decline in the discount rate applied to investors to future earnings. Heaton and Lucas devote most of their paper to an exploration of alternative mechanisms that could produce such a decline. They rightly concentrate on effects that could reduce the equity premium (the expected excess return on equities over short-term debt), since real interest rates have not historically moved closely with the stock market.

Heaton and Lucas first consider an increase in the stock-market participation rate. Intuitively, if aggregate equity risk is now shared more broadly, then the amount of risk borne by any single investor has declined, justifying a decline in the equity premium. In thinking about this effect, it is important to keep in mind that investors should be weighted by their wealth. The right measure of the participation rate is not the fraction of individuals who invest in stocks, but the fraction of wealth controlled by individuals who invest in stocks. As Heaton and Lucas admit, wealthy individuals have always tended to participate in the stock market, so there is little evidence for a dramatic increase in the wealth-weighted participation rate.

Heaton and Lucas take the participation rate as exogenous, determined by unmodeled forces such as transaction and information-processing costs. They build a fairly realistic, but correspondingly complicated, model to explore the effects of the participation rate on the equity premium. Unfortunately they find it very hard to generate a large equity premium when the participation rate is above 30% or so. The reason for this is hard to see in their model, but Gollier (1999) suggests a simpler framework that can be used to gain insight.

Gollier assumes a static atemporal market in which a claim to random output $\tilde{y}$ is traded for a riskless claim. The price of the output claim is P. Agents have utility u over final wealth and choose the portfolio share of the output claim, α, to maximize

$$V(\alpha) = E[u(P + \alpha(\tilde{y} - P))]. \tag{1}$$

The first-order condition is

$$E[(\tilde{y} - P)u'(P + \alpha(\tilde{y} - P))] = 0. \tag{2}$$

Equilibrium requires that the total supply of the output claim (normalized to one) be held. When all agents participate in the financial market, this requires $\alpha = 1$, or

$$E[(\tilde{y} - P)u'(\tilde{y})] = 0. \tag{3}$$

If only a fraction k of wealth is controlled by agents who can hold equity, however, then for these agents equilibrium requires $\alpha = 1/k$, so we get

$$E\left[(\tilde{y} - P)u'\left(\frac{\tilde{y}}{k} + \left(\frac{k-1}{k}\right)P\right)\right] = 0. \tag{4}$$

Gollier calibrates these equations to data on real per capita output in the United States over the period 1963–1992. Consistent with the results of Heaton and Lucas, he finds little effect of the participation rate k on the expected return of the output claim for RRA = 2 and $k > 0.3$.

To understand the source of this result, I now take a second-order Taylor approximation of marginal utility around the mean of output, $\bar{y}$:

$$u'(\tilde{y}) \approx u'(\bar{y}) + u''(\bar{y})(\tilde{y} - \bar{y}) + \tfrac{1}{2}u'''(\bar{y})(\tilde{y} - \bar{y})^2. \tag{5}$$

Substituting into (3), assuming that $\bar{y}$ has a symmetric distribution, and assuming constant relative risk aversion γ, I find that with full equity participation ($k = 1$), the expected return on equity is

$$\frac{\bar{y}}{P} - 1 = \frac{1}{1 - \gamma\sigma^2[1 + \gamma(\gamma + 1)\sigma^2/2]} - 1 \approx \gamma\sigma^2, \tag{6}$$

where $\sigma^2 \equiv \mathrm{Var}(\bar{y})\bar{y}^2$ is the proportional volatility of output, and the second approximation is accurate for small σ^2. This can be understood by recalling the well-known rule of thumb that the optimal portfolio share in a risky asset is the expected excess risky return, divided by relative risk aversion times the variance of the excess risky return.[2] To achieve an optimal portfolio share of one, the expected excess risky return must equal relative risk aversion times the variance.

Similar analysis of the case with limited participation ($k < 1$) shows that in general,

$$\frac{\bar{y}}{P} - 1 \approx \frac{\gamma\sigma^2}{k}. \tag{7}$$

Limited participation by investors who control a fraction k of wealth is equivalent to scaling up the variance of dividends by a factor $1/k$. Once again, this can be understood by using the rule of thumb for optimal risky investment. To achieve an optimal risky portfolio share of $1/k$, the expected excess risky return must be $1/k$ times larger than it would be if the optimal risky portfolio share were only one.

Equation (7) has two important implications. First, a change in equity participation has a larger effect on the equity premium if the participation rate is initially low than if it is already high. A doubling of participation from 5% to 10% cuts the equity premium in half in just the same way as a doubling from 50% to 100%; and the absolute change in the equity premium is much larger in the former case. This explains why both Gollier, and Heaton and Lucas in their more elaborate model, find little participation effect for k larger than about $\frac{1}{3}$. Second, limited equity participation has a larger effect on the equity premium if relative risk aversion and dividend volatility are high than if they are low. Limited participation can amplify a high equity premium caused by high dividend volatility or high risk aversion, but an unrealistically small k is

2. This rule of thumb is exact in a continuous-time model in which the risky asset's price follows a geometric Brownian motion (Merton, 1969). Friend and Blume (1975) used this approach to estimate risk aversion.

required to produce a high equity premium in the absence of these conditions.[3]

Given their finding that increases in participation from medium to high levels have little effect on the equity premium, Heaton and Lucas emphasize an alternative story. They argue that the typical investor used to hold a poorly diversified portfolio containing only a few stocks. With the growth of mutual funds and especially index funds over the last few decades, however, the typical investor is now better diversified. Diversification makes equities a more appealing investment by reducing the risk associated with any given average return. Heaton and Lucas show that a simultaneous increase in participation and reduction in equity risk can account for a large decrease in the equity premium. In terms of equation (7), Heaton and Lucas simultaneously reduce σ^2 (by a factor of 4) and increase k (by a factor of 2) to get a much more powerful effect on the equity premium than can be achieved by a change in k alone.

Heaton and Lucas also argue that an undiversified portfolio is likely to have a negatively skewed return because any single firm can go bankrupt. They find that negative skewness further increases the equity premium. To understand this effect within the simple framework presented above, one can drop the assumption that $\tilde{y}$ has a symmetric distribution. This adds a term $-\gamma(\gamma + 1)SK/2k^2$, where SK is the proportional skewness of $\tilde{y}$, to the equity premium in equation (7). Negative skewness increases the equity premium, and this effect is more powerful when stock-market participation is limited.

Although many investors are undoubtedly better diversified today, I doubt that this is the cause of a major decline in the equilibrium equity premium. The problem is that diversification, like equity participation, should be measured on a wealth-weighted basis. Most stocks have always been held by wealthy investors who are more likely to diversify their holdings. Even if the typical *portfolio* has been undiversified, the typical *share of stock* is likely to have been held in a diversified portfolio. Increased diversification by small investors need not have a large effect on equilibrium asset prices.

Furthermore, diversification can only have had a large impact on the equity premium if the gains from increased diversification were historically large, certainly much larger than the direct costs of increasing the number of stocks held in a typical portfolio. Thus the diversification story creates a new puzzle—why were investors historically reluctant to hold diversified portfolios?—and this seems little easier to resolve than

3. In a similar spirit, Campbell (1999) uses the results of Constantinides and Duffie (1996) to argue that heterogeneous risk in labor income cannot have a large effect on the equity premium unless risk aversion is high.

the original equity-premium puzzle—why were investors historically reluctant to hold equities?

Both the effects that Heaton and Lucas emphasize—increased participation and diversification—are long-run trends that may help to explain why valuation ratios are higher now than they were in the early postwar period, but do not specifically explain the runup in prices during the late 1990s. An important clue, ignored by Heaton and Lucas, is the fact that this runup has occurred during a period of robust economic growth. This is also characteristic of bull markets in previous decades such as the 1920s and the 1960s.

Campbell and Cochrane (1999) present a model of stock-market behavior in which valuation ratios are driven entirely by cyclical variation in consumption. Increases in consumption drive up risky-asset prices relative to dividends, not by increasing expected future dividend growth (which is constant by assumption), nor by decreasing real interest rates (which are also constant in the model), but by increasing the risk tolerance of investors. Investors' preferences are assumed to display *habit formation:* they have power utility whose argument is not the absolute level of consumption, but the level of consumption relative to a subsistence level, which is a nonlinear moving average of current and past consumption. When consumption is close to the subsistence level, only a small fraction of consumption is available as a surplus to generate utility, and even small shocks to consumption can have a large effect on this surplus. In such circumstances, investors become extremely risk-averse. As consumption increases relative to the subsistence level, however, their risk aversion declines and the equity premium is driven down.

The use of habit formation to generate time variation in the equity premium is appealing because there are other reasons to think that people judge their well-being by relative rather than absolute consumption. For example, it is common to compare a recession period unfavorably with a much earlier period of strong growth, even if the absolute level of consumption is higher in the recession than in the earlier boom. Habit formation explains this by the fact that surplus consumption, which generates utility, may be lower in the recession.

One objection to Campbell and Cochrane's model is that it requires high risk aversion to explain the historical average value of the equity premium. Barberis, Huang, and Santos (1999) have recently proposed a variant of the model in which investors are "loss-averse" (Kahneman and Tversky, 1979). Investors derive utility from the level of wealth relative to a reference point, which adjusts only gradually in response to changes in wealth. Furthermore, there is a kink in preferences at the reference point: the absolute value of marginal utility is higher for losses than for gains. In periods of weak economic growth, investors' wealth is close to the reference point and the kink in the preferences at that point makes them extremely risk averse. In cyclical expansions, however, wealth increases far above the reference point and risk aversion declines. The Barberis–Huang–Santos model uses loss aversion to generate high aversion to wealth risk even with moderate aversion to consumption risk.

Both these models have an additional advantage relative to the framework used by Heaton and Lucas. Because risk aversion varies in these models, risky asset prices more relative to dividends and so the volatility of stock returns can be much higher than the volatility of dividend growth. This is a feature of the data that is not easily matched by models with constant risk aversion. Heaton and Lucas do not report the volatility of stock returns in their constant-risk-aversion model, but it is probably close to the underlying volatility of dividend growth. Even though Heaton and Lucas calibrate their model with greater dividend volatility than has historically been observed, the model probably understates the volatility of stock returns, and this makes it harder to generate a large equity premium.

In my view cyclical factors of the sort emphasized by Campbell and Cochrane and by Barberis, Huang, and Santos are at least as important for stock prices as the secular changes in participation and diversification emphasized by Heaton and Lucas. But in the end, it is important to recognize that the recent runup in stock prices is so extreme relative to fundamental determinants such as corporate earnings, stock-market participation, and macroeconomic performance that it will be very hard to explain using a model fit to earlier historical data. The relation between stock prices and fundamentals appears to have changed, and it may be a long time before a definitive interpretation of this change is possible. In the meantime investors should keep in mind that a return to historical valuation ratios would imply extremely large negative returns, while a continuation of current ratios would imply mediocre returns unless there is a historically unprecedented acceleration of corporate earnings growth.

REFERENCES

Barberis, N., M. Huang, and T. Santos. (1999). Prospect theory and asset prices. Cambridge, MA: National Bureau of Economic Research. NBER Working Paper 7220.
Campbell, J. Y. (1999). Asset prices, consumption, and the business cycle. Forthcoming in *Handbook of Macroeconomics*, J. B. Taylor and M. Woodford (eds.). Amsterdam: North-Holland.
———, and J. H. Cochrane. (1999). By force of habit: A consumption-based explanation of aggregate stock market behavior. *Journal of Political Economy* 107:205–251.

————, and R. J. Shiller. (1998). Valuation ratios and the long-run stock market outlook. *Journal of Portfolio Management*, Winter, pp. 11–26.

Cole, K., J. Helwege, and D. Laster. (1996). Stock market valuation indicators: Is this time different? *Financial Analysts Journal*, May/June, pp. 56–64.

Constantinides, G., and D. Duffie. (1996). Asset pricing with heterogeneous consumers. *Journal of Political Economy* 104:219–240.

Friend, I., and M. E. Blume (1975). The demand for risky assets, *American Economic Review*, 65:900–922.

Gollier, C. (1999). *The Economics of Risk and Time.* Forthcoming. Cambridge, MA: MIT Press.

Graham, B., and D. L. Dodd. (1934). *Security Analysis*, 1st ed. New York: McGraw-Hill.

Kahneman, D., and A. Tversky (1979). Prospect theory: An analysis of decisions under risk, *Econometrica*, 47:313–327.

Merton, R. (1969). Lifetime portfolio selection under uncertainty: The continuous-time case. *Review of Economics and Statistics* 51:247–257.

Modigliani, F., and R. A. Cohn. (1979). Inflation, rational valuation, and the market. *Financial Analysts Journal*, March–April, pp. 24–44.

Sharpe, S. (1999). Stock prices, expected returns, and inflation. Board of Governors of the Federal Reserve System. FEDS Paper 99–02.

Discussion

In replying to the discussants, both authors agreed that increasing participation rates alone could not explain the current level of stock prices. John Heaton emphasized that much of the effect of increasing participation occurs as the economy moves from low to moderate participation, but we are now moving from moderate to high participation. Deborah Lucas expressed skepticism that adding capital accumulation to the model would change this result. As an alternative explanation, which is more fully developed in the published version of the paper, she noted that stock investors are now holding more diversified portfolios, which increases their aggregate risk-bearing capacity.

Mark Gertler asked whether there might be some benefit to studying stock prices at a more disaggregated level. For example, there is a great deal of variation among stocks in price–earnings ratios, with internet stocks like Amazon.com at the upper extreme. John Campbell remarked that explaining the pricing of "growth" stocks raises interesting issues: One hypothesis is that such stocks are priced high because optimistic investors with upward-biased earnings expectations are more likely to hold them. Another story is that, as the discount rate falls for whatever reason, growth stocks experience large effects because of the long average duration of their expected earnings streams.

Martin Feldstein argued that it is important to incorporate tax considerations. Because of their tax treatment, share buybacks are a much more efficient way to pay out to individual shareholders. To the extent that buybacks are becoming a more important share of payouts, net-of-tax returns have increased.

Martin Eichenbaum asked whether participation is defined to include holding stocks in a retirement account. Heaton responded that the contribution data reflect holdings of defined-contribution retirement accounts, and that the increase in such accounts may explain part of the measured rise in participation. Jonathan Parker noted that some people who are technically participants in the market at earlier times held only one or two stocks, whereas today they might hold one or two well-diversified mutual funds. This would support the idea that average diversification rather than participation per se is what is important. As another example of how financial innovation can reduce required yields, Michael Mussa mentioned the "liquification" of the below-investment-grade bond market by Michael Milken.

The identity of the "the marginal stockholder" was the subject of some discussion. Julio Rotemberg suggested that the marginal stockholder might be very rich and not very risk-averse. Heaton remarked that the characteristics of stockholders' noninvestment income are important, particularly the correlation of this other income with the market. For example, if the marginal stockholder is a wage earner rather than the owner of a business, the reduction in the required risk premium may be greater, all else equal.

Fernando Alvarez and Marcelo Veracierto
UNIVERSITY OF CHICAGO, UNIVERSIDAD T. DI TELLA, AND NBER; AND
FEDERAL RESERVE BANK OF CHICAGO

Labor-Market Policies in an Equilibrium Search Model

1. Introduction

Labor markets perform quite differently across countries. An often cited example is the sharp contrast in unemployment rates between Europe and the United States. There are large and persistent differences in labor-market policies as well.[1] The goal of this paper is to explore to what extent differences in labor market policies can generate differences in labor-market performance. In particular, the paper builds a general equilibrium model to evaluate the aggregate effects and welfare consequences of a variety of labor-market policies and institutions, mainly minimum wages, firing restrictions, unemployment insurance, and unions. The model embodies a McCall search model in a general-equilibrium production economy by modifying Lucas and Prescott's (1974) island model to incorporate undirected search and out-of-the-labor-force participation.

Production takes place in a large number of separate locations called islands, which use labor as an input of production in a decreasing-returns-to-scale technology. In each island there are a fixed number of firms which share a common productivity shock. Productivity shocks follow a Markov process, and are identically and independently distrib-

We thank Jeff Campbell, Larry Jones, Alan Krueger, Robert Lucas, Giuseppe Moscarini, Julio Rotemberg, Nancy Stokey, and Edward Prescott for their comments, as well as seminar participants at Carnegie-Mellon, Duke, Northwestern, ITAM, Federal Reserve Bank of Chicago, University of Chicago, and the 1999 NBER Macro Annual Conference. We also thank Enric Fernandez for excellent research assistance. The views expressed here do not necessarily reflect the position of the Federal Reserve Bank of Chicago or the Federal Reserve System.
1. This has been documented in a number of OECD Jobs Studies and surveyed and analyzed by Nickell (1997), among others.

uted across islands. At the beginning of a period, there is a given distribution of agents across islands. After shocks are realized, agents decide whether to leave their islands and become nonemployed, or stay and work. Nonemployed agents must decide whether to search or engage in home production. If an agent searches, he is randomly assigned to an island the following period. In this sense search is undirected.

Labor markets are competitive within each island: firms and workers take the process for spot wages as given. We also assume that firms and workers have access to a complete set of state-contingent securities indexed by the shocks to each island. Given this market structure, workers and firms maximize the expected discounted value of their earnings. The model abstracts from any insurance role of labor-market policies. In Alvarez and Veracierto (1998) we analyzed unemployment insurance and severance payments in a model with incomplete markets and found that the insurance role of these policies was quantitatively very small.[2] Their welfare implications were dominated by their effects on productivity, search decisions, and firm dynamics. Those findings motivate our current assumption of complete markets; it considerably simplifies the analysis, allowing us to analyze a richer set of policies while still capturing most of the effects of these policies.

The model is general equilibrium in the sense that: (1) wages are consistent with market clearing in each island, (2) the cross-sectional distribution of employment and wages is endogenous, (3) the endogenous distribution of wages across islands is consistent with the incentives to search, and (4) aggregate employment is consistent with the number of workers that search and the aggregate labor supply.

The model is closely related to two strands in the literature. First, it incorporates important elements of industry equilibrium models where the job creation and destruction process is determined by changes in the labor demand of firms. Examples of these models include Bertola and Caballero (1994), Bentolila and Bertola (1990), Hopenhayn and Rogerson (1993), Campbell and Fisher (1996), and Veracierto (1995). Second, it incorporates features of standard search models where the job creation and destruction process is determined by the accept–reject decisions of workers. Examples of these models include McCall (1970), Mortensen (1986), Wolpin (1987), and Lundqvist and Sargent (1998).

Industry equilibrium models (e.g., Hopenhayn and Rogerson (1993)) have typically abstracted from unemployment decisions, focusing on the employment–nonemployment decision. Most equilibrium models of unemployment that have been used for policy analysis (e.g.,

---

2. Also see Costain (1997), Hansen and Imrohoroglu (1992), and Valdivia (1996).

Millard and Mortensen (1997)) have abstracted from the employment–nonemployment decision and studied production units that consist of single workers. The model in this paper incorporates all three margins: (1) the employment decision of firms, which allows to study firms dynamics; (2) home vs. market production decisions, which allows us to analyze labor-force participation; and (3) the search decisions of workers, which allows us to study unemployment.[3] In fact, the labor-market policies that we analyze will have important consequences for all of these margins.

We start by considering a laissez-faire regime. Since this is an economy where the laissez-faire equilibrium is efficient (despite the search frictions), we use it as a benchmark when comparing the effects of different policies. We show how to modify the basic environment to introduce minimum wages, unions, firing taxes, and unemployment benefits. In all cases, we consider stationary equilibria only. We select parameter values by matching model moments with selected U.S. statistics under a stylized version of U.S. policies.

Minimum wages are introduced as in textbook analyses: if equilibrium wages in a given island are lower than the minimum wage, jobs must be rationed in some way until wages equal the minimum wage. We experiment with different ways of rationing the supply of workers. For instance, we allow for a distinction between "insiders" and "outsiders." We find that the aggregate effects of minimum wages are extremely small in all the cases.

We introduce unions, by assuming that the workers in a certain fraction of the islands sector are unionized. As in textbook analyses, unions restrict employment in order to increase total wage earnings. As a consequence, unionized islands generate higher unemployment rates than competitive islands. We consider two models of unions, with quite different implications. In one version, a union is consistituted by the coalition of all workers present in the island at a given period of time. The workers collude to extract rents from the fixed factor, sharing the benefits equally among themselves. In the other version, the union is dominated by a "union boss" who appropriates all the rents from the fixed factor, and pays workers their opportunity cost. We find that in the coalition model of unions, higher degrees of unionization increase the unemployment rate and decrease welfare levels substantially. This is due to the incentives to search for a unionized island in order to appropriate rents.

---

3. On the other hand, our model abstracts from entry and exit and from any search done by firms, two margins that have been analyzed in previous studies.

The rationing of employment in unionized islands contributes to larger flows into unemployment as well.

Following Bentolila and Bertola (1990) and Hopenhayn and Rogerson (1993), we introduce firing restrictions as a tax on employment reductions. This tax makes the firms' employment decisions dynamic, since increasing current employment exposes firms to future firing costs. Firms react to the firing taxes by firing and hiring workers less often, leading to higher unemployment duration and lower unemployment incidence. Under our parametrization, the decrease in unemployment incidence dominates the increase in unemployment duration. As a consequence, firing taxes reduce the unemployment rate in the economy. Similarly to previous studies, we find that firing taxes equivalent to one year of wages have large negative welfare effects. However, firing taxes of similar magnitudes to the severance payments observed in OECD countries produce relatively small negative effects.

Finally, we model unemployment insurance (UI) benefits as payments that accrue to workers after a job separation. In our model, unemployment benefits have similar effects to firing subsidies.[4] In particular, agents choose to stay out of the labor force and not search as long as they are eligible for UI benefits. We find that UI benefits have large effects on unemployment rates, since they increase both the duration and the incidence of unemployment. For instance, doubling the present value of UI benefits (from U.S. values) increases unemployment rates by about 1%.

Our quantitative analysis indicates that the responses of the unemployment rate and employment to changes in UI benefits, degree of unionization, minimum wages, and firing taxes are broadly consistent with estimates in the empirical literature (Nickell, 1977, for example). This provides some confidence about the structure of our model economy and the welfare results obtained.

The paper is organized as follows. Section 2 describes the economy. Section 3 describes the laissez-faire equilibrium. Section 4 introduces different policies/institutions into the basic model. Section 5 explains our choice of parameter values. Section 6 describes the effects of the different policies in the calibrated economy. Finally, Section 7 compares these effects with estimates provided by the empirical literature.

2. The Economy

The economy is populated by a measure one of ex ante identical agents with preferences given by

---

4. In fact, they are completely equivalent when the UI benefits are small.

$$E \sum_{t=0}^{\infty} \beta^t \left(\frac{c_t^{1-\gamma} - 1}{1 - \gamma} + h_t \right),$$

where c_t is consumption of market goods, h_t is consumption of home goods, $\gamma \geq 0$, and $0 < \beta < 1$.

The market good is produced in a continuum of islands. Each island has a production technology given by

$$y_t = F(g_t, z_t) \equiv z_t g_t^{\alpha},$$

where y_t is output, g_t is the labor input, z_t is an idiosyncratic productivity shock, and $0 < \alpha < 1$. The productivity shock z_t evolves according to the following AR(1) process:

$$\ln z_{t+1} = a + \rho \ln z_t + \epsilon_{t+1},$$

where $\epsilon_{t+1} \sim N(0, \sigma^2)$ and $0 < \rho < 1$. Realization of z_t are assumed to be independent across islands. Throughout the paper we will refer to Q as the corresponding transaction function for z_t, and to $f(g_t, z_t) = \partial F(g_t, z_t)/\partial g_t$ as the marginal productivity of labor.

Home goods are produced in a nonmarket activity which requires labor as an input of production. If an agent spends a period of time at home, he obtains w^h units of the home good. Home and market activities are mutually exclusive: agents cannot engage in both at the same time.

At the beginning of every period there is a given distribution of agents across islands. An island cannot employ more than the total number of agents x_t present in the island at the beginning of the period. If an agent stays in the island in which he is currently located, he produces market goods and starts the following period in that same location. Otherwise, the agent leaves the island and becomes nonemployed.

A nonemployed agent has two alternatives. First, he can leave the labor force and engage in home production during the current period. In this case, the following period the agent will remain nonemployed. The second alternative is to search. If the agent searches, he obtains zero home production during the current period, but becomes randomly assigned to an island at the beginning of the following period. A key feature of the search technology is that agents have no control over which island they will be assigned to, i.e., search is undirected. In particular, we assume that searchers arrive uniformly across all islands in the economy.

Hereafter, we refer to agents doing home production as being *out of the labor force*, agents working in the islands sector as *employed*, and agents searching as *unemployed*.

We now describe feasibility for stationary allocations.[5] An island is indexed by its current productivity shock z and the total number of x agents available at the beginning of the period. Feasibility requires that the island's employment level, denoted by $g(x,z)$, cannot exceed the number of agents initially available:

$$g(x,z) \leq x.$$

The number of agents in the island at the beginning of the following period, denoted by x', is given by

$$x' = U + g(x,z),$$

where U is total unemployment in the economy. Note that this equation uses the fact that unemployed agents become uniformly distributed across all islands in the economy.

The law of motion for x and the Markov process for z generate an invariant distribution μ which satisfies

$$\mu(X',Z') = \int_{\{(x,z)\,:\,g(x,z)\,+\,U\,\epsilon\,X'\}} Q(z,Z')\mu(dx \times dz)$$

for all X' and Z'. This equation states that the total number of islands with a number of agents in the set X' and a productivity shock in the set Z' is given by the sum of all islands that transit from their current shocks to a shock in Z' and chose an employment level such that x' is in X'.

Aggregate employment N is then given by

$$N = \int g(x,z)\mu(dx \times dz),$$

and aggregate consumption by

$$c = \int F(g(x,z),z)\mu(dx \times dz).$$

Both expressions are obtained by adding the corresponding magnitudes across all islands in the economy.

5. Since our analysis will focus on steady-state equilibria, we restrict our discussion of feasibility to stationary allocations.

Finally, the number of agents that stay out of the labor force cannot be negative:

$$1 - U - N \geq 0.$$

3. Laissez-Faire Competitive Equilibrium

In this section we describe a competitive equilibrium with complete markets. For expository purposes, we first discuss the case where the market good and the home good are perfect substitutes, i.e., where $\gamma = 0$. The case $\gamma > 0$ will be discussed at the end of the section. When both goods are perfect substitutes, agents seek to maximize the expected discounted value of their wage earnings and home production. We assume competitive spot labor markets in every island. As a consequence wages are given by the marginal productivity of labor, f.

Let consider the decision problem of an agent who begins a period in an island of type (x,z) and must decide whether to stay or leave, taking the employment level of the island $g(x,z)$ and the aggregate unemployment level as given. If the agent decides to stay, he earns the competitive wage rate $f(g(x,z),z)$ and begins the following period in the same island. If the agent decides to leave, he becomes nonemployed and obtains a value of θ (to be determined below). His problem is then described by the following Bellman equation:

$$v(x,z) = \max \left\{ \theta, f(g(x,z),z) + \beta \int v(g(x,z) + U,z')Q(z,dz') \right\}, \tag{1}$$

where $v(x,z)$ is the expected value of beginning a period in an island of type (x,z).

At equilibrium, the employment rule $g(x,z)$ must be consistent with individual decisions. In particular,

1. if $v(x,z) > \theta$ (agents are strictly better off staying than leaving), then

$$g(x,z) = x; \tag{2}$$

2. if $v(x,z) = \theta$ (agents are indifferent between staying or leaving), then

$$g(x,z) = \bar{g}(z), \tag{3}$$

where $\bar{g}(z)$ satisfies

$$\theta = f(\bar{g}(z),z) + \beta \int v(\bar{g}(z) + U,z')Q(z,dz'). \tag{4}$$

Figure 1 EMPLOYMENT DETERMINATION, LAISSEZ-FAIRE

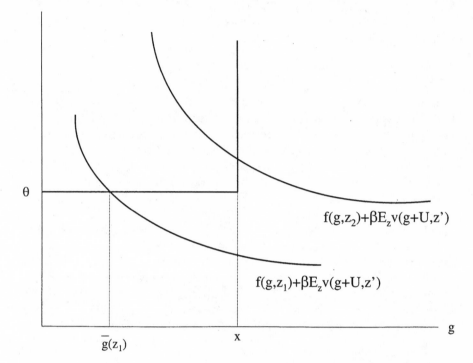

θ

$f(g,z_2)+\beta E_z v(g+U,z')$

$f(g,z_1)+\beta E_z v(g+U,z')$

$\bar{g}(z_1)$

x

g

Figure 1 illustrates the labor market within an island. Between 0 and x, the labor supply is infinitely elastic at θ, since at that value agents are indifferent between staying and leaving. For values larger than θ all agents prefer to stay, so the labor supply becomes inelastic at x. For values lower than θ all agents prefer to leave, so the labor supply becomes inelastic at zero.

The downward-sloping curve is the marginal value of a worker at the island, which can be interpreted as a demand function for labor. If the intersection of both curves occurs at the left of x, the equilibrium employment level is $\bar{g}(z)$. Otherwise, the equilibrium employment level is x.

Figures 2 and 3 depict the equilibrium values $v(x,z)$ and equilibrium employment $g(x,z)$ that correspond to Figure 1. If x is larger than $\bar{g}(z)$, the equilibrium employment is $\bar{g}(z)$ and the equilibrium value is θ. If x is smaller than $\bar{g}(z)$, the equilibrium employment is x and the equilibrium value is the marginal value of labor evaluated at x.

Let us now consider the problem of a nonemployed agent who must decide whether to go home and obtain home production or search for a

Figure 2 VALUE FUNCTION, LAISSEZ-FAIRE

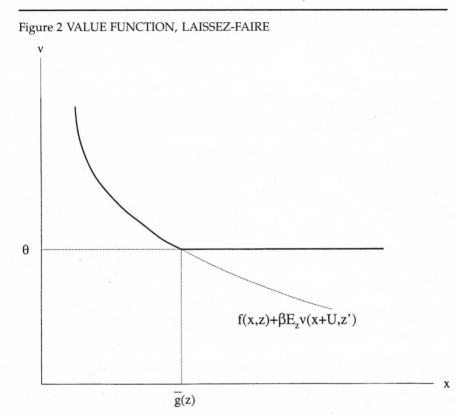

job. If the agent chooses to stay out of the labor force, he obtains w^h of home goods during the current period but remains nonemployed the following period. If the agent decides to search, he obtains no home production during the current period but gets a new draw at the beginning of the following period from the invariant distribution μ of islands. Thus the problem of a nonemployed agent is described by the following equation:

$$\theta = \max \left\{ w^h + \beta\theta, \beta \int v(x,z)\mu(dx \times dz) \right\}. \tag{5}$$

If $w^h + \beta\theta < \beta\int v(x,z)\mu(dx \times dz)$ (nonemployed agents strictly prefer searching to staying at home) no one stays at home and the employment feasibility becomes

$$U + \int g(x,z)\mu(dx \times dz) = 1. \tag{6}$$

Figure 3 EMPLOYMENT POLICY, LAISSEZ-FAIRE

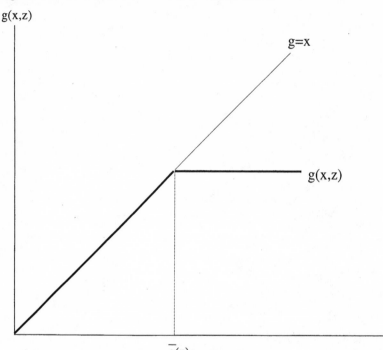

g(x,z)

$g=x$

$g(x,z)$

$\overline{g}(z)$

x

If $w^h + \beta\theta = \beta\int v(x,z)\mu(dx \times dz)$ (nonemployed agents are indifferent between searching and staying at home) some agents may stay out of the labor force and employment feasibility becomes

$$U + \int g(x,z)\mu(dx \times dz) \leq 1. \tag{7}$$

The inequality $w^h + \beta\theta > \beta\int v(x,z)\mu(dx \times dz)$ implies that $U = 0$, which is inconsistent with an equilibrium (see Alvarez and Veracierto, 1999). It follows that

$$\theta = \beta \int v(x,z)\mu(dx \times dz). \tag{8}$$

In Alvarez and Veracierto (1999) we show that despite the search frictions, this is an economy where the welfare theorems hold: laissez-faire competitive allocations coincide with the stationary solutions to a Pareto problem. We also establish the existence and uniqueness of stationary competitive equilibria. Moreover, our proof provides an efficient algorithm to compute the unique steady-state equilibrium.

When $\gamma > 0$ market goods and home goods are imperfect substitutes, which is the preference specification used by Hopenhayn and Rogerson (1993) to analyze the employment and welfare effects of firing taxes. Following them, we assume that agents have access to employment lotteries and financial markets where they can diversify the income risk associated with search and employment histories.[6] The employment lotteries are not realistic. Nevertheless, we think that the tractability that they bring to the problem more than compensates for their lack of realism.

The case of $\gamma > 0$ requires only minor modifications to the equilibrium conditions presented above. If θ is interpreted as the present value of search in terms of market goods, equation (8) is satisfied by definition and the functional equation (1) still describes optimal behavior by agents and firms within the islands sector. The only equilibrium condition that must by modified is the one that determines the optimal mix of agents between market and home activities. The new relevant condition is

$$\frac{w^h}{1 - \beta} \leq c^{-\gamma}\theta.$$

The left-hand side of this equation gives the present-value gain of increasing by one unit the number of agents in the home sector. The right-hand side represents the present-value loss of decreasing by one unit the number of agents that search: it is the present value of forgone wages in terms of consumption goods, θ, times the marginal utility of consuption, $c^{-\gamma}$. At equilibrium, both sides must be equal if there is a positive number of agents at home. If the right-hand side is larger than the left-hand side, no one must be at home in equilibrium.

In Alvarez and Veracierto (1999) we show that the equilibrium unemployment rate is independent of the value of γ. Instead γ determines the elasticity of the labor supply, with $\gamma = 0$ corresponding to an infinitely elastic labor supply and a large γ corresponding to a low elasticity.

In the description that follows of the equilibrium conditions for the different policies we focus on the case where $\gamma = 0$ to simplify the exposition. The case where $\gamma > 0$ would require modifications to the optimal nonemployment decisions analogous to the ones just described.

---

6. Prescott and Rios-Rull (1992) show how to use classical competitive equilibrium analysis to study a similar economy by using lotteries.

4. Labor-Market Policies

In this section we introduce a variety of labor-market policies and institutions into our model economy. In particular, we consider minimum wages, unions, firing taxes, and unemployment insurance.

4.1 MINIMUM WAGES

The first labor-market policy we consider is minimum-wage legislation. If equilibrium wages in an island are lower than the mandated minimum wage $\underline{\omega}$, employment must be rationed. In this case, a lottery determines who becomes employed. The losers of the lottery are forced to leave the island and become nonemployed.[7] Throughout the section we denote by $\tilde{x}(z)$ the maximum employment level consistent with $\underline{\omega}$ and z, i.e.,

$$\underline{\omega} = f(\tilde{x}(z),z).$$

Let's consider the problem of an agent that begins a period in an island of type (x,z). If $g(x,z) < \tilde{x}(z)$, the minimum wage does not bind in the island and the problem of the agent is similar to laissez-faire:

$$v(x,z) = \max\left\{ \theta, f(g(x,z),z) + \beta \int v(g(x,z) + U,z')Q(z,dz') \right\}.$$

But if $g(x,z) = \tilde{x}(z)$, the minimum wage binds and an employment lottery takes place. Since the lottery treats all agents the same way, the probability that the agent wins is given by $\tilde{x}(z)/x$. In that case he receives the minimum wage $\underline{\omega}$ during the current period and begins the following period in the same island. His expected value is then given by[8]

$$v(x,z) = \frac{\tilde{x}(z)}{x}\left(f(\tilde{x}(z),z) + \beta \int v(\tilde{x}(z) + U,z')Q(z,dz') \right) + \frac{x - \tilde{x}(z)}{x}\,\theta.$$

Figure 4 illustrates the labor market when the minimum wage binds. At the equilibrium employment level, wages are lower than the minimum wage. Hence, the labor supply must be rationed down to $\tilde{x}(z)$ workers.

The decision problem of nonemployed agents as well as the rest of the equilibrium conditions are the same as under laissez-faire.

---

7. In actual computations we allow the losers of the lotteries to stay in the islands if they so desire. But (except for extreme cases) we found that they always preferred to leave rather than to stay without working. As a consequence, here we describe the more restrictive but simpler case where agents are forced to leave. In Alvarez and Veracierto (1999) we discuss the more general case.
8. In Alvarez and Veracierto (1999) we show that $f(\tilde{x}(z),z) + \beta \int v(\tilde{x}(z) + U,z')Q(z,dz') > \theta$: agents always prefer going through the employment lottery to leaving directly.

Figure 4 EMPLOYMENT DETERMINATION, MINIMUM WAGES

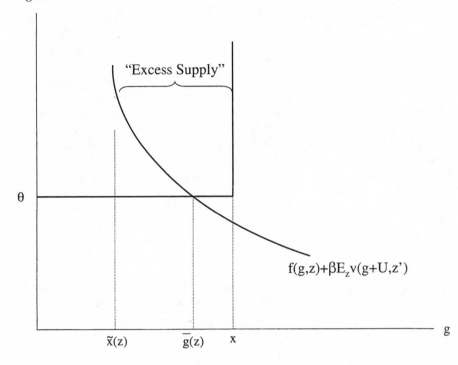

4.1.1. Insider–Outsider Model of Minimum Wages   We explore a variation on the previous case in order to capture the distinction between insiders and outsiders. In this case we assume that when the minimum wage is binding, the rationing scheme gives priority to the previously employed agents. More specifically, the agents that worked in the island last period (the *insiders,* of whom there are $x - U$) are given priority over the ones that searched last period and just arrived (the *outsiders,* of whom there are U). We assume that if rationing must take place, one of the following two cases applies: either (1) all insiders stay employed and the remaining $\tilde{x}(z) - x - U$ positions are rationed among the U outsiders, or (2) the available $\tilde{x}(z)$ positions are rationed among the $x - U$ insiders, and none of the U outsiders are employed.

The analysis of minimum wages for this case is similar to the previous one, but it requires some additional notation to consider the different problems of outsiders and insiders. The details of the analysis can be found in Alvarez and Veracierto (1999).

4.2 UNIONS

We assume that a fraction λ of the islands are unionized. In these islands a union determines the total labor supply, taking the wages of the rest of the economy as given. Once the union decides how many agents are permitted to work in the island, there is a competitive market in which workers are paid their marginal productivity. Agents that are restricted from entering this competitive labor market leave the island and become nonemployed. We explore two extreme assumptions on the distribution of the rents generated by the union. In the first case, which we label the *coalition model*, we assume that rents are shared equally among all current union members. In the second case, which we label the *union-boss model*, we assume that they are entirely captured by one individual.

We use a simple story to illustrate the two models. Consider an economy made out a large number of piers, where cargo must be unloaded from ships, and where the number of ships arriving at each pier is random. Workers are distributed across piers and take one period to move between them. There is a gate in each pier, on the other side of which ship managers hire workers in a competitive spot market. The two model of unions differ on the assumption about the control over the gate. In the coalition model the gate is controlled by all the workers present in the pier at the beginning of the period. In the union-boss model the gate is controlled by a union boss.

4.2.1 The Coalition Model   We denote the total expected discounted earnings of the coalition in an island of type (x,z) by $u(x,z)$. Since we assume that the monopoly rents of the coalition are shared equally among all workers in the island, each agent receives a value $u(x,z)/x$. The union maximizes the expected discounted value of earnings of its current members. Hence, u satisfies

$$u(x,z) = \max_{0 \le g \le x} \left\{ f(g,z)g + \theta[x - g] + \beta \int \frac{g}{g + U} u(g + U,z')Q(z,dz') \right\}, \quad (9)$$

where g is the number of agents that the union allows to work—i.e. those allowed to cross the gate. The present discounted value of total earnings of the agents that leave the island equals $\theta[x - g]$. On the other hand, the total current wage earnings of the agents that become employed equal $f(g,z)g$. Each of these agents receive a value $u(g + U,z')/(g + U)$ starting the following period, since they will form a coalition with the U new agents that will arrive to the island. The total expected discounted value of the g members that are allowed to stay is given by last term in equation (9).

The Bellman equation in (9) has a nonstandard structure due to the endogenous discount factor $\beta g /(g + U)$. However, in Alvarez and Veracierto (1999) we show that a unique value function u satisfies this Bellman equation, that it is concave and differentiable, and that its optimal employment policy is described by a threshold rule of the same form as in the competitive islands.

Competitive islands behave exactly the same as under laissez-faire. The employment decision rule of unionized islands generates an invariant distribution μ^u, while the employment decision rule of competitive islands generates an invariant distribution μ. The decision problem of nonemployed agents is then given by

$$\theta = \max\left\{ w^h + \beta\theta, \right.$$

$$\left. \beta\lambda \int \frac{u(x,z)}{x} \mu^u(dx \times dz) + \beta(1 - \lambda) \int v(x,z)\mu(dx \times dz)\right\}.$$

Note that agents that search have no control over whether they will arrive at a unionized island or not. As in the previous cases, if the right-hand side of this expression is larger than the left-hand side, no one stays out of the labor force.

4.2.2 The Union-Boss Model In a unionized island a union boss acts as a monopolist with respect to the competitive firms and as a monopsonist with respect to the workers. The union boss maximizes his own expected discounted revenue net of payments to workers, so he solves

$$V(x,z) = \max_{0 \leq g \leq x}\left\{ f(g,z)g - g\theta(1 - \beta) + \beta \int V(g + U,z')Q(z,dz') \right\}, \qquad (10)$$

where g is the number of workers that he allows to work. Letting θ denote the equilibrium nonemployment value for a worker, note that a worker is indifferent between working at the wage $\theta(1 - \beta)$ and leaving the island. The union boss can then charge an access fee to workers, so that after paying this fee they receive only $\theta(1 - \beta)$. In Alvarez and Veracierto (1999) we show that the optimal employment policy is described by a threshold rule similar to that which characterizes employment in competitive islands.

Letting μ^u and μ be the invariant distribution corresponding to unionized and competitive islands, optimality of search decisions requires that

$$\theta = \max \{w^h + \beta\theta, (1 - \lambda)\beta \int v(x,z)\mu(dx \times dz) + \lambda\beta\theta\},$$

where we use the fact that the value for a worker of arriving at an unionized island is θ.

4.3 FIRING TAXES

In this subsection we consider a competitive equilibrium with firing taxes: whenever a firm reduces employment below its previous-period level, the firm must pay a tax τ per unit reduction in employment. The proceeds are rebated as lump-sum transfers.

Because of the firing cost τ, the firms' maximization problem now becomes dynamic. The individual state of a firm is given by (x,n,z), where n is its previous-period employment level. The firms's problem is described by the following Bellman equation:

$$R(x,n,z) = \max_{0 \le g \le x} \left\{ F(g,z) - w(x,z)g - \tau \max \{n - g, 0\} \right.$$
$$\left. + \beta \int R(G(x,z) + U,g,z')Q(z,dz') \right\}, \tag{11}$$

where g is current employment, $F(g,z)$ is output, and $\tau \max\{n - g, 0\}$ are the firing taxes. The firm behaves competitively, taking the equilibrium employment level $G(x,z)$ of the island, the equilibrium wage rate $w(x,z)$, and the number U of agents that search as given. We denote the optimal employment decision rule for this problem by $g(x,n,z)$.

Note that at equilibrium, the islands' employment rule must be generated by the individual decisions of firms. In particular,

$$g(x, x - U, z) = G(x,z) \qquad \text{for all } x,z,$$

where $x - U$ is the previous-period employment level of the island.

The problem of a worker in an island of type (x,z) is given by the following Bellman equation:

$$H(x,z) = \max \left\{ w(x,z) + \beta \int H(G(x,z) + U,z')Q(z,dz'), \theta \right\}, \tag{12}$$

where θ is the value of nonemployment. The worker chooses to leave the island whenever the expected discounted value of wages in the island is less than the value of nonemployment. Similarly to firms, workers behave competitively, taking the island's employment level $G(x,z)$, the equilibrium wage rate $w(x,z)$, and the number U of agents that search as given.

Figure 5 illustrates the behavior of an island's labor market under firing taxes. The supply curve is similar to that under laissez-faire: it is infinitely elastic at θ, and becomes inelastic at x for values larger than θ. On the contrary, the demand for labor is substantially different. In par-

Figure 5 EMPLOYMENT DETERMINATION, FIRING TAXES (FIRMS PAY TAX)

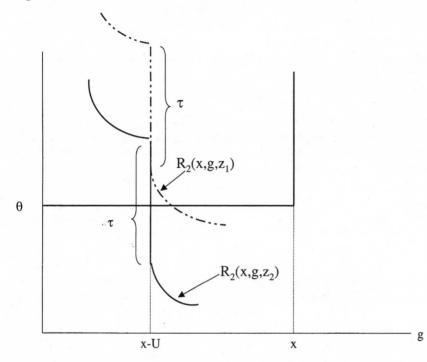

ticular, the firing tax introduces a wedge between the marginal value of hiring and the marginal value of firing a worker. This translates into a jump of size τ at the previous-period employment level n, which in equilibrium equals $x - U$. Note that only large enough shocks induce firms to hire or fire workers. For intermediate shocks, firms will leave their labor force unchanged.

The decision problem of nonemployed agents and the rest of the equilibrium conditions are the same as under laissez-faire, so we omit them. Note that equilibrium wages $w(x,z)$ are not equal to marginal productivities $f(g(x,z),z)$. Instead, wages have to be lower than marginal productivities, effectively making workers prepay the firing taxes.

In Alvarez and Veracierto (1999) we show that a competitive equilibrium with firing taxes coincides with the stationary solution to a constrained Pareto problem, where the planner treats the employment separation costs as technological. This is an important result. It establishes that the spot labor contracts considered above are sufficient to exploit all mutually beneficial trades, even in the presence of search frictions and firing taxes. We also show that the equilibrium described above coincides (except for equilibrium wages) with a competitive equilibrium where the firing taxes are paid directly by the workers. The advantage of this alternative decentralization is that it is much simpler to analyze, since it requires only a small variation on the arguments used in the laissez-faire case.

4.4 UNEMPLOYMENT INSURANCE

In this subsection we introduce an unemployment insurance system in which the government plays unemployment benefits b to eligible agents, financing the system with lump-sum taxes. Nonemployed agents may or may not be eligible for benefits. Whenever an agent leaves an island where he was employed during the previous period, he becomes eligible for benefits with probability κ. Eligible agents lose their eligibility for the following period with probability ψ. Agents that lose their benefits cannot regain eligibility within the same spell of unemployment.[9]

Given the nature of the unemployment insurance system, we must keep track not only of whether nonemployed agents are out of the labor force or unemployed, but of whether they are eligible for benefits or not.

Let θ_0 be the expected value of being nonemployed without benefits, θ_1 the value of being nonemployed with benefits, U_0 the number of new arrivals (i.e., agents that searched during the previous period) who are not eligible for benefits during the current period, and U_1 the number of new arrivals who are eligible for benefits during the current period. Note that $U = U_0 + U_1$. Agents learn whether they are eligible for benefits or not at the beginning of the period.

The problem of an agent who was employed during the previous period in an island with current state (x,z) is described by the following Bellman equation:

$$v(x,z) = \max \left\{ \begin{array}{l} \kappa\theta_1 + (1 - \kappa)\theta_0, \\ f(g(x,z),z) + \beta \int v(g(x,z) + U,z')Q(z,dz') \end{array} \right\},$$

where $g(x,z)$ and U are taken as given by the agent.

The problem of an agent who searched the previous period, has UI eligiblity i, and arrives at an island with current state (x,z) is given by

$$u_i(x,z) = \max \left\{ \theta_i, f(g(x,z),z) + \beta \int v(g(x,z) + U,z')Q(z,dz') \right\},$$

where $i = 1$ if the agent is eligible for benefits, and $i = 0$ otherwise.

9. We model the eligibility and duration of the benefits as stochastic to reduce the dimension of the state in the agent's problem.

We now consider the nonemployment decisions of eligible and ineligible agents. If an agent not eligible for UI benefits decides to stay at home, he obtains home production w^h during the current period. The following period he will be nonemployed and ineligible for benefits, obtaining a value θ_0. If he decides to search, he will draw an island of type (x,z) under the invariant distribution, obtaining a value $u_0(x,z)$. His problem is then described by

$$\theta_0 = \max \left\{ w^h + \beta \theta_0, \beta \int u_0(x \times z)\mu(dx \times dz) \right\}.$$

If an agent eligible for UI benefits decides to go home, he obtains home production w^h during the current period. The following period he will become ineligible for benefits with probability $1 - \psi$ and will still be eligible for benefits with probability ψ, obtaining values θ_1 and θ_0 respectively. If the agent decides to search, he will draw an island type (x,z) under the invariant distribution, obtaining a value $u_0(x,z)$ with probability $1 - \psi$ and a value $u_1(x,z)$ with probability ψ, depending whether the agent loses his eligibility for UI benefits or not. His decision problem is then described by the following equation:

$$\theta_1 = b + \max \left\{ \begin{array}{l} w^h + \beta[\psi\theta_1 + (1 - \psi)\theta_0], \\ \beta \int [\psi u_1(x,z) + (1 - \psi)u_0(x,z)]\mu(dx \times dz) \end{array} \right\}.$$

Note that the agent receives UI benefits independently of whether he stays out of the labor force or searches.

We denote by $\phi_i \in [0,1]$ the fraction of nonemployed agents with eligiblity $i = 0, 1$ that decide to search. The equilibrium values of ϕ_i must be consistent with the optimal nonemployment decision described above. In particular,

$$w^h + \beta\theta_0 > \beta \int u_0(x,z)\mu(dx \times dz) \quad \Rightarrow \quad \phi_0 = 0,$$
$$w^h + \beta\theta_0 < \beta \int u_0(x,z)\mu(dx \times dz) \quad \Rightarrow \quad \phi_0 = 1,$$

and correspondingly for ϕ_1.

To describe aggregate consistency, it is useful to introduce the following notation. Let H_i be the number of nonemployed agents that stayed home during the previous period and have eligibility i during the current period, and let D_i be the total number of agents with eligibility i that leave the islands during the current period. Note that D_1 includes two types of agents: (1) agents who searched during the previous period, whose benefits have not expired during the current period, and who reject employment, and (2) all previously employed agents who decide to leave their islands and gain eligibility. In particular,[10]

$$D_1 = \int \min \{U_1, x - g(x,z)\} \, \mu(dx \times dz)$$
$$+ \kappa \int \max \{ \min \{ x - U_1 - U_0, x - U_1 - g(x,z)\}, 0\}.$$

On the other hand, D_0 consists of (1) all new arrivals without benefits who decide not to accept employment, and (2) all previously employed agents who leave and do not gain eligibility:

$$D_0 = \int \max\{U_0 - g(x,z), 0\} \, \mu(dx \times dz)$$
$$+ (1 - \kappa) \int \max\{\min\{x - U_1 - U_0, x - U_1 - g(x,z)\}, 0\}.$$

In steady state, U_0, U_1, H_0, and H_1 satisfy their laws of motion:

$$U_0 = \phi_0(D_0 + H_0) + (1 - \psi)\phi_1(D_1 + H_1),$$
$$U_1 = \psi\phi_1(D_1 + H_1),$$
$$H_0 = (1 - \phi_0)(D_0 + H_0) + (1 - \psi)(1 - \phi_1)(D_1 + H_1),$$
$$H_1 = \psi(1 - \phi_1)(D_1 + H_1).$$

The market-clearing condition is given by

$$U_0 + H_0 + U_1 + H_1 + \int g(x,z)\mu(dx \times dz) = 1.$$

4.4.1 UI Benefits, Firing Subsidies, Firing Taxes, and Severance Payments   We conclude this section with a brief analysis of the relationship between UI benefits, firing taxes, firing subsidies, and severance payments. Define p as the expected discounted payments that an agent is entitled to after a job separation, contingent on not becoming employed until the expiration of benefits, so that

$$p = \kappa \frac{b}{1 - \psi\beta}. \tag{13}$$

In Alvarez and Veracierto (1999) we show that nonemployed agents with benefits search ($\phi_1 > 0$) only if all nonemployed agents without benefits search ($\phi_0 = 1$). Moreover, we establish that for small values of p, equilib-

---

10. Since $\theta_1 > \theta_0$, the first agents to leave an island are those who have just arrived and are eligible for benefits, the second group to leave are those who were employed the previous period, and the last agents to leave are those who have just arrived and are not eligible for benefits.

ria with UI benefits have $\phi_1 = 0$ and $0 < \phi_0 < 1$. In words, agents that receive UI benefits do not seach, and agents that have no UI benefits are indifferent between searching and staying out of the labor force. It follows that the only feature that is important in the UI benefits system is the expected discounted value of payments (p), regardless of the particular combination of duration (ψ), benefits per period (b), and eligiblity (κ). Since agents eligible for benefits do not search, this results shows that in our model UI benefits are equivalent to a firing subsidy in the amount p.

The previous result has the following two important corrolaries about the combined effects of firing taxes and UI benefits, whose proofs can be found in Alvarez and Veracierto (1999). First, these policies can be summarized by a single number: the expected discounted value of UI benefits minus of the value of firing taxes. In particular, if $p' \equiv p - \tau > 0$, then the equilibrium is the same as with a firing subsidy of p'. Alternatively, if $p' < 0$ the equilibrium is the same as with a firing tax of size p'. Second, if we interpret severance payments as a tax on the firms proportional to the employment reductions and a simultaneous subsidy to each worker that leaves the firm, then one obtains that severance payments have no effect. This is a known result for competitive markets; see for example Lazear (1990). What is interesting is that it holds even in the presence of the search frictions.

5. Calibration

To explore the effects of the labor-market policies described above, we parametrize the economy in the following way. There are six structural parameters to determine: (1) the Cobb–Douglas parameter α, (2) the time discount factor β, (3) the home productivity w^h, (4) the curvature parameter in the utility function, γ, (4) the persistence of productivity shocks, ρ, and (5) the variance of the innovations, σ^2. Additionally we have to choose the model period. Parameter values are chosen to reproduce selected U.S. observations under a policy regime that resembles the U.S. unemployment insurance system. We select a model period of one and a half months as a compromise between computational costs and our interest in matching the short average duration of unemployment in the United States.

A characteristic of the U.S. system is that it is financed by experience-rated taxes. Experience-rated taxes work as firing taxes: they increase the tax liabilities of employers when workers are fired. Anderson and Meyer (1993) report that they are quite substantial in magnitude: for each dollar that the government pays as unemployment insurance, about 60 cents are paid by employers as experience-rated taxes. For this reason we want to consider a policy regime with both unemployment insurance and experience-rated taxes. We use the property of the model described in Section 4.4.1 to introduce both policies in a parsimonious way. We interpret the experience-rated UI tax as a firing tax and set the UI benefits in the model equal to the present value of the UI benefits net of this firing tax. In particular, we consider the "net" UI benefits to be 40% of the U.S. unemployment insurance benefits.

In a sample of agents that collected insurance benefits between 1978 and 1983, Meyer (1990) found an average replacement ratio of about 66%. Given Anderson and Meyer's estimate of experience-rated taxes and our previous discussion, we select a replacement ratio which is 60% of Meyer's, or 26%. Meyer (1990) also reported that the average duration of agents in his sample is 13 weeks. Since we are proceeding under the assumption that agents that collect benefits do not search, we identify the 13 weeks with the average duration of UI benefits. Given a model period of 6 weeks, this translates to a persistence of UI benefits, ψ, of about 0.50.

The probability κ that an agent becomes eligible for UI benefits at the start of an unemployment spell is chosen as follows. Let h be the escape rate from unemployment, and I the flow out of employment. Then in steady state

$$hU = I. \tag{14}$$

Let H_1 be the number of agents that stay out of the labor force collecting UI benefits. Note that

$$(1 - \psi)H_1 = \kappa I, \tag{15}$$

since the flow out of H_1 is given by the number of agents that lose their benefits, and the flow into H_1 is equal to a fraction κ of the flow out of employment. At steady state the two flows must be equal. Substituting (14) in (15), we obtain

$$\kappa = \frac{1 - \psi}{h} \frac{H_1}{U}.$$

Note that H_1/U is the ratio of the number of agents that receive UI benefits to the total number of agents that are unemployed. In OECD (1994, Table 8.4), we find that this ratio is about 0.35 for the U.S. economy. On the other hand, a 4-month average duration of unemployment in the U.S. suggests a value of $1/h$ equal to 2.66 model periods. The value of κ consistent with these magnitudes is 0.50.

The Cobb–Douglas parameter α was set to match a labor share of 0.64, which is the value implicit in the NIPA accounts. The discount factor β was selected so that its reciprocal reproduces an annual interest rate of 4%, a compromise between the return on equity and the return on bonds.

Given all the previous choices, the persistence of the productivity shocks (ρ) and the variance of its innovations (σ^2) were selected to generate an average duration of unemployment equal to 4 months and an unemployment rate of 6.2%. Note that there is no analytical relation between these parameters and the corresponding observations; we experimented until a good fit was obtained.

In Alvarez and Veracierto (1999) we show that the productivity of home production, w^h, affects only the labor-force participation ratio, leaving all other ratios unchanged. The productivity w^h was then selected to reproduce a labor force participation of 0.79, which is the ratio of labor force to working-age population in the United States (OECD, 1994, Table 8.4).

The curvature parameter γ in the utility function determines the degree of substitutability between home goods and market goods, but has no effect on steady-state observations (it only affects the value of w^h that is needed to reproduce a given labor-force participation). However, γ is an important determinant of the elasticity of labor supply. In particular, it can be shown that the elasticity of labor-force participation with respect to labor taxes is equal to

$$\epsilon = -\frac{1}{1 - \alpha - \alpha\gamma} \frac{\tau}{1 - \tau}, \tag{16}$$

where τ is the labor tax.

One way of selecting γ is then to use equation (16) to calibrate to some empirical estimate of the elasticity ϵ. The regression coefficients in Nickell (1997, Table 7) indicate that a cross-country elasticity ϵ equal to 0.18 is not unreasonable. Since the average labor tax in Nickell's sample is about 50%, our choice of α requires a value of γ equal to 8 to reproduce such an elasticity.

Another way of selecting γ is to use macro observations. One stylized fact that has been emphasized in the macroeconomic literature is that wages have increased substantially over long period of times, while total hour worked have displayed no trend. To reconcile this observation with the theory, preferences where income and substitution effects cancel

Table 1

Parameters		
α	Cobb–Douglas parameter	0.64
β	Time preference	0.9951
γ	Substitution between market and home goods	1
ρ	Persistence of z	0.98724
σ^2	Innovation variance of z	0.00838
w^h	Productivity at home	0.817

U.S. Observations	
Labor share	0.64
Interest rate	4% (annual)
Employment/population	0.79
Average duration of unemployment	4 months
Unemployment rate	6.2%

U.S. Policies	
Average duration of UI benefits collected	3 months
UI recipients/unemployed	35%
Replacement ratio	66%
Experience rating	60%

each other are needed. This requires a choice of $\gamma = 1$ under our preference specification. This parameter value is not only consistent with macro secular observations (and consequently common in the macroeconomic literature), but is what Hopenhayn and Rogerson (1993) have used to estimate the welfare costs of firing taxes. As a consequence we will treat it as our benchmark, but we will also report results under $\gamma = 0$ and $\gamma = 8$.

Table 1 reports selected parameter values under the benchmark case.[11]

6. Experiments

This section analyzes the effects of the labor-market policies and institutions introduced above for the parameters selected in the previous section. In each subsection we report how the corresponding policy affects laissez-faire, which serves as our benchmark case.

Tables 2 through 5 show the results. To illustrate the role of the elasticity of labor supply, the tables report results for different values of γ. The efects on the unemployment rate, the average duration of unemployment, and the rate of of incidence into unemployment are presented at the top of each table since they are independent of γ. The rest of each table shows results under $\gamma = 0$ (the case where home and

---

11. Parameter values under $\gamma = 0$ and $\gamma = 8$ are available upon request.

market goods are perfect substitutes), $\gamma = 1$ (our benchmark log utility case), $\gamma = 8$ (the case of low elasticity of labor supply). For each of these we report the following: (1) total unemployment (i.e. the total number U of agents that search in the model economy), (2) total employment, (3) total market output, and (4) total home output. Each of these numbers is normalized by its corresponding laissez-faire value. Additionally a welfare measure is provided. It is defined as the permanent increase in consumption that must be given to agents in the laissez-faire economy to attain the same utility level as under the policy considered.

6.1 MINIMUM WAGES

Table 2a describe the effects of minimum wages. The third column corresponds to laissez-faire, while the fourth and fifth columns correspond to minimum wages equivalent to 85% and 90% of average wages, respectively. In the first case only 5% of employed agents receive the minimum wage; in the second case the fraction is 27%.

We see in Table 2a that introducing a minimum wage into an otherwise laissez-faire economy increases the incidence of agents into unemployment. The reason is that employment must now be rationed in islands where the minimum wage becomes binding. For the same reason it becomes more difficult for unemployed agents to find employment. As a consequence the average duration of unemployment increases. Both effects tend to increase the unemployment rate relative to laissez-faire. However, we find that the effects are small: a minimum wage equal to 85% of average wages increases the unemployment rate only from 5.3% to 5.4%. Higher minimum wages can increase the unemployment rate further. But even a minimum wage which is large enough so that 27% of employed agents receive it increases the unemployment rate from 5.3% to only 6.6%, a small effect compared to other policies.

The minimum-wage regulation has the effect of increasing average wages. As a result, the number of agents that search for a job (U) increases until indifference between working at home and at the market is restored [i.e. until equality in equation (8) is obtained]. Table 2a shows that when home and market goods are perfect substitutes ($\gamma = 0$), a minimum wage equal to 90% of average wages increases the number of agents unemployed (U) by 24.7%. However, employment falls by 1.9% because the increase in the unemployment rate is large relative to the increase in the number of agents unemployed. The fall in employment dominates the increase in unemployment, and labor-force participation decreases. This leads to an increase in home output of 1.8% and a decrease in market output of 0.5%.

At the other extreme, when $\gamma = 8$, the effects are quite different. The

Table 2   MINIMUM WAGES AS PERCENTAGE OF AVERAGE WAGES

| | | | Value | |
| | | | Minimum Wage | |
γ	Quantity	Laissez-Faire	85%	90%
(a) No Priority				
	Unemployment rate	5.3	5.4	6.6
	Avg. duration of unemployment	2.4	2.4	2.8
	Incidence of unemployment	2.3	2.3	2.6
0.0	Employment	100.0	99.9	98.1
	Unemployment	100.0	102.1	124.7
	Market output	100.0	100.0	99.5
	Home output	100.0	100.1	101.8
	Change in welfare[a]	0.0	0.0	−0.2
1.0	Employment	100.0	99.9	98.6
	Unemployment	100.0	102.1	125.4
	Market output	100.0	100.0	99.8
	Home output	100.0	100.0	100.0
	Change in welfare[a]	0.0	0.0	−0.2
8.0	Employment	100.0	99.9	98.9
	Unemployment	100.0	102.3	126.0
	Market output	100.0	100.0	100.0
	Home output	100.0	100.0	99.0
	Change in welfare[a]	0.0	0.0	−0.1
(b) Priority				
	Unemployment rate	5.3	5.4	6.6
	Avg. duration of unemp.	2.4	2.4	2.8
	Incidence of unemp.	2.3	2.3	2.5
0.0	Employment	100.0	100.0	97.8
	Unemployment	100.0	102.3	124.8
	Market output	100.0	100.1	99.3
	Home output	100.0	99.8	102.5
	Change in welfare[a]	0.0	0.0	−0.2
1.0	Employment	100.0	99.9	98.5
	Unemployment	100.0	102.2	125.7
	Market output	100.0	100.0	99.7
	Home output	100.0	99.9	100.1
	Change in welfare[a]	0.0	0.0	−0.2
8.0	Employment	100.0	100.0	98.9
	Unemployment	100.0	101.4	125.6
	Market output	100.0	100.1	100.0
	Home output	100.0	99.7	98.9
	Change in welfare[a]	0.0	0.0	−0.2

[a]Percentage of consumption, with respect to laissez-faire.

fall in market output increases the marginal utility of market goods so much that agents respond by substituting away from home activities towards market activities. As a consequence, the labor-force participation increases and home production decreases. Employment still decreases, because the increase in labor-force participation is small compared to the increase in the unemployment rate. However, the fall in market output now becomes negligible.

The welfare effects of minimum wages are extremely small. Even for a minimum wage equal to 90% of average wages, the welfare cost is only about 0.2% in terms of consumption.

In Table 2b we compute the effects of minimum wages when the employment rationing scheme gives priority to insiders over outsiders. This feature could potentially increase the duration of unemployment, since outsiders—agents that search—are rationed more often. However, the results are virtually the same: we still find small effects of minimum wages.

6.2 UNIONS

Table 3a reports the effects of the coalition model of unions. Table 3b reports the effects of the union-boss model. In both cases we compare laissez faire with economies that have 20%, 40%, 60%, and 80% of their islands unionized.

We describe the coalition model of unions first. Recall that a union obtains monopolistic rents from the fixed factor by restricting the labor supply of its members. As a consequence, unionized islands have higher unemployment rates than competitive islands (for instance, with 20% of the labor force unionized, the unemployment rate is 4 percentage points smaller in the competitive sector than in the unionized sector). As the number of unionized islands increases, the aggregate unemployment rate of the economy increases due to a composition effect. Moreover, as the size of the unionized sector becomes larger, the average duration of unemployment and the incidence into unemployment in both sectors tend to increase. The reason is that agents demand better conditions to become and remain employed, since it is easier for them to find monopolistic rents somewhere else. As a consequence, a larger unionized sector unambiguously increases the aggregate unemployment rate in the economy. In fact Table 3a shows that the effects of unions are surprisingly large. When 60% of the islands become unionized, the unemployment rate increases from 5.3% to 12.5%.

Since unions extract rents from the fixed factor, average wages increase with the size of the union sector (since the opportunity cost of becoming employed in the competitive sector increases, wages increase in the competitive sector as well). When home and market goods are

Table 3

(a) Unions as Coalitions

γ	Quantity	Laissez-Faire	Value			
			Islands Unionized			
			20%	40%	60%	80%
	Unemployment rate	5.3	7.1	9.5	12.5	16.3
	Avg. duration of unemp.	2.4	3.0	3.6	4.5	5.5
	Incidence of unemp.	2.3	2.7	3.0	3.4	3.7
	Wage Premium[a] (%)		12.5	10.9	8.9	6.6
0.0	Employment	100.0	96.5	91.0	83.9	75.6
	Unemployment	100.0	132.8	171.7	215.9	264.5
	Market output	100.0	98.3	95.1	90.7	85.5
	Home output	100.0	105.2	114.9	128.4	144.7
	Change in welfare[b]	0.0	−0.7	−1.9	−3.4	−5.3
1.0	Employment	100.0	98.2	95.7	92.5	88.5
	Unemployment	100.0	135.2	180.6	238.0	309.3
	Market output	100.0	99.4	98.2	96.6	94.5
	Home output	100.0	99.6	99.4	99.5	99.6
	Change in welfare[b]	0.0	−0.7	−1.9	−3.5	−5.6
8.0	Employment	100.0	99.0	97.9	96.7	95.0
	Unemployment	100.0	136.4	184.8	248.8	332.2
	Market output	100.0	99.9	99.7	99.3	98.9
	Home output	100.0	96.5	90.9	82.9	72.5
	Change in welfare[b]	0.0	−0.7	−1.8	−3.2	−4.8
	Competitive islands:					
	Unemployment rate		6.6	8.0	9.6	11.3
	Avg. duration of unemp.		2.7	3.1	3.6	4.0
	Incidence of unemp.		2.6	2.8	3.0	3.2
	Unionized islands:					
	Unemployment rate		10.6	13.0	15.6	18.3
	Avg. duration of unemp.		3.8	4.4	5.1	5.8
	Incidence of unemp.		3.1	3.4	3.6	3.8

(b) Union-Boss Model

			Value			
			Islands Unionized			
γ	Quantity	Laissez-Faire	20%	40%	60%	80%
	Unemployment rate	5.3	4.8	4.2	3.5	2.4
	Avg. duration of unemployment	2.4	2.3	2.2	2.0	1.7
	Incidence of unemployment	2.3	2.2	2.1	1.9	1.5
0.0	Employment	100.0	92.2	82.9	71.0	53.3
	Unemployment	100.0	83.5	65.8	46.1	23.5
	Market output	100.0	94.4	87.6	78.6	64.1
	Home output	100.0	125.8	155.9	193.7	249.3
	Change in welfare[b]	0.0	−0.3	−1.0	−2.2	−5.2
1.0	Employment	100.0	97.6	94.6	90.4	83.1
	Unemployment	100.0	88.5	75.1	58.6	36.7
	Market output	100.0	97.9	95.3	91.7	85.2
	Home output	100.0	109.9	122.3	139.1	167.1
	Change in welfare[b]	0.0	−0.3	−0.7	−1.5	−3.7
8.0	Employment	100.0	100.2	100.5	101.0	101.9
	Unemployment	100.0	90.8	79.8	65.5	44.9
	Market output	100.0	99.6	99.1	98.4	97.1
	Home output	100.0	101.2	102.2	103.6	104.2
	Change in welfare[b]	0.0	−0.2	−0.5	−1.1	−2.4
	Competitive islands					
	Unemployment rate		4.6	4.8	2.9	1.7
	Avg. duration of unemployment		2.2	2.0	1.8	1.5
	Incidence of unemployment		2.2	2.0	1.7	1.2
	Unionized islands					
	Unemployment rate		6.0	5.1	4.0	2.6
	Avg. duration of unemployment		2.6	2.4	2.1	1.7
	Incidence of unemployment		2.4	2.2	2.0	1.6

[a](Average earnings per union member)/(average competitive wages).

perfect substitutes and 60% of the islands become unionized, the number of agents unemployed (U) must increase by 115.9% before agents again become indifferent between participating in market activities and working at home [i.e. before equality in equation (8) is restored]. However, the unemployment rate increases so much that employment falls by 16.1%. The fall in employment dominates the increase in the number of agents unemployed, leading to a decrease in labor-force participation and a consequent increase in home production of 28.4%. Market output falls by 9.3% because of the large fall in employment. Note that the effects of unions are qualitatively similar to those of minimum wages, since both regimes transfer rents from firms towards workers. However, the effects of unions are much larger, since minimum-wage legislation extracts rents only when the minimum wage becomes binding (i.e., only wages in the lower tail of the distribution are affected), while unions extract rents at all levels.

When $\gamma = 8$, the marginal utility of home goods increases so much when market output falls that agents substitute away from home activities to sustain the level of market output. In this case, the labor-force participation increases, and home output consequently falls by 17.1%. The increase in the labor force is not enough to outweigh the higher unemployment rate, and employment still falls by 3.3%. However, market output now decreases only by 0.7%.

We find that the welfare cost of unions is extremely large: when $\gamma = 1$ and 60% of the islands become unionized, the welfare loss is 3.5% in terms of consumption.

We now turn to the results under the union-boss model, as described in Table 3b. We see that the effects are very different from the coalition model: larger unionized sectors lead to lower unemployment rates. To understand this difference, notice that in this case it is the union boss who retains all monopolistic rents; workers in the union sector are paid only their opportunity cost. As a consequence, average wages fall as the size of the unionized sector increases. With lower average wages, both union bosses and competitive firms hire more workers, and unemployment rates decrease in each sector. Observe that the unemployment rate is always higher in the unionized sector than in the competitive sector, since union bosses restrict the labor supply. However, the composition effect doesn't dominate: unemployment rates fall so rapidly in each sector as the degree of unionization increases that the economy-wide unemployment rate decreases. In fact, as the fraction of islands unionized increases to 60%, the unemployment rate decreases from 5.3% to 3.5%.

When home goods and market goods are perfect substitutes ($\gamma = 0$), the fall in average wages is so large when 60% of the islands become unionized that the number of agents that search (U) must fall by 53.9% before agents again become indifferent between working at home and working in the market [i.e., before equality in equation (8) is restored]. The fall in unemployment is so large that employment decreases by 29%, despite the fall in the unemployment rate. The consequent reduction in labor-force participation leads to an increase of 93.7% in home output. In contrast, market output decreases by 21.4%.

When $\gamma = 8$, the fall in market output increases the marginal utility of market goods so much that agents substitute away from home activities to sustain the level of market output. Even though this effect is large enough to increase employment by 1%, it is not enough to increase labor-force participation: home output still increases, but only by 3.6%. As a counterpart, market output decreases by merely 1.6%.

Notice that even though unemployment rates are lower, the negative welfare effects of unions are quite large. For instance, with 60% of the labor force unionized the welfare cost of unions is equivalent to a 1.5% permanent reduction in consumption under $\gamma = 1$.

Since the two models of unions predict such different effects on unemployment rates, it is important to discuss what evidence favors one type of model over the other. Note that in the coalition model of unions, union members receive higher wages than workers in the competitive sector. The opposite is true in the union-boss model. Thus, an indirect test of the relative relevance of the two models would be provided by the sign of the union wage premium in the data. Card (1996) provides such evidence. Using panel data from the 1987 and 1988 Current Population Surveys, he reported that the union wage premium is about 15% in the U.S. economy. The sign of this premium favors the coalition model of unions over the union-boss model. However, the evidence in favor is stronger than this. In order to obtain a wage premium of the magnitude reported by Card, about 20% of the islands must be unionized (the generated wage premium is 12.5%). Under this degree of unionization we verify that 13% of the work force is employed in the unionized sector. This is surprisingly close to the empirical counterpart of 15.6% reported by Nickell (1997), providing additional confidence about the quantitative relevance of the coalition model of unions.

6.3 FIRING TAXES

Table 4 shows the effects of firing taxes that range between 3 months and 12 months of average wages. To understand these results, note that in the presence of firing taxes firms change their behavior in two important ways: (1) they become less willing to fire workers (as they try to avoid current taxes), and (2) they become less willing to hire workers (as they

Table 4 EFFECTS OF FIRING TAXES

			Value		
				Firing Tax[a]	
γ	Quantity	Laissez-Faire	3.0	6.0	12.0
	Unemployment rate	5.3	4.6	4.2	3.7
	Avg. duration of unemp.	2.4	3.7	4.2	5.1
	Incidence of unemp.	2.3	1.3	1.1	0.1
0.0	Employment	100.0	93.7	90.1	86.1
	Unemployment	100.0	81.0	71.5	60.0
	Market output	100.0	94.9	91.9	88.0
	Home output	100.0	121.6	133.7	147.3
	Change in welfare[b]	0.0	−0.6	−1.2	−2.3
1.0	Employment	100.0	98.7	98.1	97.9
	Unemployment	100.0	85.3	77.8	68.2
	Market output	100.0	98.1	97.0	95.5
	Home output	100.0	106.8	110.3	112.7
	Change in welfare[b]	0.0	−0.6	−1.2	−2.3
8.0	Employment	100.0	101.2	102.1	103.9
	Unemployment	100.0	87.4	80.9	72.3
	Market output	100.0	99.7	99.5	99.2
	Home output	100.0	98.5	96.6	91.8
	Change in welfare[b]	0.0	−0.6	−1.1	−2.1

[a]In months of average wages.
[b]Percentage of consumption, with respect to laissez-faire.

try to avoid future taxes). These effects tend to reduce the incidence of unemployment and increases the average duration of unemployment, respectively. Depending on which effect is larger, the unemployment rate can decrease or increase. Under our choice of parameter values we find that the effect on the firing rate dominates: the unemployment rate decreases from 5.3% to 3.7% with firing taxes equal to 12 months of wages.

The distortions in the firing and hiring process introduced by the firing taxes reduce the productivity in the islands sector quite substantially. As a consequence wages fall considerably. When home and market goods are perfect substitutes ($\gamma = 0$), this induces the number of agents that search for employment to decrease by 40% before agents become indifferent between searching and staying at home. The fall in the total number of agents unemployed is so dramatic that it drags employment down with it, despite the decrease in the unemployment rate. In particular, employment decreases by 13.9%. The consequent fall in labor-force participation increases home output by 47.3%. On the other hand, market output decreases by 12%, both because of the decrease in employment and because of the distortions introduced in the job reallocation process.

When $\gamma = 8$, the decrease in market output is so large that the marginal utility of market goods increases quite dramatically. This induces agents to substitute away from home activities towards market activities. As a consequence the total number of agents unemployed falls by only 16.7%. This is a small decrease compared to that in the unemployment rate, leading to an increase in employment of 3.9%. Labor-force participation increases so much that home output falls by 7.2%. In contrast, market output falls only by 0.8%.

It is interesting to compare our results with those obtained by Hopenhayn and Rogerson (1993), who calculated the costs of firing taxes in a frictionless economy without unemployment, where labor could freely reallocate across production units. Since they considered log preferences, we restrict our discussion to the case $\gamma = 1$.

Table 3 in Hopenhayn and Rogerson (1993) reports that a firing tax equivalent to one year of wages lowers output by 4.6%, decreases employment by 2.5%, and lowers welfare by 2.8% in terms of consumption in their model economy. Table 4 in this paper shows that the same policy produces a fall of 4.5% in output, a decrease in employment of 2.1%, and a welfare cost of 2.3% in our model economy. These results are surprisingly similar, and consequently they are robust to the search frictions introduced. However they are not robust to the preference parameter γ. As in Hopenhayn and Rogerson (1993), the effects of firing taxes on employment and output depend on the income and substitution effects on the labor supply. If the substitution effect dominates (as in the case $\gamma = 0$), employment decreases; if the income effect dominates (as in the case $\gamma = 8$), employment increases.

6.4 UNEMPLOYMENT INSURANCE

In Table 5 we analyze the effect of introducing unemployment compensations with different expected discounted value of benefits into the laissez-faire economy. We measure the generosity of the UI system by the present value of UI benefits p, given by $\kappa b/(1 - \beta\psi)$, where κ is the fraction of separations that qualified for UI benefits, b is the number of the benefits per period, ψ is the per-period probability of maintaining UI benefits, and β is the reciprocal of the gross interest rate. In Table 5 we

Table 5   EFFECTS OF UNEMPLOYMENT BENEFITS

			Value				
			Present Value of Unemployment Benefits[a]				
γ	Quantity	Laissez-Faire	0.28	0.50	0.75	1.00	1.25
	Unemployment rate	5.3	6.2	7.3	9.1	11.9	15.0
	Avg. duration of unemployment	2.4	2.7	2.9	3.4	4.1	5.0
	Incidence of unemployment	2.3	2.5	2.7	2.9	3.3	3.6
0.0	Employment	100.0	105.0	108.0	111.6	115.2	118.5
	Unemployment	100.0	125.5	153.3	201.9	279.4	377.8
	Market output	100.0	103.8	106.2	109.2	112.1	114.7
	Home output	100.0	81.2	68.0	49.5	26.5	0.7
	Change in welfare[b]	0.0	0.0	−0.3	−1.2	−3.0	−5.6
1.0	Employment	100.0	101.2	101.7	102.2	102.7	103.3
	Unemployment	100.0	120.9	144.3	184.9	249.2	329.2
	Market output	100.0	101.4	102.2	103.2	104.2	105.1
	Home output	100.0	92.4	86.5	77.2	63.7	47.2
	Change in welfare[b]	0.0	0.0	−0.3	−1.0	−2.5	−4.6
8.0	Employment	100.0	99.4	98.9	98.2	97.5	97.0
	Unemployment	100.0	118.8	140.3	177.6	236.4	309.0
	Market output	100.0	100.2	100.4	100.6	100.8	100.9
	Home output	100.0	98.7	96.4	91.6	82.5	70.2
	Change in welfare[b]	0.0	0.0	−0.2	−0.8	−2.1	−3.6

[a]In model periods of average wages.
[b]Percentage of consumption, with respect to laissez-faire.

calculate the equilibrium for different values of p, starting with the one that corresponds to our depiction of U.S. policies (see Section 5 above for the details). Recall that for the U.S. we select p to be 0.28 average model period of wages, where the model period equals one and a half months. The other values of p considered are 0.5, 0.75, 1.0, and 1.25 model periods of wages.

As the size of the UI benefits increases, workers are more willing to leave an island after a bad shock. This increases the rate of incidence into unemployment. On the other hand, there are two effects on the average duration of unemployment. First, agents tend to accept employment more easily, since they obtain eligiblity for UI benefits. This leads to a decrease in average duration. Second, since searching for a job becomes more attractive than staying at home without UI benefits, the number of agents that search (U) must increase until agents are once again indifferent between the two activities [i.e., equality in equation (8) is restored]. This leads to an increase in the average duration of unemployment. In Table 5 we observe that this general equilibrium effect dominates: larger UI benefits increase the average duration of unemployment. Since both the rate of incidence and the average duration of unemployment increase, the unemployment rate increases quite substantially. We see that a present value of UI benefits equivalent to one model period of wages increases the unemployment rate from 5.3% to 11.9%.

When market goods and home goods are perfect substitutes ($\gamma = 0$), the general-equilibrium effect described above is large: the total number of unemployed (U) increases by 179.4% on moving from laissez-faire to a present value of UI benefits equivalent to 1 model period of wages. This increase in the total number of unemployed is so important that employment increases by 15.2% despite the increase in the unemployment rate. This leads to such an increase in labor-force participation that home output falls by 73.5%. Market output increases by 12.1%.

Under $\gamma = 8$, the higher market output decreases the marginal utility of market goods, inducing agents to substitute away from market activities. As a consequence, the total number of unemployed (U) increases by a more moderate 136.4%, and employment falls by 2.5%. The lower labor-force participation dampens the fall in home output to only 17.5%. On the other hand, market output increases by merely 0.8%.

The welfare costs of introducing UI benefits are quite large: a present value of UI benefits equivalent to 1 model period of wages reduces welfare by 2.5% in terms of consumption under $\gamma = 1$.

7. A Comparison with the Empirical Evidence

We end the paper by contrasting our results with some of the empirical evidence available on the effect of different policies/regimes.

7.1 MINIMUM WAGES

While empirical studies for the U.S. economy have traditionally found that minimum wages affect teenage employment with an elasticity of about −0.1, the evidence has become more tenuous over time (see Card and Krueger, 1995). The evidence that minimum wages affect adult employment is even weaker, suggesting that minimum wages have little effect on the aggregate unemployment rate and employment level.

Card and Krueger (1995) observe that in the U.S. economy only 5% of workers are paid the minimum wage. Since in Table 2a the economy with a minimum wage equal to 80% of average wages generates a similar proportion of recipients, we identify it with the U.S.[12] Given the small differences between that economy and laissez-faire, we find our results to be broadly consistent with the empirical evidence.

While a large empirical literature has investigated the effects of minimum wages on income inequality, our model is not well suited to address those issues. The only heterogeneity that our model generates is due to time variation in wages: all agents face the same stochastic process for wages. As a consequence, the wage distribution that the model produces is more concentrated than the data (the standard deviation of wages in the benchmark U.S. case is only 13%). To analyze distributional issues we would have to incorporate different income groups, but that would complicate the model considerably and is outside the scope of this paper.

7.2. UNIONS

In Section 6.2 we argued in favor of the coalition model of unions over the union-boss model, due to its ability to generate jointly an empirically relevant union wage premium and degree of unionization. We now compare its predictions with some of the estimates found in the empirical literature.

Nickell (1997) reports that union densities vary widely across countries: from 9.8% in France and 11% in Spain, up to 72% in Finland and 82.5% in Sweden. Table 3a considered degrees of unionization on this range and found that the effect is to increase unemployment rates from 7.1% to 16.3%. We consider the magnitude of these effects to be consistent with empirical findings. In particular, the coefficients in Nickell's regressions indicate that the elasticity of the unemployment rate with respect to union density is about 0.48. The corresponding elasticity underlying Table 3a is 0.38, which is very close to Nickell's estimate.[13]

Nickell's regression coefficients also indicate an elasticity of employment relative to union density of about -0.05. Di Tella and MacCulloch

---

12. In order for 5% of workers to be subject to the minimum wage, the minimum wage has to be 80% of average wages in the model economy. In the U.S. the minimum wage is only 26% of average wages (see Card and Krueger, 1995). The reason for the difference is that the wage distribution is more concentrated in the model than in the data. See the comments in the next paragraph.

13. We calculated each of the elasticities of change relative to the economy with 20% of unionization, and then we averaged them.

(1999) provide a similar estimate. As has been previously discussed, the corresponding elasticity in the model economy depends on the substitutability between home and market goods given by the parameter γ. For $\gamma = 1$ the model elasticity is -0.03, which is also close to Nickell's estimate.

7.3 FIRING TAXES

Table 4 reported the effects of firing taxes between three months and one year of wages. We saw that firing taxes equal to one year of wages decreased the unemployment rate from 5.3% to 3.7% and decreased employment by 2.1% in the benchmark case ($\gamma = 1$). These are large effects. However, firing taxes equal to one year of wages are large compared to observed policies in OECD countries. Table 6 reports the sum of advance-notice and severance payments (adjusted for tenure) as multiples of average model-period wages. According to this measure, one year of firing taxes (equal to 8 model periods) is at the upper end of what is observed.[14]

Ths sign of the relation between unemployment rate and firing taxes in the model economy is consistent with Nickell's results: in his regression of unemployment rate he finds a negative coefficient on a measure of employment protection. On the other hand, Lazear (1990) reports a positive coefficient for severance payments. Neither of the two coefficients is statistically significantly different from zero. Di Tella and MacCulloch (1999) find a negative effect of labor-market flexibility on unemployment rate, controlling for random effects, but the result is not significant when they control for both country and year fixed effects.

Nickell (1997), Lazear (1990), and Di Tella and MacCulloch (1999) find that larger employment protection reduces aggregate employment. In our model economy, the sign of that relation depends on the degree of substitution between home and market goods. However, for the benchmark economy ($\gamma = 1$) we find a negative relation. Lazear (1990) reports that moving from laissez-faire to three months of severance payments reduces the employment–population ratio by about 1%. In our benchmark case of $\gamma = 1$ we find that three months of severance payments reduce the employment–population ratio from 73.6% to 72.7%, which is consistent with Lazear's estimate.

14. Moreover, as explained at the end of the next subsection, in the model economy severance payments can be undone perfectly. To the extent that in actual economies severance payments can be partially undone, the relevant measure of firing taxes will be lower than shown in Table 6. For instance, if severance payments could be undone perfectly, firing taxes would only include expected legal costs of litigation. For Germany, Italy, France, and the United Kingdom, Bentolila and Bertola (1990) report that these costs are well below one month of wages.

Table 6 GENEROSITY OF UI BENEFITS AND FIRING TAXES

Country	Maximum Duration of Benefits[a]	Benefit Recipients per Unemployed	Monthly Hazard out of Unemployment[b]	Replacement Ratio[c]	Present Value of Unemployment Benefits[d,e]	Estimated Severance Payments[d,f]	Present Value of "Net" UI Benefits[d]
Belgium	32.00	1.48	0.08	0.66	7.88	1.52	6.36
Canada	7.69	1.29	0.26	0.67	2.23	NA	NA
Denmark	19.85	1.13	0.19	0.73	2.73	0.46	2.27
Finland	16.00	1.12	0.13	0.75	4.23	NA	NA
France	19.85	0.98	0.03	0.71	6.75	6.31	0.44
Germany	7.94	0.89	0.09	0.71	2.78	1.38	1.40
Ireland	9.92	1.07	0.03	0.64	3.11	0.00	3.11
Italy	3.97	NA	0.09	0.47	NA	9.41	NA
Japan	4.62	0.36	0.13	0.42	0.78	0.00	0.78
Netherlands	23.82	1.05	0.05	0.77	8.70	1.33	7.37
Portugal	8.60	0.41	0.14	NA	NA	3.45	NA
Spain	15.88	0.59	0.02	0.75	5.76	4.16	1.60
Sweden	9.23	0.93	0.17	0.84	3.10	0.51	2.59
Switzerland	7.69	0.53	NA	0.89	NA	0.67	NA
U.K.	8.00	0.71	0.09	0.51	2.01	0.60	1.41
U.S.	4.00	0.34	0.34	0.68	0.45	0.00	0.45

[a] In model periods; from Table 7.2 in OECD Jobs Study (1994).
[b] Monthly flow rate out of unemployment for ages 25–54 from Table 1.9 in OECD, *Employment Outlook*, 1995 (most recent year).
[c] From Table 2.1 in OECD, *Employment Outlook*, 1996 (net replacement rates at APW level of earnings for couple with two children).
[d] In model periods of average wages.
[e] Computed as $p = b \times (1 - \beta \psi)$.
[f] Sum of severance and advance-notice payments (Lazear, 1990), in month's wages. The severance payments, given by Lazear at 10 years' tenure, are adjusted to median tenure as given in Table 5.5 of OECD, *Employment Outlook*, 1995.

7.4 UNEMPLOYMENT INSURANCE

Table 5 reported how changes in the present value of UI benefits affect unemployment rates and employment levels. We found large effects. But the present values considered ranged up to 5 times the benchmark value for the U.S. economy. While we evaluated relatively large present values of UI benefits, we consider that the responsiveness of the model to UI benefits is within what the empirical evidence suggests.

Nickell (1997) reports regression coefficients that imply an elasticity of the unemployment rate, with respect to the UI-benefit replacement ratio, of about 0.62. The average elasticity in Table 5 is 0.34, which is smaller than Nickell's estimate, but is of the right order of magnitude. Observe that our theory predicts that the elasticity of the unemployment rate with respect to the replacement ratio is the same as with respect to benefit duration [see equation (13)]. The elasticity that Nickell reports with respect to benefit duration is about 0.20, which is lower than his estimated elasticity with respect to the replacement ratio. However, his coefficient on benefit duration is estimated with a larger standard deviation.

The elasticity of employment with respect to UI benefits in Nickell's calculations is -0.02.[15] While the results in the model economy depend on the substitutability between market and home goods, for the benchmark economy ($\gamma = 1$) the average elasticity in Table 5 is -0.01. This elasticity is lower than Nickell's estimate but again is of the correct order of magnitude.

REFERENCES

Alvarez, F., and M. Veracierto. (1998). Search, self-insurance and job security provisions. Federal Reserve Bank of Chicago. Working Paper 98–2.
———, and ———. (1999). Equilibrium search and labor market policies: A theoretical analysis. University of Chicago. Working Paper.
Anderson, P., and B. Meyer. (1993). The effects of unemployment insurance taxes and benefits on layoffs using firm and individual data. Northwestern University. Working Paper.
Bentolila, S., and G. Bertola. (1990). Firing costs and labour demand: How bad is eurosclerosis? *Review of Economic Studies* 57(3):381–402.
Bertola, G., and R. J. Caballero. (1994). Cross-sectional efficiency and labour hoarding in a matching model of unemployment. *Review of Economic Studies* 61(3):435–456.
Campbell, J., and J. Fisher. (1996). Aggregate employment fluctuations with microeconomic asymmetries. Cambridge, MA: National Bureau of Economic Research. Working Paper 5767.
Card, D. (1996). The effects of unions on the structure of wages: A longitudinal analysis. *Econometrica* 66(4):957–979.
———, and A. Krueger. (1995). *Myth and Measurement: The New Economics of the Minimum Wage.* Princeton, NJ: Princeton University Press.

15. Di Tella and MacCulloch (1999) also estimate negative elasticities.

Costain, J. (1997). Unemployment insurance in a general equilibrium model of job search and precautionary saving. University of Chicago. Ph.D. Thesis.

Di Tella, R., and R. MacCulloch. (1999). The consequences of labor market flexibility: Panel evidence based on survey data. Harvard Business School. Working Paper.

Hansen, G., and A. Imrohoroglu. (1992). The role of unemployment insurance in an economy with liquidity constraints and moral hazard. *Journal of Political Economy* 100(1):118–142.

Hopenhayn, H., and R. Rogerson. (1993). Job turnover and policy evaluation: A general equilibrium analysis. *Journal of Political Economy* 101(5):915–938.

Lazear, E. (1990). Job security provisions and employment. *Quarterly Journal of Economics* 105:699–726.

Lucas, R., and E. C. Prescott. (1974). Equilibrium search and unemployment. *Journal of Economic Theory* 7(2):188–209.

Lundqvist, L., and T. Sargent. (1998). The European unemployment dilemma. *Journal of Political Economy* 106(3):514–550.

McCall, J. (1970). Economics of information and job search. *Quarterly Journal of Economics* 84(1):113–126.

Meyer, B. (1990). Unemployment insurance and unemployment spells. *Econometrica* 58:757–782.

Millard, S., and D. T. Mortensen. (1997). The unemployment and welfare effects of labor market policy: A comparison of U.S. and U.K. In *Unemployment Policy: How Should Governemnts Respond to Unemployment?* D. Snower and G. de la Dehesa (eds.). Cambridge: Cambridge University Press.

Mortensen, D. (1986). Job search and labor market analysis. In *Handbook of Labor Economics,* Vol. 2, O. Ashenfelter and R. Layard (eds.). New York: Elsevier Science, pp. 849–919.

Nickell, S. (1997). Unemployment and labor market rigidities: Europe versus North America. *Journal of Economic Perspectives* 11(3):55–74.

OECD. (1994). *Jobs Study.*

Prescott, E. C., and J.-V. Rios-Rull. (1992). Clasical competitive analysis of economies with islands. *Journal of Economic Theory* 57(1):73–98.

Valdivia, V. (1996). Policy evaluation in heterogeneous agent economies: The welfare impact of unemployment insurance. Northwestern University. Ph.D. Thesis.

Veracierto, M. (1995). Essays on job creation and job destruction. University of Minnesota. Ph.D. Thesis.

Wolpin, K. (1987). Estimating a structural search model: The transition from school to work. *Econometrica* 55(4):801–817.

Comment

GIUSEPPE MOSCARINI
Yale University

1. Introduction

Equilibrium search models have been quite useful and successful in the investigation of labor-market dynamics. We are now at an early stage of their practical application to policy analysis. Alvarez and Veracierto (AV) provide one of the first quantitative and comprehensive evaluations of labor-market policies in a general-equilibrium search environment. Their model combines ideas from two parallel traditions, the Lucas–Prescott (1974) island model and the *matching* or *flow approach* to labor markets (e.g., Blanchard and Diamond, 1990, or Mortensen and Pissarides, 1994). Although closer in spirit to the former, AV also pursue normative goals that have attracted special attention in the latter part of the literature. I find this modeling choice very appropriate for investigating the four labor-market policies of interest (albeit unions are better described as institutions than as policies).

The main innovation in AV is the simultaneous consideration of the three labor-market states—employment, unemployment, and non-participation—as well as of the elasticity of labor supply. Such ingredients appear in different combinations in previous contributions to the literature, but their full interaction with labor-market policies has hardly been explored from a quantitative viewpoint, in general equilibrium, or with heterogeneous production units. On methodological grounds, AV build upon a classical theoretical framework to obtain an efficient algorithm for quantitative analysis, fully illustrated in a companion paper (1999). The exercise presented here is elegant, well executed, and clearly explained.

I find the results of these experiments greatly informative as far as the minimum wage and, to a more limited extent, unions are concerned. The insights that this exercise offers are still limited on three dimensions. First, most interesting welfare effects of labor-market policies are shut down *ex ante*. Second, AV follow the literature and posit without regrets a random-matching technology, which appears somewhat artificial in the context of the economy they describe, and of course determines in part the outcome of the policy experiments. Third, the equilibrium that emerges from their simulations, meant to replicate salient aspects of the U.S. economy, looks "stiff": Compared with the magnitudes that macroeconomists have learned to consider normal, churning and ongoing reallocation appear subdued. The absence of aggregate shocks certainly plays a major role in this respect. In this comment I elaborate further on these three points, and then indicate how they affect the results of each policy experiment.

2. Insurance and Welfare Analysis

Simulations of a structural equilibrium model anchored to data have two advantages over standard econometric analysis: They avoid identification fallacies, and they allow welfare evaluation. Eventually, AV refer to the findings of some empirical literature to corroborate their results. But their most interesting message is the magnitude of welfare consequences. It is then unfortunate that they account for only part of the social costs and for none of the benefits of the labor-market policies in question.

Costs would be greatly enhanced by the presence of capital. The substitution of capital for labor by firms would amplify the impact of these policies on labor participation and unemployment. This is in fact a major theme of the current debate on Euorpean unemployment. It is fair to say, however, that such an extension would be highly nontrivial.

It is equally fair to say that the main goal of these institutions, at least in the minds of the policymakers who promote them, is to provide insurance against idiosyncratic labor-market uncertainty. In AV's world this is a nonissue, as workers have access to employment lotteries to diversify away this risk. I do not begrudge the tractability granted by this assumption, but one is left wondering about the meaning of the welfare analysis. AV claim to have dismissed important insurance effects in a companion paper; but this claim must depend on the degree of idiosyncratic risk that workers face, which is rather scant in the essay of this volume. The relevance of this issue is witnessed by the fast-growing literature on the macroeconomic consequences of uninsurable labor-market risk.

A similar role to lotteries is played by the assumption of competitive wage setting at the local (island) level, from Lucas and Prescott (1974). Without wage bargaining (the standard assumption in the other strand of equilibrium search literature), AV avoid altogether the familiar congestion-type externalities. To many readers, decreasing returns to scale and perfect competition may appear a virtue of the model. Yet, by their very nature, search frictions do generate rents, and labor-market policies appear more interesting in nonefficient scenarios. But this may be a matter of taste.

It is less disputable that competitive wage setting appears somewhat artificial in the absence of entry by firms into the island. It is natural to expect that, in each island, the fixed number of firms extract rents from the variable population of workers who happen to land there and then face a cost to move out. With no free entry, the value of a vacancy net of capital costs cannot be always zero. Indeed, workers effectively prepay for the firing tax through a 1:1 reduction in the competitive wage.

3. Undirected Search

Search models explicitly recognize the importance of heterogeneity in labor markets and have successfully accommodated increasing degrees of heterogeneity among agents and technologies. AV are no exception, allowing for idiosyncratic productivity shocks and uneven distribution of employment across islands, as well as for partial unionization and varying UI eligibility status among workers. This trend in the literature, however, has not been matched by a corresponding sophistication in the description of the search technology. In the model that AV propose, as in most of its predecessors, workers cannot direct their effort to locate more productive or unionized jobs, not even in a noisy way. This simplification, analogous to random matching, has served the equilibrium search literature well, but I take this occasion to say that it is time to move on and explore the implications of richer allocation mechanisms. The first attempts in this direction go back at least to Salop's (1973) discussion of systematic job search in partial equilibrium; Lucas and Prescott (1974) themselves sketch an analysis of directed search in general equilibrium. Since then, technical advances in the solution and simulation of equilibrium models have made it possible to manage successfully other projects of similar complexity, so I believe this exploration should now resume.

As for any polar case in theoretical analysis, undirected search provides useful insights into more realistic descriptions of the matching process. But, absent a comprehensive investigation, it is hard to conclude that partially directed search would simply result in a convex combination of Walrasian frictionless economies and random matching. The possibility of steering job search towards more attractive labor markets is an extra margin that responds autonomously to the introduction of the four policies and simply does not exist in either polar case. In Moscarini (1998) I investigate a frictional two-sector ecnomy where *ex ante* heterogeneous workers and firms may choose to be more or less selective in their search, both on and off the job. Agents on both sides of the markets adjust their search strategies to both sectoral and aggregate productivity shocks, and they do so in a systematic way that moderates the response of unemployment duration. For instance, in bad times workers become less selective and probe a wider range of jobs, reducing match quality but also the unemployment rate. It is reasonable to expect similar implications from the introduction of labor-market policies. I will discuss later in some detail the consequences of directed search in the AV model of unions.

4. Churning Intensity and Other Calibration Issues

The third major point I wish to raise concerns the amount of reallocation emerging from the numerical experiments. I find the choice of four months (17 weeks) for average unemployment duration too high in the

light of available empirical evidence for the United States. The Bureau of
Labor Statistics CPS series indicate 13 weeks for the whole postwar
period, and 15 weeks for the post-oil-shock period. The upward trend in
U.S. unemployment duration, documented by Murphy and Topel in the
1987 *NBER Macroeconomics Annual,* has since then leveled out and, if
anything, mildly reversed, as manifest for example from the series mentioned above. The choice of 17 weeks is representative of the first half of
the 1990s, and leads to a rather "stiff" picture of the economy. The other
source of rigidity is the absence of search while employed, a major
component of worker turnover. The very low incidence of unemployment that AV obtain from their experiments is the other side of the same
coin. These choices thus imply a high persistence and low variance of
idiosyncratic shocks, with intuitive consequences for policy evaluation
that I will take up shortly.

The other open end of the calibration is the utility curvature parameter
γ. A value $\gamma = 8$ may appear high, and indeed the results of the experiments conducted under this assumption are the least appealing, leading
the authors to select $\gamma = 1$ as the benchmark value. But in fact the
procedure that delivers $\gamma = 8$, based on equation (16), is perfectly reasonable and suggests an even higher number. Since $\tau/(1 - \tau)$ is a convex
function of the labor tax rate $\tau \in [0,1]$, which is known to vary substantially across countries, by Jensen's inequality the implied value of γ is
larger than the above value 8 obtained by simply substituting into equation (16) the empirical average of τ (50%). In any event, AV conduct an
excellent robustness analysis on γ, but cannot find much robustness.
Unfortunately, this brings us back to the beginning: we are left to evaluate the quantitative performance of a macromodel on the basis on a
labor-supply-type preference parameter, which is hardly pinned down
unambiguously by different calibrating procedures. In particular, as
usual, micro and macro data suggest quite different numbers.

I now turn to policy modeling and numerical experiments. The minimum-wage exercise is quite convincing, both in its implementation and
in its results, so I will limit my comments to the other three exercises.

5. Unions

I restrict attention to the coalition model of unions, which I consider the
empirically relevant one. A union is a local monopolist of labor that sets
quantity and lets the wage adjust. In the real world unions often bargain
for a wage rate, conditional on securing employment for their members.
The authors' choice shifts action from the employment margin to the

wage margin, and yet the effects of unions on the former are "surprisingly large" in their experiments.

One way to dampen these effects is to introduce directed job search, which should drive union membership up and dilute rents. Suppose workers may direct their job search towards unionized islands, as long as a wage premium is paid there, still bearing the same opportunity costs of search, namely discounting and home production. The Bellman equation for the value of joblessness θ reduces to

$$\theta = \max \left\{ w^h + \beta\theta, \beta \int \frac{u(x,z)}{x} \mu^u(dx \times dz), \beta \int v(x,z)\mu(dx \times dz) \right\},$$

the three possibilities corresponding to home production, search for a unionized job, and search for a competitive job. *Ceteris paribus*, θ obviously rises (compare the Bellman equation above with the equation for θ in AV's Section 4.2). Labor participation also rises, as job search gains a "technological edge" over home production. The higher θ also sustains the value of being employed in both unionized [u; cf. AV's equation (9)] and competitive [v, equation (1)] islands, a familiar feedback that contributes to raising θ further. As a consequence, unemployed workers increase their reservation wage, and the marginal productivity of labor must rise in competitive islands. Workers must then relocate to unionized islands until indifferent between the two subsectors, as equilibrium requires continuous arrivals to competitive islands (see Alvarez and Veracierto, 1999). In conclusion, it is natural to expect a less dramatic employment reduction than the one we observe in the union experiment with undirected search.

Instead, a new distortion originates from the incentives that unions provide for outsiders to become insiders, rather than (say) pursue their natural talents or human-capital accumulation. Although outside the scope of this paper, this and other important consequences of labor-market institutions are obliterated by the assumption of undirected search.

6. Firing Taxes

Just as in Bentolila and Bertola (1990), firing taxes discourage firms from both firing and hiring, with opposite effects on unemployment, but the first effect always dominates. It is useful to learn that these well-known implications survive in a general-equilibrium context.

In quantitative terms, the benchmark configuration of parameters predicts a mild impact of empirically plausible firing taxes (cf. Section 7.3 of AV) on the unemployment rate, while again welfare changes are sizable but do not take insurance benefits into account. Hence, one would be tempted to deem excessive the time and energy currently spent in Europe debating the reform of firing restrictions.

I suspect that such weak unemployment effects depend to a large extent on the high persistence of idiosyncratic shocks, which skew toward zero the distribution of employment adjustments in the laissez-faire economy, thus reducing the "bite" of firing taxes. Indeed, a major concern in many European countries is that firing restrictions make firms totally unwilling to hire in the face of *temporary* and even predictable changes in profitability, choking off exit from unemployment and giving rise to long-term joblessness. Not surprisingly, proposals to reduce firing costs go hand in hand with the promotion of part-time jobs. In addition, both this model and Hopenhayn and Rogerson (1993), who found similar responses, abstract from aggregate shocks with their transitory components.

Although an average unemployment duration of 17 weeks may appear too low for several European countries, this number refers to an unobservable laissez-faire economy. The actual magnitudes could as well originate from less persistent shocks that amplify the impact of firing restrictions, a different image from the one depicted by AV.

7. Unemployment Insurance (UI)

In the absence of uninsured unemployment risk, unemployment benefits amount to search subsidies because employment is necessary to regain UI eligibility. The authors choose to fund unemployment benefits with a lump-sum tax levied on each worker irrespective of her labor-market status, rather than (more realistically) only on active jobs, say on wages and profits. This feature reduces the relative desirability of nonemployment over employment, understating the impact of UI on unemployment duration and rate. In spite of this bias, the model exaggerates the aggregate implications of UI vis à vis the available empirical evidence.

AV also show analytically that unemployment benefits and firing taxes offset each other. Again, an employment tax on wages and/or profits would compound, rather than neutralize, the incentives to unemployment provided by UI.

REFERENCES

Alvarez, F., and M. Veracierto. (1999). Equilibrium search and labor market poli-
cies: A theoretical analysis. University of Chicago. Unpublished Working Paper.
Bentolila, S., and G. Bertola. (1990). Firing costs and labor demand: How bad is
Eurosclerosis? *Review of Economic Studies* 57(3):381–402.
Blanchard, O., and P. Diamond. (1990). The cyclical behavior of the gross flows
of U.S. workers. *Brookings Papers on Economic Activity* 2:85–155.
Hopenhayn, H., and R. Rogerson. (1993). Job turnover and policy evlauation: A
general equilibrium analysis. *Journal of Political Economy* 101(5):915–938.
Lucas, R., and E. C. Prescott. (1974). Equilibrium search and unemployment.
Journal of Economic Theory 7(2):188–209.
Mortensen, D., and C. Pissarides. (1994). Job creation and job destruction in the
theory of unemployment. *Review of Economic Studies* 61(3):397–415.
Moscarini, G. (1998). Excess worker reallocation. Dept. of Economics, Yale Uni-
versity. Mimeo.
Murphy, K., and R. Topel. (1987). The evolution of unemployment in the United
States: 1968–1985. In *NBER Macroeconomics Annual 1987*, S. Fischer (ed.). Cam-
bridge, MA: MIT Press.
Salop, S. (1973). Systematic job search and unemployment. *Review of Economic
Studies*, 40:191–201.

Comment

ALAN B. KRUEGER
Princeton University

This paper provides a model with homogeneous production by homogeneous workers with homogeneous tastes on different islands that are hit
by random shocks. In commenting on this paper, I have to confess that I
feel a little like I've landed on a different kind of island—where the
workers use a different production technology and possibly have different tastes. Nonetheless, I think it is healthy for the economic science to
have many islands that employ different techniques, and to have the
workers visit each others' islands from time to time.

I have two types of comments on this paper. The first concerns the
modeling assumptions; I will try to relate what we've learned from micro
studies about the type of model the authors have assumed, and the
parameter values they build into the model. The second involves evaluating the models' predictions in light of the available evidence.

I have little quarrel with the elasticities the authors have assumed. If
used in the right model, these seem quite sensible to me, and consistent

with the consensus of thought among mainstream labor economists.[1] I also like the fact that the authors make employee search a prominent feature of their model; this also seems consistent with many of the findings in the labor literature. What seems more problematic to me, however, is that the authors have disregarded *employer search*. Workers are presumed to show up at employers' doorsteps without so much as a help-wanted ad. Firms never have vacancies in the model the authors employ. This seems inconsistent with an important feature of labor markets. Moreover, it is a modeling assumption that matters, because it implies that the elasticity of labor supply to firms is infinite. I think it would be more realistic and appropriate to model the labor market as entailing both employer- and employee-side search frictions, and to have the duration and incidence of vacancies at individual firms depend on the generosity of the compensation they offer.

Burdett and Mortensen (1998) and Dickens, Machin, and Manning (1999), for example, provide search models in which employers cannot instantly and costlessly fill their vacancies. As a result, these papers find that a wage floor that is modestly above the prevailing wage (e.g., imposed by a government minimum wage or union) can actually raise employment. In essence, the firm-side search costs bestow employers—even small employers—a small degree of monopsony power, since they can fill their vacancies more quickly if they pay a higher wage.[2] But, as in a static Joan Robinson monopsony model, employers would not choose to pay a higher wage voluntarily, because they already employ some workers, and it is not profitable to offer a higher wage to everyone. Also, as in static monopsony models, if the mandated wage is too high, employers would return to their demand curve and choose to fill fewer jobs. This type of model predicts an inverted-V-shaped pattern between employment and the wage floor and can explain other phenomena, such as a firm-size wage premium.

The asymmetric treatment of search frictions in this paper casts some of the policies the authors examine in as unflattering a light as possible. Nonetheless, the simulation results are rather encouraging for some of the policies. It is not unusual that I receive papers in the mail that report finding "very small employment effects of the minimum wage," as this paper does. But it is unusual that I receive such papers with return addresses in Chicago. Even setting the minimum wage at 85% of the average

1. For evidence on the consensus labor supply and demand elasticities, see Fuchs, Krueger, and Poterba (1998). The authors' assumed labor supply elasticity of 0.18, though low, is higher than the median estimate among labor economists.
2. One might think that the current model, with just one employer per island, would be a natural situation to consider firms as monopsonists.

wage (which is more than twice the U.S. level in 1998), the authors find that employment is unchanged from the no-minimum-wage counterfactual. And, as I stated above, the model the authors employ is likely to exaggerate the distortionary effect of a minimum wage. I think a valuable extension of this work would be to calculate the welfare effects of a minimum wage for workers and capital owners. My suspicion is that the authors will find that the minimum wage raises low-wage workers' welfare because their employment hardly changes, although their pay increases substantially.

An interesting implication of the authors' island-based model is that it implies a substantial spike at the minimum wage. Actual wage distributions clearly display such a spike. This finding, which only became known after microdata were available, was not predicted by George Stigler and early neoclassical critiques of the minimum wage. Stigler (1946), for example, expected wage distributions to be truncated at the minimum.

The analysis of unions could have benefited from a stronger connection to the previous literature. There is a tradition in labor economics of general-equilibrium analysis of unions (see, for example, Johnson and Mieszkowski, 1970), and I would have been interested in the authors' perspective on how their results extend this literature. Moreover, the union-boss model strikes me as equivalent to the efficient-bargains literature (see Oswald, 1985, for a survey). There are also additional alternative views of unions, such as the voice model.

In any event, the U.S. union penetration rate has been steadily declining for the last 25 years, and is currently below 10% in the private sector. The authors simulate the effect of unions on the economy, assuming a union penetration rate between 20% and 80%.[3] I would have found some simulation results for a union rate of around 10% useful, especially since the results presented suggest that the percentage of islands unionized has a nonlinear effect on the outcomes of interest. Cross-country studies often find that unions are associated with better macroeconomic outcomes when the institutional structure is such that unions bargain at a national level.

The assumptions of random eligibility for UI benefits and random duration of benefits strike me as more simplistic and artificial than necessary. For example, in the United States, a worker generally must work a certain number of quarters to qualify for 26 weeks of UI benefits. Why not build this into the model and allow for endogenous UI participation?

---

3. I presume that if X% of islands are unionized, approximately X% of workers are also unionized.

Furthermore, the split treatment of UI benefits and the firing tax strikes me as odd. Since in practice in the United States UI benefits are funded by an experience-rated tax on employers (akin to the firing tax in this model), it was not clear to me that anything is gained by treating UI benefits and firing costs separately.

In any event, my impression is that the generosity and duration of UI benefits are the only robust variables found in cross-country studies of unemployment. Layard, Nickell, and Jackman (1991), for example, find that countries with more generous UI benefits tended to have higher unemployment rates in the 1980s. And, unlike most of their explanatory variables, the UI variable tends to have a similar effect in later years (see Forslund and Krueger, 1996). Several compelling microeconometric studies (some involving randomized field trials) have also found that more generous UI benefits are associated with longer spells of unemployment.[4]

A few comments about the general approach taken in this paper are also called for. First, it seems to me that the piecemeal aproach (e.g., evaluate minimum wage, then unions, then UI) that the paper follows is sensible enough, but what would really be helpful would be to consider some policies in tandem. Policies have interactions that can either offset or exacerbate each others' distortions. For example, it is plausibly argued that an effect of the Earned Income Tax Credit is to lower market wages, and the minimum wage can offset this distortionary effect. The approach developed in this paper could be used to evaluate the optimal combination of policies designed to achieve a certain aim (in this case, raising the welfare of low-income workers).

Second, it is unclear to me how the results from the elaborate simulation exercise in this paper differ from a more simple (simple-minded?) partial equilibrium analysis. For example, with the parameters chosen, how different would the predicted effects of a minimum wage or union wage floor be in a textbook partial-equilibrium model? My guess is that the predictions would be quite similar, which makes me wonder whether the additional complexity that the authors introduce is worth the cost.

Third, and perhaps most importantly, it seems to me that we are a long way from being in a position where we know enough about the structure and operation of the labor market to model economic behavior with the fully specified general-equilibrium approach taken here. Personally, I think that the effort would be better spent identifying natural and actual experiments that yield insight into the modeling assumptions required for this type of work (estimating parameter values, understanding employer search behavior, etc.) than jumping to a full-scale model

4. See, for example, Meyer (1995), Solon (1985), and Katz and Meyer (1990).

based on an unknown set of primitives. But, as I noted earlier, I think there is benefit from diverse research methods, and it is reassuring to know that the machinery is available for the type of analysis in this paper when economics is in a position to model the labor market more confidently some time in the next millennium.

REFERENCES

Burdett, K., and D. Mortensen. (1998). Wage differentials, employer size and unemployment. *International Economic Review* 39(May):257–274.
Dickens, R., S. Machin, and A. Manning. (1999). The effects of minimum wage on employment: Theory and evidence from Britain. *Journal of Labor Economics* 17(1):1–22.
Forslund, A., and A. Krueger. (1997). An evaluation of the Swedish active labor market policy: New and received wisdom. *The Welfare State in Transition*, R. Freeman, B. Swedenborg, and R. Topel (eds.). Chicago: University of Chicago Press.
Fuchs, V., A. Krueger, and J. Poterba. (1998). Why do economists disagree about policy?. *Journal of Economic Literature* 36(3):1387–1425.
Johnson, H. G., and P. Mieszkowski. (1970). The effects of unionization on the distribution of income: A general equilibrium approach. *Quarterly Journal of Economics* 84(4):539–561.
Katz, L., and B. Meyer. (1990). Unemployment insurance, recall expectations and unemployment outcomes. *Quarterly Journal of Economics* 104:973–1002.
Layard, R., S. Nickell, and R. Jackman. (1991). *Unemployment: Macroeconomic Performance and the Labor Market.* Oxford: Oxford University Press.
Meyer, B. D. (1995). Lessons from the U.S. unemployment insurance experiments. *Journal of Economic Literature* 33(March):91–131.
Oswald, A. (1985). The economic theory of trade unions: An introductory survey. *Scandinavian Journal of Economics* 87(2):160–193.
Solon, G. (1985). Work incentive effects of taxing unemployment benefits. *Econometrica* 53:295–306.
Stigler, G. (1946). The economics of minimum wage legislation. *American Economic Review* 36:358–365.

Discussion

In response to the discussants, Veracierto said that they did not consider search by firms because they consider their work complementary to that of Mortensen and Pissarides, who emphasize very different margins. He defended the assumption of perfect insurance markets by citing other work by the authors, in which they consider the case of borrowing-constrained agents with no access to insurance markets. Although workers in this alternative model can only self-insure through saving, their behavior appears very similar to what is found under the assumption of complete markets. The reason for the similarity in results is that the average duration of unemployment in the United States is only about three months. The resulting risk is sufficiently small that it can be effectively handled through sef-insurance. Veracierto concluded that it is reasonable to abstract from borrowing constraints and market incompleteness, and that the main effects of policy appear to operate through search incentives (for workers) and hiring incentives (for firms).

Continuing his response, Veracierto conceded that undirected search is a strong assumption. He said, however, that experiments by the authors with directed search in the context of unemployment insurance actually strengthened the results. He also thought that including capital would enhance the effects that they find. Veracierto agreed with Krueger that their simulations are not successful in capturing the cross-sectional wage distribution, a result of their assumption of worker homogeneity.

Robert Shimer disagreed with the presumption that workers can effectively self-insure against unemployment, since even though spells are short on average they tend to be repeated and may lead to wage losses. He expanded on the criticism of complete markets by noting that several of the policies analyzed, such as unemployment insurance and firing taxes, make little sense in such a world. Effectively, in this setup, UI serves only as a subsidy for search. Several people noted that incorporation of permanent shocks, such as aggregate productivity shocks, would increase the need for insurance by workers. Mark Gertler suggested that self-insurance would work well only if agents were very long-lived, allowing them to spread the effects of shocks out over many periods. The authors replied that such long lives are necessary only if the shocks are relatively persistent.

Christopher Foote agreed with the authors that a general-equilibrium framework is necessary to think about firing taxes, since firing taxes reduce aggregate productivity and thus the return to work. He also pointed out that the welfare cost of firing taxes calculated here is very close to that found by Hugo Hopenhayn and Richard Rogerson in related work. The authors noted that their work differed from that of Hopenhayn and Rogerson mainly in that the latter allowed for entry and exit of firms.

Ben Bernanke suggested the incorporation into the model of two classes of workers of different productivity, or with different endowments of labor supply, in order to allow for a more realistic spread in the wage distribution. He thought that the analysis of the minimum wage would be particularly interesting in that extension. He also suggested supplementing the steady-state analysis with analyses of one-time shocks followed by transition to the steady state. The authors indicated an interest in doing future work that includes worker heterogeneity.

Jonathan A. Parker
PRINCETON UNIVERSITY

Spendthrift in America? On Two Decades of Decline in the U.S. Saving Rate

1. Introduction

During the past two decades, the personal saving rate in the United States has fallen dramatically. From a typical and quite steady level of around 8% during the sixties and seventies, it has declined to below 2% in 1997, and preliminary estimates put the rate at $\frac{1}{2}$% in 1998 and negative so far in 1999. Figure 1a displays the U.S. personal saving rate from 1959 to 1998 and makes clear the magnitude of the change.[1]

This change does not merely reflect labelling or measurement issues. In particular, for the majority of this decline, it is not the case that businesses or governments have increased their saving with national saving unaffected. Since the National Income and Product Account (NIPA) definitions of savings rates are neither transparent nor representative of basic economic concepts, the simplest way to judge the importance of this shift in the U.S. economy is to examine whether consump-

For useful comments and discussions, I am grateful to Ben Bernanke, Angus Deaton, Michael Horvath, Rodolfo Manuelli, Julio Rotemberg, John Karl Scholz, and participants at the NBER Macroeconomics Annual conference, particularly my discussants, and especially Pierre Olivier Gourinchas and Kenneth West. Eric Hurst and Joe Lupton provided invaluable consultations on using the early release PSID data. I thank Karen Dynan for sharing her understanding of NIPA saving measures. Grigori Kosenok provided excellent research assistance with the aggregate series. This paper was written while I was at the University of Wisconsin. I alone am responsible for any errors.
1. An October 1999 revision in the calculation of personal saving raises these numbers but does not alter the twenty-year decline nor any of the main conclusions of this paper. The personal saving rate is defined as one minus the ratio of personal outlays to disposable income. In the national accounts, personal outlays are personal consumption expenditures plus interest paid by persons and personal transfer payments abroad; disposable income is labor income, proprietors' income, rental income, personal interest and dividend income, and transfer payments to persons less personal contributions for social insurance and personal tax and nontax payments.

Figure 1 (a) U.S. PERSONAL SAVING RATE, 1959–1998; (b) U.S. PERSONAL
CONSUMPTION EXPENDITURES AS A SHARE OF GDP, 1959–1998

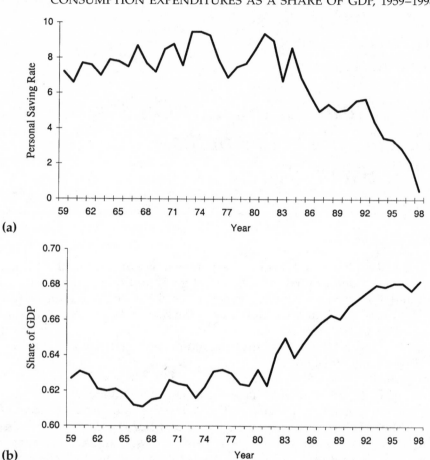

(a)

(b)

tion has risen as a share of national output. Figure 1b shows that the
decline in personal saving has largely been mirrored on the expenditure side of the national accounts. The ratio of consumption to GDP in
the United States was roughly constant from 1950 to 1980, and has risen
by 6 percentage points during the past two decades.[2]

While the ratio of consumption to income has risen significantly since

2. Since this paper was written (and of importance to the discussion), the Bureau of
   Economic Analysis has released a major revision of the National Accounts that reclassi-
   fies expenditures on software as investment, treats government pension plans in the
   same manner as private pension plans, and removes some asset transfers from disposable income. The revised data still show an 8 percentage point decline in the personal
   saving rate and a 5 (rather than 6) percentage point increase in the consumption share of
   GDP in the past twenty years.

1980, it is worth noting that this ratio has not risen in the past few years. The recent decline in the personal saving rate that has received so much attention from journalists and policymakers is not reflected in the ratio of consumption to output. As the next section shows, this decline is more than offset by increases in saving by governments and businesses.

This paper focuses on the fundamental and significant change in the allocation of the output of the U.S. economy documented in Figure 1b: Why has the largest economy in the world increased its consumption expenditures by 6% of output in a twenty-year period? This change poses a basic challenge to economists as those who seek to explain economic outcomes. Do we understand the allocation of resources?

This consumption boom also has import for the economic future of the United States. Saving is the accumulation of resources on which to base future consumption. Absent offsetting changes in the national economy, higher consumption generally leads to a lower capital stock and thus affects wages and national output in the future. If the present low saving rate represents an optimal response of well-functioning markets to fundamental improvements such as new technologies, then policies designed to stimulate saving are at best unnecessary, since the future is rosy. On the other hand, if high consumption rates are the results of imprudent fiscal policies or malfunctioning markets, then anemic saving signals an avoidably worse future.[3]

Despite the basic prediction that lower saving and investment lowers the capital stock, the aggregate wealth-to-income ratio has actually increased during the period of the consumption boom. While new investment has slowed, the revaluation of existing assets has kept wealth levels high relative to national output, raising the possibility that the capital-to-income ratio is not declining. Put differently, the saving rate including capital gains has not fallen. As is clear from the paper and comments on the value of the stock market in this volume, however, high stock prices may not reflect only high expected future dividends. It seems imprudent to simply assume that saving is in some sense high and that the capital stock is larger than would be inferred from past investment. Instead, this paper considers whether the appreciation of assets, whatever the driving mechanism, can explain the changing allocation of current output. If it can, this suggests that households perceive the increase in the value of the stock market as real wealth creation. As this paper demonstrates, however, the increase in wealth alone does not explain the consumption boom.

This paper begins by laying out the basic facts surrounding the decline

3. While uncovering significant evidence about the behavior of the consumption ratio, this paper does not enter this debate directly. For examples of these arguments see Bernheim and Shoven (1991), Bernheim and Scholz (1993), Gustman and Steinmeier (1998).

in national saving and how a canonical aggregate model can account for these changes. I focus both on several recently observed changes in the U.S. economy and on the main current theories of the increased consumption of output.[4]

I employ two main sources of data to study the increase in the consumption of output. First, the paper uses U.S. national accounts data to compare the timing of the consumption boom with the timing of the candidate driving forces, and to ask what expected changes would be required to rationalize observed household consumption behavior. Second, the work evaluates cross-sectional implications of the theories using a custom-built panel dataset on U.S. households. As first suggested in Skinner (1987), I impute consumption of nondurable goods and services for each household in the Panel Study of Income Dynamics (PSID) using information from the Consumer Expenditure Survey (CEX) and the U.S. national accounts. The resulting dataset contains 80,000 observations on household income, consumption, wealth, and demographic characteristics covering the period of interest.

The analysis leads to the following main results.[5]

First, the decline in measured saving is not purely due to a rise in expenditures without an associated rise in consumption. That is, households are not simply spending more on durable goods and thereby shifting the composition of their savings.

Second, the consumption boom cannot be explained by decreased government purchases "crowding in" consumption. The sum of government and household expenditures on goods and services has also risen over this period. Further, the declines in government spending that would have to be expected to rationalize the consumption boom are, to the author, implausibly large.

Third, the data suggest that at most one-fifth of the increase in the ratio of consumption to income can be explained by changes in the ratio of household wealth to income. The consumption boom precedes the recently observed increases in wealth, and the national saving rate has actually risen coincident with the stock-market boom of the late 1990s. Additionally, the increases in consumption-to-income ratios

4. There is no shortage of theories that can "explain" the decline in saving, once one allows any combination of changing structural parameters or shifting definitions as plausible candidates. This paper limits the scope of its investigation to the main current theories and looks at the data with these explanations in mind. Further, this paper focuses on ruling out monocausal explanations and upon describing behavior.

5. While much relevant literature is cited where appropriate, the literature is too large to cover in detail here. See Browning and Lusardi (1996), Hayashi (1997), and Attanasio (1997b) for an overview of the state of empirical research on saving.

across groups are not related to the distribution of wealth, homeownership, or pension participation. Changes in asset values are not the main force driving the relative increase in consumption.

Fourth, during this period of rising consumption share, the growth rate of real consumption per capita was low and real interest rates were relatively high. Absent a run of expectational errors, the consumption Euler equation implies that the actual or effective discount rate of the representative agent was high. Additionally, there is a strong correlation between the real interest rate and consumption growth within the period of consumption boom. That is, the aggregate consumption Euler equation provides a better description of the data during this period than in previous periods.

Fifth, turning to evaluating explanations that are consistent with such increased impatience, the changing age distribution and income-by-age distribution of the population are not important causes of the consumption boom. Nor, sixth, can financial innovation which relaxes liquidity constraints and potentially reduces precautionary saving be blamed for the consumption boom. Given the observed increases in debt, this source can generate at most one-third of the increase in consumption observed to date.

Seventh, the consumption-to-income ratio of each generation is larger than that of the generation before it.[6] This implies that intergenerational fiscal transfers alone cannot account for the decline in saving. Thus, either different factors have increased the consumption of different generations, or general optimism or a preference shift has increased the consumption-to-income ratios of all households.[7]

In sum, the analysis reveals that each of the major current theories of the decline in the U.S. saving rate fails on its own to match significant aspects of the macroeconomic or household data. The concluding section of the paper discusses some combinations of theories that are consistent with the stylized facts uncovered in this paper and with the limited roles found for the monocausal explanations.

The paper is organized as follows. The next section describes the history of the decline in the personal saving rate and its relationship to the allocation of output. Section 3 presents a canonical aggregate model

---

6. As will be shown, this can be explained either by a time effect increasing everyone's consumption-to-income ratio or by true cohort effects, as is described here. In this latter case, while the changing age distribution of the population is irrelevant, who is at each age is very relevant.

7. An example of such a combination of factors is federal transfers from future generations to the elderly and financial innovations that allow the young to consume more out of future income.

and the classes of explanations for the consumption boom that the paper considers. Section 4 evaluates a subset of the theories using U.S. national accounts data and in doing so provides a more detailed description of the aggregate facts. Section 5 describes the main features and construction of the household-level dataset that is used to further test the theories in Sections 6, 7, and 8. These sections differ by methodology: Section 6 decomposes the consumption-to-income ratios into age, time, and cohort effects; Section 7 models the cohort effect and estimates consumption functions; Section 8 estimates Euler equations. Section 9 concludes. A data appendix is provided.

2. The Decline in the U.S. Saving Rates

Before turning to the theoretical determinants of the consumption ratio and evaluating these determinants using the aggregate data, this section presents the stylized facts concerning the declining U.S. saving rates.[8] It is important to clarify what has occurred before turning to possible explanations. The section is structured as being about saving because it is national saving (plus international capital flows) that equals total national investment.

Is the precipitous decline in personal saving shown in Figure 1a leading to lower national saving, or is public and business saving offsetting the decline? Actually, from private-saving data, it is not even clear that households themselves are saving less. National accounts data misallocate several categories of saving between private and business saving. Personal saving includes the saving of noncorporate, nonfinancial businesses, such as sole proprietorships, partnerships, and nonprofit organizations, which might be better included in business saving. Additionally, because disposable personal income includes nominal rather than real interest payments to businesses, personal saving is overstated relative to business saving.[9]

Given that personal saving is confounded with business saving, the first question is what has happened to their sum, private saving. Figure 2a displays the private saving rate—the ratio of private saving to national income—over the past forty years.[10] Prior to the precipitous de-

---

8. In contemporaneous research, Gale and Sabelhaus (1999) analyze the aggregate data on saving and wealth and reach similar conclusions to those of this section.
9. See Hendershott and Peek (1988) and Summers and Carroll (1987).
10. NIPA saving-rate measures have recently been revised so as to exclude the capital gains distributions of mutual funds from both saving and disposable income. This is consistent with the national accounts' purpose of describing the allocation of newly produced, final value added. Unfortunately, this revision only goes back to 1982, so that there is a break in the savings series in that year. However, these distributions account

Figure 2 (a) GROSS SAVINGS RATES 1959–1997; (b) HOUSEHOLD ASSETS
AND NET WORTH

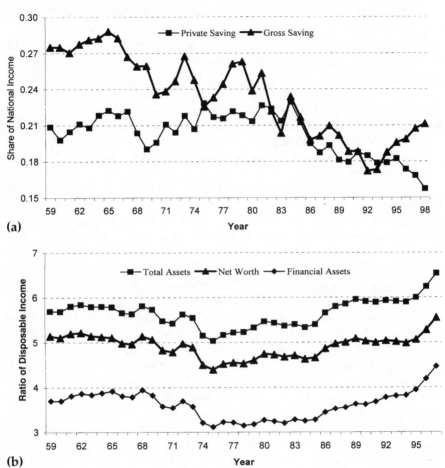

(a)

(b)

cline in personal saving, the private saving rate was nearly constant.
This stable relationship was known as Denison's law (Denison, 1958),
but this law appears to have been repealed.[11]

for only $\frac{1}{4}$ percentage point of the saving rate in the 1980s. Thus, while this revision
lowered measured private saving in the 1990s significantly, carrying the revision back
farther would have negligible effect on measured saving rates and the conclusions of
the present analysis.

11. In part, Denison's law is also based on an observed high negative correlation between
personal and business saving. Hendershott and Peek (1988) argue that mismeasurement generates most if not all of this negative correlation and thus that Denison's
law was never passed in the first place.

Turning now to government saving, higher saving by the government, holding expenditures constant, leads to lower taxes in the future. The principal of Ricardian equivalence states that if taxes are nondistortionary, this offset is complete: households observing higher government saving save less themselves, if government purchases of goods are held constant. Figure 2a also shows that government saving— the difference between private and gross saving—declined through the 1950s, 1960s, and 1970s and has only rebounded from near zero in the early 1990s.[12] Thus gross saving declined steadily from the late 1960s to the early 1990s and has risen recently. We can conclude that while the last five years of declining private saving have been offset by increased government saving, national saving has still fallen substantially in the past twenty years.

One reason for pausing to examine national saving—and not simply focusing on consumption-to-income ratios throughout—is that saving and investment have moved in lockstep over most of the postwar period. Capital inflows have not offset the decline in saving, either because of an offsetting temporal pattern of changes in the world economy or because of any one of the proposed rationalizations of the Feldstein– Horioka puzzle. Nevertheless, declining national saving has been associated with a large decline in new investment as a share of GDP over the past twenty years. Ultimately, and ceteris paribus, one would expect this decline of roughly one-fifth in gross investment to lower the U.S. capital stock per worker by one-fifth.

As discussed in the introduction, however, the value of extant assets, has not declined. The stock of wealth in the U.S. has risen as a share of income over the past twenty years. Figure 2b shows that net worth, as measured in the flow-of-funds data, has increased as a share of disposable income during the period of declining saving. While the flow of the share of output stored for future production is declining over time, the value of the stock is rising. Put slightly differently, while active saving has decreased, the change in household wealth as a share of income has increased.[13]

These coincident trends raise two puzzles. First, why has wealth risen while saving has fallen? This question is addressed elsewhere in this volume. Second, what has driven the decline in active saving and the

---

12. This is the official measure of government saving, which does not include changes in government debts associated with social security and the implicit and violable promises to future generations. Officially, government obligations held by the public rose by about 20% of GDP from 1979 to 1995 and have declined by about 5% since.

13. This fact is also present in the PSID data that will be used subsequently (Hurst, Luoh, and Stafford, 1998).

increasing consumption of output? In the rest of this paper we focus on the latter question.

3. The Canonical Theory and Main Explanations

This section discusses the main explanations for the consumption boom in the context of a canonical macroeconomic model. In subsequent sections, these explanations are evaluated using aggregate time-series evidence and panel data on household behavior.

To provide a framework for analyzing the decrease in saving and the increase in the consumption share of output, I begin with a standard Ramsey economy. Aggregate output, Y, is produced from the aggregate capital stock, K, and total labor in the economy, N, using a constant-returns-to-scale production technology:

$$Y = F(K, AN),$$

where A is an exogenous Harrod-neutral technology that grows at rate a. Let the labor force grow at exogenous rate n, and let capital depreciate at rate δ. Then one can rearrange the standard capital accumulation equation to solve for the consumption share of output:

$$\frac{c}{y} = 1 - g - (n + a + \delta)\frac{k}{f(k)} - \frac{\dot{k}}{f(k)}, \tag{3.1}$$

where C is aggregate consumption, lowercase letters denote per-effective-worker values (e.g., $c \equiv C/AN$), g is the rate of government consumption of output in steady state, and $f(k) \equiv F(k,1)$. In steady state, the consumption ratio is related only to the accumulated capital stock, the share of output consumed by the government, and the exogenous rates of technology growth, population growth, and depreciation.

In the canonical Ramsey model with a single infinite-lived representative agent maximizing the present discounted value of per capita utility flows, the steady-state real interest rate and thus the capital–output ratio are tied down by the modified golden rule. Assuming a Cobb–Douglas production function, the consumption share of output in steady state is

$$\frac{c}{y} = 1 - g - \frac{\alpha(n + a + \delta)}{r + \delta} \tag{3.2}$$

$$= 1 - g - \frac{\alpha(n + a + \delta)}{n + \frac{a}{\sigma} + \rho + \delta}, \tag{3.3}$$

where r is the real interest rate, ρ is the discount rate of the representative agent, α is the share of output that is paid to capital, and σ is the intertemporal elasticity of substitution of the representative agent. The consumption ratio is increased by increases in impatience and by decreases in government spending, the growth rate of population, the capital share, and the intertemporal elasticity of substitution.[14] A decrease in the depreciation rate has a theoretically ambiguous effect but, for reasonable parameter values, increases the consumption share of output. Similarly, an increase in the growth rate of productivity has an ambiguous effect but, for reasonable parameter values, increases the consumption share of output.

Of the large number of possible factors that can increase the consumption share according to equation (3.3), this paper focuses on several that are noticed in the literature or suggested by recently observed changes in the economy. First, the share of output consumed by the government has declined over the past twenty years. A declining rate of government spending causes a consumption boom. Second, household wealth has increased despite low active saving, as documented in Figures 1 and 2. An increase in the capital stock causes a transitory consumption boom.

Finally, an increase in the discount rate of the representative agent increases the consumption share of output. While this cannot be observed directly, several existing theories imply an increase in the effective discount rate of the aggregate consumer.[15] First, the social security system is currently making large transfers from future generations to those alive today. Considering the representative agent derived from a life-cycle model, this increased intergenerational redistribution temporarily increases the effective discount rate of the representative agent.[16] Thus the social security system is considered as a potential explanation for the increase in the consumption share. Second, since households at different ages have different propensities to consume out of total resources, changes in the age distribution of the population change the effective discount rate of the representative agent. The aging of the baby boom generation and the increased life span of the typical American have changed the demographic structure of the U.S. and may also have driven up the consumption share of output.

14. For all of these effects, the change in consumption share at impact is the same as in the long run except that a decrease in the capital share can cause the consumption share to decline at impact.
15. I do not consider one potential explanation, advanced in Carroll and Weil (1994) and Paxson (1996). Habit formation tends to lead the growth rate of consumption to decline slowly following a slowdown in growth.
16. That is, in a certainty model, intergenerational transfers to the present increase the propensity of the representative agent to consume out of current and expected output.

Third, in a model in which some households face large idiosyncratic risk or liquidity constraints, some saving is driven by precautionary or liquidity concerns. In the past twenty years, there has been an increase in the financial instruments employed by Americans and a significant increase in the ratio of debt to income. Thus I consider relaxed liquidity constraints as a possible explanation for the increase in the consumption-to-income ratio.[17] Finally, while not observed, there has been speculation that saving behavior differs by cohort. One version of this story is that households who did not live through the Great Depression have a lower propensity to save than those who did. I examine whether there is evidence of an increase in the discount rate of the representative agent due to more patient older generations being replaced by more impatient younger ones.

4. A Quick Tour of Aggregate Evidence

In this section, I analyze which if any of the explanations just discussed are consistent with the observed changes in the aggregate economy. I focus on timing, on relative magnitudes, and on the composition of aggregate consumption. This first pass at the data is complemented later in the paper by a thorough evaluation using household-level survey data.

Before seeking to explain the increase in the consumption share, this section dismisses the possibility that consumption expenditures have increased while consumption has not. Suppose that there were a relative preference shift or price decline such that the representative household sought to increase the share of its consumption flows that are due to durable goods. Since the NIPA measure expenditures rather than consumption, an increase in the share of consumption coming from the service flows from durable goods would generate a boom in consumption expenditures. In fact, however, the observed increase in consumption expenditures relative to income would not represent a decline in saving rates, but rather a shift of saving from capital to durable consumption goods.[18]

This supposition is easily rejected by an examination of household budget shares. Working with reference to GDP rather than total consumption, the ratio of expenditures on durable goods to GDP has re-

---

17. See Caballero (1991), Ayagari (1993), and Carroll (1997).
18. Durable goods do not include housing. Housing services are counted as consumption, while housing-stock depreciation and investment are counted as capital consumption allowance and investment. Changes in household wealth due to changing homeownership patterns are correctly reflected in the figures on saving. See Bureau of Economic Analysis (1987, 1997).

mained steady since 1959, falling by a tenth of a percentage point from 1959 to 1979 and rising by a tenth of a percentage point since.

Turning now to the main explanations proposed in the previous section, we will see that there is little aggregate evidence that declines in government spending or appreciation of existing assets caused the increase in consumption to income. Since during the past twenty years the real interest rate was relatively high and the growth rate of consumption relatively low, the data do suggest that the effective discount rate of the representative agent has increased.

4.1 REDUCTIONS IN GOVERNMENT PURCHASES

Is the consumption boom driven by a decreasing share of output purchased by the government, due to the so-called "peace dividend" for example? In steady state, the canonical model of Section 3 implies that the share of national output consumed by households and the government together is constant [equation (3.3)].

A steady-state explanation can be quickly dismissed. Figure 3 shows that the share of output devoted to the purchases of both households and governments has risen over the past twenty years. The purchases of goods and services by governments have fallen by about 3 percentage points of GDP over the past ten years, but this decline is concentrated after most of the increase in the consumption share.[19] A small piece of evidence is provided by the real interest rate. The real interest rate should be unchanged by a decrease in the demand for output by the government. During the past twenty years, the real interest rate has been singificantly higher than it was in the previous twenty.

There is however the possibility that a non-steady-state explanation could work. That is, could the consumption boom be due to the expectation of both the currently observed decline in government spending and further declines in government spending in the future? This hypothesis is consistent with a high real interest rate and a high consumption share of output. If households expect lower government purchases in the future, consumption of the extra output available is smoothed by reducing investment and the capital stock in the present, thus increasing the real interest rate.

To evaluate this explanation, I ask what changes would have to be expected to rationalize the observed consumption boom. To keep matters transparent, general, and easily reproducible, the present values are calculated holding the real interest rate constant. Such experiments pro-

---

19. Also, the constant consumption share and the declining share of government purchases over the past five years suggests no "crowding in" of consumption in response to the reduction in the share of government expenditures.

Figure 3 CONSUMPTION AND GOVERNMENT SPENDING AS A SHARE
OF GDP

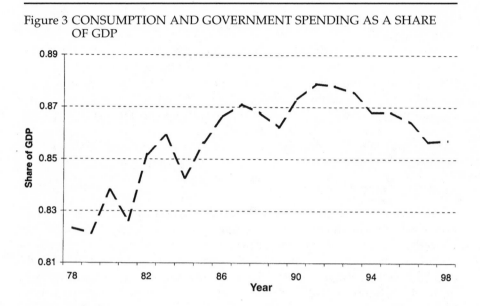

vide a lower bound on the expected future declines in government
spending.[20]

First, what is the expected steady-state share of government spending? The average ratio of government and consumption purchases to
GDP from 1959 to 1979 is 84%. Given the current ratio of personal consumption expenditures to GDP of 68%, equation (3.3) implies that the
expected steady-state ratio of government spending to output is 16%.

Second, what accumulated value from the consumption boom must be
recovered from lower government spending? Consider first the counterfactual that the consumption ratio remained at its 1959–1979 value over
the 1979–1998 period. The present value of the excess of the observed
consumption series over this alternative stands at 5782 billion 1992 dollars, or three-quarters of a year of GDP, when accumulated at a 3% real
interest rate. The decline in government spending as a share of GDP

20. The fact that the partial equilibrium experiment provides a lower bound can most easily
be seen in two steps. First, consider the household budget constraint. Because the
capital stock declines as consumption rises and then rises as government spending
further declines, the real interest rate is high when the household is borrowing from
the future (reducing capital below the steady-state level). Thus, to "pay off" the early
consumption boom requires greater saving (a greater decline in government spending
in the future) than if the interest rate had been constant. Second, since we see that the
current ratio of consumption to income and the real interest rate should decline as we
get to steady state, the steady-state consumption-to-income ratio is actually higher
than the observed one, thus requiring a still-lower steady-state level of government
spending.

since its local peak of 21% in 1987 cumulates to only 1400 billion 1992 dollars to date.

One path of government purchases that can rationalize the consumption boom is that the ratio of government purchases to GDP declines by half a percentage point a year to 13%, stays there for 15 years, and rises again by half a percentage point a year to 16%. Thus, to rationalize the consumption boom from this source requires expectations of extreme declines in government purchases. To date, no government spending movements have occurred that can rationalize more than a small fraction of the consumption boom.

4.2 APPRECIATION OF EXISTING ASSETS

As shown in Figure 2b, the value of assets owned by the representative household has been increasing relative to its income. Can this rise explain the increase in the consumption-to-income ratio?

First, what might generate the large increases in the ratio of net worth to income while the investment share is low and the real interest rate is high? If households realize that the capital stock was higher than they had thought, then the consumption share would increase, but, counterfactually, the real interest rate would be low. Instead suppose that households expect a big increase in output in the future. Then households should decumulate capital, the real interest rate rise, and consumption rise as a share of output. These real-interest-rate, consumption, and output movements are as observed in the data. If, in addition, firms must invest now, for example in information technologies, in order to reap these future productivity gains, then it is also possible for the theory to predict an increase in the ratio of net worth to income, as in Greenwood and Yorukoglu (1997). If this investment is not measured as output or investment, then consumption rises as a share of output.[21]

An alternative theory is simply that asset prices follow fads or bubbles. In either case, two problems are encountered in trying to explain the consumption boom with the increase in wealth.

First, the timing is wrong. The increase in the wealth-to-income ratio is mainly due to the increases in the values of financial assets—largely stocks—as shown in the lowest curve in Figure 2b. This increase occurs primarily in the last five years, a time when personal saving is declining but the consumption-to-output ratio is constant.

Second, focusing on the years over which the consumption share of

---

21. See Greenwood and Yorukoglu (1997) and Greenwood, Hercowitz, and Krusell (1997), or assume that the future increase in productivity is associated with certain existing pieces of capital. Another possible shift in technology is a decrease in the capital share of the economy.

income increased, we see that the total increase in the ratio of net worth to income from the late 1970s to the mid-1990s equals about one-third of a year of GDP. The marginal propensity to consume out of wealth must be one-sixth to rationalize the consumption boom. If one assumes such a high marginal propensity to consume, however, then the lack of a consumption response to recent increases in wealth is puzzling.

A role for wealth accumulation becomes more plausible if one ignores timing and simply observes that budget constraints relate consumption to wealth. The increase in the ratio of net worth to income from the late 1970s to 1997 amounts to two-thirds of a year of GDP. The marginal propensity to consume out of wealth need now only be 9% to rationalize the consumption boom.[22] Thus, while the aggregate data cast some doubt on the role of wealth, this explanation for the consumption boom is a main focus of the subsequent analysis of household data.

4.3 INCREASES IN IMPATIENCE OR THE PROPENSITY TO CONSUME

As noted at the end of Section 3, several current explanations argue that the effective discount rate or the propensity to consume of the representative agent has increased. Such an increase is consistent with two main coincident facts. First, as already mentioned, the real interest rate was high during the consumption boom relative to the previous two decades. This suggests that the demand for output is relatively high. Second, as documented in the first two rows of Table 1, the growth rate of real consumption per capita actually has slowed. Within the context of a Ramsey economy, the Euler equation governs consumption growth. Without a change in the effective discount rate, a higher real interest rate should be associated with a higher average growth rate of consumption, not a lower one.

I now turn to two of the explanations discussed at the end of Section 3: increases in government transfers from future to present generations, and financial innovation and increases in debt. These explanations are also evaluated in Sections 6, 7, and 8, using cross-sectional implications of these theories and household data.

4.3.1 Increasing Government Transfers to Older Generations   During the period of the increasing consumption share of output, the U.S. government has increased its reallocation of wealth from future to current generations. In a pure life-cycle model, the beneficiaries of these transfers

---

22. Poterba and Samwick (1995) and Ludvigson and Steindel (1999) also demonstrate that the high-frequency relationship between stock-market value and consumption is weak.

Table 1 CONSUMPTION GROWTH AND EXPENDITURE SHARES

	Real Per Capita Annual Growth Rate (%)			
	1959–69	1969–79	1979–89	1989–98[a]
Total PCE	3.0	2.4	2.0	1.6
Nondurable goods and services	2.8	2.3	1.8	1.4
	Change in Share of GDP (%)			
	1959–69	1969–79	1979–89	1989–98[a]
Total PCE	−1.2	0.7	3.8	2.1
Durable goods	0.3	−0.4	0.3	−0.2
Nondurable goods	−3.5	−1.4	−3.0	−1.9
Services	2.0	2.5	6.5	4.2
Medical care	1.3	1.6	2.6	1.7
Other services	0.8	0.3	2.3	1.9
Housing	0.0	0.0	1.2	0.2

[a] 1998 estimates are preliminary.

consume more than their pretransfer wealth, while other generations consume less. In the United States, social security and Medicare are the largest of these programs, and the payments to the elderly have been consistently rising, as has the share of medical care in total consumption. Gokhale, Kotlikoff, and Sabelhaus (1996) argue that this redistribution can explain the consumption boom.

To provide a first evaluation of this explanation, the second panel of Table 1 presents the budget shares of different categories of consumption, including medical care. The boom in consumption is more than entirely due to increased consumption of services, of which medical care is a major component. The output share of purchases of goods—nondurable and durable—has declined by nearly 10 percentage points since 1959. Two-thirds of this decline is a steady decrease in the share of consumption that is food. Within services, the largest increases in consumption are due to spending on medical care and on other services.[23] From 1979 to 1998, the growth in the share of medical care is 4.3% and the growth in the share of other services is 4.2%, both large when compared to the 5.9% increase in the total consumption to GDP ratio. This

23. Other services include transportation services and household operations (which are usually their own categories) and miscellaneous services related to clothing, accessories, and jewelry (such as cleaning, repair, and storage); personal business such as banking, legal, and funeral services; recreational services such as cable TV, club memberships, theater tickets, and pet-related costs; religious activities; foreign travel; and finally education and other day-care costs. See Bureau of Economic Analysis (1990).

seems to suggest that the consumption boom can largely be explained by government provision of medical care free of charge to the elderly.

However, a slightly different picture emerges if one compares these recent changes, which occurred contemporaneously with the consumption boom, with the changes that occurred over the previous twenty years, during which the consumption-to-GDP ratio was constant. Table 1 again reveals that services growth is, at least in an accounting sense, the cause of the recent consumption boom. But, relative to growth over the previous twenty years, the increased consumption of services is more evenly distributed among nonmedical nonhousing services, medical services, and housing. The change in medical services as a share of output from 1979 to 1998 exceeds the change over the previous twenty years by 1.4 percentage points. It is also worth noting that the transition to Medicare was largely completed prior to the consumption boom.[24]

In sum, there is evidence that the consumption boom is concentrated in spending on services, but not that this increased spending on services is disproportionately concentrated on medical care. Since this evidence is far from conclusive, I later evaluate the role of intergenerational transfers, including Medicaid, by studying which households were "overconsuming" relative to their ages, wealth, and incomes, and asking whether these households are in cohorts that are receiving large intergenerational transfers. In good macroeconomic tradition, the remainder of the paper will focus on output as one good.

4.3.2 Financial Innovations and Increases in Debt During the past twenty years, gross debt has risen as a share of disposable income. As shown in Figure 2b, the difference between the ratios of total assets to disposable income and net worth to disposable income have increased from 0.7 to nearly 1. If this increase represents relaxed liquidity constraints or financial innovation that allows previously constrained households to borrow to support consumption, then that innovation would lead to a transitory consumption boom. During the past twenty years, credit cards have become more widely available and an increasing amount of debt is held on them. Also, the minimum down payment required to purchase a house has declined, and the number and visibility of financial instruments available to borrow against home equity have increased.

Financial innovations are not able to account for a large increase in consumption. As noted in the previous subsection, the share of expenditures on housing services rises during the consumption boom. However, the increase in the ratio of debt to output is just over 20%. As calculated

24. See Bosworth (1996).

in Section 4.1, the present value of the consumption boom is three-quarters of one year of GDP. If the increase in the debt ratio were entirely caused by an exogenous increase in households' ability to borrow, then financial innovation could explain at most 30% of the increase in consumption to income to date.

4.4 THE LIMITS OF AGGREGATE EVIDENCE

Using only aggregate data, a significant difficulty in understanding the decline in the saving rate is lack of exogeneity. Thus this paper now turns to household-level data. This approach has three advantages. First, the composition of households has changed significantly over the past twenty years. There are more retirees, more single-parent families, and greater dispersion in household income. This paper uses household-level data to evaluate whether such changes have caused the decline in the saving rate. Second, several possible causes of the consumption boom give strong predictions about the cross-sectional distribution of consumption ratios. For example, intergenerational transfers are expected to raise consumption by the currently elderly and reduce it for the currently young. Finally, absent full consumption insurance, household propensities to consume out of idiosyncratic asset values and income levels can be used to estimate the response of the aggregate economy to these variables.

The next section describes the construction of a novel dataset that combines information from two household-level survey datasets and NIPA data to generate a panel dataset with information on consumption, income, and wealth at the household level. The remainder of the paper uses this dataset to evaluate theories of the increase in aggregate consumption relative to income.

5. Constructing a Household-Level Dataset

In order to study the consumption behavior of households, I employ the Consumer Expenditure Survey (CEX) to impute the consumption of services and nondurable goods to each household in the Panel Study of Income Dynamics (PSID) from 1979 to 1994. This yields a panel dataset on consumption of households that includes a large set of demographic and income information as well as three years of detailed wealth information. [Skinner (1987) pioneers the use of the CEX to impute consumption to the PSID.] This section briefly describes my procedure for imputation and the important features of the final dataset. Additional details are provided in the Appendix.

5.1. THE PSID

The PSID has been used extensively to study year-to-year fluctuations in consumption, and the main characteristics of the dataset are reasonably well known. For the present analysis, using PSID households as the unit of analysis has three main advantages. First, the survey provides panel data over much of the time period of interest on over 5000 households per year. Data from 1979 to 1994 are used to match the timing of the consumption boom.[25] The PSID provides weights so that the means in any year or category of household can be aggregated to produce a nationally representative sample.

Second, the Survey has repeated measures of food consumption and excellent information on household income. The main measure of consumption is usual weekly food consumption, and this information has been gathered in every year of interest except 1988 and 1989. Food consumption is measured with error, and this has hampered studies working with Euler equations and relating annual consumption changes to observable variables. In much of this study, the focus of interest will be long-term movements or movements across groups of people, so that this mismeasurement creates fewer difficulties. The fact that food consumption is not typical of all consumption expenditures is more of a concern, and this concern leads to the joint use of the CEX, as subsequently described.

Income in the PSID is total posttransfer, pretax income, so that it is not completely comparable to national income in the NIPA. Nonetheless, as demonstrated in the appendix, the ratio of food consumption to income constructed from aggregating the PSID data has the same temporal pattern as that of the NIPA. The correlation between the PSID series and the NIPA series is 0.93.

Third, and most importantly, the survey contains accurate information on wealthholding of households in 1984, 1989, and 1994, a time period covering the heart of the consumption boom. Such information is not available in the CEX alone. The PSID data on wealth include wealth held in saving and checking accounts, money market accounts, certificates of deposit, bonds, stocks, mutual funds, IRAs, cash value of life insurance, trusts and estates, main home, second homes, investment real estate, cars, trucks, boats, motor homes, farm and business wealth, and collections of things for investment purposes (e.g., baseball cards), all less credit card, mortgage, and "other" debts. The wealth data are comprehen-

---

25. These include income information from the Survey year 1995. The 1994 and 1995 data are in early-release form, and thus the relevant variables must be constructed from raw data.

sive and do an excellent job of reproducing the wealth of the bottom 99% of the wealth distribution in these categories of wealth (Juster, Smith, and Stafford, 1999). The only real shortcoming of the PSID wealth data is that pension wealth is unavailable. The PSID does report whether the household has a pension, and that information is used here.

In order for a household to be included in the analysis, it must have all the necessary information for the year in question. Further, the observation is dropped if any of the necessary information is a major assignment made by the PSID staff.

5.2 THE CEX

In order to use the PSID to analyze the increase in the consumption share of output, this work imputes the consumption of nondurable goods and services for each household. I first estimate the relationship between this larger measure of consumption and a household's level of food consumption and demographic characteristics, using data from the Consumer Expenditure Survey (CEX). The consumption of nondurable goods and services of households in the PSID is then predicted using this estimated relationship.

The CEX is conducted by the Bureau of Labor Statistics in order to construct baskets of goods for use in the bases for the Consumer Price Index and has been run continuously since 1980. The survey has excellent coverage of consumption expenditures, reasonable data on liquid assets, and income information of moderate quality.[26] The survey interviews about 5500 households each quarter and has households keep records of consumption expenditures, which are then collected by the survey at the end of four three-month interview periods. About half of all households make it through all the interviews, and sample weights are given so that a representative sample of nonrural households can be recovered. The CEX represents the best source of information on household consumption across a large set of categories.

The data used here come from the family files of the CEX from 1980 to 1993 and from extracts made publicly available by the Congressional Budget Office and John Sabelhaus through the NBER.[27] Each household contributes one data point to the employed sample. I drop any household that is classified as an incomplete income reporter, that has any of the crucial variables missing, or that does not report an income measure contemporaneous with the consumption data.[28] I construct variables

26. See Lusardi (1996), Attanasio (1994), and Branch (1994).
27. See Bureau of Labor Statistics (1993) and http://www.nber.org/ces_cho.html.
28. This procedure cuts nearly all households that are listed in the CBO/Sabelhaus/NBER data as not completing all the interviews. The weights adjusted by the CBO for attrition are employed.

measuring food consumption and consumption on all NIPA categories of nondurable goods and services consumption. Income is pretax total family income to match the concept in the PSID.

Finally, as for the PSID, I construct the ratio of food consumption to income from the CEX and compare this with the NIPA series. The correlation between the CEX and NIPA series is 0.78, which is not as high as that from the PSID. However, as discussed in the Appendix, it is an acceptable level for present purposes.

5.3 IMPUTING EXPENDITURES ON NONDURABLE GOODS AND SERVICES

Turning to the imputation of consumption for households in the PSID, two important factors drive the specification of the imputation. First, what are the correct theoretical concepts that shift the relative utility of consumption of food and nonfood items? Given that food has declined significantly as a share of consumption over the period of interest, to impute nondurable and services consumption to households it will be necessary to recognize both that the relative price of food changes through time and that food is a necessity, so that its budget share declines with increasing wealth. Further, household characteristics such as family size, number of earners, and retirement status may shift the relative utility of food consumption vs. consumption of other goods.

Second, what variables are measured in similar ways in both surveys? The imputation is only valid if the regressors used in the estimating equation are the same variables as those in the predicting equation. As discussed in the Appendix, there is some variation in the relative levels of the consumption and income series, but the factors of interest are the time trends. For all the regressors, the survey questions, the levels, and the time trends are compared between the surveys, and they match reasonably well.

The imputation proceeds in four steps. First, using the CEX data, the log of expenditures on nondurable goods and services is regressed on a cubic polynomial in the log of food consumption and a set of regressors designed to allow preferences for relative consumption to vary by family size, age, education level, labor-force status, and retirement status. To capture differences in relative prices of goods over time, the mean is allowed to vary by year. The regression employs 37,730 households and explains 80% of the variation in household consumption.

Second, the estimated parameters are used to predict consumption of nondurable goods and services for each household in the PSID. Third, the imputed consumption for each household is treated as a relative consumption level, and the total consumption across households is scaled up to include medical purchases by the government. This step is similar to that of Gokhale, Kotlikoff, and Sabelhaus (1996), who assign medical consumption across ages. Their medical-care adjustments employ more detailed age-specific adjustments but do not assign these expenditures in relation to individual consumption. Finally, the consumption of nondurable goods and services in the NIPA in each year is allocated across households in proportion to each household's consumption from the third step.

After this imputation, I have a true panel dataset that covers 16 years from 1979 to 1994 and contains measures of income, nondurable and service consumption (for all years except 1988 and 1989), and wealth in 1984, 1989, and 1994. I turn now to describing the evolution of consumption ratios across broad groups of the population. All nominal data are made real using a price index constructed by dividing nominal consumption of services and nondurable goods by the same real quantity, where nondurable and services consumption is made real using the NIPA chained price indexes. Data for the second quarter of the year of interest are used.

From here on the term "consumption" is used interchangeably with the more cumbersome term "consumption of nondurable goods and services."

6. Growth and Demographic Structure: Age, Cohort, and Time Effects in Consumption

The United States has experienced a large increase in the share of the population that is over 65 years of age and a bulge in the population distribution associated with the aging of the baby boom generation.[29] If households of different ages have different propensities to consume out of lifetime income, then there is variation in the representative agent's discount rate. For example, middle-aged households wish to consume at a greater rate than young or old households since they tend to have more members. Thus an economy in which a population bulge is entering middle age looks like a canonical Ramsey economy with a temporarily higher effective discount rate. Are the observed fluctuations in the U.S. age distribution leading to fluctuations in the discount rate of the representative agent that are in turn pushing up the consumption-to-income ratio?

---

29. In addition, there is a long-term trend towards slower population growth in the United States.

Table 2   CELL SIZES FOR AGE AND COHORT GROUPS

Cohort Born	Cell Size	Age Group	Cell Size
1905–09	1,722	19–24	7,090
1910–14	2,799	25–29	12,838
1915–19	3,264	30–34	13,075
1920–24	3,973	35–39	10,427
1925–29	4,725	40–44	7,319
1930–34	4,488	45–49	5,263
1935–39	4,135	50–54	4,702
1940–44	5,462	55–59	4,421
1945–49	9,331	60–64	4,225
1950–54	13,024	65–69	3,850
1955–59	13,627	70–74	3,063
1960–64	8,339	75–85	3,208
		85+	583
1893–05[a]	1,176		
1965–73[a]	3,999		

[a]Partially observed.

6.1 WHO ARE CONSUMING MORE OF THEIR INCOME?

Over the period in question, the elderly as a group have increased their share of consumption. This fact suggests an important role of decreasing lifetime wealth of the young and/or increasing transfers to the elderly. However, this trend significantly predates the current data and the consumption boom.[30] Following in the footsteps of previous studies using micro data, the analysis of the household data begins by describing the evolution of consumption and consumption ratios across different age groups and time periods.[31] Next, this section uses a simple life-cycle framework to identify the role of demographics in the consumption boom.

The analysis first groups the data into birth cohorts and age groups. Table 2 shows the cells and the cell sizes chosen for the analysis. Ages are grouped into 13 five-year cells, and the cohorts are also split into 12 cells.[32] The number of households in each cohort cell and age group

30. See Gokhale, Kotlikoff, and Sabelhaus (1996, Figure 1).
31. This approach is employed in the study of consumption and saving by Deaton and Paxson (1994), Attanasio (1997a), Deaton and Paxson (1997), and Alessie, Kapteyn, and Lusardi (1998).
32. Two *partial* cohorts are in the sample for too little time to properly identify their actual cohort effect. Of these cohorts, the youngest is only observed in the relevant age range for about half the sample. The oldest has some members in the sample in every year,

varies over time. There are 14 years of data, spread over the 16 years 1979 to 1994. In general, each cohort group and age group will be denoted by the middle age or year in its range. The number of data afforded by the PSID is a significant advantage: there are over 80,000 observations on household consumption and income. This is an unweighted look at the data. Sample weights imply quite a different age and cohort distribution of the data, one that is representative of the U.S. noninstitutional population.

To begin, I use the sample weights and data in each cohort group to construct a measure of the average log consumption of each cohort at each age. Figure 4a displays the consumption of each cohort at different ages. The life-cycle pattern of hump-shaped consumption is clearly visible.[33] Also noticeable is the artificially sudden rise in consumption that occurs at age 65 due to the allocation of medical expenditures by the imputation procedure.[34] The figure shows, for any cohort, the combination of both age and time effects at work. None of the effects are separately identified. It could be that all households have the same lifetime wealth and that the "endpoints" of each segment do not join due to time effects that raise the endpoint of each cohort's age series of consumption. However, productivity growth implies that younger cohorts are richer and so consume more than their elders did at the same age. If there were no time effects, then consumption profiles of younger cohorts would lie above those of their elders due solely to cohort effects, which would be due in turn to productivity growth. To identify the separate effects of age, time, and cohort requires identifying assumptions, which are provided shortly.

Figure 4b displays the same set of information as Figure 4a, but by year and for only four cohorts. This figure shows that over the period of the consumption boom, the cohort whose consumption has risen the most is that of households born between 1955 and 1959, the youngest cohort. While this would seem to be evidence that this younger group is, in an accounting sense, the cause of the consumption boom, in fact, the age profile of consumption for this cohort should be increasing.

Figure 5a and b show the total consumption of each cohort divided by

---

but fewer than 50 in each year of the 1990s. These partial cohorts are used only in a subset of the analysis, and when this is done it is noted.

33. This pattern has many interpretations and has been the subject of much debate; see for example Carroll and Summers (1991), Attanasio and Browning (1995), and Gourinchas and Parker (1997).

34. In the analysis of consumption levels, this feature of the imputation only biases the estimated age effects. In the growth-rate regressions, the artificial consumption growth over these years is removed by a dummy variable.

Figure 4 LOG NONDURABLES CONSUMPTION (a) BY AGE AND COHORT, (b) BY YEAR AND COHORT

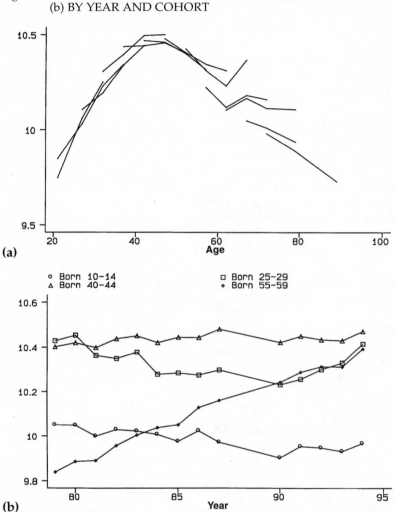

(a)

(b)

the total income received by that cohort by age and time respectively. Figure 5a emphasizes the clear life-cycle pattern of consumption ratios, in which the young save and the elderly dissave. Again these patterns are confounded by the inability to see people of different cohorts at the same age and in the same year. Looking at the general shape of the profile, one sees a mixture of effects at work. That is, since the profiles for different cohorts nearly join neatly or overlap when observed at the

Figure 5 NONDURABLES CONSUMPTION TO INCOME RATIOS (a) BY AGE
AND COHORT, (b) BY YEAR AND COHORT

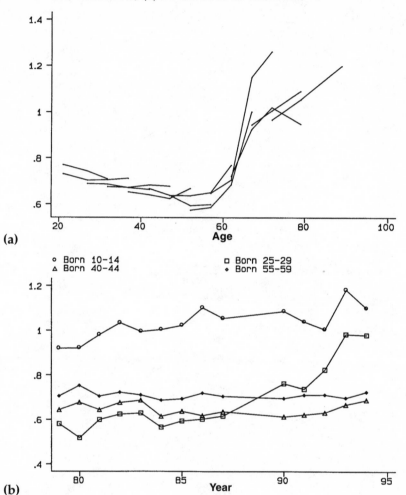

(a)

(b)

same ages, it may seem that the effect of cohort on saving behavior is
small. In fact, however, these profiles may not join or overlap if time
effects are removed. Figure 5b displays the combination of the effects of
age and time on each cohort of households. The cohort born between
1925 and 1929 clearly has the sharpest rise in consumption ratio over the
period; however, the same caveat that applies to the increasing consumption of the young applies here. During the 16-year period examined, the

Figure 6 LOG NONDURABLES-CONSUMPTION GROWTH (a) BY AGE AND COHORT, (b) BY YEAR AND COHORT

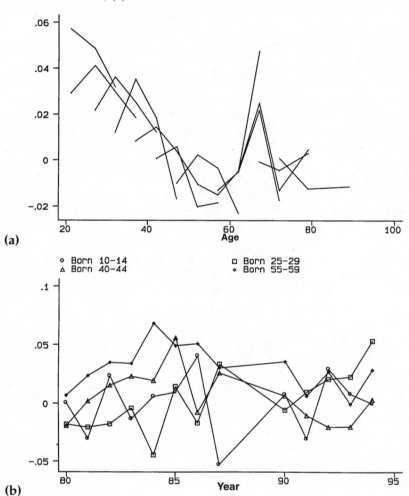

(a)

○ Born 10–14   □ Born 25–29
△ Born 40–44   ◆ Born 55–59

(b)

youngest households in this cohort age from 50 to 65 and the oldest households in this cohort move from 54 to 69. Thus, life-cycle considerations suggest that this group should move from saving to dissaving.

Finally, Figure 6a and b display the profiles of the average of household-level consumption growth. As is typical of household data, the growth rates of consumption display a fair amount of variation, but the life-cycle figure still captures a broad age pattern in the same way as

Figures 4a and 5a.[35] Household-level variation is potentially useful for identification of the underlying causes of the consumption boom. The profiles by time seem to have more measurement error, although the data do pick up the aggregate growth following the 1982 recession and the decline in consumption growth in the 1991 recession.

6.2 IDENTIFYING THE EFFECT OF DEMOGRAPHICS

In this section, each household's consumption and income is decomposed into a portion specific to the time period, a portion specific to its birth cohort, a portion specific to its age, and a final portion specific to the individual household. By defining the household-specific portion to have mean zero for each age, cohort, and time grouping, the aggregate consumption ratio can be reconstructed from a weighted combination of age, time, and cohort components for each time period. Separately identifying age, cohort and time effects requires an identifying assumption.[36]

The canonical methodology for separately identifying the effects of age, cohort, and time in saving-rate data is to assume either that time effects are unimportant or that they have mean zero and are orthogonal to a time trend (Attanasio, 1997a; Deaton and Paxson, 1994). Income and consumption are composed of four additive effects: a time effect specific to the year the household is observed; a cohort effect that captures permanent differences in wealth and situation; an age effect that captures the typical household's saving profile over their life; and finally a household-specific component, uncorrelated with the first three. In the absence of fluctuations, the stripped-down life-cycle model of Modigliani and Brumberg (1956) predicts identical age profiles for each generation and cohort effects that depend on lifetime resources. Attanasio (1997a) and Paxson (1996) provide evidence that age profiles over long time horizons conform reasonably well to this model.

I assume that the time effects have mean zero and are orthogonal to a linear time trend. The consumption increase can then be traced only to differential saving behavior of different generations or to different shares of the population at different ages. While this decomposition is informative without yielding a direct structural interpretation, a simple life-cycle

---

35. An alternative approach would be to average consumption by year and group first, and then to first-difference. But the amount of noise in household-level consumption growth does not seem to be sufficient to require that one look only at consumption growth by group.

36. Smoothing the data using age and cohort groups can provide an artificial identification. To avoid this, all members of a cohort are assigned to the same age, so that age = year − cohort, and the identification of the linear relationship among the effects requires an identifying assumption. The results, once identification is imposed, are substantively unchanged by this modification.

model predicts these effects. In the basic life-cycle model, the household consumption ratio, C/Y, can be written as the marginal propensity to consume at that age times the household's wealth:

$$\frac{C_h}{Y_h} = \text{MPC}_a \frac{\text{NPVY}_h + W_h + \text{NT}_h}{Y_h}, \tag{6.1}$$

where NPVY denotes the net present value of human wealth, MPC denotes the propensity to consume out of total resources, h denotes the household in question, a denotes age, W denotes financial wealth, and NT denotes the present value of net transfers. All wealth measures are as of the start of life. The marginal propensity to consume out of wealth is allowed to vary by age, presumably due to changing family size, time until death, and possibly changing preferences (or even unmodelled precautionary saving).

Taking logs yields

$$\ln \frac{C_h}{Y_h} = \ln \text{MPC}_a + \ln (\text{NPVY}_h + W_h + \text{NT}_h) - \ln Y_{h,t}.$$

So that the aggregate consumption-to-income ratio can be exactly reconstructed after the decomposition, I employ the approximation $\ln(C_h/Y_h) \approx -S_h/Y_h = C_h/Y_h - 1$, leading to

$$\frac{C_h}{Y_h} = A_h + B_h + T_h + \epsilon_h, \tag{6.2}$$

where $A_h \equiv 1 + \ln \text{MPC}_a$ plus the sample average of C/Y, B_h is the average of $\ln (\text{NPVY} + W + \text{NT})$ across households in the same cohort as h less the sample average, T_h is the average of $-\ln Y_{h,t}$ across households in the same year as h less the sample average, and finally ϵ_h is that share of the consumption ratio not explained by the three effects. Under certainty, the cohort effect depends only on lifetime resources. Fluctuations in income deliver time effects. Note that in estimation, sampling error falls naturally into a time effect.[37]

Before decomposing the ratio of consumption to income as shown in equation (6.2), I decompose household consumption into age, cohort, and time effects. Household consumption is regressed on a complete set

---

37. The existing models that yield time, age, cohort decompositions maintain the dual assumptions of certainty and a constant real interest rate.

of age dummies, a set of time dummies less two, and a complete set of cohort dummies less one. Cell weights are used in the regressions so that the relative importance of a given cell in generating the aggregate is accounted for. The regression constrains the coefficients on the time dummies to sum to zero and to be orthogonal to a time trend. The coefficients on the cohort dummies are constrained to have mean zero.

Figure 7a shows the decomposition of household-level consumption. The age profile of consumption rises with age and declines less than the rough profile of Figure 4. This difference is due to the cohort effects that steadily increase over the century. Each successive cohort consumes more, presumably because its lifetime resources are greater.[38]

Figure 7b shows the same decomposition applied to the consumption ratio, as in equation (6.2). Consumption and income are separately constructed for each cell of cohort, age, and year, and the consumption rate is constructed for each cell by dividing total consumption by income.[39] The age effects in consumption ratios show a typical profile of nondurable and service consumption rates for any generation. Households during their working lives consume less than their incomes, and a roughly constant fraction of income as they age. As income declines at age 60 and during retirement, households consume significantly more than their incomes. The implied saving profile looks quite similar to the predictions of the textbook life-cycle model.

Turning next to the cohort effects, there is clear evidence that the younger cohorts are bigger spenders than the older cohorts, relative to their incomes. The effect is large, with the cohorts born most recently on average consuming over 15% more of their income than the oldest households. What causes such large differences? Within the framework of the simple life-cycle model above, this higher level of consumption comes from younger cohorts having higher wealth relative to income, such as from net government transfers or bequests.

The role of increases in wealth will be evaluated shortly. The role of intergenerational transfers is studied closely by Gokhale, Kotlikoff, and Sabelhaus (1996), who construct certainty-equivalent wealth levels in a life-cycle model and examine saving rates from 1963 to 1989. Their decomposition blames the declining national saving on government transfers to households that are elderly by 1989. If the pattern observed in Figure 7b were due only to intergenerational transfers, the net transfers to the youngest cohorts would have to be larger than those to the older cohorts. This is somewhat implausible and inconsistent with the

---

38. The rate of increase of the cohort effects clearly slows over time, consistent with the slowing of productivity growth.
39. Similar conclusions are reached on employing separate identification of effects in consumption and income at the household level.

Figure 7 (a) NONDURABLES-CONSUMPTION EFFECTS;
(b) NONDURABLES-CONSUMPTION-TO-INCOME EFFECTS

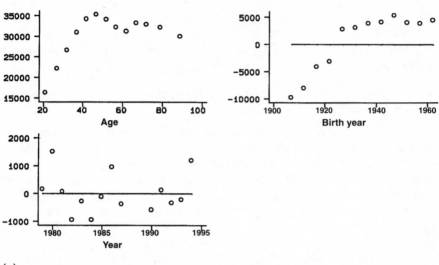

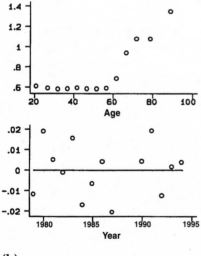

(a)

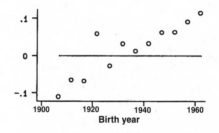

(b)

intergenerational transfer distributions constructed by Gokhale, Kotlikoff, and Sabelhaus (1996).

In sum, within the context of a basic life-cycle model, fiscal transfers across generations alone cannot explain the consumption boom. Transfers may be leading today's elderly to consume a larger share of their incomes than the elderly of two decades ago. But social security cannot explain the propensity of cohorts born more recently to consume a higher fraction of their incomes than the current elderly.

6.3 CAN CHANGING DEMOGRAPHICS EXPLAIN THE CONSUMPTION BOOM?

This subsection demonstrates that the changing distribution across age groups in the United States does not explain the increase in the ratio of consumption to income. According to the decomposition of Section 6.2, there are two possible explanations of the decline in saving. First, the weight given to different age effects may change as the shares of different age groups in the population change. For example, as the elderly have become an increasing share of the population, they may have pushed the aggregate saving rate down because the elderly consume a larger fraction of their incomes than other age groups. Second, the cohorts that are higher consumers may move to the ages at which their consumption and incomes are higher and so push up the aggregate consumption rate. Lower-consumption cohorts may also die and be replaced by higher-consumption cohorts.

This subsection uses the estimated effects to consider partial-equilibrium alternative scenarios in which different weights are given to different effects in generating the aggregate consumption ratio. The aggregate consumption-to-income ratio for each year, denoted $\left(\widehat{\frac{C}{Y}}\right)_t$, can be reconstructed as

$$\left(\widehat{\frac{C}{Y}}\right)_t \equiv \frac{\Sigma_{i \in I_t} w_i \hat{B}_i}{\Sigma_{i \in I_t} w_i} + \hat{T}_t + \frac{\Sigma_{i \in I_t} w_i \hat{A}_i}{\Sigma_{i \in I_t} w_i},$$

where i indexes age–cohort–year cells, I_t is the set of cells for which the year is equal to t, w_i is the population weight associated with that cell, $\hat{B}_i$ is the estimated birth-year or cohort effect, $\hat{T}_i$ is the estimated year effect, and $\hat{A}_i$ is the estimated age effect.

Figure 8a displays the reconstructed consumption-to-income ratio without cohort effects.[40] Figure 8b shows the consumption ratio with age

40. This analysis is conducted including the partial cohorts so as to replicate the aggregate time series. This reconstructed consumption ratio has a slightly lower increase over the

and time removed, leaving only the effect of cohorts aging. These figures show that the consumption boom is not due to the changing age distribution. Instead, the decline in saving occurred because each successive generation consumed more of its income than the previous generation at that age.[41]

This conclusion matches the general consensus of research in this area that the age distribution of the population has little effect on national saving (Bosworth, Burtless, and Sabelhaus, 1991; Paxson, 1996; Attanasio, 1997a; Deaton, 1997). All of these papers employ slightly different methodologies and data, and all blame cohort rather than age effects for declining saving rates. Attanasio (1997a) finds that those born between 1925 and 1939 account for an unusually high share of national consumption. Gokhale, Kotlikoff, and Sabelhaus (1996) attribute the decline in saving between 1960 and 1990 to the large share of resources flowing from future generations to the generation that is currently elderly.[42] The findings of the remaining sections of the present paper concur that age dynamics have little to no effect on the consumption ratio.

The balance of this paper is devoted to a fuller investigation of the structural interpretation of these all-important cohort effects. In this section, the cohort effects represent differences in lifetime resources, because the environment is assumed so simple that no other explanations are present to compete. There are two reasons to be skeptical of such a simple interpretation. First, the observed pattern of fiscal transfers is not consistent with the estimated pattern of the cohort effects. Second, there are important observed changes in the U.S. economy that call into question the simple identification scheme of this section. Differences in real interest rates, shocks to wealth, and different rates of time preference across generations all invalidate the identification assumptions employed here by altering the age profile of consumption across households.

To address these shortcomings, the next section augments the simple life-cycle decomposition. I allow for uncertainty and model the cohort effect as due both to the permanent component of income and to wealth holdings. Estimating a linear approximation to the household

---

period than the raw data, which implies that the true cohort effects for the extremely old and young are larger in absolute value than the endpoints that are used for them. Also, the changing numbers of these households over time induce some year-to-year fluctuations in the reconstructed ratio that are not due to time effects.

41. The same conclusion and similar pictures are obtained if instead I separately remove cohort effects from consumption and income at the household-level and reconstruct time series without cohort effects in either series.

42. They attribute about half of the increase in consumption to an increasing propensity of the elderly to consume, a propensity that is not identified as due to age, cohort, or time.

Figure 8 (a) NONDURABLES-CONSUMPTION RATIO AND COHORT
         EFFECTS; (b) NONDURABLES-CONSUMPTION RATIO WITHOUT
         TIME AND AGE EFFECTS

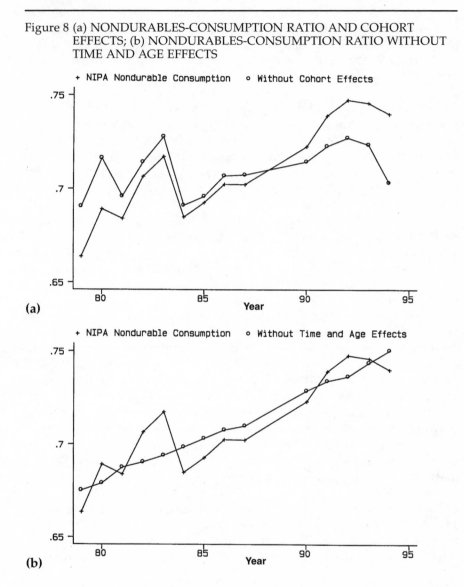

(a)

(b)

consumption policy function, I again find that the appreciation of assets alone cannot explain the consumption boom.

7. The Role of Wealth

This section considers a realistic but simple model of household behavior
and estimates an approximate consumption policy function for each

household.[43] The procedure of this section does not assume that time effects have mean zero or that the agent's environment is certain. The consumption boom is traced to the changing age distribution, time effects, and the changing distributions of wealth and the permanent component of income.

7.1 AN ORGANIZING MODEL

Each household in the economy chooses consumption to maximize expected lifetime utility:

$$\text{Max } E_s \left(\sum_{t=s}^{T} \beta^{t-s} v_a u(\Gamma_t, C_t) + \beta^{T+1-s} V_{T+1}^D(\Gamma_{T+1}, X_{T+1}) \right),$$

where E_s is the expectation operator conditional on all information available at time s, β is the discount factor, v shifts utility as households age, Γ is a family-size adjustment that normalizes consumption to per capita terms, X_t is household cash on hand, and $V^D(\cdot)$ captures the possible value of cash on hand remaining at death. Household choices are constrained by an intertemporal budget constraint that represents the evolution of liquid assets or cash on hand, X_t, and a liquidity constraint that they must maintain positive net wealth:

$$X_{t+1} = \tilde{R}_{t+1}(X_t - C_t) + (1 - \tau) Y_{t+1},$$
$$X_t \geq C_t,$$

where $\tilde{R}_{t+1}$ is the gross after-tax rate of return on the household's optimal portfolio, and Y_t is disposable nonasset, pretax income.

The household bases its consumption upon its current state and its expectations about the future. That is, household consumption is described by an optimal policy function of the payoff-relevant state variables. In order to choose its current consumption level, the household needs to know its current and expected future resources, its family size, the time horizon over which it is alive, and the possible investments and rates of return available to it. In order to forecast future income, I assume that the household only requires the permanent component of its income, P_h, the aggregate state, A_t, and its age.[44] I assume that the household requires only knowledge of the aggregate state to forecast future rates of return optimally.

Under these assumptions, the consumption function for household h

---

43. Recent work that estimates consumption functions includes Carroll (1994) and Parker (1998).
44. The permanent component will be defined shortly. I will also consider a case in which current income is necessary for predicting future income.

can be written solely as a function of family size, wealth, income, age, the permanent component of income, and the aggregate state.

$$C_h = F(\Gamma_h, X_h, \text{age}_h, P_h, A_t). \tag{7.1}$$

Since different cohorts may still have different preferences for consumption above and beyond their state variables, and since there may be a role for different intergenerational transfers by cohort, the exclusion of birth year from the consumption function is tested.

7.2 ESTIMATION STRATEGY

A log-linear approximation to the policy function is estimated in the form

$$\ln C_h = g(\Gamma_h) + h(X_h) + f(\text{age}_h) + B \ln P_h + T_t + \epsilon_h, \tag{7.2}$$

where the residual represents measurement error in the level of consumption, and T_t is a year effect that captures the aggregate state, that is, changing expectations about the future. This equation is estimated on the PSID data in 1984, 1989, and 1994, the years in which, as previously discussed, the PSID has an accurate reporting of household wealth. The data are constructed from the PSID data already employed, with the addition of these three years' wealth supplements and the following two constructions.

First, I construct a measure of consumption in 1989, a year in which the PSID does not report food consumption. Consumption from 1990 is used instead and deflated for each household by the aggregate growth in consumption between 1989 and 1990. Since any innovation to marginal utility between 1989 and 1990 should not be predictable by anything known in 1989 (such as what is on the right-hand side of the 1989 regression), this substitution should not adversely affect the results. Second, I construct the permanent component of income as the forecast of the log of current income from two lags of the log of family income, education, and age-group dummy variables. This forecast is done separately for retired and nonretired households. Note that to the extent that permanent income is mismeasured, some of its effect on consumption will be picked up by correlated variables such as wealth. Given a positive correlation between true permanent income and wealth, such mismeasurement would lead to an exaggeration of the impact of wealth on consumption.

The function $g(\Gamma_h)$ consists of the size of the family and the number of children in the family. A set of dummy variables representing the five-year age groupings capture the age effects on consumption, $f(\text{age}_h)$. Finally, wealth is included in the regressions as the log of wealth if it is positive, a dummy for wealth being zero or negative, and a dummy for whether the household has a pension.

How does this model differ from the age–time–cohort decomposition of the previous section? The key differences are two. First, the model includes directly both wealth and the permanent component of income in place of the cohort effect of the previous section. The behavior of consumption can then be traced both to this observable version of the cohort effect and to time effects and omitted elements of the cohort effect. Second, the time effects are not constrained to be orthogonal to a linear trend. Thus they can explain trend movements in consumption that are not explained by increases in wealth, the changing age distribution, and so forth.

Equation (7.2) is estimated on the entire sample of weighted data with imputed real nondurable and services consumption as the dependent variable. The time effects capture expectations, real interest rates, and all aggregate conditions. The only source of variation is cross-sectional. The goal of the exercise is to see whether the behavioral relationships estimated from household data can explain the consumption boom when time-series variation is substituted for cross-sectional variation.

7.3 BEHAVIORAL EVIDENCE ON THE CONSUMPTION BOOM

Table 3 displays the results of estimation of four different specifications and the implied increases in the ratio of consumption to income due only to changes in the distribution of wealth to income over the period.[45]

The marginal propensity to consume out of wealth is estimated to be around 4%. As noted in Section 3, ignoring timing, a marginal propensity to consume out of wealth of 9% can rationalize the entire 20-year consumption boom. Over the 10-year period being studied here, however, wealth increased in relation to income only over the first 5 years; during the second 5 years the distribution of wealth spread out, so that the number of low-wealth households increased despite no significant change in the mean wealth-to-income ratio.

The estimated relationship between consumption and wealth is not linear, in that the cluster of low-wealth households have more consumption than would be implied by the relationship between wealth and consumption for higher-wealth households. The PSID does not measure pension wealth, but the presence of a pension increases consumption by between $2\frac{1}{2}$% and 5%.

When interpreting the income variables—the current income and the

---

45. See Hurst, Luoh, and Stafford (1998) for a detailed description and analysis of the distribution of wealth in the PSID. See also Sabelhaus and Pence (1998) on the changing wealth distribution.

Table 3   CONSUMPTION-FUNCTION REGRESSIONS

Regression	1	2	3	4
Log of wealth (if not low)	0.048 (0.002)	0.039 (0.002)	0.045 (0.002)	0.036 (0.002)
Low wealth	0.330 (0.025)	0.267 (0.023)	0.301 (0.025)	0.248 (0.024)
Expected log income	0.314 (0.005)	0.175 (0.006)	0.309 (0.006)	0.172 (0.007)
Pension	0.049 (0.007)	0.028 (0.007)	0.047 (0.007)	0.027 (0.007)
Log income		0.161 (0.005)		0.160 (0.005)
Stockholder			0.041 (0.008)	0.028 (0.007)
Year 1989	0.030 (0.008)	0.030 (0.007)	0.028 (0.008)	0.029 (0.007)
Year 1994	0.053 (0.008)	0.059 (0.008)	0.048 (0.008)	0.056 (0.008)
Number of observations	11,903	11,903	11,901	11,901
R^2	0.583	0.623	0.584	0.624
Significance level for birth year	0.953	0.908	0.955	0.909
Implied increase in C/Y due to increase in W/Y:				
1984–89	0.011	0.009	0.010	0.008
1989–94	0.003	0.002	0.002	0.002
Total increase in C/Y				
1984–89	0.025	0.025	0.025	0.025
1989–94	0.030	0.030	0.030	0.030

Regressions also include family size and the number of children in the household and a complete set of age-group effects. Standard errors are in parentheses.

permanent-component or expected income—one must keep in mind that the time effects remove mean long-run correlations. That is, if the model were identified from the time dimension, then rising incomes and consumption together with the budget constraint would impose a cointegrating relationship. This is not the case in cross-sectional data, a point made famously by Milton Friedman. Even looking at predicted income, the coefficient is far from unity, suggesting only a 30% increase in consumption with income.[46]

The increase in wealth-to-income ratio explains, again in a partial-equilibrium sense, about a fifth of the increase in the ratio of consumption to income over the period. The implied increase in consumption due to the changes in wealth-to-income ratio is calculated as follows. The consumption-to-income ratio that actually occurred is compared with the consumption-to-income ratio calculated from the estimated parameters and an unchanging distribution of wealth-to-income ratio.[47] By estimating the consumption function rather than looking for evidence in Euler equations or contemporaneous relationships, this analysis exploits the long-term relationships between the variables. Thus it finds a significant effect of stock-market activity on consumption, where many studies before, focusing on high-frequency data, have found little relation.[48]

In addition to a role for wealth, the regressions in Table 3 find a significant role for both time and birth-year effects. First, the majority of the increase in the ratio of consumption to income is due to time effects.[49] This is consistent with the optimism explanation for the consumption boom, in which households believe that future output less government consumption will rise significantly. However, the null hypothesis that birth year does not belong in the regression model is rejected at the 10% level across all specifications. Thus, the wealth variable is not sufficient to capture all the cohort effects that are present in the data. The large share of the decline in saving that cannot be explained by the wealth distribution is instead explained by some combination of time effects and unmodeled cohort effects. We can conclude that neither the increase in wealth nor the changing distribution of the population can fully account for the consumption boom.

The third and fourth regressions investigate the role of stock-market participation. If some households are exogenously barred from investing in the stock market, then the consumption of households that are in the market should be higher than that of those that are out of the market, given the value of the set of state variables for that household.[50] This

46. It is most likely that this signals persistence but not permanence in the expected/permanent component of income.
47. The change in the log of wealth less the change in the log of income is multiplied by the estimated coefficient on the log of wealth and added to the change in the fraction of low-wealth households times the coefficient on low wealth.
48. See Poterba and Samwick (1995), Ludvigson and Steindel (1999), and the citation therein.
49. Changes in the age distribution contribute a small decrease in the consumption-to-income ratio.
50. The household that is not excluded can always mimic the excluded household and do at least as well.

might be the case if, for example, poor households do not find it worthwhile to pay a fixed cost that is required for access to the stock market.[51] Table 3 estimates that the benefits to participation are quite small, on the order of 3–4% of consumption. Given that the share of households in the stock market has risen by about 10% over the period studied, a partial-equilibrium model would predict a $\frac{1}{3}$% rise in consumption from increased stock-market participation. Of course, in general equilibrium, prices respond. The increased participation affects asset prices and so the wealth of those already in the market; the expectation of entering the market has effects on those not in the market; and in addition, endogenous changes in the capital stock affect all workers. From this analysis, one can only conclude that there are small but significant increases in consumption from stock-market participation above and beyond wealthholding, income, age, and the aggregate state.

In sum, this section finds a significant but small role for the appreciation of assets in the consumption boom: the increase in wealth that occurred from 1984 to 1994 increased the consumption ratio by one-fifth of its overall increase. The remaining causes of the consumption boom are due to other time and cohort effects, but not due to the changing age distribution of the population.

The next section studies the growth rate of consumption and models all time effects as due to the real interest rate or shocks to wealth.

8. Consumption Growth: Impatient Generations, Wealth Increases, and Intertemporal Substitution

This section analyzes the growth rate of consumption instead of its level. The advantages of this approach are threefold. First, the real interest rate and thus intertemporal substitution is modelled structurally. Second, the growth rate of consumption is related to wealth measures in order to evaluate whether unexpectedly high asset returns are the cause of the consumption boom. If a series of unexpectedly high stock-market returns have increased consumption significantly, the households that own stocks should have significantly higher consumption growth than those that do not. Third, the role of some preference heterogeneity is modelled by allowing different cohorts to have different discount rates.[52] To preview the findings, there is no evidence uncovered that wealthy

---

51. See Vissing-Jørgensen (1998).
52. In the levels analysis, if discount rates were heterogeneous, then the age profiles of consumption would vary with cohort and this variation would undermine the identification employed in Section 6.

households had faster consumption growth or that younger cohorts have higher discount rates.

Analysis of growth rates cannot replace examination of consumption levels for two reasons. First, growth rates of consumption at the household level are extremely variable, which weakens statistical inference. Second, household transitions like divorce, marriage, death, and leaving home imply that the analysis misses significant parts of consumption growth. For example, if young cohorts start life with high consumption and then have consumption growth over their lives that is similar to that of older cohorts, consumption growth aggregated from household consumption growth will show no consumption boom or cohort heterogeneity. The level and the growth-rate analyses are complementary.

Before presenting the analysis, it is important to note that there is a consumption boom in the first-differenced data.[53] However, for the analysis of consumption growth rates, a modified method is used to impute consumption in the PSID, as described in the Appendix. This imputation assigns NIPA consumption so that the aggregated household data match NIPA growth in real per capita consumption. The imputation does not alter the cross-sectional pattern of consumption growth, so that, for example, if stockholders have faster consumption growth than nonstockholders over the period, this will still be detected. This imputation mainly smooths out the swings in growth that occur from year to year due to sampling and measurement error.

The expected real interest rate is constructed from the after-tax nominal return on a six-year Treasury bill during the calendar year of the interview less the inflation rate calculated from the chained deflator for nondurable goods and services that is used to deflate the rest of the data. The marginal tax rate is taken from Stephenson (1998) (the series AMEITRPI).[54] The expectation is taken by predicting the real interest rate for year t (to be used as the return between t and $t + 1$) using the following variables: the once lagged second-quarter to second-quarter growth rate in national income; the twice lagged after-tax real interest rate; the once and twice lagged annual unemployment rate for white males 20 years of age and older.[55] The predicting equation is run for the period 1962 to 1997.

Finally, two steps are taken to minimize the effect of the high level of

53. See Appendix (Figure 10) and Figure 6b.
54. Using the real return on high-grade municipals which are tax-free leads to the same conclusions throughout, since the expected returns of these annual series are highly correlated.
55. The consumption data in the PSID refer to a specific point in time, and are not averages over a calendar year, although there is some debate on this point (see the appendix of Zeldes, 1989).

noise in consumption growth data.[56] First, the groupings of age and cohort are expanded to ten-year groups. The noise in consumption growth makes the identification of age and cohort groups more difficult, and the five-year groups were substantially noisier.[57] Second, changes greater than 75% in absolute value are dropped.

Identification is slightly simpler in the growth-rate regressions. In theory, the innovations in the Euler equation have mean zero and are not predictable by the other right-hand-side variables. In other words, the real interest rate captures all time effects that are not orthogonal to cohort and age effects and to the real interest rate.

However, one of the main explanations of the consumption boom is that there has been a sequence of positive shocks to wealth. Thus, as a second assumption, time effects aside from the real interest rate are allowed to differ by household wealthholding patterns. That is, the weakness of the first assumption is that innovations to wealth might be correlated with predictable movements in the real interest rate in a short panel of data. Suppose that the period from 1984 to 1994 experienced a run of innovations to wealth, due to unexpectedly strong stock-market growth. There would be increases in consumption over the period that would not have mean zero after removing the substitution effect due to movements in the real interest rate. The coefficients on the remaining regressors would suffer from a small-sample bias. To allow for this possibility, I identify the trend in cohort and age effects of all households using the nonstockholders or low-wealth households according to the first identifying assumption, and then allow the time effects or trend consumption growth rate of stockholders or high-wealth households to be different. This is done by adding a dummy variable for stockholding or the log of wealth to the Euler equation to capture the mean of the expectation errors for these households in sample.

Table 4 shows the results of estimating the following consumption Euler equation.[58]

$$\Delta \ln C_{h,t+1} = \sigma E_t[r_{t+1}] + \text{age}_{h,t} + \text{cohort}_{h,t} + \eta_{h,t+1},$$

where σ is the intertemporal elasticity of substitution. The regressions explain just over 1% of the variation of household consumption growth.

56. The same set of regressions are run in grouped data, since the measurement error is reduced by averaging, but exogenous variation is also averaged and the results are quite similar to those presented here.
57. Put another way, the groupings are informally imposing a smoothness prior on the data. Large amounts of variation across neighboring groups suggest insufficient smoothing.
58. Estimation employs two-stage least squares, and reported standard errors allow for correlation across households within a time period by including time effects.

Table 4   CONSUMPTION GROWTH REGRESSIONS

Regression	1	2	3
Expected real interest rate	0.700	0.729	0.730
	(0.120)	(0.125)	(0.125)
Cohort <09	−0.006	−0.006	−0.005
	(1.259)	(1.308)	(1.309)
Cohort 10–19	0.006	0.010	0.010
	(1.178)	(1.223)	(1.224)
Cohort 20–29	−0.009	−0.005	−0.005
	(1.065)	(1.104)	(1.105)
Cohort 30–39	−0.013	−0.011	−0.011
	(0.918)	(0.952)	(0.953)
Cohort 40–49	−0.009	−0.009	−0.009
	(0.791)	(0.825)	(0.826)
Cohort 50–59	−0.007	−0.008	−0.008
	(0.577)	(0.599)	(0.600)
Log (wealth)/100 (if not low)		−0.076	−0.096
		(0.320)	(0.433)
Stockholder		0.000	0.000
		(0.023)	(0.023)
Pension		0.003	0.003
		(0.032)	(0.032)
Homeowner			0.003
			(0.040)

Dependent variable is the first difference of log consumption. Regressions also include a complete set of age-group effects. Standard errors are in parentheses.

The first column of Table 4 presents the regression results for a standard Euler equation.

The first result of interest is that the intertemporal elasticity of substitution is estimated as 0.7. Typical estimates in the literature are significantly lower and sometimes zero.[59] This estimate is in line with Attanasio and Weber (1995), who used grouped CEX data to study Euler equations over the same period. The reasons for this finding here are three. First, consumption of nondurable goods and services typically has a higher elasticity than food. Second, the data are annual. If seasonal fluctuations in consumption and the real interest rate are to some extent driven by preferences, this confounds inference. Finally, for the decade covered by the

59. See the discussion in Deaton (1992).

Figure 9 INTEREST RATES AND GROWTH IN REAL CONSUMPTION PER
CAPITA

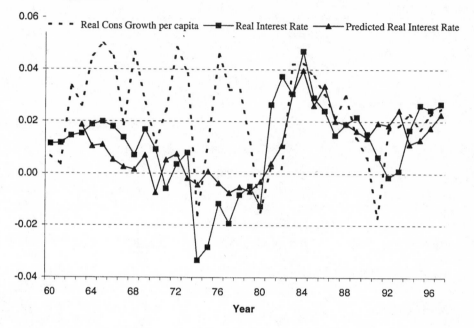

household data, consumption growth and the expected real interest rate
are highly correlated.

Figure 9 displays the expected real interest rate and the growth rate of
real consumption per capita. Over the past twenty years, the changes in
the growth rate of consumption can be rationalized by movements in the
expected real interest rate assuming an intertemporal elasticity of substitution near unity. As to explaining the consumption boom, one can ask
to what extent consumption growth would have been slower had a
lower real interest rate been in effect.[60] The expected real interest rate
from 1980 to 1994 averaged 1.5%. During the last five years the expected
rate has averaged just over 1%. Given the estimated elasticity of intertemporal substitution, consumption growth would have been 0.35%
per year slower had this lower interest rate been in effect. Over the 15
years of data on which the coefficient is estimated, consumption grew
5.5 percentage points more than income, and this alternative scenario
generates nearly exactly that excess.

60. There would of course be an associated jump in consumption with an announced
different path of interest rates, so this counterfactual is asking whether the observed
consumption growth can be rationalized by the substitution effect alone.

There are three main problems with explaining the decline in saving solely by intertemporal substitution. First, the nice fit of the Euler equation, observed roughly since Hall (1978) pointed the equation out, is not evident in the earlier data.[61] Expected income growth may be partly generating this high estimate of the intertemporal elasticity of substitution during the consumption boom. During the 1980s and 1990s, there is a strong correlation between expected income growth and the expected real interest rate.[62] Second, from 1960 to 1979, the real rate of return averaged 0.02%, and as shown in Table 1, the growth rate of real consumption per capita averaged 2.5%. That is, across the decades, high real interest rates are correlated with low rates of consumption growth. Finally, it is difficult to take seriously a story in which almost none of the movements of consumption over 14 years are driven by changes that represent new information to households.

Despite this skepticism, it is important to note that the consumption and real-interest-rate data are consistent with the impulse response of a shock to household propensity to consume in the early 1980s.

Turning to the hypothesis that different cohorts have different discount rates, Table 4 demonstrates that the cohort effects on consumption growth are small and not significantly different from one another. While the standard errors are large, even in the point estimates, there is not evidence of greater impatience in younger cohorts. It is worth noting that the mean of the cohort dummies is not separately identified from the mean of age effects. Thus one cannot construct a hypothetical consumption path along the lines of Figure 8 without some further restrictions on the data.

The second and third columns of Table 4 show that consumption growth is not significantly higher for high-wealth households, homeowners, stockholders, or households with pensions.[63] Wealth is statistically insignificant in the last column, and the magnitude of the effect is small, suggesting a 0.1% lower rate of consumption growth for a doubling of wealth.[64]

61. The usual citations are Hansen and Singleton (1983), Hall (1988), Campbell and Mankiw (1989), and Blinder and Deaton (1985).
62. Janice Eberly and John Campbell both suggested that I include expected income growth in the consumption-growth regressions. Doing so does give a statistically significant role for expected income growth, but it is economically small and does not alter the coefficient on the expected real interest rate. Given the imputations made, this is not quite a fair test of the role of expected income, but there are many in the literature.
63. In regressions using wealth data that are only available in 1984, 1989, and 1994, the most recent predetermined value is used. When this is not available, 1984 data are used. Dropping all changes prior to 1984–1985 leads to the same conclusions.
64. While not consistent with the wealthy having more positive innovations to the marginal utility of wealth over this period, the result is consistent with the wealthy having lower precautionary saving motives.

One possible reason for the insignificant results in these growth-rate regressions is the presence of large amounts of measurement error in the growth rate of consumption. One solution, which comes at the cost of a representative sample, is to regress the growth of consumption in the five years following a wealth survey on the initial wealth levels and time effects and household characteristics such as family size and age, as is done for levels in the previous section. Doing this confirms two of the three main implications of the growth-rate regressions. First, cohorts cannot be ignored even after conditioning on the wealth characteristics of households, although it is still not possible to identify a clear pattern of differing discount rates across cohorts. Second, the wealthy are again found to have slightly lower consumption growth over this period. The final main point, which cannot be meaningfully confirmed with only two observations on consumption growth, is that consumption growth and the real interest rate move in lockstep.

In sum, how does the analysis of growth rates inform what was learned in the levels analysis? The real interest rate may have played a role, but only as it propagates a positive shock to the desire to consume out of output in the early 1980s. We still find no evidence that the consumption boom is due to wealth appreciation.

9 Conclusion

This paper is motivated by a striking increase in the share of U.S. output that is consumed. This increase has occurred concurrently with a reduction in the growth rate of consumption per capita, a high real interest rate, and an increasing ratio of wealth to income. In a search for clues, the paper uses a dataset of household consumption, income, and wealth to decompose the consumption boom and confirm or reject possible culprits.

This analysis leads to several conclusions about the large increase in the consumption share of output and the decline in the U.S. saving rate.

First, a thorough examination of NIPA data shows that households and governments in the United States are consuming a greater share of output than twenty years ago. Second, this increase is not due to the changing age distribution of the U.S. population.

Third, only one-fifth of the increase in consumption to income can be explained by changes in the ratio of household wealth to income. While the wealth-to-income ratio has risen, it has done so primarily after the increase in the consumption share of output. The national saving rate has actually risen coincident with the stock-market boom of the late 1990s. The propensity to consume out of wealth estimated from the household data cannot rationalize the consumption boom. The increases in consumption-to-income ratios across groups are not related to the distribution of wealth, homeownership, or pension participation. While surely they have a role, shocks to asset values are not the main force driving the relative increase in consumption.

Fourth, prime candidates for explaining the consumption boom are factors that increase the effective discount rate of the representative agent. During this period of rising consumption share, the growth rate of real consumption per capita has fallen. At the same time, real interest rates have been relatively high. These two facts together imply a driving force that has increased actual or effective discount rates. It is also worth noting that there is a strong correlation between the real interest rate and consumption growth within the period of consumption boom. That is, the aggregate consumption Euler equation provides a better description of the data during this period than in previous periods.

This paper considers several explanations that can generate this effective impatience. The analysis reveals no evidence that the growth rate of consumption, and thus the discount rate, is higher for younger households. Further, inconsistent with an explanation that relies only on intergenerational government transfers, younger cohorts have a higher ratio of consumption to income than older cohorts. Finally, relaxed liquidity constraints could lead to an increase in debt and consumption. But the total increase in debt relative to income over the past two decades only amounts to one-third of the value of the consumption boom.

While we do not yet have a clear answer to what has caused the recent decline in saving, some speculation is possible based on the concrete findings of this paper.

Given that consumption is a forward-looking variable, households may be learning about high levels of output in the future. This explanation is untestable, and twenty years is a long consumption boom without yet seeing a shift to higher output growth. However, given that other explanations have come up short, this possibility gains credence. The strength of this explanation is that we do observe some signals of high future growth rates, such as the increase in stock prices; the weakness is that without quite a run of negative expectational errors, this explanation cannot match the slowdown in consumption growth.

A second candidate is that rather than being driven by technology or a force external to U.S. households, the decline in saving is due to a shift in the preferences of the typical household. This explanation is as hard to evaluate as the optimism explanation just discussed; however, it can fit the facts uncovered here.

A final explanation consistent with the findings of this paper is a combination of factors that work to increase the consumption of different generations. Perhaps federal transfers in the form of social security and Medicare are increasing the consumption of the elderly, while relaxed liquidity constraints are allowing the young to consume more of their incomes. This explanation can match the cross-cohort effects on the consumption-to-income ratio found in Section 6, the high real interest rate, and the slowdown in consumption growth; however, it is inconsistent with the stock-market boom.

There are many theories that can explain an increase in the consumption of aggregate output. This paper shows that the main monocausal explanations fail to match the household behavior or macroeconomic outcomes observed during the decline in U.S. saving over the past two decades. More importantly, we have an increasing number of facts that new theories or combinations of theories must fit.

Appendix. The Household Data

A.1 THE PANEL STUDY OF INCOME DYNAMICS

The main relevant features of the PSID are described in the body of the paper. Several remaining issues are noted here.

To ensure that the sample is nationally representative, the over-sampled Latino subsample is excluded from analysis.

Figure 10 demonstrates that the ratio of total household food consumption to total household income in the PSID matches well the time-series pattern of the ratio of total food consumption to national income in the NIPA data. The PSID ratio is persistently lower by about $2\frac{1}{2}\%$ of income. This is because food consumption in the national accounts includes food purchases by employers and the government, because income in the PSID includes transfers, and because the PSID seems to underestimate total food consumption expenditures by households. This claim is verified by comparing the amounts inferred from the PSID and from the CEX.

The PSID total-wealth-to-income ratio matches the net-worth-to-income ratio in the flow-of-funds data well. Both ratios rise significantly from 1984 to 1989 and are roughly the same in 1989 and 1994.

A.2 THE CONSUMER EXPENDITURE SURVEY

This section evaluates the relevant features of the CEX data. In order to perform the imputation procedure, a household's consumption must be allocated to a quarter, and to evaluate the quality of the data, it must also be allocated to a year. A household's reported consumption expendi-

Figure 10 FOOD-CONSUMPTION-TO-INCOME RATIOS

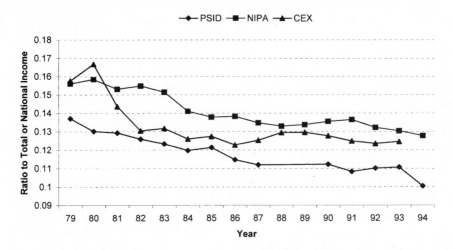

tures are allocated to the calendar quarter closest to the midpoint of the year covered by interviews. Annual data are constructed for graphing by using the average of all quarters in that year.

Figure 10 shows that the ratio of food consumption to income in the CEX declines slightly more and has a slightly lower correlation with the NIPA series than the PSID series does. In fact, this large decline in the CEX is symptomatic of a poor correlation between the ratio of total consumption to income in the CEX and that in the NIPA. While this difference is in part due to increasing purchases of medical care by the government, it is also due to an increasing difficulty for the BLS in measuring certain categories of household consumption expenditures. It turns out that this does not create an insurmountable difficulty for the analysis. Instead of taking imputed consumption expenditures as the truth, two adjustments are made so as to allocate NIPA consumption and medical care in relation to imputed household consumption. Gokhale, Kotlikoff, and Sabelhaus (1996) use the CEX in a similar manner to allocate national accounts consumption across age groups in each year. In addition, since the CEX is used to scale up food consumption in the PSID, the ratio of total nondurables and services consumption to total consumption, rather than the ratio of consumption to income is the relevant series. The ratios of nondurables and services consumption to food consumption in the CEX and NIPA track each other reasonably well, with the exception of changes between 1980 and 1982 (when the CEX improved its survey instrument for consumption) and between 1986 and 1988.

A.3 THE CREATION OF NONDURABLE AND SERVICES
CONSUMPTION IN THE PSID

The details of the regressors in the consumption imputation procedures are as follows. The main regression employs a log–log specification with a cubic polynomial of the log of food consumption. Since there are possibly different returns to scale in the household consumption of food and other items, the variables allowed to shift preferences include nine family size dummies for household sizes 1 through 9 or more. The imputation also includes dummies for whether the household head has a high-school degree or less education, some college, or a college degree or more education. To account for shifting preferences across ages, I also include a fifth-order polynomial in age for households less than age 65 and a second-order polynomial in age for households greater than 65. To allow for labor-supply interactions, the preference shifters include a retirement dummy variable, a dummy variable for whether the household is retired and younger than 65, and dummies for whether there are zero, one, or two or more earners. Finally, to capture both prices and preferences, a set of quarter dummies and a set of year dummies are included.

The four steps of the imputation are as follows.

First, using the CEX data, the log of nondurable and services consumption is regressed on a cubic polynomial in the log of food consumption and the remaining regressors just discussed. The CEX regression using 37,730 households explains 80% of the variation in household consumption, although the typical error is 30% of nondurable and services consumption. The coefficients are not reported but are reasonable. A household with a college-educated head consumes 15% percent more nondurables and services relative to food than a household with a head without a high-school degree. Retired households consume 10% more nondurables and services relative to food than a nonretired household.

Second, the estimated equation is used with the same set of regressors in the PSID to predict nondurables and services consumption for each household. The number of earners in the PSID is calculated from reports on labor income and wages of head and spouse. The quarter dummy is set equal to the second quarter, since most PSID households are interviewed in May. Similarly, the year dummy for 1979 is set equal to its value for 1980, and the year dummy for 1994 is set equal to its value for 1993. Constructing the implied consumption-to-income ratio from the imputed data gives a highly volatile series. This said, the average ratio for the first four years is 0.057 below the average for the last four, showing a reasonably good mapping to the aggregate trend.

Third, the imputed consumption for each household is treated as a relative consumption level, and the total consumption across households is scaled up to include medical purchases by the government. Medical care purchased by the government, except for Medicare, is allocated in proportion to total consumption across all households that are younger than 65 by year. This adjusts consumption of these households upwards by 1.5% to 2.5% of total consumption over the entire sample. Medicare expenditures are allocated evenly across all households age 65 or older in a similar manner, which leads to a scale factor that grows by 10 percentage points over the sample. The elderly account on average for 11% of total imputed consumption. Medicare purchases by the government rise from 1.6% to 3.2% of total consumption expenditures less government spending on health care. Without this adjustment, the consumption of the elderly would be significantly understated and, more importantly, the rise in their consumption would be understated. Income is not adjusted for this consumption that is purchased by the government for households. Interpretation of cohort and age profiles throughout the paper keeps this in mind.

Fourth, the consumption of nondurable goods and services in the NIPA in each year is allocated across households in proportion to each household's consumption from the third step. The allocation is conducted so that the consumption-to-income ratio in the micro data matches that in the NIPA in every year.

When working with the growth rate of consumption, the following modification to the imputation procedure is made. Instead of using the level of predicted consumption in the PSID to allocate NIPA consumption expenditures, the level is used only to allocate medical purchases by the government. In the fourth step of the imputation, the growth rate of NIPA real consumption per capita is allocated across households in accord with their household growth rates. One might be concerned because this procedure ignores the fact that these two series might differ due to household births and deaths. However, in the PSID data, many missing consumption growth rates are not due to birth or death but to missing data. Thus it is also not appropriate to assume that the difference between the PSID growth in consumption and that in the NIPA represents differences in true births and deaths. More importantly, the trend in the time series of consumption growth from the PSID is similar whether one calculates it from averaging levels or averaging first differences. See also the discussion in the text.

REFERENCES

Alessie, R., A. Kapteyn, and A. Lusardi. (1999). Explaining the wealth holdings of different cohorts: Productivity growth and social security. Manuscript. Center, Tillburg University, TMR Progress Report No. 5.

Attanasio, O. (1994). Personal saving in the US. In *International Comparisons of Household Saving,* James M. Poterba (ed.). Chicago: University of Chicago Press, pp. 57–124.

———. (1997a). Cohort analysis of saving behavior by U.S. households. *Journal of Human Resources* 33(3):575–609.

———. (1997b). Consumption and saving behavior: Modelling recent trends. *Fiscal Studies* 18(1):23–47.

———, and M. Browning. (1995). Consumption over the life cycle and over the business cycle. *American Economic Review* 85:1118–1137.

———, and G. Weber. (1995). Is consumption growth consistent with intertemporal optimization? Evidence from the Consumer Expenditure Survey. *Journal of Political Economy* 103(6):1121–1157.

Ayagari, R. (1993). Uninsured idiosyncratic risk and aggregate savings. *Quarterly Journal of Economics* 109:659–684.

Bernheim, B. D., and J. K. Scholz. (1993). Private saving and public policy. In *Tax Policy and the Economy,* Vol. 7, J. M. Poterba (ed.). Cambridge, MA: MIT Press, pp. 73–110.

———, and J. B. Shoven, eds. (1991). *National Saving and Economic Performance.* Chicago: University of Chicago Press.

Blinder, A. S., and A. S. Deaton. (1985). The time-series consumption function revised. *Brookings Papers on Economic Activity* 1985 (2):465–521.

Bosworth, B. (1996). Comment. *Brookings Papers on Economic Activity* 1:391–395.

———, G. Burtless, and J. Sabelhaus. (1991). The decline in saving: Evidence from household surveys. *Brookings Papers on Economic Activity* 1:183–191.

Branch, E. R. (1994). The Consumer Expenditure Survey: A comparative analysis. *Monthly Labor Review,* December, pp. 47–55.

Browning, M., and A. Lusardi. (1996). Household saving: Micro theories and macro facts. *Journal of Economic Literature* 34(4):1797–1855.

Bureau of Economic Analysis. (1987). GNP: An overview of source data and estimating methods. U.S. Department of Commerce Methodology Paper BEA-MP-4. Washington: Government Printing Office.

———. (1990). Personal consumption expenditures. Washington: Government Printing Office. U.S. Department of Commerce Methodology Paper BEA-MP-6.

———. (1997). Updated summary NIPA methodologies. *Survey of Current Business,* September, pp. 12–33.

Bureau of Labor Statistics. (1993). *Consumer Expenditure Survey, 1980–1993: Interview Survey.* Washington: U.S. Department of Commerce, Bureau of the Census; Ann Arbor, MI: Inter-university Consortium of Political and Social Research.

Caballero, R. J. (1991). Earnings uncertainty and aggregate wealth accumulation. *American Economic Review* 81(4):859–871.

Campbell, J. Y., and N. G. Mankiw. (1989). Consumption, income and interest rates: Reinterpreting the time series evidence. In *NBER Macroeconomics Annual,* O. J. Blanchard and S. Fischer (eds.). Cambridge, MA: MIT Press, pp. 185–215.

Carroll, C. D. (1994). How does future income affect current consumption. *Quarterly Journal of Economics* 109(1):111–147.

———. (1997). Buffer stock saving and the life cycle permanent income hypothesis. *Quarterly Journal of Economics* 107(1):1–56.

———, and D. N. Weil. (1994). Saving and growth: A reinterpretation. In *Carnegie-Rochester Conference Series on Public Policy,* Vol. 40. Elsevier, pp. 133–192.

Deaton, A. (1992). *Understanding Consumption*. Oxford: Clarendon Press.
———. (1997). Saving and growth. Research Program in Development Studies, Princeton University. Manuscript.
———, and C. Paxson. (1994). Saving, growth, and aging in Taiwan. In *Studies in the Economics of Aging*, David A. Wise (ed.). Chicago: University of Chicago Press for NBER, pp. 331–357.
———, and ———. (1997). Growth, demographic structure, and national saving in Taiwan. Research Program in Development Sudies, Princeton University. Manuscript.
Denison, E. (1958). A note on private saving. *Review of Economics and Statistics* 15:261–267.
Gale, W. G., and J. Sabelhaus. (1999). Perspectives on the household saving rate, *Brookings Papers on Economic Activity* 1:181–224.
Gokhale, J., L. J. Kotlikoff, and J. Sabelhaus. (1996). Understanding the postwar decline in U.S. saving: A cohort analysis. *Brookings Papers on Economic Activity* 1:315–407.
Gourinchas, P. O., and J. A. Parker. (1997). Consumption over the lifecycle. Social Science Research Insitute. Working Paper 9722.
Greenwood, J., and M. Yorukoglu. (1997). 1974. *Carnegie-Rochester Conference Series on Public Policy* 46:49–95.
———, Z. Hercowitz, and P. Krusell. (1997). Long-run implications of investment-specific technological change. *American Economic Review* 87(3):342–362.
Gustman, A. L., and T. L. Steinmeier. (1998). Effects of pensions on saving: Analysis with data from the health and retirement study. Cambridge, MA: National Bureau of Economic Research. NBER Working Paper 6681.
Hall, R. E. (1978). The stochastic implications of the life cycle permanent income hypothesis. *Journal of Political Economy* 86:971–87.
———. (1988). Intertemporal substitution in consumption. *Journal of Political Economy* 96:339–357.
Hansen, L. P., and K. J. Singleton. (1983). Stochastic consumption, risk aversion, and the temporal behavior of asset returns. *Journal of Political Economy* 91:249–268.
Hayashi, F. (1997). *Understanding Saving: Evidence from the U.S. and Japan*. Cambridge, MA: MIT Press.
Hendershott, P. H., and J. Peek. (1988). Aggregate U.S. private saving: Measures and empirical tests. In *Measures of Saving, Income and Wealth*, R. Lipsey and H. S. Tice (eds.). Chicago: University of Chicago Press, pp. 185–226.
Hurst, E., M. C. Luoh, and F. P. Stafford. (1998). The wealth dynamics of American families, 1984–94. *Brookings Papers on Economic Activity* 1:267–337.
Juster, F. T., J. P. Smith, and F. Stafford. (1999). The measurement and structure of household wealth. *Labour Economics* 6(2):253–275.
Ludvigson, S., and C. Steindel. (1999). How important is the stock market effect on consumption? Federal Reserve Bank of New York. Research Paper 9821.
Lusardi, A. (1996). Permanent income, current income, and consumption: Evidence from two panel data sets. *Journal of Business and Economic Statistics* 14(1):81–90.
Modigliani, F., and R. Brumberg. (1956). Utility analysis and the consumption function: An interpretation of cross-section data. In *Post-Keynesian Economics*, K. K. Kurihara (ed.). New Brunswick, NJ: Rutgers University Press, pp. 338–436.

Parker, J. A. (1998). The consumption function re-estimated. University of Wisconsin. Manuscript.

Paxson, C. H. (1996). Saving and growth: Evidence from micro data. *European Economic Review* 40(2):255–288.

Poterba, J. M., and A. Samwick. (1995). Stock ownership patterns, stock market fluctuations, and consumption. *Brookings Papers on Economic Activity* 1995 2:295–357.

Sabelhaus, J., and K. Pence. (1998). Household saving in the 90's: Evidence from cross-sectional wealth surveys. Congressional Budget Office. Manuscript.

Skinner, J. (1987). A superior measure of consumption from the panel study of income dynamics. *Economic Letters* 23:213–216.

Stephenson, E. F. (1998). Average and marginal tax rates revisited. *Journal of Monetary Economics* 41:389–409.

———, and C. Carroll. (1991). Consumption growth parallels income growth: Some new evidence. In *National Savings and Economic Performance*, B. D. Bernheim and J. B. Shoven (eds.). Chicago: University of Chicago Press, 305–343.

Summers, L. H., and C. Carroll. (1987). Why is U.S. national saving so low? *Brookings Papers on Economic Activity* 2:607–635.

Vissing-Jorgensen, A. (1998). Limited stock market participation. MIT. Manuscript.

Zeldes, S. P. (1989). Consumption and liquidity constraints: An empirical investigation. *Journal of Political Economy* 97:305–346.

Comment

DAVID LAIBSON
Harvard University and NBER

This paper provides a rich analysis of consumption and savings choices. It thoughtfully and productively integrates data from an impressive range of sources, including the Panel Survey of Income Dynamics, the Consumer Expenditure Survey, and the National Income and Product Accounts. Parker documents a large set of important stylized facts. Three of those findings were particularly interesting for me: First, the changing age distribution has played only a small role in the consumption boom of the 1980s and early 1990s. Second, during the consumption boom younger cohorts consumed a larger share of their income than older cohorts did at the same age. Third, younger cohorts had the same rate of consumption growth as older cohorts did at the same age. Parker has resisted the natural temptation to draw too many theoretical conclusions from these interesting findings. He should be congratulated on the scope of his empirical effort and on the modesty of his subsequent conclusions.

However, I do take issue with one underlying point of this paper. The

Meghana Bhatt provided excellent research assistance. Laibson acknowledges the financial support of the National Science Foundation (SBR-9510985) and the MacArthur Foundation.

Figure 1 TOTAL CONSUMPTION AND CONSUMPTION AS SHARES
OF GDP

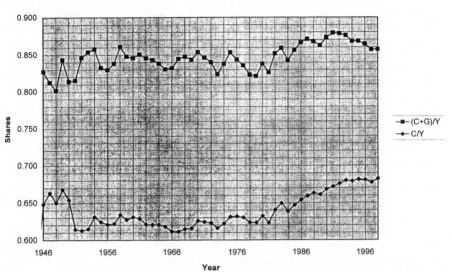

paper is motivated by the consumption boom during the 1980s and
1990s. There is clearly some evidence for such a boom. But this evidence
is not overwhelming, and it appears that the consumption boom is now
over, an important reversal that Parker underemphasizes. For example,
by historical measures, consumption is at a postwar *low* relative to standard benchmarks for human and physical capital.

To tell this story it is helpful to begin with Parker's aggregate analysis
of consumption benchmarks. Parker begins by pointing out that the
consumption share of GDP (i.e., C/Y) has risen during the past two
decades. Parker also discusses total consumption, which comprises both
household consumption and government consumption. Extended time
series (1945–1998) of C/Y and $(C + G)/Y$ are plotted in my Figure 1.

Looking at Figure 1, the boom in C is clear, but the rise in $C + G$ is
more muted. The ratio $(C + G)/Y$ reaches a postwar peak of 0.879 in
1991. But by 1998 this ratio had fallen to 0.857, a level which is less than
one standard deviation (0.023) above the 1946–1970 mean (0.838). By
these calculations, there has been a temporary boom in total consumption, but we have settled back into a fairly typical spending pattern.

However, comparing consumption with current output misses one of
the principal economic insights. Forward-looking consumers should
want to smooth consumption and hence should base consumption on
permanent income. Any effort to evaluate consumption normatively

should take some consideration of the discounted income stream upon which that consumption is ultimately based.

The following relatively transparent framework can be used to compare total consumption to permanent income. Specifically, divide total consumption (TC) by total wealth (TW):

$$\frac{\text{total consumption}}{\text{total physical and human wealth}} \equiv \frac{TC}{TW} = \frac{C + G}{NW + \dfrac{Y_L}{r-g} + GNW}.$$

My total wealth measure has three components. First, net worth of U.S. households, NW, is measured by the Federal Reserve's Flow of Funds Balance Sheets. Second, human capital of U.S. households, $Y_L/(r - g)$, represents the net present value of future labor income. Here Y_L is labor income,[1] and $r - g$ is the difference between the real interest rate and the growth rate of labor income. I assume $r - g = 0.05$. Third, governmental net worth, GNW, including federal, state, and local governments, is measured by the Federal Reserve's Flow of Funds Balance Sheets, which only include financial assets and liabilities of the government.[2] Necessarily, omitting governmental tangible assets biases down government net worth, and therefore biases up the consumption ratio at all points in time. But this level bias is not likely to bias the trend.

Figure 2 plots the total consumption to total wealth ratio, TC/TW, during the postwar period. Two properties stand out. First, the time series did increase significantly between 1980 and 1994, seemingly reversing a previous downward trend. But the 1980–1994 increase has now been entirely reversed. By the end of 1998, the series was at an all-time low for the postwar period. These results do not depend at all upon my calculation of human capital. To demonstrate this point, consider Figure 3, which ignores human capital and plots the ratio $(C + G)/(NW + GNW)$. Now there appears to be no consumption boom whatsoever, and the only prominent feature of the data is the consumption bust during the 1995–1998 period.

To develop intuition for these effects, consider just one source of new wealth in the U.S. economy. In U.S. equities markets, price-to-earnings (P/E) ratios are currently over twice their historical norm. At year-end 1998, U.S. market capitalization was $13.451 trillion,[3] implying that the

1. Specifically, I take compensation of employees from the BEA's National Income and Product Accounts.
2. To a first approximation, GNW is roughly equal to the net debt of the federal government, and hence GNW is negative.
3. Source: International Finance Corporation.

Figure 2 RATIO OF TOTAL CONSUMPTION TO TOTAL WEALTH

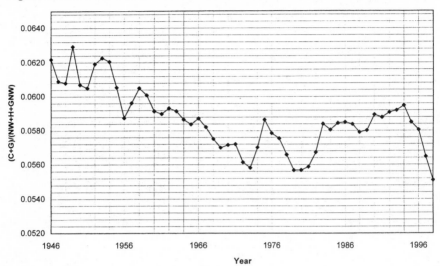

rise in P/E ratios has generated a wealth shock of approximately $7 trillion. With a marginal propensity to consume of 0.05, this wealth shock should have raised total consumption by $350 billion, or 4.1% of an $8.5 trillion economy.[4] Alternatively, note that U.S. equities have generated real returns of approximately 13% per year since 1979, 6 percentage points above the historical rate. Had U.S. equities realized historically average performance over the 1979–1998 period, the U.S. market capitalization would now be approximately $5 trillion, implying that the realized excess returns produced a wealth shock of approximately $8.5 trillion. Assuming a marginal propensity to consume of 0.05, this wealth shock should have raised total consumption by $425 billion, or 5.0% of GDP. Note that the actual long-run rise in the total consumption ratio was only 3.6% of GDP [from a $(C + G)/Y$ ratio of 0.821 in 1979—the lowest value realized in the 1970s—to a 1998 value of 0.857].

Parker is right to point out that there was an anomalous boom in consumption during the 1980s and 1990s. But my calculations suggest that since 1994 the anomaly has evaporated. High levels of total con-

4. Parker estimates an MPC of 0.04, but his estimates are almost surely biased down due to measurement error in household-level wealth data and omitted variables in his regression. For example, failing to include a measure of heterogeneity in the taste for saving will bias the MPC down, since the taste for saving covaries positively with wealth accumulation and covaries negatively (holding all else equal) with consumption.

Figure 3 RATIO OF TOTAL CONSUMPTION TO PHYSICAL WEALTH

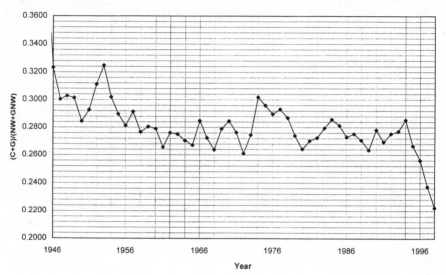

sumption are now justified by high levels of total wealth. The ratio TC/TW is now at a postwar low.

Since the rise in TC/TW was temporary, it may be relatively easy to explain. Transitory shocks like the 1980, 1981–1982, and 1990–1991 recessions, and the rapid expansion of consumer credit, can probably jointly explain a significant fraction of the temporary rise in TC/TW.

Finally, collapsing stock prices could rapidly change all of my conclusions. If stock-market wealth falls dramatically (>30%), but consumption stays the same, the consumption puzzle will be resurrected. Unfortunately, I am not able to forecast future values of either the numerator or the denominator of my ratio.

Comment

ANNAMARIA LUSARDI
Dartmouth College and Northwestern, and University of Chicago Joint Center for Poverty Research

1. What Is Saving? Some Measurement Issues

The decline in the saving rate in the United States represents a long-standing puzzle. Much research has been devoted to it, but so far there seems to be more agreement on the reasons that cannot explain the decline than on the reasons that actually can. This paper provides a very thorough investigation of saving, looking at both macro models and aggregate data, and micro evidence on saving. The empirical work on household data tries to disentangle the reasons for the decline in saving by looking at different groups in the population and also by examining the role of the increase in wealth. The main findings are that there is not a unique explanation for the decline in saving, and the paper points to a list of viable candidates.

There are several issues to address when considering saving. The first one is concerned with measurement. Consider a simple manipulation of the budget constraint:

$$W_t - W_{t-1} = rW_{t-1} + Y_t - C_t,$$

where W denotes wealth, C consumption, Y income, and r the interest rate. Saving can be derived by taking the first difference of wealth or by subtracting consumption from (capital and labor) income. At the aggregate level, saving has been measured from the National Income and Product Accounts (NIPA) as the difference between personal consumption outlays and personal disposable income, and from the Flow of Funds (FOF) of the Federal Reserve System as the household sector's net acquisition of assets (including housing) minus its net accumulation of liabilities. These two measures do not generally match, and many adjustments are needed to obtain comparable figures. The most important fact is that capital gains are not counted in the above definitions of saving. However, those gains have become so important that if one were to include them, saving would not even show a decline. Gale and Sabelhaus (1999) have examined the measures of saving from NIPA and FOF and considered several adjustments to the official statistics related to, for example, the treatments of durable goods, inflation, tax accruals, and retirement accounts. Considering those adjustments, the decline in saving is much smaller and the level of saving much higher than reported in the official statistics. On adding capital gains, however, the figures change dramatically. Saving is not only much higher than in the official statistics, but also it shows no decline over time and has actually increased in the 1990s, in particular after 1993. One of the important features of the U.S. economy is that while we observed a decline in saving (at least according to the official statistics), we did not witness a decrease in the stock of wealth.

On moving from aggregate to micro statistics, measurement issues become even more problematic. The two existing data sets on consumption, i.e., the Panel Study on Income Dynamics (PSID) and the Consumer Expenditure Survey (CEX), have serious limitations for calculating accurate measures of saving. For example, the PSID reports information only on food consumption. This measure is not only limited, but also noisy.[1] The CEX has information on total household expenditure, but suffers from severe measurement error in income, and has only limited (and noisy) information about financial assets. In addition, income is top-coded in the CEX, and this makes it difficult to calculate saving for high-income households, which are responsible for a large share of saving in the United States. It is also possible to calculate saving using wealth data from the Survey of Consumer Finances (SCF) or from the PSID, but one has to deal with the issue of how to treat capital gains, which, as mentioned before, are not included in the aggregate statistics.

These observations suggest that one should use much caution in interpreting the aggregate statistics. As far as measurement is concerned, there are different definitions of saving, and which one to choose does ultimately depend on the research question under consideration. For micro data, there is no ideal data set to study saving. The paper uses the PSID, but much data construction and imputation is needed to obtain accurate measures of consumption. More specifically, data from the CEX and NIPA are used to construct a more comprehensive measure of consumption than the one reported in the PSID.

2. Some Basic Facts

In addition to the official statistics on saving, the paper reports several important facts, which are not usually present in previous works on the decline in saving. For example, the paper documents that there has been a substantial increase in the ratio of consumption to income, in particular after the 1980s. Additionally, it shows that the household rather than the government sector is responsible for the decline in saving. As mentioned before, the paper also shows that while saving declined, wealth has increased a lot, at least in the aggregate statistics. However, one should note that aggregate data hide important differences across households. Wealth is very unequally distributed among U.S. households, and in the 1980s the distribution of wealth became more spread out.[2] In this respect, only a share of the population enjoyed capital gains on existing assets.

Household debt also surged in the past years. Figures 1 and 2 of this comment show that total debt per capita and one of its components,

1. See Runkle (1991).
2. See Wolff (1994).

Figure 1 PER CAPITA TOTAL HOUSEHOLD DEBT: 1960–1997
(IN 1997 DOLLARS)

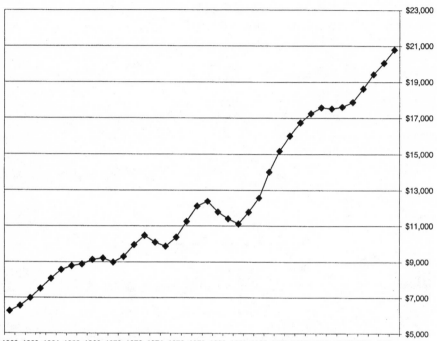

consumer credit per capita, have increased over time and accelerated during the 1990s.[3] This is also a potentially important fact, and it should be kept in mind when modeling household consumption or saving. I will return to it below.

Perhaps a less well-known fact is that the lack of saving is very pervasive among U.S. households. Recent data from the Health and Retirement Study (HRS) show that many households arrive close to retirement with little nonpension wealth. Table 1 reports the distribution of financial wealth, housing equity, and total net worth for a cohort of households whose head is close to retirement (they were 51–61 years old in 1992). Even though these households should be close to the peak of their accumulation, their median financial wealth is $6,000 and median total net worth is less than $100,000. Much of the accumulation is accounted

3. Household total debt is the sum of home mortgage and consumer credit. Consumer credit includes automobile credit and revolving credit, such as credit-card debt and unsecured personal lines of credit. These figures are from the Flow of Funds Accounts of the Federal Reserve System.

Figure 2 PER CAPITA CONSUMER CREDIT: 1960–1997 (IN 1997 DOLLARS)

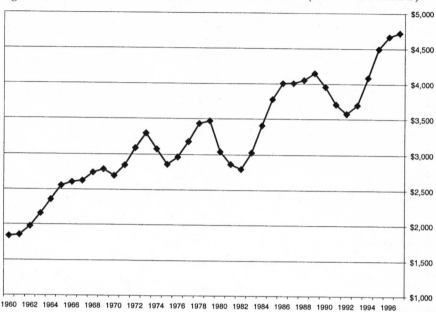

for by housing equity, but it is an issue whether or not households are using housing wealth to support their consumption at retirement.[4,5] These findings raise some concerns about the financial security of many American households. Saving is also heavily concentrated among the high-income, high-education, high-wealth households. For example, according to Kennickell and Starr-McCluer (1997), households with income of $50,000 and above (in 1989 dollars) accounted for over 75% of total saving. Households whose head had a college degree also accounted for a disproportionate share of saving; depending on the chosen sample, estimates go from 64% to 72%. Note that if saving is calculated to measure the ability of households to finance consumption in retirement, then official statistics may provide an inadequate picture, since, as mentioned before, they do not take into account the appreciation of the existing stock of assets.

4. Financial wealth is defined as the sum of checking and saving accounts, bonds, stocks, and other assets minus short-term debt. Total net worth is the sum of financial wealth, IRAs and Keoghs, housing equity, other real estate, business equity, and vehicles. Figures refer to the sample of households whose financial respondent is not retired. All values are in 1992 dollars. Figures are weighted using survey weights.
5. See Lusardi (1999) and the references therein.

Table 1   DISTRIBUTION OF FINANCIAL AND TOTAL NET WORTH,
AGE RANGE 51–61 IN 1992

Percentile	Financial Net Worth	Housing Equity	Total Net Worth
5	−6,000	0	0
10	−2,000	0	850
25	0	0	27,980
50	6,000	42,000	96,000
75	36,000	85,000	222,200
90	110,000	150,000	475,000
95	199,500	200,000	785,000
Mean	46,171	61,613	227,483
(Std. dev.)	(178,654)	(100,646)	(521,467)

Note: Author's calculations from the Health and Retirement Study.

3. Explaining the Decline in Saving

While basic facts are important, the important question is: What explains the observed figures? As mentioned before, there have been many explanations for the decline in saving in the United States. In Browning and Lusardi (1996), we reviewed as many as twelve proposed explanations. They can be summarized as follows: (1) the aging of the population; (2) changes in the saving propensities of different cohorts; (3) changes in the structure of households (e.g., divorce rates); (4) changes in the insurance provided by the government (a decrease in the precautionary saving motive); (5) changes in the distribution of income; (6) the decline in aggregate growth; (7) capital gains on housing; (8) capital gains on stocks; (9) the increased annuitization of wealth (due to Social Security and pensions); (10) cash payouts to shareholders; (11) the development of financial markets; (12) changes in the thriftiness and perception of financial security (and other reasons from economic psychology).

This list serves to emphasize that this topic has been heavily investigated, and while we can perhaps rule out some of the explanations suggested by past research, many still remain under debate. The paper adds to the existing explanations by suggesting that there is not a single culprit behind the decline in saving, but several reasons are likely to coexist. The paper offers useful and original insights with respect to previous work. On the one hand, there is an examination of a stylized macroeconomic model. How do we reconcile the movements in consumption with changes in government policies, the behavior of interest rates, and the stock-market boom? On the other hand, there is a close examination of micro data, using different methods.

It is clear that, to be able to explain the decline in saving, it is necessary to look at micro data. This makes it possible to test different hypotheses, as well as focus on well-defined demographic and economic groups and characterize their behavior. The micro-data analysis, however, is not without limitations. As mentioned before, there is not a single data set that can be used to analyze saving. Data construction is not only cumbersome, but it also requires making several assumptions about the characterization of consumption. For example, the imputation of health expenses is particularly difficult, since those data are only available at the aggregate level. The other problem is that micro data are notoriously noisy and it is hard to estimate effects with precision. Nevertheless, the analysis of household behavior is important, both because this is the sector responsible for the decline in saving and because aggregate statistics hide important differences across population groups.

The first problem in modeling household saving is determining which theoretical scheme to refer to. The paper refers broadly to the life-cycle model, even though it sometimes hints at the importance of incorporating a precautionary saving motive. By using a fairly general specification of the life-cycle model of saving, at least three explanations for the decline in saving can be rationalized. The first one is that the proportion of the elderly has increased; since they should be net dissavers, that may explain the decline in saving. This can be called an *age effect*. An additional explanation is that individuals born in different time periods display different saving behaviors. This may be due to the fact that their resources are different or that preferences are different across generations. This can be called a *generational* or *cohort effect*. A third explanation is that the behavior of the macro economy has affected saving. This can be called a *time effect*.

Unfortunately, it is not possible to decompose the observed decline in saving into age, cohort, and time effects. This is due to the well-known identification problem in using time, cohort, and age dummies: Their effects cannot be separately identified, since year of birth (or cohort) plus age is simply equal to time. There are several ways to get around the identification problem.[6] One way is to use identifying assumptions—for example, restrict the estimates on the time dummies. This approach was originally used by Deaton and Paxson (1994) and is also implemented in this paper. While it has several advantages, it leaves open the question of how to interpret cohort effects: are they due to economic conditions,

6. See Heckman and Robb (1985) and Attanasio (1998).

for example differences in the rate of productivity growth across generations, or are they due to preferences? It is not possible to disentangle
these effects by simply using cohort dummies. Another alternative is to
use better proxies for these effects than dummy variables, and/or to
model the effect explicitly. While this requires putting more structure
into a specific model of saving and making assumptions about the variables necessary to estimate the model, it may provide a clearer interpretation of the cohort effects. An additional advantage of this approach is
that it allows a more flexible specification for these different effects. For
example, it is easy to think of cases where age, cohort, and time effects
are not simply additive. Kapteyn, Alessie, and Lusardi (1998) use a
simple life-cycle model of saving and show that the introduction of a
universal social security system in the Netherlands in the mid-1950s
introduced an interaction between age and cohort effects. Rather than
using cohort dummies, they model the cohort effect in wealth and saving explicitly by constructing measures of productivity growth and the
generosity of the social security system across different generations.

Which interpretation to attach to cohort effects is a rather critical issue
in this paper. As the empirical work shows, age effects can be easily
dismissed as an explanation for the decline in saving. This is consistent
with the findings of many other papers.[7] It is almost intuitive why this is
the case. Changes in the age structure of the population are too slow to
be able to rationalize the decline in saving. Note that while the decline
started perhaps two decades ago, it has become precipitous since the
mid-1980s, at least according to the official statistics. The importance of
time effect is not clearly assessed. In one specification of the empirical
work, these effects are restricted *ex ante*. By making the assumption, as
in Deaton and Paxson (1994), that time effects are orthogonal to a linear
time trend and average to zero, all (linear) trends observed in the data
are attributed to age and cohort effects. This restriction is relaxed when
estimating a consumption function, and in that context time effects are
found to be significant in sign and magnitude.

A main finding of the paper is that cohort effects are significant and
important for explaining the decline in saving. More precisely, every
generation is consuming more than the previous generation did at a
similar age. This finding is relevant per se, even though it is open to
many interpretations. First, note that it is partly in conflict with previous
research.[8] While other authors too attribute the decline in saving mainly
to cohort effects, the cohorts that are responsible for the decline differ

7. See the discussion in Browning and Lusardi (1996) and the references therein.
8. Some studies, such as Bosworth, Burtless, and Sabelhaus (1991), report results in line
with this paper that saving has declined across every age group.

widely across studies. For example, according to Boskin and Lau (1988), the generations born after 1939 are the ones responsible for the decline in saving. This is in contrast with the findings of Attanasio (1998) that it is not the baby-boomers, but the generations born between 1925 and 1939, that shifted down their saving. In other words, it is the generations that should be at the peak of their saving during the 1980s that are saving less. Gokhale, Kotlikoff, and Sabelhaus (1996) provide yet a different explanation. According to their study, it is mainly the elderly that are responsible for the decline in saving. They document that the government redistributed resources from young and future generations to current old ones and there has been a sharp increase in the propensity of older Americans to consume out of their remaining lifetime resources.

It is not obvious why the findings are so different, and what explains the different conclusions reached by different authors, in particular among studies using similar micro data sets and similar versions of the life-cycle model of saving. We await a study that can explain those differences and generate some consensus on this topic.

Second, there is the problem of interpreting cohort effects when using cohort dummies. What do cohort effects capture—differences in economic circumstances, or differences in preferences across generations? The fact that all generations consume more than previous ones seems to indicate a plurality of reasons for the decline in saving, even though it is not obvious which are the correct ones. For example, transfers from the government are a possible explanation, but they have affected generations differentially, and it is the elderly, if any, that have benefited from them. Similarly, changes in the financial markets, and in particular in the opportunities for borrowing, should have affected the younger generations. Changes in preferences, such as impatience, could also be changing across generations. In this case it is difficult to expect a dramatic change across (adjacent) generations, and any such change should have affected prevalently the younger generations, even though it is not clear which ones (individuals born after the Great Depression, or after the war, or the late boomers?).

The paper suggests that several reasons could be at work, such as an increase in government transfers that explain the decline for the elderly combined with the development in the financial markets that changed saving for the young. While plausible, this explanation requires further investigation, since it is not easy to rule out the possibility that preferences, such as impatience or attitudes toward saving (thriftiness, expectations toward the future), have changed across generations.

In the attempt to explain cohort effects, the paper resorts to estimating a consumption function. To model cohort effects explicitly, wealth and the permanent component of income are considered in the estimation of a consumption function. Thus, the analysis allows a close evaluation of how much of the increase in consumption is attributable to the increase in wealth that was documented earlier.

The results from estimating consumption functions do not provide evidence in support of one specific explanation or set of explanations for understanding cohort effects. Overall, the estimates suggest that a rather limited share of the consumption boom can be explained by the increase in wealth. But estimates from these equations are not without difficulties. If households have financed the increase in consumption by borrowing from future resources, then low wealth (but not necessarily zero or negative, which in the estimation is treated as a separate group) can be highly correlated with high consumption, and current estimates may not adequately capture this nonlinear effect. In fact, even households with zero or negative wealth are found to have high consumption.

In addition, much attention both in the media and in some current academic research has focused on the effect of the stock-market boom. Given the importance of capital gains in the measures of saving mentioned before, this is an important issue to study. However, it is hard to evaluate the effect of the stock market from the estimates of the consumption function. Even though the dummy for stock-market participation is statistically significant, much of the effect may be due to the increase in the wealth invested in stocks, which is not separately identified.

The theoretical model that underlies the calculation of the consumption function assumes that borrowing is severely limited. More specifically, assets are assumed not to go negative. This implicitly rules out the importance of the development of financial markets. As documented in the figures shown before, many households can borrow, and they have increased substantially the amount of debt that they are holding. Similarly, it is not surprising that cohort effects are still present in the data after allowing for wealth and the permanent component of income, since those two variables could be poor predictors of future resources across cohorts.

From consumption functions the analysis shifts at the end to the estimation of Euler equations. Thus, from the examination of consumption levels the analysis goes to the examination of growth rates of consumption. However, it is hard to gain clear insights into the decline of saving from Euler equations. On the one hand, data in first differences are very noisy, and estimates are often poor and unreliable.[9] On the other hand,

---

9. See the discussion about estimating Euler equations using micro data in Browning and Lusardi (1996).

we do not know whether the Euler equations are well specified. If some households face borrowing constraints, then there should be additional terms in the Euler equation (a proxy for the Lagrange multiplier) to capture the fact that consumption grows more for constrained than for unconstrained consumers.[10] While borrowing constraints are explicitly considered in the derivation of the consumption function, they are not considered in the derivation of Euler equations. Additionally, apart from the case of quadratic preferences or the certainty equivalence case, the variance of consumption growth should also appear in the Euler equation. This is because, for households that have a precautionary saving motive, uncertainty depresses consumption and consumption should grow faster for households facing greater uncertainty. While the derivation of the consumption functions relaxed the assumption about certainty, the Euler equations do not allow for uncertainty.

Euler equations have the advantage that one does not have to specify the income process of households or their expectations about future events. Nevertheless, specific assumptions have still to be made about how to characterize preferences and the economic environment, for example whether households are impatient, whether they have a precautionary saving motive, and whether there are borrowing constraints or other market imperfections. To illustrate this point more clearly, note that in addition to the expected interest rate and a set of cohort dummies, wealth (in logs) is added to the Euler equation. The justification for adding wealth reported in the paper is to evaluate whether unexpectedly high asset returns are the causes of the consumption boom. Even though it is statistically significant only in one specification, the sign of wealth is negative rather than positive. However, as is mentioned in the paper too, wealth might be capturing precautionary saving, i.e., the fact that the wealthy have lower precautionary saving motives. Alternatively, it might be capturing the fact that the wealthy do not face stringent borrowing constraints.

In the end, the analysis of consumption from these three different angles—the decomposition of the data into age, cohort, and restricted time effects; the estimation of consumption functions; and the estimation of Euler equations—does not pin down a single explanation for the decline in saving, and sometimes it leads to somewhat different and conflicting results. It is plausible that this is the result of different identifying assumptions. On the one hand, the decomposition into age, cohort, and time effects requires making assumptions about the behavior of one set of dummies. On the other hand, the estimation of con-

10. See Zeldes (1989).

sumption functions and Euler equations requires making modeling assumptions about the preferences of individuals and the potential imperfections in the financial and insurance markets they could face. Given that there is much debate on which theoretical model can best describe saving (life-cycle models, models with intergenerational transfers, precautionary saving, etc.), there is no safe avenue for studying the decline in saving. Different methods have their own shortcomings, and overall the results of employing those different methods in this paper may also be interpreted as showing how hard it is to explain saving well and how many difficulties the traditional theories of saving have in rationalizing the empirical findings.

To summarize: this paper has taken up the difficult task of explaining the decline in saving. With respect to previous work in this area, it proposes that there are several different explanations at work that can explain saving. Among them, a combination of government transfers to the elderly, changes in preferences (impatience or attitudes toward saving) across generations, and changes in the development of financial markets seem most promising and a useful avenue for future research.

REFERENCES

Attanasio, O. (1998). Cohort analysis of saving behavior by US households. *Journal of Human Resources* 33:575–609.
Boskin, L., and L. Lau. (1988). An analysis of postwar consumption and saving: Part II. Emprical results. Cambridge, MA: National Burea of Economic Research. NBER Working Paper 2606.
Bosworth, B., G. Burtless, and J. Sabelhaus. (1991). The decline in saving: Evidence from household surveys. *Brookings Papers on Economic Activity* 1: 183–256.
Browning, M., and A. Lusardi. (1996). Household saving: Micro theories and micro facts. *Journal of Economic Literature* 34:1797–1855.
Deaton, A., and C. Paxson. (1994). Saving, growth and aging in Taiwan. In *Studies in the Economics of Aging*, D. Wise (ed.). Chicago: Chicago University Press, pp. 331–357.
Gale, W., and J. Sabelhaus. (1999). Perspectives on the household saving rate. *Brookings Papers on Economic Activity*, 1:181–214.
Gokhale, J., K. Kotlikoff, and J. Sabelhaus. (1996). Understanding the postwar decline in US saving: A cohort analysis. *Brookings Papers on Economic Activity* 1:315–407.
Heckman, J., and R. Robb. (1985). Using longitudinal data to estimate age, period and cohort effects in earnings equations. In *Cohort Analysis in Social Research Beyond the Identification Problem*, W. Mason and S. Fienberg (eds.). New York: Springer-Verlag.
Kapteyn, A., R. Alessie, and A. Lusardi. (1998). Explaining the wealth holdings of different cohorts: Productivity growth and social security. University of Chicago. Mimeo.

Kennickell, A., and M. Starr-McCluer. (1997). Household saving and portfolio change: Evidence from the 1983–89 SCF panel. *Review of Income and Wealth* 43:381–399.

Lusardi, A. (1999). Information, expectations and savings for retirement. Forthcoming in *Behavioral Dimensions of Retirement Economics*, H. Aaron (ed.). Brookings Institution and Russell Sage Foundation.

Runkle, D. (1991). Liquidity constraints and the permanent income hypothesis: Evidence from panel data. *Journal of Monetary Economics* 27:73–98.

Wolff, E. (1994). Trends in household wealth in the United States: 1962–1983 and 1983–1989. *Review of Income and Wealth* 40:143–174.

Zeldes, S. (1989). Consumption and liquidity constraints: An empirical investigation. *Journal of Political Economy* 97:305–346.

Discussion

In his reply Parker noted that the biggest increase in the ratio of government and household consumption to GDP occurred in the 1980s; during the past 4–5 years, as the stock market rose, the consumption ratio declined. These facts pose a problem for the view that the consumption boom is the result of rising asset prices. Responding to Annamaria Lusardi, Parker argued for the usefulness of estimated Euler equations. He said that the correlation of consumption growth and the real interest rate during the 1980s, which he uncovered by looking at Euler equations, is both interesting and a potentially important clue to the source of the savings decline.

Mark Gertler asked about the role of fiscal policy. He noted that the rise and decline of the Reagan-era deficits might help explain movements in the broad consumption ratio in the 1980s. Michael Mussa noted that declines in defense spending amount to a gain in wealth for households, which might account for some increased consumption. Parker pointed out that defense spending increased during the early 1980s; this buildup should have crowded out consumption, but there is no evidence that it did. Similarly, the recent decline in government purchases as a share of GDP has not had a positive effect on consumption. Gertler remarked that the means of financing of government spending, i.e., whether through debt or taxes, may also matter.

Giuseppe Moscarini asked about the role of medical expenses, which are treated as consumption but might better be thought of as including an investment component. Some studies have found increased spending on medical services to be a large part of the increase in measured consumption. Benjamin Friedman noted the possible effects of the "marketization" of the economy, i.e., services once provided in the home or without monetary compensation are now bought and sold in markets and are thus counted as consumption. Examples are elderly people living independently (and thus paying rent) rather than staying with children, and women entering the labor force who now purchase housework and child-care services in the market. Friedman suggested looking at consumption subaggregates by age group to see if this hypothesis makes sense. Ben Bernanke noted that marketization adds to measured income as well as consumption, which moderates though it does not reverse the effect on the consumption-to-income ratio.

Friedman also noted that in some sense we have no option but to save wealth created by asset revaluations, since current consumption can be increased only at the expense of current investment or by running a larger current-account deficit, both limited options. Indeed, if individuals tried to consume their capital gains, those gains would vanish as everyone tried to sell their shares. Pierre-Olivier Gourinchas noted that U.S. net foreign assets have switched from large positive to large negative in past decades, so that the willingness of foreign lenders to finance the U.S. consumption boom should not be downplayed. Agreeing with Friedman, Daron Acemoğlu said there is no easy way of reconciling the behavior of the stock market, savings, consumption, and the real interest rate with a partial-equilibrium model and that a general-equilibrium approach is needed.

Bernanke wondered whether a decline in precautionary savings, arising from low unemployment and easier access of households to credit, might explain the trends. Parker agreed that young households can borrow much more easily today than in the past and that they appear to be taking advantage of that, in that young households are consuming more and middle-aged households consuming less than a generation ago.

The discussion turned to the cross-sectional differences in saving and wealth. Deborah Lucas worried about the adequacy of the savings of many older individuals. Lusardi cited work showing that a large fraction of people close to retirement have both low saving and low wealth. Parker suggested this might be partially due to the increased variance in wealth. He also noted that for low-income households, low saving rates might be rational, if social security plus any private pension replace a large share of working-life income.